THE MARKET FOR TRAINING

For Heather, Robert, Bethan and Ann

The Market for Training

International perspectives on theory, methodology and policy

Edited by
ROBERT McNABB
KEITH WHITFIELD
Cardiff Business School
University of Wales
College of Cardiff

Avebury
Aldershot · Brookfield USA · Hong Kong · Singapore · Sydney

Published by
Avebury
Ashgate Publishing Ltd
Gower House
Croft Road
Aldershot
Hants. GU11 3HR
England

Ashgate Publishing Company
Old Post Road
Brookfield
Vermont 05036
USA

British Library Cataloguing in Publication Data

Market for Training: International Perspectives
  on Theory, Methodology and Policy
  I. McNabb, Robert   II. Whitfield, Keith
  331.2592
ISBN 1 85628 599 5

Library of Congress Cataloging-in-Publication Data

The market for training : international perspectives on theory,
  methodology and policy / Robert McNabb and Keith Whitfield, editors.
    p. cm.
"The chapters in this volume were originally presented at the International
Conference on the Economics of Training at the Cardiff Business School
in September 1991"-- Pref.
  Includes index.
  ISBN 1-85628-599-5 : £40.00 ($69.95 U.S. : est.)
  1. Occupational training--Congresses. 2. Employees--Training of-
-Congresses. 3. Vocational education--Congresses. I. McNabb,
Robert. II. Whitfield, Keith.   III. International Conference on the
Economics of Training (1991 : Cardiff Business School)
HD5715 M375 1994
331.25'92--dc20   94-18853
                                                               CIP

Printed and Bound in Great Britain by
Athenaeum Press Ltd, Newcastle upon Tyne.

Contents

List of contributors

Abebe Assefa, University of Warwick
Meredith Baker, University of Melbourne
Derek Bosworth, UMIST
Clair Brown, University of California, Berkeley
Peter Dolton, University of Newcastle
Peter Elias, University of Warwick
Francis Green, University of Leicester
Christine Greenhalgh, University of Oxford
John Ham, University of Pittsburgh
Jaap de Koning, Netherlands Economic Institute
Robert LaLonde, University of Chicago
Robert McNabb, University of Wales, College of Cardiff
Gerry Makepeace, University of Hull
Judith Marquand, University of Sheffield
Geoff Mason, NIESR
George Mavrotas, University of Oxford
Rebecca Maynard, University of Pennsylvania
Joan Payne, University of Oxford
John Treble, University College of North Wales, Bangor
Bart Van Ark, NIESR
Eric Verdier, CEREQ, France
Keith Whitfield, University of Wales, College of Cardiff
Robert Wilson, University of Warwick

Acknowledgements

The current volume reflects the effort of a large number of individuals and organisations. We would like to thank all of them for helping us bring to fruition a project which we believe to be important for the development of research in a key strategic policy area.

We are in indebted to the authors of the chapters for not only presenting interesting and incisive contributions but also showing an admirable willingness to modify their papers between the conference and the submission for this volume.

Similarly the discussants at the conference - Paul Ryan, Ken Mayhew, John Creedy, David Stanton and David Finegold - all made excellent contributions. Both the subsequent debate and the development of the papers benefited from their insights. We are particularly indebted to Paul Ryan for his objective summarising of a paper in his session following the last minute withdrawal of the presenter.

A number of organisations provided financial and practical support of the conference. We are especially indebted to the major sponsor, the Employment Department Group. The assistance of British Gas, the Chemical Bank, Edwards Geldard (Solicitors), Ernst and Young, the South Glamorgan Training and Enterprise Council, the Welsh Development Agency and Welsh Water is also much appreciated.

The turning of a collection of (albeit first-rate) papers into a volume such as this is no easy task and the brunt of the secretarial input fell on the shoulders of Carole Bulman. We are extremely grateful for her good humour and patience in helping with this task, as well as the able way in which she coped with our frequently vague instructions.

Robert McNabb
Keith Whitfield

Preface

The chapters in this volume were originally presented at the International Conference on the Economics of Training at the Cardiff Business School in September 1991. They have been revised in line with comments made at that conference and in the light of further reflections by the authors themselves.

The subsequent volume highlights some of the main theoretical and methodological questions facing economists who are analysing training. It represents the coming together of a group of researchers from a wide range of countries who are at the forefront of research in their particular areas. The result is a thought-provoking and incisive set of analyses on the of the key issues of our time.

Training has become a central concern in the debate about national economic performance and there is widespread opinion that a prime cause of Britain's slow underlying growth rate is the inadequacy of its education and training system. The latest government initiative in this area is the devolution of responsibility for training provision to the Training and Enterprise Councils. This mirrors schemes enacted in a number of overseas countries.

A number of key questions have arisen in the growing policy debate on training. Among these are: What are the determinants of whether firms/individuals undertake training? What are the benefits of training to those involved? How should training programmes be evaluated? What lessons can be drawn from the approaches adopted in other countries?

Economists have made major contributions to the understanding of such issues. In particular, they have been concerned to develop a rigorous analytical base for the addressing of complex and multi-facted questions. This has involved a lively debate which has promoted a number of differing perspectives on theory, methodology and policy.

Four main issues are addressed in this volume. The first concerns the contribution of economic theory to our understanding of training matters. Substantial criticisms have been made of the orthodox economic approach to theory and these are well articulated in the contributions contained herein. However, it is clear that most of the authors accept that orthodox theory has something to offer research on training and accept that it offers a base which is far superior to the casual empiricism of much (non-economic) work in the area. Differences, however, relate to the degree to which the orthodox model is adhered to in the development of theoretical models.

The second set of issues addressed are more methodological in nature and principally concern the evaluation of training initiatives. They focus around the reliability of current, largely non-experimental, analyses of training effects. Experimental research undertaken in the United States of America has indicated that such methods offer results which are very different from those derived from randomised experiments. This has called non-experimental techniques (particularly those of the more simplistic kind) into question. However, it is by no means certain that the experimental methods are free of bias themselves. A related debate concerns the ethics of undertaking randomised experiments, whereby some individuals are denied access to programmes that may be of benefit to them.

A third set of issues addressed is that of the access to training. Of particular concern is the ability of disadvantaged groups to obtain sufficient training to mitigate or even eradicate their poor labour market positions. Research has clearly shown that the more advantaged groups have greater access to training and are thereby able to further improve their relative advantage. The mechanisms generating this result and the key variations in its applicability are less well understood, however.

Both are crucial if training provision is to contribute to greater equity as well as efficiency.

The final set of key issues addressed relates to training policy. In short, this involves the development of an economic and social environment in which training will flourish. Past research has shown that there are no simple answers to this question. This is reflected in the multiplicity of policy initiatives which have been developed throughout the world. National governments have increasingly sought to improve their country's training performance in the hope of obtaining competitive advantage in increasingly competitive international markets. A variety of strategies have been followed, including the development of vocational education at the secondary level, the instigation of training levies and the encouragement of market processes. No government has seemed to find the holy grail, however.

The papers in this volume do not provide easy answers to the difficult questions in the training area. At the very least, however, they do indicate why such answers are so difficult to obtain and how we might go about obtaining them. More than this they indicate that the economics of training is a thriving area and that economists have made major contributions to the myriad of debates on this important topic.

Robert McNabb and Keith Whitfield
Editors

1 The market for training: An overview

Robert McNabb and Keith Whitfield

Introduction

Training has become a key issue in the debate about national economic performance and there is widespread opinion that a prime cause of Britain's slow underlying growth rate is the inadequacy of its education and training system. It is generally believed that Britain under-trains its workforce, although there is considerable disagreement about the causes of this shortfall. Economists have made major contributions to this debate over a number of years, particularly in the development of a rigourous theoretical and methodological base for the analysis of training.

For many years, the economics of training was narrowly focused, being mainly concerned with the benefits to individuals of training and with evaluations of government training schemes. Since most training is provided by firms and has a considerable informal element to it, this emphasis was recognised by many economists as either incomplete or inappropriate. More recently, however, economists have extended their analysis and considered a much wider range of questions. In particular, issues such as what determines whether firms and/or individuals undertake training and the nature of the training provided and received have been considered. Attention has also been directed at establishing the most appropriate methodologies to be adopted in evaluating training programmes. The economist has brought to the area of training an approach and set of techniques which offer the potential for understanding such issues.

The work of economists on training has, however, reflected the main disagreements to be found in the main training debate and consequently a number of differing theoretical and methodological perspectives can be observed. While this can be disconcerting to the non-economist, it is most properly seen as a considerable strength - a menu for choice containing a wide variety of excellent dishes.

The principal objective of this paper is to outline the various concepts and techniques adopted by economists in their analyses of training. The next section focuses on theoretical issues and the following section is concerned with methodological issues. The paper concludes with an overview of the current state of play in this area.

Theoretical issues

In attempting to answer the sorts of questions frequently asked in the training area, economists have adopted a variety of theoretical perspectives. Some choose to apply the standard tools of mainstream economics, whilst others have applied a more descriptive approach which explicitly recognises the role of institutions and the way these shape the labour market.

The debate concerning the merits and shortcomings of the different theoretical perspectives is, moreover, not simply a matter of academic interest but is equally relevant for practitioners in the training field. The various theories provide the hypotheses that try to explain observed relationships and the causal mechanisms involved, and thus provide the basis for prediction and evaluation. Without such a theoretical basis empirical investigation would operate in a vacuum, making interpretation impossible. To observe a series of 'facts' cannot in itself provide a basis for evaluation or prediction. Only by understanding how observed relationships arise is it possible to evaluate training programmes and provide a basis for public policy.

In this section, therefore, we shall provide an overview of the different perspectives economists have brought to their analysis of training. In fact, economists have adopted a broad spectrum of theoretical viewpoints and the demarcation between them is not always clear cut. To aid exposition we shall use the standard neoclassical model as our point of reference against which other theoretical contributions can be compared. Since the 1960's, models of the labour market employing the tools of neoclassical micro-economics have established themselves as the mainstream. There is, however, a considerable body of economists who believe that despite its impeccable logic and mathematical rigour, the neoclassical box of tricks is inadequate in being able to provide a useful basis for labour market analysis. In particular, these critics point to the absence of an institutional content to neoclassical models. They suggest that by ignoring the way institutions in an economy constrain the decisions of workers and firms in the labour market, the neoclassical model cannot possibly provide a basis for explaining labour market outcomes.

In what follows we shall first provide a description of the neoclassical model as contained in the human capital theory. The shortcomings of this approach and several developments of the model are then considered. This is followed by an outline of several theories that we shall consider under the heading of 'institutional' but which are in fact diverse in nature and in the extent to which they maintain a neoclassical outlook.

The neoclassical approach to the economics of training

According to the neoclassical model, labour market outcomes are determined by the interaction of supply and demand considerations. In the present context, the supply side is explained according to the human capital theory whilst the marginal productivity theory underlies the demand side.

In its most extreme form the human capital theory proposes that all productivity differences between individuals reflect differences in the amount of human capital they possess. Individuals acquire human capital in a variety of ways including education, training and migration. The important feature of this acquisition, however, is that it is an investment in the sense that the individual foregoes current income for increased earnings potential in the future. Assuming that individuals wish to maximise the present value of their lifetime earnings, they will accumulate human capital up to the point where the marginal benefits - the discounted expected incremental income that arises from the investment - equals the marginal cost of acquiring it.

On the demand side, profit maximising firms will employ labour up to the point where the wage equals the value of the marginal product with technology and capital taken as exogenous parameters. Competition will then ensure that wage differentials reflect the value of the extra output made possible by the higher level of education or training.

This version of the human capital theory was developed by Ben Porath (1967) to explain the optimum life cycle pattern of human capital accumulation. In essence, the theory in terms of its application to training is basically a theory of occupational choice. Workers choose between jobs that offer different amounts of training opportunities. Those workers who choose jobs with training receive lower current earnings but higher future earnings than those who enter jobs with less training. This choice primarily reflects differences in individual preferences though subsequent work by Becker(1975) extended the model to accommodate differences in ability and family background;, and the differential access individuals have to the resources necessary for funding education and training programmes.

Perhaps the most restrictive assumption underlying this analysis is that it has very little to say both about the nature of the skills individuals acquire and the about the nature of the training activity itself. The former is important because it has implications for the financing training and is conditioned by the institutional framework within which it takes place. The latter has implications not only for the efficient provision of training but also brings into question the way people acquire skills.

Within the standard human capital model training is assumed to take place primarily on-the-job and is simply an extension of the schooling decision in which there is less than complete specialisation in education. This is only valid if the training involved is general in the sense that the individual's productivity gain can be applied in any job and not just in the one in which the training was received. In this case the concept of a firm as an institutional entity is irrelevant. Such an assumption is, of course, highly restrictive and has been relaxed by several human capital theorists. Becker's model of general versus specific training is especially relevant.

The idea that some skills can increase productivity only in the firm or on the job where the training is received has a number of implications for the human capital model. In the first place, the relevant time period over which the benefits accrue are no longer the individual's lifetime but the expected duration of the employment contract with the firm or the expected duration of the job itself. Second, it is no longer the case that the optimum pattern of lifetime investment is one that is heavily loaded during the earlier parts of an individual's working life. Again the important consideration is the expected duration of the job.

4

Perhaps the most important consequence of introducing the distinction between general and specific skills concerns the question of how training is financed. In the case of general training employers have no incentive to finance training since it would be impossible to recoup their expenditures: workers are free to take their newly acquired skills to the highest bidder making it impossible for firms to set a wage below the marginal product. General training can therefore be expected to be financed by the individuals who receive it.

Where skills are specific, workers will be less inclined to finance the investment. Since they cannot transfer these skills to other firms or jobs, individual workers will be concerned that they will not recoup the costs of such training should they lose their jobs. Employers on the other hand will also be reluctant to commit themselves to high training expenditures for fear that employees leave before the benefits of the training are fully recouped. The optimum strategy is that the costs of specific training are shared and that both sides agree on employment relationships that reduce turnover.

In practice, of course, most skills contain both general and specific elements so the distinction is only useful as a convenient analytical tool. It does, however, raise the question of what determines the mix between general and specific training firms provide.

One feature of the training process that also receives very little attention in the human capital model is the nature of the training activity itself. It is implicitly assumed that individuals spend part of their working time learning technical skills and as a result become more productive workers. However, many critical job skills are the informal outcome of doing the job itself. Such learning-by-doing may be an unavoidable feature of doing a particular job or may depend on custom and social relationships at the workplace. In either case the relevance of the human capital individual decision making framework is called into question. Both Rosen (1972) and Parsons (1980) have attempted to formulate human capital models in which the characteristics of the training activity itself are accommodated.

Developments within the neoclassical framework

The assumption that training provides individuals with cognitive and technical skills that directly enhances an individual's productivity has been questioned by some neoclassical economists. Alternative models have been developed in which hiring workers is an uncertain investment. This uncertainty arises because a worker's productivity is unobserved at the time of hiring and can only be gauged after they have been employed for a length of time. Under these circumstances, firms will use signals which they believe are indicators of individual productive capacity to screen workers. Such signals will include amongst other things a willingness to undertake on-the-job training, though this would only be a good indicator of potential productivity if training is more costly to undertake for less productive workers.

Criticisms of the human capital model

Human capital theory has over the years given rise to a vast literature, though much of this has been narrowly focused and has simply attempted to establish the impact that human capital investment has on a narrow range of labour market outcomes. Very little attention has been directed to the question of why some individuals have access to training whilst others do not. Similarly, the human capital theory has very little to say about the demand side of the labour market. For example, why do some firms offer more training than others and what determines the type of training they offer? It is hardly surprising therefore that labour market institutions receive very little attention.

Some economists are, however, not simply critical of the absence of an institutional/demand side analysis. They also question the way human capital theory describes the mechanisms through which training is acquired and the role it plays in wage and employment determination. They emphasise the informality of training within firms and that it involves learning-by-doing and being 'show the ropes'(Blaug 1976). Training is seen more as a form of socialisation at the workplace that involves the internalisation of the norms and values of the firm and existing workers. Training is thus not considered to be an endogenous variable determined within the choice theoretic framework of neoclassical economics.

Institutional economists are also critical of the simple application of one relationship or theory to all workers irrespective of the institutional frameworks and divisions within which groups of workers operate. Not all workers have equal access to groups of jobs and as a result not all will

6

benefit equally from training. In order to understand how labour markets function it is therefore deemed necessary to understand how institutions and market imperfections develop and change through time and how they affect and are affected by workers and employers.

It is also important to note that the human capital model will generate an efficient amount of training only under a very restrictive set of assumptions. In particular, a competitive labour market comprised of maximising individuals and firms will be efficient as long as all workers have access to capital at the social rate of interest, job changing is costless, there are a large number of firms demanding the particular skills concerned and there are no externalities.

As a result doubts have been expressed that a model based on such restrictive assumptions can have any value in explaining what happens in the real world. Imperfect capital markets and uncertainty about future incomes can give rise to significant underinvestment in training by individuals. Limited labour mobility may encourage firms to bear part of the costs of general training or reduce the premium paid to workers with specific skills to reduce turnover. Trade unions can affect pay structures in favour of unskilled workers reducing the return to training or by pushing up the pay of trainees thus reducing the amount of training or the skill intensity of training.

These are just a few examples of how market imperfections can distort the efficient provision of training that would result under the conditions assumed by human capital theorists. More importantly, they highlight the way particular labour market institutions shape economic forces and determine labour market outcomes.

The institutional approach

The modern development of an institutional alternative to the neoclassical analysis of training has its origins in the work of John Stuart Mill. Mill was critical of the market orientated analysis of Adam Smith and who proposed that institutional factors were too significant and prevalent to be seen as simple short term deviations from the competitive equilibrium. Rather he suggested that the labour market comprised non-competing groups of workers. Within each group, wage and employment determination (including opportunities for training) differ and are determined by custom and institutional rules. Access to groups of jobs is similarly constrained by custom and social norms.

The institutional alternative was further developed by the American institutional economists of the 1940's and 1950's who proposed the concepts of balkanised and structured labour markets to describe the role played by institutional factors in determining the way labour markets operate.

The contemporary institutional literature is diverse though it owes much to the recent work of Doeringer and Piore (1971) and their development of the concept of internal labour markets. Such markets are concerned with wage determination and the allocation of labour within the firm, including the availability and nature of training. The internal labour market can be seen as an efficiency response of firms in the face of uncertainty, fixed employment costs and the specific nature of skills. Doeringer and Piore, however, emphasise their institutional and social nature and the mechanisms through which firms are able to develop rules and procedures that are isolated from external economic forces.

Within this framework the labour market can be seen as comprising favourable jobs in structured internal labour markets and more disadvantaged jobs in unstructured internal labour markets. Access to favourable employment opportunities is not based on the productivity related characteristics individuals possess but on social acceptability and custom. Indeed productivity is related to the job an individual does and is not the result of human capital decision making. This is reinforced by the fact that training is acquired through learning-by-doing which is an integral part of the job but which requires the cooperation of co-workers and the acceptance of group norms.

For some institutionalists, productivity is a technical relation determined by the types and quantity of machines available, whilst others offer a more radical analysis in which productivity is rooted in social relations and the power relations between social classes. In both cases, however, a worker's productivity arises out of the job he or she does.

For institutionalists, therefore, the labour market is seen as being subject to external influences that condition the impact of economic forces. As a result the labour market no longer conforms to one based on occupational labour markets with outcomes determined by the forces of competition. The fact that firms incur a significant proportion of both general and specific training costs, Marsden suggests, has led them to internalise labour markets (Marsden, 1986).

Not all protagonists in the debate consider the two approaches as alternatives and various attempts have been made to introduce institutional factors into a neoclassical framework. An example of this is Thurow's job competition model. This includes many of the components of the institutional approach already mentioned. Productivity is assumed to be an attribute of jobs rather than workers, reflecting the capital intensity of the production process. Workers will receive the necessary skills to perform their jobs through both informal (learning by doing) and formal training programmes. The main consideration for firms is then to minimise training costs. Workers are seen to queue for jobs, with their position in the job queue determined by their 'trainability'. Since this is not observable, firms will use as signals those characteristics that it feels are associated with lower training costs. These characteristics will include such factors as education, age, sex, and race.

Once a worker as obtained access to a good job and received training the costs associated with training him or her for the next job on the job ladder are less relative to an outside candidate. This internal promotion and employment will then give rise to internal labour markets. Specific skills will encourage the firm to try and reduce turnover further and thus act as an additional force in the development of structured internal labour markets.

Overview

The plethora of theoretical perspectives present in the economic analysis of training leaves those interested in better understanding issues in the training area with a large menu for choice. On the one hand, there is the highly rigourous Ben-Porath human capital model with minimal institutional content and, on the other hand, the more descriptive approach deriving from the institutional tradition. In between are numerous eclectic approaches which combine elements from these polar types.

The choice made by those attempting to develop their understanding of training issues depends on a number of factors, primarily personal preference and the nature of the analysis to be undertaken. There are no hard and fast rules for this choice. The one certainty, however, is that such a choice will be made, either explicitly of implicitly. At this point it is appropriate to remember the oft-quoted words of John Maynard Keynes, 'The ideas of economists and political philosophers ... are more powerful than is commonly understood. Indeed the world is ruled by little else. Practical men, who believe themselves to be quite exempt from any intellectual influences, are usually the slaves of some defunct economist.'

Methodological issues

The main purpose of using a scientific method in a research programme is to mitigate any bias which might otherwise be inherent in any conclusions drawn. Such bias can emanate from a variety of sources - data which contain an inherent bias (information bias), methods which fail to allow adequately for observed differences between members of a sample (observed heterogeneity bias) and methods which fail to allow adequately for unobserved differences between members of a sample (unobserved heterogeneity bias). Economists in the training area have focused their attention on the second and third of these and have become increasingly concerned with developing techniques for mitigating the bias caused by unobserved heterogeneity.

Information bias

Information bias emanates from two main sources. The first concerns the use of a sample which is not a random selection of the overall population to which the results are to be generalised. This could occur for a variety of reasons, including biased selection procedures and the failure of some sample members to respond to the request for information. The second major source of information bias results from questions which do not obtain accurate and/or consistent information about the phenomenon under analysis. This can result from poorly worded questions which are interpreted differently by different members of the sample, leading questions which suggest particular responses to respondents or questions which define key concepts in a manner which is different from that of the researcher.

Economists have generally been much less prone to collect their own data than other social scientists. While this is less true in the training area

10

than in a number of other specialist areas, much economic research on training has typically used secondary data which has been collected for reasons other than the research itself. This has varied from large aggregative data-sets such as the Labour Force Survey and the General Household Survey to more disaggregative information such as that to be found in Youth Cohort Surveys. Little attention has been paid to the potential biases which are inherent in these data-sets, despite substantial evidence that, first, the samples from which they are drawn are not random and, secondly, that questions in the training area are not unproblematic.

The most extensive data-set for analysing training in Britain is the National Training Survey (NTS). It was undertaken in 1975 and 1976 and is therefore now extremely dated. It is based on retrospective work histories, which were collected by interview. The definition used of training was extremely broad - anything which may have helped an individual to learn to do his or her work (Greenhalgh and Stewart, 1987). Economists have not used this survey extensively and it is unlikely that this body of work will be extended in the future (except perhaps by historians). The major economic analysis of this data set was by Greenhalgh and Stewart (1987) on the effects and determinants of training.

National data sets collected by the Central Statistical Office typically contain little information on training. The General Household Survey (a survey of 10,000 households) has recently included some broad questions on training by asking respondents to identify any 'education, training or self-instruction that would help with (your job or) a job that you might do in the future.' It has been used by Francis Green for his paper to this conference and so we shall leave further discussion of its potential to later.

The Labour Force Survey also contains material on training. It requests information on training received in the period immediately prior to the survey and on vocational qualifications obtained. It is an annual survey which is based on 60,000 to 80,000 households. These data have been used by Green (1991) and by Christine Greenhalgh and George Mavrotas for their paper.

Less aggregative data sets have been more extensively used by economists to analyse training. Prime examples are the Youth Cohort Surveys. These are panel data sets which are based on the collection of

11

broad background and retrospective work history information from cohorts of 16 to 19 year olds in England and Wales. An equivalent survey has been undertaken for Scotland. They contain questions relating to on- and off-the-job training and on the obtaining of vocational qualifications. To date, however, these data-sets have largely been used to evaluate the labour market effects of participation on the Youth Training Scheme; see, for example Main and Shelly (1990) and Whitfield and Bourlakis (1991). YCS has also been used by Dolton, Makepeace and Treble for their paper in this conference. A major problem with YCS is that the populations on which it is based are nor random samples of the relevant cohort. This reflects both the fact that the original sample only included state schools and that there is a major attrition bias which is caused by the failure of some members of the original sample to respond to all of the questionnaires.

Other data-sets of this type which have been used by economists to analyse training are the National Child Development Survey, the British Social Attitudes Survey, Training in Britain and the Survey of Graduates and Diplomates.

All of the above-mentioned analyses are secondary analyses in the sense of using data collected by someone other than the researcher. The nature of the research has therefore been constrained by the type and range of questions asked. This has generally proved to be extremely limiting and has prevented the research from addressing many of the issues raised by the theoretical work or even adequately operationalising the main analytical concepts, such as skill transferability or the general/specific training divide. A key problem concerns the definition which is accorded to the term 'training'. This not only tends to be very loose but it varies substantially between data-sets. It is therefore probable that studies based on different data-sets are tapping different dimensions of what is meant by the term 'training'.

A more detailed overview of data available for the analysis of training can be found in Peter Elias' paper, including information on data which will only become available in the future.

Observed heterogeneity bias

Economists have been much more concerned to mitigate biases originating from observed heterogeneity than from data sources. Such biases result from the fact that persons undertaking training or firms engaging in training differ from those which do not in a number of important respects, about which we have information. For example, it is possible that large firms undertake more training than small firms and that older individuals undertake less training than younger. Unless we allow for such heterogeneity in the most appropriate manner, estimates of, say, the effect of training on profitability or earnings will be biased.

Allowing for observed heterogeneity bias has involved the use of a wide range of multivariate techniques, most of which are based on the method of ordinary least squares. The estimation techniques used have largely developed from research on earnings functions and unemployment. They initially revolved around the use of simple ordinary least squares regression analysis to allow for observed differences between sample members but there has been increasing use of maximum likelihood estimation techniques in more recent research, reflecting the discrete nature of many of the important outcomes in the training area and the increasing ability of computers to handle the complexities of maximum likelihood estimation.

Research on the effect of training on earnings has primarily developed out of human capital research. Most earnings functions which are estimated follow the basic Mincer log-linear specification and include explanatory variables, such as age/experience, age/experience squared and years of schooling, which are to be found in most human capital analyses. It is also common, however, to see variables relating to family background, marital status and occupational position that do not yield direct human capital interpretations. Moreover, some of the key concepts of human capital theory, such as the general/specific training divide, are rarely operationalised in earnings analysis. An exception is the paper by Francis Green in this volume.

Research on the effect of training on employment/unemployment has been concerned with both the probability that a person will be in one state or another at a particular point and the probability that an individual will leave either state (particularly unemployment) within a certain time. The main concern of the former has been the analysis of regression models with dichotomous dependent variables (discrete regression models) and has involved a plethora of techniques ranging from the linear probability model to probit and logit analysis. The latter has been more concerned with the estimation of hazard functions and has drawn heavily on the extensive literature on the influence of unemployment benefits of the duration of unemployment; for a review of this literature see Kiefer (1988).

Research on the determinants of training has also focussed on the use of discrete regression models, particularly logit and probit. These typically include explanatory variables which are akin to those found in human capital earnings functions, such as age, age squared and tenure, although these are rarely justified in human capital terms. Such functions are reduced forms which reflect behaviour on both the supply and demand sides of the training market. They are typically estimated on data relating to individuals. Examples of such analyses are Greenhalgh and Stewart (1987) and Green (1991).

Unobserved heterogeneity bias

Of most concern to economists in the training area in recent years has been the mitigation of bias emanating from non-random selection for training. Such bias can arise either because of self-selection processes or from the decisions made by administrators of training schemes. The former could result, for example, from the fact that only the more motivated members of a population undertook training. It is to be expected that they would, say, earn more than their less motivated counterparts even in the absence of training. Consequently any analysis which related the propensity to train and earnings would involve an upward bias for the effect of training on earnings unless the joint effect of motivation on training and earnings was properly estimated. Such a bias could also occur if training programme administrators selected, say, those most likely to benefit from the programme and excluded others. It should be noted, however, that such bias only occurs if we do not have sufficient information on the factors causing non-random selection to estimate their separate effects, that is the bias is caused by unobserved heterogeneity.

The most common example of such bias in the literature concerns the effect of undertaking a training programme on earnings, although there are many other examples of potential selectivity bias in the training area. A standard procedure of someone attempting to estimate whether participation on a training programme increased a person's earnings would be to estimate an earnings function using ordinary least squares

14

regression analysis with a vector of explanatory variables including a proxy for training. The coefficient on the training variable would be taken as an estimate of the training effect. However, such a technique will yield consistent estimates only if entry into training is random. Otherwise those undertaking training can be expected to earn different amounts from those who do not and the coefficient will reflect that in addition to the independent effect of training.

A number of techniques have been developed to mitigate such selectivity bias. These have typically involved complex econometric techniques which are based on strong assumptions about the processes relating entry to training and the generation of earnings differences. The econometric techniques used can be classified into two main types. The first are known as one-step estimators and are typically based on the assumption that the bias in the earnings equation is a fixed effect which is eliminated if the earnings equation is differenced; see, for example, Bassi (1984). The second are known as two-step estimators, the most commonly used of which is Heckman's correction technique (Heckman,1976). It is based on extremely strong assumptions about the relationship between participation in training and earnings. This has been used, *inter alia*, by Main and Shelly (1990) and Whitfield and Bourlakis (1991).

Such techniques are only as valid as the assumptions on which they are based. An indirect test of these assumptions has been provided by the comparison of the results of randomised experiments and those which would have been generated by the same data using econometric procedures. In randomised experiments a population is randomly divided into a treatment group which undertakes training and a control group which does not. This prevents selectivity bias from occurring by design. Tests using the data from such experiments have suggested that, in many cases, the econometric procedures derive results which are very different from those of the experiments and that established econometric specification tests are not good guides between better and worse results (see, for example, LaLonde, 1986 and Fraker and Maynard, 1987). They do, however, suggest a number of indicators of how to improve on past performance. In particular, two-step estimators are seen to be superior to one-step and analyses using longitudinal data tend to perform better than those without. Issues in this area are examined in this conference in the papers by Rebecca Maynard and Robert LaLonde.

An interesting variant on the use of experimental methods is the construction of matched samples of either individuals or firms. This has been undertaken by the National Institute of Economic and Social Research (NIESR) in their work on the relationships between training and a number of key economic variables. They construct matched samples of plants in particular industries in different countries in an attempt to ascertain the relationship between training and qualifications and productivity levels. Such an approach considerably reduces the amount of heterogeneity inherent in the comparison but it certainly does not eliminate it. For example, the average size of plant may vary in different countries; consequently there is a need to allow for this factor via some form of multivariate technique. Furthermore, it is probable that the plants differ in some important but unobservable ways. Consequently great care must be taken in analysing the results to allow for both observed and unobserved heterogeneity bias. Nonetheless the NIESR method does focus attention on the major differences in training processes and work organisation in different countries. Geoff Mason and Bart van Ark's paper outlines some of the most recent research by the NIESR.

The current state of play

The economics of training area is in the state of considerable flux at present for the best of all reasons - a lot of people are contributing interesting and far-reaching ideas about theory and methodology and are using these ideas to illuminate a wide range of key issues in the training domain. Above all, there is a conscious attempt to develop and apply a rigourous analytical approach to a complex and multi-faceted phenomenon.

In the theoretical area there is no doubt that the human capital approach is dominant. There is, however, an increasing awareness that, at the very least, it needs to be augmented with concepts from a more sociological or institutional approach. In the methodological area it is well recognised that selectivity bias is a major problem and that the search for techniques to handle it has not been completely successful. The careful use of experimental data has, however, guided this search towards more fruitful avenues.

The question might therefore be asked of what the economist has to offer the analysis of training. This review has suggested three main contributions. The first is an awareness of the complexity of the issues in the training debate. While this might not be popular in an era in which people are valued for their abilities to bring solutions rather than problems to the ears of their leaders, it is an essential part of the search for long-term improvements in the efficiency of training. The second contribution of economists to the training debate is a rigourous approach to analysing such issues which is, at the same time, sufficiently flexible to accommodate a wide range of standpoints. Thirdly, economists offer to those involved in the training domain a set of best practice techniques which have been tried and tested. These offer the best possibility for the mitigation of bias in evaluations of the effectiveness of given training programmes.

References

Bassi, L.J. (1984), 'Estimating the effect of training programs with non-random selection', *Review of Economics and Statistics*, 66, pp. 36-43.

Fraker, T. and Maynard, R. (1987), 'The adequacy of comparison group designs for evaluations of employment-related programs', *Journal of Human Resources*, 22, pp. 194-227.

Green, F. (1991), 'Sex discrimination in job-related training', *British Journal of Industrial Relations*, 29, pp. 295-304.

Greenhalgh, C. and Stewart, M. (1987), 'The effects and determinants of training', *Oxford Bulletin of Economics and Statistics*, 49, pp. 171-190.

Kiefer, N. (1988), 'Economic duration data and hazard functions', *Journal of Economic Literature*, 26, pp. 646-676.

LaLonde, R. (1986), 'Evaluating the econometric evaluations of training programs with experimental data', *American Economic Review*, 76, pp. 604-20.

Main, B.G.M. and Shelly, M.A. (1990), 'The effectiveness of YTS as a manpower policy', *Economica*, 57, pp. 495-514.

Whitfield, K. and Bourlakis, C. (1991), 'An empirical analysis of YTS, employment and earnings', *Journal of Economic Studies*, 18, pp. 42-56.

2 Workforce training in the Thatcher era – market forces and market failures

Christine Greenhalgh and George Mavrotas

Introduction

It is widely believed that the poor economic performance of the UK economy over the post-war period is in part attributable to inadequate workforce skills, particularly an absence of middle level technical qualifications (Prais 1990). Recent government initiatives in the fields of education and training have attempted to provide a better environment for the creation of a skilled workforce, but in the main the provision of skill training, especially for those already at work, has been left to market forces. The direct expenditures of government have been concentrated in the two areas of labour market entry and re-entry, focusing on the transition from school to work and the retraining of the long term unemployed (Employment Institute 1990). Thus employers and/or their workers have financed most of the training which has taken place for the adult employed population.

The economic theory of training markets suggest that, left to itself, the market will be unlikely to provide either the right level or the best balance of general (transferable) and specific skills; rather it will tend to under provide general skills. Too little general training will be financed by employers because they cannot ensure that all the returns to this investment will accrue to their business, due to staff turnover. The deficit will not be made good by employees financing their own training since they face constraints on their liquidity and uncertainty about the future value of the skills.

Despite the gloomy predictions of economic theory there is evidence that the proportion of the workforce receiving some training has risen sharply over the last decade. In this paper we document the rise in training propensity in Britain as evidenced by data from the Labour Force

Survey (LFS). We examine whether this is a substantive rise, perhaps due to a change of incentives and attitudes towards training or an illusion based on simple but uniformative average statistics.

We begin with a short summary of the changing patterns of sectoral and occupational employment in the period 1979-1989, which delineate the constraints against which the career decisions of individual workers and the hiring decisions of individual firms were made. We then describe the changing patterns of training be sector and evaluate how far the observed changes represent an improvement of the skill base for manufacturing and traded services.

Changing employment patterns in the 1980s

The factors contributing to changes in the level and structure of employment in the first half of the Thatcher era can broadly be summarised as those of weakening international competitiveness, labour saving technological change in production methods, and a changing balance of public an private production.

The period 1979-84 was characterised by a sharp loss of employment in the traded goods sector, because of both long standing weaknesses in product quality and short term problems of an overvalued currency. Whilst the loss of output markets caused job losses at all levels of skill in the firm which went bankrupt, there was also a significant amount of job loss due to the introduction of computer aided design and manufacture, which was felt more keenly by certain types of workers in manufacturing (Daniel 1987, Northcott and Walling, 1988). Table 2.1 shows that as the share of manufacturing employment (particularly engineering) fell, that of distribution rose with other factors remaining fairly constant.

An alternative way of delineating sectors is given in Table 2.2 where, instead of the customary grouping of product types, we adopt a grouping based on the industry's technology and trade characteristics; (for the bases of the groups also Greenhalgh, Taylor and Wilson, 1991). It can be seen that the largest part of the decline in manufacturing employment was in the high technology sector; the share of total employment in technology-using non-manufacturing (mostly services) rose. The more standard technology industries and the non-tradeable sector absorbed a slightly higher share of workers than before.

20

Table 2.3 documents the uneven incidence of these changes for broadly defined occupational groups. It can be seen that the demand for plant and machine operatives fell more sharply than for other skills and craft occupations were also less in demand by 1984. In contrast, the share of jobs classified as senior and highly skilled rose sharply. These trends reflect the erosion of the role of semiskilled workers by automated processes (Northcott and Walling, 1988) and the continuing rise in the demand for multiskilled supervisors, to oversee and maintain complex manufacturing processes and equipment or to provide professional services (Wilson and Bosworth, 1987; Institute for Employment Research, 1989).

The directions of change in the sectoral distribution of employment were similar in the second half of the Thatcher era, but the speed of change was more muted, given the rise in manufacturing output. The exceptional positive element was the rapid rise in the share of employment in business services, which displaced distribution as the fastest absorber of labour. But of course not all those looking for work could be easily accommodated with a job offer in the expanding sectors. Tables 2.4A and 2.4B show the degree of sectoral specificity of occupational employment in 1979 was extremely high for men and women who were working at the levels most affected by technological redundancy.

The rising unemployment rates in 1979-84 (and increased inactivity rates for men) are documented in Table A1, Appendix I below. Despite some authors claims that structural change and technological change did not cause rising unemployment in this period (Jackman and Roper, 1987; Nickell and Kong, 1989) we would argue that these factors together with losses of traded goods markets were important. The large redundancy rate in manufacturing, coupled with sector specific skills and work experience formed a large part of the causes of the rise in unemployment and the fall in participation rates from 1979-84. Although unemployment eventually fell it is interesting to note that the inactivity rate for men remained high, even in the boom years during which the female participation rate rose sharply.

Training Flows and Stocks in 1979

The proportion of the workforce who were receiving vocational training at the time of the 1979 Labour Force Survey was rather small - one in twenty men and one in thirty women were undertaking formal training either full or part time. Those reporting any training during their work history were a minority for both men and women and the most common pattern was to have received only one spell (see Appendix I Table A2). Amongst men apprenticeships were the most prevalent type of course and the higher training rate for males is largely explained by the smaller proportion of women taking this type of training, which was most often associated with employment in the manufacturing or construction sectors at craft level (Table 2.5).

Training rates differed by sector (Table 2.6) with the highest rates being observed in business and public services, and the lowest in distribution for men and manufacturing for women. The higher incidence in the two high training service sectors was accompanied by a higher propensity to undertake short courses; thus over time a larger share of the workforces in these sectors experienced a short spell of training but the degree to which their skills were enhanced by the course would be perhaps rather limited (Table 2.7). Regrouping the industries into the technology/trade subgroups shows less differences between sectors overall but reveals a slightly higher training rate in the high-tech manufacturing group compared to middle-tech (Table 2.8).

Table A2 compares the training history of the unemployed with that of workers in 1979, whilst Table A3 shows recent training incidence for the larger stock of unemployed in 1984. Whilst in both cases the training measures are lower for those without work, there is still a considerable proportion of skills in this latter group.

Who financed the training of those who were on courses at this time? The 1979 Labour Force Survey shows that 60% of all trainees received help from a private employer, a further 17% were aided by government (including both as employer and special schemes) whilst only 22% were reliant entirely on private resources. It is safe to assume that for the vast majority of training experiences for those in work there was a sharing of total direct and indirect costs between employers and workers who, even if they had course fees paid had to put in extra effort or spend leisure time studying.

Training needs and the signals to providers 1984

Combining the facts of UK training practices in the 1970s with the labour market experiences of the early 1980s enables us to gain an indication of the signals about the returns to different types of training, as they would have been perceived by employers and workers in the mid 1980s. Employers in manufacturing were faced with a slack labour market with an excess supply of male workers with traditional apprenticeship skills, but were not increasing the size of their workforces nor seeking more of these kinds of workers because of trends in process technology. The CBI skill shortages indicator for manufacturing firms was at an all time low during the early 1980s. In these circumstances it would be expected that manufacturers would seek to reduce the number of apprenticeships they offered. Equally, new entrants to the labour market would be dissuaded from entering traditional craft apprenticeships by the lack of certainty that these skills would be required in future.

However there is reason to suppose that in other areas of the occupational spectrum that there was an excess demand for skilled workers; Table 2.3 shows that there was increasing employment for those in occupation groups 1-3. These were also (Table 2.4) the least sector-specific occupations, requiring the general training which the market is least well able to provide. These signals would be expected to produce a market response of shorter courses of training to an increasing proportion of the workforce. This would avoid the risks inherent in lengthy apprenticeships, which would have looked unattractive to both sides of the market, but go some way to supplying the rising demand for higher level and multiskilled workers as the economy recovered.

Training incidence and duration 1984-89

Did the market for training respond in this way? Table 2.9 shows the training incidence and duration measures available in the Labour Force Survey, which at first sight entirely confirm these expectations.

First, comparing training incidence for 1984 with 1979 there is no evidence of decreased incidence of training during the depression; despite the common perception that training is a pro-cyclical activity. Although the measures available in these years are not exactly comparable due to changes in the questions asked in the LFS, it is possible to see from Table 2.9 that even the level of off-the-job training per week was as high in 1984 as the total amount of training in 1979 including both on and off job spells. At the 1984 low point in the business cycle profit shares had only recently revived, business failures were high by historical levels and perceived skill shortages in manufacturing had been low for four years. However it appears that the structural shifts in employment and the changes in process technology were stimulating the training market as a whole.

The rise in training continued and accelerated during the economic upswing of 1984-89. In this period there was a very rapid increase in the incidence of training for those at work, which rose 50% by 1989. By this time women's training propensity had surpassed that of male workers, a feature which entirely reverses previous male-females relativities (Green, 1991a and 1991b).

The third feature of interest is the changing pattern of durations of training courses. The major part of the increase in training is in short courses lasting less than one month; although the longest courses of more than three years may have risen from 1984 to 1986 (statistics not entirely comparable) they later fell in importance from 1986 to 1989. Separate evidence of the number of apprentices in engineering can be obtained from the Engineering Industry Training Board (Stevens, 1991). This confirms that there was a rapid reduction in traditional apprenticeships. Evidence from the Training in Britain study (Training Agency 1989) also confirms the picture of more people experiencing training at work over the years 1984-86 (Rigg, 1989).

Table 2.10 tabulates the incidence of training for each occupational group over the decade. These figures show that the incidence of training rose most quickly in occupation of a professional and technical nature (group 2 and 3) which were a rising share of all jobs. Training propensity for women rose particularly fast for these occupations, reflecting the greater skill shortages for such workers. Relative to craft occupations, training incidence also increased in clerical, service and sales jobs, but the small number of mostly male workers taken on in the declining craft field were not deprived of the opportunity to train as rates rose in all occupations.

Who financed the increased burden of training in the late 1980s? The Rigg report shows that for the adult worker aged over 25 there are very few instances of training by the individual for younger workers. In our interpretation of the causes of the rise in training therefore we shall continue to assume that employers were major financiers for most of the training incidents reported in the LFS.

From the point of view of the economy and its potential for competitiveness and growth in the future the types of skills being obtained are crucial. In Tables 2.11 and 2.12 (and Table A5) we tabulate the training incidence and duration measures by sector of employment. This shows the incidence of training to have risen most rapidly for the static share of the workforce employed in the non-tradeable sector.

Essentially women have achieved their high training incidence by being disproportionately employed by government, which always offered them greater parity, and by private services which have been hiring and training at an increasing rate. It is useful if government sets the standard for workforce training as part of a package of remuneration and conditions of work, but the contribution of this training to the underlying shortages of skills in the private sector is likely to be minimal unless there is a high degree of intersectoral mobility and the skills obtained are relevant.

Tables A6A and A6B repeat the cross tabulation of occupations by sector for 1989. As in 1979 (Table 2.4) the employment of many highly skilled women (occupations 2 and 3) was still concentrated in the public sector. For both men and women the pattern of sector concentration of occupations changed only to a limited degree, reflecting the loss of level 5 and 8 jobs in manufacturing and the growth of level 2 and 3 jobs in private business services.

Within the traded goods and service sectors there is some evidence of higher training rates in the most technologically active industries, a feature which has also been observed for the United States (Tan 1990), but there is little if any change in the relative propensity to train by sector during the late 1980s. Muellbauer and Murphy (1990) have shown that investment in the 1980s was concentrated in the least traded sectors of the economy. Whilst the training record does not look quite so starkly biased as their results for capital investment it is still worrying to find that non-tradeables lead other sectors.

Training and turnover

In attempting to judge how valuable is the observed rise in training we also have to consider how much it has added to the skill base given the forces operating to make existing skills redundant. Training can be offered either to an employee of long standing to upgrade his/her skills or to newly hired employees as part of their induction into the firm. In a labour market experiencing a rapid rate of restructuring and redeployment it would be expected that the incidence of induction training would rise, as this is almost a necessary consequence of hiring a worker into a new field of work. In this situation the gross rate of investment will exceed the net rate, both for the worker and for the economy, to the extent that old skills are being scrapped.

However the consequences of deindustrialisation and economic depression are not all negative for training activity, because as redundancies rise the level of voluntary quits tends to fall. Employers facing the opportunity to choose between a worker coming to him directly from a similar job and one who has been unemployed or inactive will almost certainly face lower induction training costs for the former. (This is the root of the so-called poaching problem). But if employee quit rates are depressed during a down swing then there will be less opportunity to poach and, for those employers who train, there will be some relief from this private wastage of training effort. Employers will thus be more inclined to engage in upgrading skills of existing workers. Thus, in a labour market with falling quit rates and increasing new hires from non-employment both induction and upgrading could rise and the level of social net investment may be improved to the extent of the upgrading.

We can investigate the relative importance of induction and upgrading by looking at the movement of labour between jobs and the training received by stayers and movers in the workforce. Whilst this cannot reveal an entirely accurate separation of training into net investment, which augments total human capital stock in the economy, and retraining, which only repairs the skill mismatch caused by de-industrialisation and technical change or makes good population retirement, it gives some guidance in this respect.

Tables 2.13-2.15 give the proportions of current employees who were stayers (with the same employer as one year ago), movers (with a different employer than one year ago) and entrants (not employed one year ago), together with training incidence and duration statistics for each sub-group in the comparison years.

Considering first the turnover figures for the first sub-period, it is clear that between 1979 and 1984 total hiring rates hardly changed as a proportion of the workforce, but there was less job to job mobility in 1984 and thus more hiring from non-employment (unemployment, previous non-participation or education). The need for induction rose whilst the opportunity to capture returns to employer-financed upgrading for existing workers also increased.

Comparing training rates for comparable groups shows that to counter their increased share of hirings, some economy was effected in the induction of new entrants, particularly for male workers; simultaneously slightly more training was provided for stayers and job movers relative to new entrants. Training incidence was raised and brought closer to male patterns for female workers. Thus between 1979 and 1984 market responses to changing costs and benefits, as well as the changing composition of demand, benefited existing male workers and women at the expense of new male entrants.

From 1984 to 1989 the rate of hiring from non-employment remained at the 1984 level, but the number of job to job moves rose sharply. Total turnover was thus considerably higher by the top of the labour market boom, but with new entrants forming a smaller share. That this was neither entirely a cyclical effect, nor purely a compositional effect arising from the increased share of employment in shorter duration services sector jobs, can be seen in Table 2.16A/B, which document mobility by occupation in the comparison years. Although average job to job mobility was higher in lower skilled service jobs and lowest in the skill shortage occupations 2 and 3, the trend for all occupations was towards higher turnover rates comparing 1979 with 1989, (which were both peak years for labour markets).

Training incidence for new male entrants in 1989 was restored to 1979 levels and followed a similar pattern of course duration to 1984. For these new workers there was no shortening of training durations in the upswing; modal length was 1-3 years in both 84 and 89. Therefore the observed average shortening of course length was not evidence of the system short-changing new entrants. Rather it was a reflection of the rise in short duration training incidence for the majority of workers who had

27

been in employment for at least one year, (but not necessarily with the same employer).

What impact has the rise in training had on the balance between general and specific skills and on the transparency of the skill levels of trained workers? In a study of the intermediate technical qualification level of skill (Steedman, 1990) shows that the UK has not made progress in catching up with European levels between 1979 and 1988. Thus it seems likely that many of the recorded training experiences were ad hoc short courses which did not contribute by a process of accreditation to workers obtaining nationally recognises portable skills. This confirms the picture obtained by Hart and Shipman (1991) who investigated responses to skill shortages by employers in 1988.

Earlier research on the individual returns to training have shown that if a spell of training is not resulting in a recognised qualification then it might as well be short, since longer spells obtained no greater return (Greenhalgh and Steward, 1987). However the same study shows that returns to vocational qualifications are quite large in relation to training with no resultant certificate.

Training needs and the signals to providers in 1989

The sharp rise in the CBI skill shortage indicator by 1989 and the rise in turnover, together with the documentary evidence of surveys such as Skill Needs in Britain (Training Agency 1990) indicate that the British economy still faces an underlying deficit of skilled workers at full employment levels of output. Recruitment difficulties were highest in the engineering sector at the height of the boom.

However, the good news is that there is evidence of increased training in all sectors of the economy; most of the increase has taken the form of more short courses so the proportion of the workforce being exposed to training has risen even faster. Women now get as much training as men, partly as a consequence of their being over-represented in the sectors with the highest propensity to train. The bad news is that short courses are not likely to provide the necessary amount of upgrading, to close the gap with our competitors in the area of intermediate technical skills which are lacking in industry; and furthermore the high technology manufacturing sector has shown no sign of closing the gap between its own training rate and that of the non-traded sector.

The main difficulty which contributes to the continuation of short termism in the market for training is the inability of individual employers to capture all the returns to their investment. With average job to job mobility running at 11-13% and the total yearly hiring rate being 19% for men and 27% for women before the recent downturn began, it is hardly a surprise if employers were sponsoring short courses with no certification, rather than long ones which award easily understood certificates.

If the system of training provision is to overcome these difficulties it has to achieve a better matching of investment and returns.

Policy reform in the training market

The solutions for internalising these positive externalities take broadly one of three forms: training subsidy by government to providers, better definition of property rights which can be marketed, or provision of training as a local public good by a club of providers who share the benefits. Do recent reforms to the UKs training institutions and the relations between government and private providers conform to any of these solutions?

The subsidies which exist at present (Youth Training Scheme, Employment Training Scheme and Training Credits) are targeted on those in transition between school or unemployment and work. There is no universal subsidy to trainees already at work, other than the tax rebate for course fees. Thus it appears that public funds are seen as appropriately directed to sustain gross investment, to make good depreciation from either natural wastage or structural change. However subsidy is not generally seen as being required to overcome either the employer's externality problem or the worker's financial and informational constraints to increase the rate of net training investment for the majority of adult workers. The recent provision of Career Development Loans by government shows some importance is being attached to the question of liquidity constraints but take-up is still low, suggesting that information on the value of the training is still the major constraint.

Can either workers or employers be invested with complete property rights over the skills embodied in workers? With the exception of actors, pop stars and sportsmen there is no universal system of payment to personal agents,or of contracts involving transfer fees, to ensure the correspondence of effort and reward in the creation of skills. For workers with ordinary (non-unique) skills these complex and expensive contractual arrangements would not be likely to improve social welfare, so this does not seem to be a promising route for reform.

Certification of training quality plays a role in permitting property rights to be defined and hence to become more marketable. The government has correctly perceived that there are too many separate types of vocational qualifications and these are not being harmonised under the National Vocational Qualification umbrella. Whilst this should improve the portability of skills, giving stronger returns to individual investment, this will only be the case if the new standards are meaningful. Prais (1990) has argued strongly that a system which does not require both written and practical examinations validated by external examiners, not simply by training providers, will never achieve consistent standards and this will weaken the informational value of these certificates.

Training and Enterprise Councils are the piece de resistance of the current policy reforms. Do they represent the right club for the provision of training by employers as a local public good? The answer to this depends on a number of empirical features of the employment market. These including the extent to which employers requiring the same kinds of skills are clustered geographically, the rates of mobility and/or long distance commuting habits of workers, and the degree of correspondence between the area designated for the TEC and the effective definition of the labour market defined by catchment area for skills in short supply.

Unfortunately the government appears to have ignored the fact that the poaching problem could be quite severe for an active TEC with a good training record, if it is next door to a less active one whose employers are not prevented from engaging their trained workers. TECs may therefore not have any effect in encouraging employers to allocate more resources than at present to vocational training for their adult workers, but rather they may remain useful agencies for the execution of government training programs for the young and unemployed, whilst having more effect on enterprise than training.

Conclusion

Trends in the demand for skilled workers appear to have generated a significant rise in the provision of training in Britain in the past decade. The patterns of training by occupation broadly reflect the relative scarcities of workers, given the decline of manufacturing and the rise of services. The pattern by gender reflects the relative flexibility and availability of women for the expanding jobs. The short duration of training reflect profit maximising responses to high labour turnover which has increased over this period.

Thus in a number of respects the market has worked well in response to incentives and private industry has shouldered a significant training burden of restructuring the distribution of employment. Equally it has not been profitable for trainers to provide a new skill base for declining manufacturing industries. Firefighting responses to skill shortages cannot hope to reverse the vicious circle operating in industries which lack international competitiveness precisely because of an inadequate skillbase, which is needed to support basic research, innovative design of new products, and complex automated production.

Notes

Funding for this study was obtained from the ESRC under grant no. R00023 1985. Data tapes of the Labour Force Survey were supplied by the ESRC Data Archive. We are grateful to Jane Roberts for assistance in obtaining the data. Peter Elias provided us with information which greatly assisted the mapping of occupations into a consistent basis for comparison.

Table 2.1
The changing sectoral distribution of jobs

Commodity Sector	Working Men			Working Women		
	1979	1984	1989	1979	1984	1989
I Primary & Utilities	7.1	8.3	6.7	1.9	2.4	1.8
II Manufacturing	36.6	29.5	28.1	23.8	17.0	15.3
(of which Engineering)	(18.6)	(14.4)	(13.5)	(8.2)	(5.4)	(5.0)
III Construction	11.3	12.0	12.8	1.3	1.6	1.6
IV Distribution & Transport	20.0	23.9	25.2	25.1	29.1	28.5
(of which Distribution)	(11.0)	(15.7)	(16.8)	(22.3)	(26.3)	(25.1)
V Business & Miscellaneous Services	11.3	11.8	14.2	17.8	20.7	24.1
VI Non-marketed Services	12.8	13.8	12.8	29.0	28.7	28.7
(of which Health & Education)	(5.4)	(6.2)	(5.4)	(22.7)	(21.2)	(20.9)
Sample (employed or self employed)	60,245	39,797	41,660	39,373	28,399	32,640

Table 2.2
Employment by technology and trade sector

Technology/trade Sector	Working Men			Working Women		
	1979	1984	1989	1979	1984	1989
A Tradeable - High technology manufacturing	28.9	21.3	20.1	14.3	9.7	8.9
B Tradeable - medium technology manufacturing	7.9	8.2	8.0	9.7	7.4	6.4
C Tradeable - non-manufacturing technology users	44.6	51.4	55.5	45.1	52.9	55.2
D Non-tradeables	17.8	18.5	16.2	30.0	29.6	29.3
Sample (employed or self employed)	60,245	39,807	41,660	39,373	28,379	32,640

Table 2.3
The changing occupational distribution of employment

Occupation	Working Men			Working Women		
	1979	1984	1989	1979	1984	1989
1 Managerial & admin	13.1	16.0	16.5	5.2	7.0	8.0
2 Professional	7.8	9.5	9.3	6.0	6.2	7.1
3 Associate professional and technical	6.0	7.1	8.1	8.2	10.4	11.3
Sub Total 1-3	26.9	32.6	33.9	19.4	23.6	26.4
4 Clerical, secretarial	8.7	7.2	7.2	29.9	28.3	28.6
5 Craft occupations	28.8	27.2	25.1	6.1	4.7	4.0
6 Service occupations	4.5	5.3	4.6	13.3	14.8	8.3
7 Sales occupations	4.4	4.7	5.2	10.9	11.4	11.4
8 Plant & machine operatives	17.1	13.6	12.9	8.7	5.9	5.3
9 Other occupations, or unknown	9.6	9.5	11.1	11.5	11.5	16.0
Sub Total 5+8	45.9	40.8	38.0	14.8	10.6	9.3

Table 2.4A
Occupations by sector 1979 (% by row)

Sector Occupation	I Primary & Utilities	II Manufacturing	III Construction	IV Distribution & Transport	V Business & Miscellaneous Services	VI Non-marketed Services
			Working Men			
1. Managerial & admin	13.7	25.2	5.3	34.5	13.6	6.9
2. Professional	3.3	22.3	5.3	3.3	20.3	44.7
3. Associate professional & technical	3.0	30.3	5.4	10.1	24.7	25.8
4. Clerical, Secretarial	4.5	30.7	2.1	22.6	19.0	20.3
5. Craft occupations	6.8	44.6	24.7	11.1	7.9	4.2
6. Service occupations	1.2	8.5	0.5	19.0	17.6	52.3
7. Sales occupations	1.3	28.5	1.8	48.6	18.9	0.4
8. Plant & machine operatives	3.8	60.1	4.9	25.6	2.0	3.0
9. Other occupations, or unkown	19.2	23.6	18.2	21.7	5.6	11.1

Table 2.4B
Occupations by sector 1979 (% by row)

Working Women

Sector Occupation	I Primary & Utilities	II Manufacturing	III Construction	IV Distribution & Transport	V Business & Miscellaneous Services	VI Non-marketed Services
1. Managerial & admin	4.4	11.9	1.9	60.5	13.4	7.0
2. Professional	0.4	1.7	0.2	1.1	4.5	91.4
3. Associate professional & technical	0.4	6.6	0.1	2.8	16.8	72.4
4. Clerical, Secretarial	2.8	23.2	3.4	19.5	26.9	23.2
5. Craft occupations	1.3	88.8	0.5	4.7	2.4	1.8
6. Service occupations	0.6	3.6	0.1	20.8	36.8	37.2
7. Sales occupations	0.7	3.5	0.4	89.1	5.2	0.7
8. Plant & machine operatives	1.3	86.2	0.2	8.6	1.9	1.4
9. Other occupations, or unkown	4.0	15.5	0.8	20.4	14.7	43.6

Table 2.5
Recent training 1979

Location and Type Training Last Week	Working Men		Working Women	
	No.	(%)	No.	(%)
General Education	214	(6.9)	252	(18.8)
Apprentice (full-time)	1529	(49.4)	268	(20.0)
Public centre (part-time)	704	(22.7)	417	(31.2)
Other (full-time)	332	(10.7)	226	(16.9)
Other (part-time)	316	(10.2)	174	(13.0)
All trainees in employment	3095	(100)	1337	(100)
Number in employment	60,245		39,373	
Trainees as % of persons in employment	5.1		3.4	

Notes

1. 'In employment' comprises both employees and self-employed workers, all ages.

2. Training last week was surveyed for persons aged 16-60.

Table 2.6
Recent training by commodity sector 1979

Working Men - Training Incidence (Last Week)

Sector Type of Training	Primary and Utilities	Manu- facturing	Construc- tion	Distrib- ution and Transport	Business and Miscell	Non- Marketed Services	All Sectors
General Education	0.3	0.1	0.1	1.0	0.3	0.3	0.4
Vocational at Work	2.9	3.6	4.4	1.8	4.0	2.5	3.1
Vocational at public centre	1.2	1.0	0.8	0.8	1.9	3.2	1.4
Vocational at private centre	0.2	0.2	0.1	0.2	0.8	0.3	0.3
Not training	95.5	95.0	94.6	96.2	93.0	93.8	94.9

Working Women - Training Incidence (Last Week)

Sector Type of Training	Manu- facturing	Distrib- ution and Transport	Business and Miscell	Non- Marketed Services	All Sectors
General Education	0.1	1.6	0.4	0.4	0.6
Vocational at work	0.8	0.6	1.8	1.9	1.2
Vocational at public centre	0.1	0.2	0.3	0.2	0.2
Not training	98.1	96.9	95.8	95.5	96.6

Note

In Tables 6 & 7, Primary and Utilities, and also Construction, were not reported because of the small numbers of women employed in these sectors.

Table 2.7
Length of training by commodity sector 1979

Working Men - Training Durations (Last Week)

Sector Type of Training	Primary and Utilities	Manu- facturing	Construc- tion	Distrib- ution and Transport	Business and Miscell	Non- Marketed Services	All Sectors
Less than 100 hours	0.8	0.9	0.5	0.7	1.5	1.5	1.0
100 or more hours	3.7	4.2	4.9	2.5	5.8	5.1	4.2
D.K./N.A	95.5	94.8	94.6	96.8	92.7	93.3	94.8

Working Women - Training Durations (Last Week)

Sector Type of Training	Manu- facturing	Distrib- ution and Transport	Business and Miscell	Non- Marketed Services	All Sectors
Less than 100 hours	0.8	0.6	1.3	1.5	1.0
100 or more hours	1.3	1.0	3.1	3.4	2.2
D.K./N.A.	98.0	98.4	95.7	95.1	96.8

Table 2.8
Recent training by technology and trade sector 1979

Sector Training	High Technology Manufacturing	Medium Technology Manufacturing	Non-manufac- turning tech- nology users	Non- tradeables	All Sectors
Working Men					
Training incidence:	5.4	3.5	4.9	6.0	5.1
Type of training:					
General Education	0.1	0.1	0.6	0.3	0.1
Vocational at Work	3.9	2.3	2.9	2.9	3.1
Vocational at public centre	1.1	0.9	1.1	2.7	1.4
Vocational at private centre	0.2	0.2	0.3	0.3	0.3
Working Women					
Training incidence:	2.3	1.2	3.5	4.5	3.4
Type of Training:					
General Education	0.1	0.1	1.1	0.4	0.6
Vocational at Work	1.0	0.7	1.0	1.9	1.2
Vocational at public centre	1.1	0.4	1.1	2.0	1.3
Vocational at private centre	0.1	0.0	0.2	0.2	0.2

Table 2.9
Training patterns in economic recovery

Training incidence:	Working Men			Working Women		
	1984	1986	1989	1984	1986	1989
Some job related training or education in last 4 weeks	8.5	10.2	12.6	7.8	9.7	13.6
None	84.0	87.0	84.2	83.3	84.7	80.4
DK/NA	7.5	2.8	3.2	8.9	5.6	6.0
Training incidence: (alternative measure)						
last 4 weeks	1.9*	3.7	4.9	1.7	3.2	5.0
Training still continuing	4.5*	6.5	7.6	3.4	6.4	8.5
Sub-total	6.4*	10.2	12.5	5.0	9.6	13.5
Duration of training:						
Less than 1 month	1.8*	3.6	4.9	1.5	3.2	4.9
1-12 months	1.2*	2.0	1.8	1.3	2.5	2.7
1-3 years	1.4*	2.1	2.2	1.4	2.4	2.5
More than 3 years	1.9*	2.4	1.6	0.7	1.4	1.0
Sub-total	6.3*	10.1	10.5	4.9	9.4	11.2
Sample E/SE	39,807	39,795	41,990	28,411	30,023	32,640

* These figures relate to training which involved at least some off-the-job elements.
All other figures reflect both on-the-job and off-the-job training.

Table 2.10
Incidence of training by occupational group

Working Men

	Managerial & admin	Professional	Associate professional and technical	Clerical Secretarial	Craft occupations	Service occupations	Sales occupations	Plant & machine operatives	Other occupations, or unknown	All occupations
1979*	2.0	6.9	9.6	5.3	7.6	4.4	4.4	2.6	2.8	5.1
1984	6.4	16.1	15.2	10.6	8.0	11.7	9.3	3.8	3.5	8.5
1989	10.9	24.7	21.4	14.9	11.0	16.1	13.6	5.8	6.2	12.7

Working Women

	Managerial & admin	Professional	Associate professional and technical	Clerical Secretarial	Craft occupations	Service occupations	Sales occupations	Plant & machine operatives	Other occupations, or unknown	All occupations
1979*	1.7	6.1	9.2	3.2	1.7	3.5	4.6	0.8	0.7	3.4
1984	6.3	19.8	15.7	8.0	2.9	5.7	7.5	1.9	1.5	7.8
1989	12.7	35.0	24.1	13.5	5.7	13.0	10.6	4.3	4.5	13.6

* In 1979 the measure of training incidence refers to training last week. In 1984 and 1989 the measure relates to the last 4 weeks.

Table 2.11
Training by technology and trade sector in 1986

Working Men

Sector		Tradeables		
Training	High Technology Manufacturing	Medium Technology Manufacturing	Non-manufacturing Technology users	Non-tradeables
Training incidence in last 4 weeks	9.8	6.8	8.9	16.0
Training Duration				
Less than 1 month	3.2	2.3	3.0	6.4
1-12 months	1.9	1.3	1.6	3.4
1-3 years	1.8	1.5	2.0	2.9
More than 3 years	2.8	1.5	2.2	3.1

Working Women

Sector		Tradeables		
Training	High Technology Manufacturing	Medium Technology Manufacturing	Non-manufacturing Technology users	Non-tradeables
Training incidence in last 4 weeks	7.7	4.5	8.8	13.0
Training Duration				
Less than 1 month	2.3	1.2	2.8	4.6
1-12 months	2.8	1.4	2.3	3.1
1-3 years	1.7	1.4	2.3	2.8
More than 3 years	0.7	0.4	1.1	2.2

Table 2.12
Training by technology and trade sector in 1989

Working Men

Sector		Tradeables		
	High Technology Manufacturing	Medium Technology Manufacturing	Non-manufacturing Technology users	Non-tradeables
Training				
Training incidence in last 4 weeks	12.2	8.6	11.0	20.1
Training Duration	(10.4)	(7.8)	(9.3)	(16.0)
Less than 1 month	4.5	3.3	4.2	8.6
1-12 months	2.0	1.3	1.4	3.1
1-3 years	2.0	2.1	2.2	2.5
More than 3 years	1.9	1.1	1.5	1.8

Working Women

Sector		Tradeables		
	High Technology Manufacturing	Medium Technology Manufacturing	Non-manufacturing Technology users	Non-tradeables
Training				
Training incidence in last 4 weeks	10.5	5.6	11.9	19.2
Training Duration	(9.2)	(4.9)	(10.0)	(15.8)
Less than 1 month	4.3	1.9	4.0	7.7
1-12 months	2.3	1.6	2.5	3.6
1-3 years	1.9	1.1	2.7	2.7
More than 3 years	0.7	0.3	0.8	1.8

Note

Training duration total is less than incidence because in some cases duration was not known for uncompleted spells of training.

Table 2.13
Turnover, entry and training 1979

Working Men	Same employer	Changed employer	New or re-entrant	All Workers
Training incidence last week	4.1	4.9	20.7	5.1
Training type:				
General education	0.1	0.2	3.8	0.4
Vocational at work	2.5	2.5	14.1	3.1
Vocational at public centre	1.2	1.8	2.6	1.4
Vocational at private centre	0.3	0.4	0.2	0.3
Proportion staying or moving	85.8	8.3	5.9	100

Working Women	Same employer	Changed employer	New or re-entrant	All Workers
Training incidence last week	2.4	4.0	9.4	3.4
Training type:				
General education	0.2	0.4	3.4	0.6
Vocational at work	0.9	1.6	3.2	1.2
Vocational at public centre	1.1	1.7	2.5	1.3
Vocational at private centre	0.1	0.4	0.4	0.2
Proportion staying or moving	79.0	8.5	12.5	100

Table 2.14
Turnover, entry and training 1984

Working Men	Same employer	Changed employer	New or re-entrant	All Workers
Training incidence i)	7.6	10.4	16.3	8.5
last 4 weeks ii)	5.7	6.2	12.8	6.4
Training Duration (ii):				
Less than 1 month	1.9	2.4	1.1	1.8
1-12 months	1.0	1.0	2.9	1.2
1-3 years	0.9	1.5	5.5	1.4
More than 3 years	1.8	1.2	3.3	1.9
Proportion staying or moving	85.5	6.1	8.5	100

Working Women	Same employer	Changed employer	New or re-entrant	All Workers
Training incidence i)	6.7	10.7	12.0	7.8
last 4 weeks ii)	4.4	5.6	8.3	5.0
Training Duration (ii):				
Less than 1 month	1.6	1.5	1.3	1.5
1-12 months	1.0	1.8	2.3	1.3
1-3 years	1.0	1.4	3.3	1.4
More than 3 years	0.6	0.8	1.3	0.7
Proportion staying or moving	77.9	7.5	14.5	100

Notes

(i) Reflects positive answers to question on 'education or training connected with your job' (or a future job).

(ii) Reflects the subset of (i) which involved at least some training away from job, i.e. it excludes training which was only obtained 'on-the job'.

Table 2.15
Turnover, entry and training 1989

Working Men	Same employer	Changed employer	New or re-entrant	All Workers
Training incidence last 4 weeks	11.5	14.0	21.1	12.5
Training Duration				
Less than 1 month	5.1	5.6	2.4	4.9
1-12 months	1.6	2.5	2.5	1.8
1-3 years	1.5	2.1	9.3	2.2
More than 3 years	1.4	1.1	4.5	1.6
Proportion staying or moving	80.8	10.9	8.3	100

Working Women	Same employer	Changed employer	New or re-entrant	All Workers
Training incidence last 4 weeks	12.5	16.2	16.4	13.5
Training Duration				
Less than 1 month	5.1	5.9	3.0	4.9
1-12 months	2.4	4.2	3.3	2.7
1-3 years	1.8	2.3	6.5	2.5
More than 3 years	0.9	1.1	1.5	1.0
Proportion staying or moving	72.9	12.7	14.4	100

Table 2.16A
Job mobility by occupation - working men

Occupation Year	1 Manag	2 Prof	3 Tech	4 Sec	5 Craft	6 Service	7 Sales	8 Oper	9 Other	All Occupations
1979										
Same employer	91.0	88.6	85.5	86.3	85.6	83.4	80.6	85.7	80.2	85.8
Changed employer	6.7	6.9	8.8	6.8	8.2	10.2	11.3	9.3	9.7	8.3
New or re-entrant	2.3	4.5	5.7	6.9	6.2	6.4	8.1	5.0	10.1	5.9
1984										
Same employer	91.7	90.1	86.8	84.2	85.2	82.5	75.8	87.0	75.3	85.5
Changed employer	5.0	5.2	6.0	5.6	5.7	8.6	10.4	6.0	6.7	6.1
New or re-entrant	3.4	4.7	7.1	10.2	9.1	8.9	13.7	7.1	18.0	8.5
1989										
Same employer	88.1	85.7	82.6	78.9	80.1	77.4	69.4	80.1	70.1	80.8
Changed employer	8.3	9.4	11.0	10.7	11.1	12.4	15.9	12.0	12.8	10.9
New or re-entrant	3.6	5.0	6.4	10.3	8.7	10.2	14.7	7.8	17.1	8.3

Table 2.16B

Job mobility by occupation - working women

Year / Occupation	1	2	3	4	5	6	7	8	9	All Occupations
1979										
Same employer	86.4	84.4	80.8	79.3	78.7	77.2	73.0	79.3	78.5	79.0
Changed employer	8.0	5.8	8.5	9.8	8.1	7.7	9.4	8.2	7.3	8.5
New or re-entrant	5.6	9.8	10.7	10.9	13.2	15.0	17.7	12.5	14.2	12.5
1984										
Same employer	87.2	83.0	83.0	80.3	76.3	73.8	67.6	77.7	75.1	77.9
Changed employer	4.8	6.3	6.6	8.1	8.1	8.1	9.1	7.5	6.7	7.5
New or re-entrant	7.9	10.7	10.4	11.6	15.6	18.1	23.4	14.8	18.2	14.5
1989										
Same employer	80.5	81.5	80.0	74.4	72.4	66.8	62.4	69.5	69.1	72.9
Changed employer	11.2	9.5	10.5	14.0	12.2	13.4	16.2	13.9	11.1	12.7
New or re-entrant	8.3	8.9	9.5	11.6	15.4	19.8	21.4	16.7	19.8	14.4

Appendix I
Table A1
Activity of those aged 16-59 who were not working

		Men		Women	
		No.	%	No.	%
1979	Unemployed	2788	4.6	2446	6.2
	Inactive	2557	4.2	23,153	58.8
	Student 16+	2945	4.9	2806	7.3
	Working (all ages)	60,245	100	39,373	100
		Men		Women	
1984	Unemployed	5335	13.5	3449	12.1
	Inactive	3108	7.8	15,909	56.0
	Student 16+	2061	5.2	1807	6.4
	Working (all ages)	39,797	100	28,399	100
		Men		Women	
1989	Unemployed	3343	8.0	2518	7.7
	Inactive	3503	8.4	13,805	42.3
	Student 16+	2252	5.4	1889	5.8
	Working (all ages)	41,660	100	32,640	100

Note

% represents no. in category as percentage of those working.

Appendix I
Table A2
Training history of labour force 1979

No. of spells of training	Men		Women	
	Working	Unemployed	Working	Unemployed
2 or more	12.8	6.2	7.6	6.5
1 only	17.6	16.0	12.8	14.5
None	28.1	48.4	40.6	55.4
DK/NA	41.4	29.5	39.0	23.5

Duration of most recent spells	Men		Women	
	Working	Unemployed	Working	Unemployed
300 + hours	19.2	14.3	10.2	11.0
200-300 hours	2.3	1.8	1.8	2.1
under 200 hours	2.5	1.5	2.1	2.0
DK/NA	76.0	82.4	85.8	84.9

Note

Reported figures relate to those aged 16-44.

Appendix I
Table A3
Training for the non-employed in the recovery

	Men		Women	
	1984	1989	1984	1989
Unemployed				
Training ended in last 4 weeks	0.6	1.0	0.8	1.4
Training still continuing	3.0	3.2	4.5	4.8
Sub-total	3.6	4.2	5.3	6.2
Sample unemployed	5355	3343	3449	2518
Inactive				
Training ended in last 4 weeks	0.1	0.3	0.1	0.2
Training still continuing	0.5	0.7	0.7	1.4
Sub-total	0.6	1.0	0.8	1.6
Sample Inactive	3108	3503	15,909	13,805

Note

Figures represent training incidence within each sub-group.

Appendix I
Table A4
Training by technology and trade sector in 1984

Sector		Tradeables			
		High Technology Manufacturing	Medium Technology Manufacturing	Non-manufacturing technology users	Non tradeables
Training					
Working men:					
Training incidence	(i)	8.1	5.6	7.3	13.3
last 4 weeks	(ii)	6.2	4.5	5.8	9.5
Training Duration (ii)					
Less than 1 month		1.6	1.0	1.6	3.1
1-12 months		0.9	0.7	1.0	2.0
1-3 years		1.2	0.8	1.3	2.0
More than 3 years		2.4	1.0	1.7	2.1
Working Women					
Training incidence	(i)	6.0	3.0	6.9	11.0
last 4 weeks	(ii)	3.9	1.5	4.2	7.6
Training Duration (ii)					
Less than 1 month		1.0	0.3	1.1	2.7
1-12 months		0.8	0.5	1.1	1.9
1-3 years		1.3	0.3	1.3	1.7
More than 3 years		0.7	0.3	0.6	1.1

Notes

(i) Reflects positive answers to question on 'education or training connected with your job' (or a future job).

(ii) Reflects the subset of (i) which involved at least some training away from job, i.e. it excludes training which was only obtained 'on-the-job'.

Table A5 A
Occupations by sector 1989 (% by row)

Working Men

Sector Occupation	I Primary & Utilities	II Manufacturing	III Construction	IV Distribution & Transport	V Business & Miscellaneous Services	VI Non-marketed Services
1. Managerial & admin	11.9	21.2	6.0	36.3	16.2	8.2
2. Professional	4.0	20.8	5.5	5.0	27.1	37.4
3. Associate professional & technical	2.9	22.8	5.5	7.7	38.4	22.7
4. Clerical, Secretarial	4.6	22.2	2.5	26.9	24.4	19.3
5. Craft occupations	6.8	36.7	28.6	19.1	4.9	3.8
6. Service occupations	1.1	5.4	0.6	26.5	18.7	47.6
7. Sales occupations	1.4	20.7	2.6	61.8	13.0	0.3
8. Plant & machine operatives	4.1	55.1	5.3	29.5	2.6	3.2
9. Other occupations, or unkown	15.5	12.8	20.0	30.6	11.1	9.9

Table A5 B
Occupations by sector 1989 (% by row)

Working Women

Sector / Occupation	I Primary & Utilities	II Manufacturing	III Construction	IV Distribution & Transport	V Business & Miscellaneous Services	VI Non-marketed Services
1. Managerial & admin	2.5	11.1	1.4	49.5	26.2	9.2
2. Professional	0.5	3.2	0.1	2.8	11.9	81.4
3. Associate professional & technical	0.6	7.0	0.3	3.8	24.8	63.4
4. Clerical, Secretarial	2.4	15.1	4.2	21.1	35.6	21.6
5. Craft occupations	2.9	77.0	1.6	12.4	3.3	2.7
6. Service occupations	0.4	2.6	0.1	35.3	35.5	25.9
7. Sales occupations	0.5	4.9	0.3	88.1	5.6	0.6
8. Plant & machine operatives	1.4	81.1	0.2	13.5	2.0	1.8
9. Other occupations, or unkown	3.3	5.2	0.7	23.2	25.7	41.7

References

Daniel, W. (1987), *Workplace Industrial Relations and Technical Change,* Policy Studies Institute.

Employment Institute (1990), *Economic Report* Vol. 5 (2).

Green, F. (1991a), 'Sex discrimination in job-related training', *British Journal of Industrial Relations*, 29.

Green, F. (1991b), 'The determinants of training of male and female employees in Britain', University of Leicester Department of Economics Discussion Paper No. 153.

Greenhalgh, C. and Steward, M. (1987), 'The effects and determinants of training', *Oxford Bulletin of Economics and Statistics*.

Greenhalgh, C., Taylor, P. and Wilson, R. (1991), 'Innovation and export volumes and prices - disaggregated study', University of Oxford Applied Economics Discussion Paper 107.

Hart, P. and Shipman, A. (1991), 'Policies to ease skill shortages in Britain', *National Institute Economic Review*.

Institute for Employment Research (1989), *Review of the Economy and Employment,* University of Warwick.

Jackman, R. and Roper, S. (1987), 'Structural unemployment', *Oxford Bulletin of Economics and Statistics*, February.

Muellbauer, J. and Murphy, A. (1990), 'The UK current account deficit - is it sustainable?', *Economic Policy,* 11.

Nickell, S. and Kong, P. (1989), 'Technical progress and jobs', Centre for Labour Economics Discussion Paper No. 366.

Northcott, J. and Walling, A. (1988), *The Impact of Microelectronics: Diffusion, Benefits and Problems in British Industry,* Policy Studies Institute Research report 673.

Office of Population Censuses and Surveys (1990), *Standard Occupational Classification*, Vol. 1, H.M.S.O.

Prais, S. ed. (1990), *Productivity, Education and Training,* National Institute for Economic and Social Research.

Rigg, M. (1989), *Training in Britain: Individuals Perspectives,* HMSO.

Steedman, H. (1990), 'Improvements in workforce qualifications: Britain and France 1979-88', *National Institute Economic Review*.

Stevens, M. (1991), *Some issues in the economics of training*, M.Phil, University of Oxford.

Tan, H. (1990), *Training in the US - who gets it and why,* Rand Corporation.

Training Agency (1989), *Training in Britain* Vol. I Main Report.

Training Agency (1990), *Skill Needs in Great Britain*, IFF Research Ltd.

Wilson, R. and Bosworth, D. (1987), *New Forms and New Areas of Employment Growth: Final Report for the United Kingdom,* Commission of the European Communities.

3 A human capital approach to training: Second draft

Derek Bosworth, Rob Wilson and Abebe Assefa

Introduction

A conference on the economics of training would be incomplete without a paper describing and, indeed, broadly in favour of the human capital approach. In a paper on the demand for education, for example, Freeman (1986, pp. 357-8) argues that:

> ...we have made considerable progress along the paths developed in the late 1950s and early 1960s by T.W. Schultz, G. Becker and others on the economic analysis of the demand for education. While there are exceptions, the past two decades' work supports the general proposition that economic analysis of rational behaviour under specified market and informational conditions goes a long way to understanding the interplay between education and the economy.

During the 1970s and 1980s the emphasis of the literature shifted from the economics of education to the economics of training. This shift produced new challenges for human capital theory, as the provision of training in market economies is only partly controlled by the State and cannot, therefore, be treated as analogous to education, where State involvement and control is much more important. Thus, there is not only the issue of private versus social returns, but also the distribution of private returns between individuals and, for the most part, firms (ie the principal alternative source of training provision). The earliest explanation of the distribution of the rewards from training focused on the distinction between specific versus general training. While this distinction is still relevant, other alternative explanations of the returns have since emerged which have resulted in important generalisations of human capital theory.

The paper deals with the optimal training decisions of both individuals and firms. A major theme of this study is that there is a 'market for training' and the demand for and the supply of trained individuals jointly determine the extent and nature of training activity. Sometimes this market can be seen in operation explicitly, with educational establishments providing the product of increased knowledge or skills (although government intervention may mean that the market does not operate freely); sometimes the market remains cloaked within the employment contracts between individuals and firms, where the employer provides the training; sometimes it is a combination of the two (ie. the individual demands training, the employer funds some part of it and it is provided by some specialised training establishment). The present paper attempts to show that, within the context of a 'market for training', the distinction between specific and general training no longer provides a complete explanation of the allocation of the costs and benefits of training. The current paper proposes a game theoretic approach which yields both non-cooperative and cooperative solutions.

Finally, the paper examines a number of reasons why there may be underinvestment in the market for training. One of these explores the analogy between the theories of R&D and human capital. Indeed, it is argued that, with some modification, investment in R&D can be viewed as a specialised form of training. In this case, the bulk of the new knowledge is embodied in the R&D staff and is passed on from one generation of R&D staff to another by a variety of forms of formal and informal training. It should be noted, however, that the R&D function itself is concerned with the development of new knowledge, while training is largely to do with the dissemination of existing knowledge.

Productivity, performance and human capital

The concept of human capital

This paper adopts an overall measure of human capital, Q_t, which is a reflection of innate ability and the accumulation of knowledge and skills through learning and earlier education and training. In general, Q_t will not be directly observable, but will be partially measured in two distinct ways: first, through examinations and tests of subsets of the individual's knowledge or skills, giving some tested performance, π_t; second, through the impact of human capital on productivity within the production process, PR_t. To simplify the notation and discussion, we assume that human capital is analogous to the 'quality of labour', even though, in practice, the latter depends on a variety of other factors. Given that Q is generally unobserved, economists might proxy it by π or PR as appropriate, for example, π might be used to represent Q in an empirical specification of the production function. Just how tenuous a link this might prove becomes clearer from the discussion below.

Human capital accumulation

The principal building block of human capital theory is the capital accumulation identity, which corresponds closely with theories of investment in physical plant and machinery. The basic idea is that, for any given level of intellectual ability, the more effort/resources put into the learning process, the greater the resulting stock of knowledge or skills. The fundamental equation can be written,

$$Q_t = Q_{t-1} + q_t - \delta Q_{t-1} = (1-\delta)Q_{t-1} + q_t \qquad (1)$$

where Q_t denotes the stock of human capital at the end of period t; q_t is the investment in further human capital during the period and δ is the rate of depreciation of existing knowledge. Thus, $q_t - \delta Q_{t-1}$ shows the net addition to knowledge during period t. Note that, if no time or resources are allocated to training, the individual's performance will be determined by their current state of knowledge (ie. at the end of period t-1 or beginning of period t), the rate at which knowledge is acquired informally (ie. outside the training scheme) and the rate of depreciation of knowledge.

Clearly, this is a fairly simplistic view of the accumulation process. In principle, considerably greater sophistication can be introduced through closer correspondence with the vintage theories of the accumulation of physical capital. In practice, surprisingly perhaps, the analogy with vintage theory has not been widely developed or utilised by human capital theorists.

Investment in human capital

The extent of investment in human capital can be specified in terms of the amount and quality of resources devoted to studying. For the purposes of illustration, the analysis assumes that this can be represented by the amount of time the individual spends training, T. Thus, the addition to human capital is written,

$$q_t = c(T_t) = CT_t{}^{\Gamma} = C(S\text{-}H_t\text{-}L_t)^{\Gamma} \tag{2}$$

where: S is total (non-sleeping) time available, H are hours of work (non-training) and L is leisure, $T = S - H - L$; $C > 0$ and $\Gamma > 0$ are 'technical' efficiency parameters in the transformation of time into training performance. We abstract initially from the fact that the precise values of these two parameters are likely to be influenced by personal (including innate ability), family background and training-provider characteristics (for a more general form, see equation 31 below). For the moment, therefore, the equations relate to any particular individual; we return to differences between individuals and the role of accumulated human capital in this process below.

Other factors will be at work, that will become apparent in more detailed specifications of the individual's optimisation problem. It seems likely, for example, that the ability to transform hours of school work into improved knowledge will be related to the level of their prior knowledge (which is predetermined at the end of period t-1, Q_{t-1}). A simple way of representing this in the above model is to allow the parameters C and L to be a function of Q ($C = C(Q_{t-1})$ and/or $\Gamma = \Gamma(Q_{t-1})$). For instance, prior knowledge may increase the productivity of the learning process. This occurs in a number of ways. First, individuals with more accumulated human capital know what sort of questions to ask and what to look for - they are more skilled and equipped for the learning process. Second, the learning process is designed sequentially around a groups of students. Thus, lessons are intended to reinforce facts or provide new knowledge for individuals of a certain standard. Nevertheless, if the pupil has not reached the 'planned standard' they will be disadvantaged in the learning process. More general specifications of this transformation process allow for the possibility of increasing (or decreasing) returns to education and training.

Human capital and productivity

There is an important distinction between the outcome of education and training as measured by formal tests and examinations and the productivity of the individual in the enterprise. Both can be assumed to be a function of the individual's human capital. Consider first measures of academic and other abilities from formal tests. Assume that skills or knowledge are tested at times t and t+1. Thus, some (continuous) measure of performance at the end of period t, πt, as revealed by the formal tests can be written,

$$\pi_t = f(Q_t) = \pi\{(1\text{-}\delta)Q_{t\text{-}1} + q_t\} \tag{3}$$

for any given individual. Tested performance can be measured in a variety of ways, including academic examination, speed and efficiency in completing a number of prespecified tasks, etc. The link between human capital (quality) and tested performance may, in principle, be quite complex, but assume for the moment that,

$$\pi = BQ^\Theta \tag{4}$$

where B and Θ are predetermined constants. By implication,

$$\delta\pi/\pi = \Theta \; \delta Q/Q \tag{5}$$

a one per cent increase in human capital leads to a Θ per cent increase in the measured performance, π^t. We return to this idea below.

The relationship between human capital and productivity as revealed by actual economic performance has been a key area of controversy. This question is linked to the relationship between training and the development of skills or knowledge and the relevance of these skills and know-how to production. This uncertainty has been fuelled by the assertion (without proof) by growth accounting theories that this link exists (Denison, 1962; Jorgenson and Griliches, 1967; Jorgenson and Fraumeni, 1992), although there have been a limited number of attempts to examine the relative contributions of different types of labour in the production and cost function literature. In the final analysis, the debate turns on the impact of some measured level of knowledge or skill, Q, on the output, Y, and thereby on the productivity; of the enterprise, PR.

The implications are easily illustrated based on a simple log-linear production function,

$$Y = f(K,E,Q) = AK^{\alpha}E^{\beta}Q^{\phi} \tag{6}$$

where Y denotes output, K is capital stock and E denotes the number of employees and Q, the measure of human capital, is an index of labour quality; A, α, ß and ϕ are the technical production parameters, where, in particular, A represents the level of technology and the remaining parameters reflect the marginal productivity of the various inputs. In practice, with this simple log-linear technology, each parameter (α, ß and ϕ) is equal to the ratio of the marginal to the average product, for example:

$$\alpha = (\delta Y/\delta K)/(Y/K) \tag{7}$$

Taking logs of equation (6) and differentiating with respect to time, dividing by Y and rearranging yields the rate of growth in demand for labour,

$$(E/E) = (Y/\text{ß}Y)-(A/\text{ß}A)-(\alpha K/\text{ß}K)-(\phi K/\text{ß}Q) \tag{8}$$

where X denotes the derivative of X with respect to time. In this simple specification, the quality of labour is a substitute for all other inputs and an increase in the quality of labour reduces the rate of growth of employment for any given rate of change in output; in other words, it increases labour productivity. This effect is more important the larger is ϕ (which reflects the marginal product of labour quality) and the smaller is ß (which reflects the marginal product of worker numbers).

There are a number of things to note about this result. First, equation (8) is derived from the assumed underlying technology of production, nothing has been said about optimisation by the firm (although the production function itself may say something about technical efficiency).

Second, the technology defines a potential link between human capital and output such that,

$$\delta Y/Y = \phi \, (\delta Q/Q) \tag{9}$$

This expression implicitly defines a relationship between productivity and human capital. It has the same form as the relationship between human capital and the performance measure, π, in equation (5). Thus, depending on the relationship between tested performance and quality, we would expect some link between the 'tested performance' measure, π, and productivity, PR, $\Theta = \Theta(\phi)$. Third, it is worth adding that the results obtained may be quite different where the underlying technology of production takes some other form than the simple log-linear equation outlined above.

A number of variants of human capital theory, in particular, growth accounting theories, assume that factors are paid their marginal products (we return to the validity of this assumption in the next section). In essence, this assumes that product and factor markets are perfectly competitive and that firms maximise profits. In the absence of adjustment costs, minimisation of costs subject to an output constraint yields,1

$$E/E \;=\; 1/\Omega \;(Y/Y) - 1/\Omega \;(A/A) + \alpha/\Omega \;(r/r) + \phi/\Omega \;(w_1/w_1) - ((\alpha+\phi)/\Omega)/(w_0/w_0) \tag{10}$$

where $\Omega = \alpha + \beta$. Thus, the rate of growth in employment is positively related to the rate of growth of output and negatively related to the rate of technological change; it is positively related to the rate of increase in capital prices and to the rate of increase in the 'price' of the quality of labour, but negatively related to the cost per employee of given quality.

Human capital, productivity and wages

The theory above outlines the way in which production theory sees the links between human capital (the quality of labour) and productivity. In addition, equation (10) makes the traditional assumption that factors are paid their marginal products. This further linkage arises via the optimisation behaviour of the firm (ie. minimisation of costs subject to an output constraint, etc.). The existence of this linkage has been a basic and controversial assumption of human capital theory. Returning to the problem outlined above, minimise,

$$LG = rK + (w_0 + w_1 Q)E + \Phi\{Y - f(K,E,Q)\} \tag{11}$$

$$\delta LG/\delta K = r - \Phi \delta f(\ )/\delta K = 0 \tag{12}$$

$$\delta LG/\delta E = w_0 + w_1 Q - \Phi f(\ )/\delta E = 0 \tag{13}$$

$$\delta LG/\delta Q = w_1 E - \Phi \delta f(\ )/\delta Q = 0 \tag{14}$$

Thus, it can be seen that the firm's optimisation procedure indicates that all factors are employed to the point where their marginal productivity is some constant, $1/\Phi$, of their per unit factor cost (note that the unit price of capital is r, the wage rate for workers of given quality, Q°, is $\{w_0 + w_1 Q^\circ\}$ and the 'price of quality' of a given number of employees, E, is $\{w_1 E^\circ\}$. In the case of a log-linear production function, equations (11)-(14) yield,

$$\begin{aligned} rK/\Phi Y &= \alpha \\ ((w_0 + w_1 Q^\circ)E)/\Phi Y &= \beta \\ (w_1 E^\circ)Q/\Phi Y &= \phi \end{aligned} \tag{15}$$

Note that in this result, the price of employment is specified for some level of the quality of labour, Q°, and the price of quality is, likewise, specified for some level of employment, E°.

Of course, these are conditional solutions (ie. E depends on the precise value of Q° and Q on E°), the optimal values of K, E and Q are jointly determined and obtained by solving the simultaneous set of equations given by the first order conditions. The key solution, relating to the quality of labour, can be written,

$$Q^* = w_0.\phi/(\beta - \phi).w_1 \tag{16}$$

It shows that the optimal value of the quality of labour within the firm is postively related to the productivity of quality, ϕ, negatively related to the marginal productivity of employees of a given quality, β, negatively related to the 'price of quality', w_1, and positively related to the price of employees of given quality, w_0 (note the slight reinterpretation of the two price variables vis à vis equation 15 above). This solution was derived under the assumptions of given values of the technology parameters and given factor prices (r, w_0 and w_1), indeed on the assumption of perfectly elastic factor supplies at these prices. The solution, however, can be rewritten to illustrate the relationship between the 'price of quality' and the marginal productivity of quality around the optimum point,

$$\delta w_1/\delta \phi \;=\; w_0 \beta / Q^* (\beta - \phi)^2 \tag{17}$$

which can be seen to be positive. In other words, close to their equilibrium, firms are willing to pay higher prices for a given level of quality, the higher the marginal productivity of quality.

Individual investment decisions

The individual will be willing to invest in training as long as this results in an increase in their wages over untrained individuals (the reason why wages are higher is largely irrelevant from an individual perspective). Net benefits should include non-pecuniary advantages associated with different forms of employment, but human capital theory is normally outlined on the assumption, explicit or implicit, that non-pecuniary advantages and disadvantages are identical across different jobs. In this way the theory concentrates primarily on the pecuniary costs and benefits. The individual is assumed to maximise the present value of future expected life-time net earnings, where net earnings are take-home pay (adjusted, where possible, by the pecuniary value of fringe benefits) minus any direct human capital investment costs incurred, such as the costs of training. Thus, in comparing different labour market supply decisions in the long-run, it is assumed that the individual will compare the present value of the different possible income streams.

The following formula represents the present value of future expected income from a particular long-run decision,

$$PV = \sum_{\tau=1}^{n} (W''\tau - W'\tau)/(1+i)^\tau = (W_1'' - W_1')/(1+i)^1 \ldots + (W_n'' - W_n')/(1+i)^n$$

(18)

where : PV denotes present value; n = the number of years for which the net income is considered; w"t-w't = the net expected income in year t (w" denotes with training and w' without training); and, given a perfect capital market, i = the rate of interest at which every individual could borrow funds. Thus, in this simple model, the individual invests if PV>0. An alternative way to viewing the human capital investment decision is in terms of the internal rate of return. In this case, equation (18) is modified to compute the private (internal) rate of return to the investment,

$$O = \sum_{\tau=1}^{n} (W''_\tau - W'_\tau)/(1+r)^\tau$$

(19)

where: r is the (gross) rate of return to the investment; W''_t is the income in year t if the individual undertakes the training, and W'_t if the individual doesn't undergo training (in practice, W" needs to be adjusted for the direct costs of training, as we demonstrate below). Thus during the period of training $W''_t - W'_t$ may be a negative figure (indeed, it may take some time for W" to overhaul W'). The internal rate of return r, is the rate at which the discounted net lifetime earnings of the trained individual equal the corresponding figure for the untrained person. In this simple illustrative model, the internal rate of return, r, is then compared with the rate of interest, i, at which every individual could borrow funds in the perfect capital market. If the internal rate of return exceeds the rate of interest (r>i) then the individual will invest.

Freeman (1986, p. 376) demonstrates that, in the simplest model of the individual undertaking education or training as an investment good, it is possible to define a continuous time version of the rate of return to training (r) as,

$$\int_{\tau}^{\tau+n'} W_\tau' \, e^{-r\tau} = \int_{\tau+n^\circ}^{\tau+n''} W_\tau'' \, e^{-r\tau} + \int_{\tau}^{\tau+n^\circ} \{W_\tau^\circ - D\} \, e^{-r\tau}$$

(20)

where: $W°$ is the wage during training; W' is the wage for individuals without the relevant training; $W"$ is the wage after completion of training; $n°$ is the length of training period; n' is the length of working life for individuals without training; $n"$ is the length of working life for individuals with training (ie. including the period of training); and D are the direct costs of training.

Freeman goes on to demonstrate the derivation of the simplest of earnings functions. This particular function requires three further simplifying assumptions. First, we focus on earnings net of any affects of age or experience (ie. age and experience are included in the empirical version of the equation as right hand side variables). Second, in order to simplify the analysis, assume that net earnings are zero during the training period. Third, it is assumed that trained workers retire $n°$ periods later than untrained workers (ie. $n° = n" - n'$). Equation (20) then simplifies to yield,

$$\log(W") = \log(W') + rn° \ (+ \ \text{other terms}) \qquad (21)$$

The details of the derivation can be found in Freeman (1986, p. 376). The other terms will include key variables such as years of experience. Equation (21) is the simplest of earnings functions, where the log of earnings is regressed on the number of years of education or training. The associated coefficient on $n°$ is a rough estimate of the rate of return to the investment. A number of variants of this equation can be found in the literature (ie. Mincer, 1974 and Heckman and Polachek, 1974).

Human capital theories often attempt to take into account periods of unemployment. The wage variables may or may not take unemployment into account, depending on how their values are calculated. If W represents the earnings of those employed continuously for the period in question (ie. the weekly wage multiplied by the number of working weeks per year) then it will not account for wages lost through unemployment. On the other hand, if W is the earnings from the year, allowing for the likely duration of unemployment, then it implicitly allows for the probability of unemployment. There are examples of rate of return calculations that allow for unemployment in this way (Wilson, 1980). Note, however, that this treatment implicitly adopts identical weights to unemployment as to wages. In practice, the individual's utility function could be more general to allow for the possibility of other factors affecting the relative weights (ie. stigma effects associated with unemployment and the costs of job change). This is an empirical question.

This exposition has been an over-simplification in the sense that it has implicitly assumed that there are two possible courses of action: undertaking a period of education or training or no human capital investment at all. There are of course a range of possible forms of human capital investment each of which has its own rate of return. These will vary according to the level and subject/discipline area. The individual will in theory choose that with the highest rate of return, given their likelihood of successfully completing the course.

Individual decision

Stylised facts

Killingsworth (1983, pp 207-209) outlined three major stylised empirical facts about life-cycle behaviour of men and women that appear with surprising regularity in a variety of different kinds of data. First, information about males suggests that time profiles of labour supply or market time, wage rates and earnings per year are all concave. Annual hours of work and annual earnings actually decline for the typical man, as retirement approaches, although hourly wage rates do not appear to decline, or, if they do fall, only slightly at the end of working life. So the fall in annual earnings towards the end of working life would appear to be mainly due to a decline in hours worked per year. Second, the typical man spends the first part of his life at school (sometimes starting to work while still at school, usually after the school-leaving age), and works more or less continuously until retirement. Having retired he usually remains out of the labour force until death. Female patterns are more diverse: some women work more or less continuously until retirement while others spend little or no time in the labour force; it has become increasingly common, however, for women to leave the labour force during the early stages of child care and to return after their children have started school (often returning initially to part time and, later, to full time employment).

The 'stylised facts' can be extended to cover training over the life-cycle. Early in life, because the individual's current earning potential is low, so are the earnings they forego whilst undertaking training. On the other hand, wages are typically higher later in life, the opportunity cost of training at a later stage is therefore higher and the required payback period is shorter. Some training may be undertaken quite late in life, however, partly to off-set the effects of human capital depreciation. Nevertheless, as retirement approaches, the pay-back period becomes much shorter and the returns to human capital investment become much smaller and the cost relatively large, such that little or no further investment is likely to be undertaken. The pattern of the market productivity of the individual over time, therefore, is jointly determined with gross additions to human capital, depreciation and obsolescence. Total human capital depreciation (ie. the rate of depreciation multiplied by the stock of human capital) initially increases with time, even if the rate of depreciation is constant, as the stock of human capital is growing. However, given declining additions to the stock of human capital over time as investment in training falls away, eventually human capital depreciation exceeds additions through new investment, and the stock of human capital begins to decline; this, in turn, reduces the total size of human capital depreciation. By implication, the market productivity of the individual (and, therefore, the potential wage) tracks the stock of human capital and therefore exhibits a broadly inverse 'U' shape. The individual's wage rate is positively related to their market productivity and, at a given point in time, negatively related to the amount of time they spend in training. Thus, their wage follows broadly the same pattern, but peaks after their productivity. In addition, there may be a discontinuity at the time the individual ceases to invest in training, and a steeper slope thereafter.

Dynamic labour supply

Main features of dynamic models
Since the 1970s a major literature has developed focusing on the labour supply decisions in a dynamic or life-cycle framework, attempting to explain these 'stylised facts'. There are essentially two variants depending on whether wages are exogenous or endogenous; the latter focus on the individual's education and training activity. In dynamic

70

models, the behaviour of labour supply over time is the net result of an efficiency effect (which makes individuals work more during periods in which the wage is higher), an 'interest rate' effect making individuals work more at first and less later on (effectively 'banking' some part of their earnings to earn high rates of compound interest) and a 'time preference rate' effect, which tends to make individuals work less at first and more later (ie. arising from a natural desire to take leisure now and put off work to a later date) (Weiss, 1972). In the short-run the individual's labour supply choice is constrained by the skills possessed; in the long-run individuals can choose to extend their skills or capacity to work by investing in education or training. Human capital theory suggests that individuals consider the various potential streams of expected costs and benefits over their lifetime and choose to supply labour in such a way as to maximise the present value of future expected net benefits. Human capital theories are encompassed in this branch of dynamic labour supply models.

Exogenous wages
Unlike static labour supply theories, the assumption that all income is consumed in each period is untenable in a multiperiod, dynamic model; savings and, thereby, the individual's stock of financial assets must be endogenous. However, it is often assumed that the individual plans to consume all of their wealth by the time they die. In addition, such theories assume inter-temporal substitutability (ie. that the marginal utility of goods or leisure consumed at time t is independent of the amount of goods and leisure consumed at other times) in which the life-cycle is treated as a sequence of separate and independent periods, so that life-time utility is simply the sum of the utilities from each individual period (Brown and Deaton, 1972 and Deaton, 1974). The instantaneous utility function is assumed strictly convex at every point in time.

The individual's decision problem, therefore, is to,

$$\text{Max}_{(G(t),H(t),\mu)} = \sum_{0}^{n} e^{-\sigma t} u(G(t), 1-H(t))dt + \mu\{F(0) + \sum_{0}^{n} e^{-it}(w(t)H(t)-p(t)G(t)) \tag{22}$$

where: G denotes the consumption of goods; L is leisure (and hours, $H = 1-L$); i is the interest rate; σ is the rate of intertemporal substitution; p is an index of output prices; F(0) is the initial wealth. The resulting first order conditions, associated with an interior solution form three equations in three unknowns (ie. G(t), H(t) and μ). The Lagrangian constant, μ, represents the perceived marginal utility of the initial financial wealth, ie. the imputed value or shadow price of such wealth (Killingsworth, 1983, p. 225). Corner solutions are also possible and are discussed in Killingsworth (1983, p. 217). The period of integration is also an issue: in many instances n has been assumed to be infinite; although this assumption is clearly more appropriate for younger than for older workers.

Provided u(t) is well behaved, the second order conditions are satisfied and, by the implicit function theorem, the first order conditions are, in principle, sufficient to yield explicit solutions for the unknowns (see Silberberg, 1978, pp. 134-9). The dynamic utility maximisation problem subsumes the static equilibrium condition and can be obtained by setting $t = T = 0$ in the first order conditions from equation (22). Killingsworth (1983, pp. 228-229) shows that, under the further simplifying assumption,

$$\dot{p}(t)/p(t) = 0 \quad \text{for all t} \tag{23}$$

then the path of H over time can be written,

$$\dot{H}(t) = a\dot{w}(t)/w(t) + b(\sigma-i) \tag{24}$$

The first term of equation (24) forms the 'efficiency effect' and the second term, the 'time effect'. The efficiency effect induces individuals to work when the wage rate is higher and to take their leisure when it is lower. This is analogous to the traditional substitution effect in static models of supply. Time effects, on the other hand, are divided into an interest rate effect (associated with i) and a 'time preference rate effect' (associated with σ). The interest rate effect persuades individuals to work earlier, 'banking' their earnings to earn the going rate of interest. The time preference rate effect tends to make individuals work less now and more later, simply because there is a natural tendency to postpone less pleasurable activities. Note that the sign of the time effect changes depending on whether i is greater or less than σ. Further discussion can be found in Weiss (1972) and Killingsworth (1983, p. 216).

The comparative dynamics of the model are quite complicated. They can be divided into two categories: first, adjustments made where changes in the exogenous variables are perfectly anticipated; and second, those adjustments made because of an unanticipated shift in one or more of the exogenous variables. Anticipated changes at some date τ_1 (which revert back to the original profile at time τ_2) are derived by differentiating the first order conditions derived from equation (22), to yield a system of three equations in three unknowns ($d\mu$, dH(t) and dG(t)) in terms of three exogenous variables (dF(0), dw(t) and dp(t)). For some given change in the wage profile between τ_1 and τ_2, a two stage solution shows that $dH(\tau^*)/dw(\tau^*)$, $\tau_1 < \tau^* < \tau_2$, can be decomposed into 'wage effects' (given the initial value of wealth) and 'wealth effects' (given the change in the wage profile at time τ^*). If however, the individual takes a decision based on an assumed wage profile which proves to be inaccurate, they will undertake some 'replanning' in the light of the unanticipated changes (ie. in w(t), p(t), i, σ, or the tax rate). For a discussion of 'replanning' see MaCurdy (1981 and 1985) and Bover (1989).

Endogenous wages
A second class of dynamic labour supply models make the wage a function of the individual's productivity in employment, which is assumed to be determined by their stock of human capital, Q(t),

$$w(t) = w(PR(t)) \qquad (25)$$

where PR(t) denotes the individual's market productivity,

$$PR(t) = v(Q(t)) \qquad (26)$$

Thus, wages are endogenised because the individual can influence their investment in human capital. The adjustment to human capital can be represented by a stock-flow relationship described by equation (1). Two types of labour supply models with endogenous wages are distinguished in the literature (Killingsworth, 1983, p. 303). First, 'training models' which include both the 'job-choice' theories and the 'allocation of time' formulations. Second, there are the 'experience models', which are based on 'learning-by-doing' formulations.

Training models

One variant of the training model is the 'job-choice' formulation, in which the individuals choose not only between work and leisure, but also between jobs with different combinations of training and earning potential. In essence, firms purchase labour services and 'sell' training opportunities. Jobs with more training offer lower wages, other things being equal. Thus, denoting the amount of training offered (ie. the training index) as T,

$$w(t) = w(Q(t), T(t)) = x(T(t))PR(t) \qquad (27)$$

where most models assume separability, as shown in equation (27); $dw(t)/dQ(t) > 0$ and $dw(t)/dT(t) < 0$. Various forms have been assumed for equation (27) in the literature; Blinder and Weiss (1976) and Rosen (1972), for example, assume $x()$ is strictly concave. The term $x(T(t))$ measures the fraction of market productivity which is realised in terms of current wages (ie. $x(T(t)) = w(t)/PR(t)$). The model also subsumes pure education/training and pure work outcomes as special cases (ie. $T=1$ and $T=0$ respectively). For a discussion, see Becker (1964) and Rosen (1972).

A second variant is the 'allocation of time' formulation. In this instance, the individual does not choose between jobs with differing amounts of training, but decides on the amount of time to be devoted to training activity, $T(t)$, where training time is the difference between the hours spent at work and the time devoted to market activities, $T(t) = H(t) - M(t)$. Note, that, following the normal convention, $1 = H(t) + L(t)$, where $L(t)$ denotes leisure taken at time t. The individual's remuneration reflects the fact that, when they are training, their productive time is less than the total number of hours they spend working for their employer,

$$w(t) = PR(t). M(t)/(H(t)) \qquad (28)$$

By implication, the individual is spending $PR(t)(T(t)/H(t))$ per hour on training. Additions to human capital, $q(t)$, are defined by a production function,

$$q(t) = q(T(t), \quad Q(t), \quad Z(t)) \tag{29}$$

where: $T(t)$ denotes the amount of time devoted to training at time t; $q(0,Q(t))=0$, $qi>0$ and $qii<0$, for $i=T,Q$; Z denotes personal and other characteristics. Note that the productivity of the investment in terms of the time devoted to training is influenced by the amount of human capital the individual already holds.

If $x(T(t))$ from equation (27) is defined as a linear function and $q(T(t),$ $Q(t))$ has the form $q(T(t) \; Q(t))$, then $T(t)$, the index of training from the job-choice model is the same as $T(t)/H(t)$, the proportion of total hours spent on training, from the allocation of time model. For further discussion, see Heckman (1976a and 1976b) and Ryder, et al. (1976). The main distinction between the two approaches is that the job choice model interprets the individual's investment in training in terms of the fraction of their market productivity that is not realised in the wage; the allocation of time model views the investment in training in terms of the amount of market time not used for work. Both models, however, emphasise the trade-off between current and future earnings: the individual gives up some proportion of current earnings in order to achieve higher levels of future wages.

Experience models
This group of models focuses on the impact of learning-by doing (see Arrow, 1962; Flueckiger, 1976; Rosen, 1972). Individuals who spend more time in market work learn more, and this raises their productivity and their wages. Such models assume that learning is costless for the individual in the sense that it involves no reduction in earnings in the current period. However, individuals may still bear a cost and be said to invest, because they spend longer at work than they would have done without any learning effects (and give up some additional amount of their valuable leisure time in return for the higher future income that the additional learning brings). In the learning models, additions to human capital are again defined by a production function,

$$q(t) = q(H(t), Q(t)) \tag{30}$$

where $q(0,Q(t))=0$; $q_i>0$ and $q_{ii}<0$ for $i=H(t),Q(t)$. However, the assumption that the direct costs of learning are zero has been criticised in the literature (Becker, 1964; Mincer, 1974). It has been argued, for example, that there is an incentive for individuals to leave jobs with lower learning opportunities and to supply themselves to jobs with greater opportunities. This creates a differential supply which lowers wages in the higher learning opportunity jobs, effectively creating the situation described in the job-choice model described above.

Models with learning and training
Given the two groups of models (ie. the training and experience models) can coexist, it is possible to produce a formulation that contains the main features of both (Killingsworth, 1982 and 1983). Killingsworth (1983, pp. 309-310), for example, outlines a 'general model' that combines aspects of the allocation of time and learning-by-doing formulations. In this model, additions to human capital are defined by the production function,

$$q(t) = q(T(t),H(t),Q(t)) \tag{31}$$

where $\delta q/\delta k_i>0$ for $k_i=T(t),H(t),Q(t)$; $q(t)>0$ if $H(t)>T(t)>0$ (ie. individuals have positive hours and some of these are spent training) or if $H(t)>T(t)=0$ (ie. individuals undertake no training but still learn by doing during the hours they spend in market work), but $q(t)=0$ otherwise. The wage rate is determined by,

$$w(t) = w(T(t),PR(t)) \tag{32}$$

where $wT<0$ and $wPR>0$; such that, $w(t)=0$ if $T(t)=H(t)$ (ie. individuals are not paid by the firm if they are effectively full-time students) and $w(t)=PR(t)$ if $T(t)=0$ (ie. individuals are paid their full market productivity if they spend no time training). Finally, the individual's earnings are defined by,

$$W(t) = w(t)H(t) \tag{33}$$

The pattern of hours over the life cycle is again determined by efficiency, interest rate (i) and time preference rate (σ) effects. Thus, the expression for the change in hours in the training model is almost identical to equation (24) above (which was developed on the assumption that wages were exogenous). In this instance,

$$\dot{H}(t) = a(t)(\dot{PR}(t)/PR(t)) + b(\sigma\text{-}i) \qquad\qquad (34)$$

where the sign on the second term changes depending on whether σ is greater, equal or less than i. Thus, if i > σ, then the peak in hours of work occurs earlier, rather than later (the individual 'banks' their income at a compound rate of interest. On the other hand, if i < σ, then the individual puts off work until later. Whatever, the outcome from the interest and time preference rate effects, the efficiency effect tends to dominate time preference effects as long as PR grows sufficiently rapidly. Hence, H rises early in life, but, later on, as PR grows more slowly, the efficiency effect which raises hours gets weaker and, eventually, the time effect outweighs the ever weaker efficiency effect and hours tend to fall. By implication, the earnings profile will also be an inverted 'U' shape.

Towards a more general theoretical framework

Main areas of criticism
The dynamic labour supply models are able to replicate the main 'stylised facts' of the life cycle labour supply and training activity of the individual. One area of criticism has concerned the amount and nature of information available to the individual in undertaking human capital investment decisions (Freeman's caveat relating to 'informational conditions'). This issue is discussed in Section 3.3.2. It is clear from this discussion that, in reaching education and training decisions, individuals also take other factors than income into account. Section 3.3.3 therefore reports an attempt to present a more general socio-economic framework, outlining the way in which the human capital approach is a special case of a more general model. Social and institutional factors are clearly likely to influence the individual (and firm) decision making processes. The key question is presumably the

extent to which education and training decisions are 'driven' by economic motives, with the associated investment decisions constrained by social and institutional factors vis à vis the extent to which education and training are 'driven' by social and institutional forces. To some extent this is an unresolved problem although we touch on it in subsequent sections, but Section 3.3.4 develops the theme that social and institution factors may themselves be influenced by economic forces in the longer term. Sociologists are probably much happier with some societal ranking of jobs or associated occupations; human capital per se says little about jobs. Section 3.3.5 therefore attempts to bridge this gap and shows how the more general framework developed in Section 3.3.3 can be used to provide an ordering system and a 'job choice' model, with implicit education and training decisions.

Imperfect information

The life-cycle framework highlights the demanding nature of the information set necessary for the individual to optimise their human capital investments. Researchers themselves have encountered a corresponding problem to the individual whenever they have attempted to construct quantitative information about earnings. Much of the early human capital work was undertaken using cross-sectional data bases of age-earnings profiles, when, in practice, what really counts is how wages develop over time. Only more recently has the emphasis has shifted to longitudinal data (Jorgenson and Fraumeni, 1991). On the other hand, human capital theorists would not claim perfect knowledge or that individuals make perfectly accurate decisions; individuals can make decisions on the basis of imperfect information and get them wrong. Thus, one strand of human capital theory focuses on the revisions to investment decisions in the light of these mistakes. On the other hand, such theorists would dispute that the information is so imperfect to make individuals reject such an approach and, thereby, to completely invalidate the underpinnings of the theory. Perfect information requires that the individual knows what will happen to their salary over time with and without training. A variety of pieces of evidence have come to light to suggest that at least certain market actors have quite sophisticated knowledge about income streams. Some of this evidence comes from the collection of individuals' ex ante views about age-earnings profiles (Williams and Gordon, 1981; Bosworth and Ford, 1985a).

Undergraduate expected income streams not only exhibit the stylised life cycle patterns outlined in Section 3.1, but also reflect both levels (by discipline area) and distributional characteristics. Freeman (1986) provides evidence of the sensitivity of potential educational entrants to variations in relative earnings. These pieces of evidence suggest that individuals do carry a considerable amount of earnings and employment related information from which, in principle, they can take decisions.

The utility function
A number of studies suggest therefore that individuals not only possess but also use this information to inform their decisions, although they also take many other factors into account (Bosworth and Ford, 1985b). Maximisation of some discounted stream of net incomes should therefore be seen as some special case of a more general model of individual behaviour. A more general model would focus on utility maximisation and might take the following form,

$$U = f(C_t,...,C_{t+s}, SC_t,...,SC_{t+s}, W_t,...,W_{t+s}, UN_t,...,UN_{t+s},$$
$$WC_t,...,WC_{t+s},...) \tag{35}$$

where: C denotes the private consumption benefits of knowledge (ie. language training for a company might have important private benefits for the individual); SC represents the social class of the individual (ie. the individual's perception of how other people see their position in society); W denotes the earnings of the individual while in employment; UN represents some measure of unemployment in each period; finally, WC denotes the working conditions of the individual.

First, however, we adopt a somewhat more general notation for the utility function,

$$U_t = f\{X(1)_t,...X(1)_{t+n}, ...,X(s)_t,...X(s)_{t+n}\} \tag{36}$$

$$= g\{\phi(1)_t X(1)_t, ..\phi(1)_{t+n} X(1)_{t+n}, ..,\phi(s)_t X(s)_t, ..\phi(s)_{t+n} X(s)_{t+n}\}$$

$$\tag{37}$$

where $\phi(i)_\tau$, $i=1,...,n$ and $\tau=t,...t+s$. Thus, at any given point in time, τ, the relative weights given to the arguments of the utility function can be written,

$$\phi(i)_\tau \Big/ \sum_{i=1}^{s} \phi(i)_\tau \tag{38}$$

Likewise, for any given argument, i, the weight given to that influence varies with the period it is 'consumed',

$$\phi(i)_\tau \Big/ \sum_{\tau=t}^{t+n} \phi(i)_\tau \tag{39}$$

The simplest of the human capital models can now be derived as a special case of equation (37). This is obtained by setting,

$$\phi(i)_\tau = 0 \tag{40}$$

for all i except i$=$W and adopting a simple exponential discounting procedure by simplifying equation (39) to represent the individual's discount rate by an exponential function of time,

$$\phi(i)_\tau = e^{-\sigma\tau} = e^{-i\tau} \tag{41}$$

This assumption is derived from the principle of investing money at a given real rate of interest, i. Clearly, both assumptions make the human capital approach a special case.

Social class and training
The following discussion demonstrates that human capital's focus on future earnings is almost certainly only part of the story. The essential point is that, at any given point in time, human capital decisions take place within a given institutional framework, but, while this framework is fixed in the short run, it may be modified in the longer term. The greater the economic incentives to modify the framework, the shorter the period in which it is likely to be changed; the greater the extent to which the

80

framework forms ingrained, custom and practice, the longer it takes to change. Economic analyses have something to offer in discussing the costs and benefits of modifying the institutional factors that influence the amount and nature of training decisions.

In essence, we might distinguish between human capital theories and their more institutional alternatives in the following way. In human capital theory, individuals are assumed to make optimising decisions about investment in training, subject to certain social or institutional constraints. These decisions are often framed within a wholly financial context: the net contribution attributable to training, discounted by some interest rate and compared with the direct costs and the opportunity costs of the foregone leisure. Financial considerations are often not the only and sometimes not even the major motivation for this type of investment. However, the human capital approach can be made much more general than its traditional focus on the marketability of the associated skills. The sociological literature, for example, refers to the concept of cultural capital (Ashton, 1989).

Alternative theories to the traditional human capital approach, often view the constraints as too serious to be treated in this way; the constraints themselves form the principal determinants of training. In some theories, the importance of the constraints, including imperfect information are argued to undermine the whole idea of optimisation. Such theories, for example, often point to the assumption of infinite time horizons as precluding dynamic optimisation. In addition, they often argue that there are non-pecuniary costs and benefits associated with training, which are not adequately encapsulated in the largely financial variables or the constraints which are imposed on the optimisation decision.

Job characteristics: good-jobs/bad-jobs
Up to this point in time, the human capital based theory has been largely devoid of the concept of a job, requiring certain personal and other characteristics to fulfil the associated set of tasks. Sociologists and institutionalists, however, are probably happier conceptualising employment, education and training in terms of jobs with given characteristics, although a number of economists have also thought of the problem in this way (Elias and Blanchflower, 1988). Section 3.3.3

provides a mechanism which enables the discussion to be recast in terms of jobs which exist within some given occupational hierarchy.

Each job can be thought of as comprising a set of current and future characteristics that influence individual utility, $X(1)_t,...X(1)_{t+n}$, ...,$X(s)_t,...X(s)_{t+n}$ (see equation 37 above). Given that employers are heterogeneous, the expected utility may be a weighted function of the expected values of the various characteristics,

$$\epsilon(Uij) = f\{\phi(1)_t \; \epsilon \; [X(1)]_t, \; ...\phi(s)_{t+n} \; \epsilon \; [X(s)]_{t+n}\} \qquad (42)$$

Thus, each individual is able to construct some ranking based on the relative importance placed on the various characteristics of jobs. From this, each individual can calculate the difference in (gross) utility (ie. excluding the costs associated with changing jobs) between any two jobs j and k, $\epsilon(U_{ijk})$. Thus, if there are m alternative jobs, then there is an mxm change in utility matrix (whose leading diagonal is zero). Sequences of jobs with different spells in each, which form a work history, can be treated as if they are different jobs and evaluated in the same way. In addition, $\epsilon(DUijk)$ denotes the expected disutility incurred because of the change. This function represents the expected utility 'distance' between any two jobs which reflects the additional human capital, other individual characteristics and search costs that would be incurred in order for the individual to change jobs. Thus, each individual perceives a matrix of net gains of changing from any job j to job k, $\epsilon(N_{ijk})=\epsilon(U_{ijk}) - \epsilon(DU_{ijk})$. In this simplistic model, jobs can be ordered in terms of their net addition to utility and individuals will move in the direction of the highest expected net gain. It can be seen that $\epsilon(N_{ijk})$, $\epsilon(U_{ijk})$ and $\epsilon(DUijk)$ may be the expected utilities from some future streams of benefits and costs. The human capital formulation simply assumes that utility is determined by income; thus, $X(1)_t, ...X(s)_{t+n}$ might refer to earnings in different years, and the determinants of the costs of change may now relate to the additional education and training required to change jobs, as well as the cost of search.

Thus, if per unit search and other costs decrease with the length of time over which adjustment takes place, wage differentials between jobs will reflect differences in investment in human capital, other things being equal. Of course, other things are not equal; there are many other nonpecuniary advantages and disadvantages of different forms of employment. As soon as this assumption is dropped, then the wage which would induce an individual to supply labour to an occupation requiring training will not be that which compensates for the monetary costs of training: if the individual associates non-pecuniary advantages with the skilled occupation as against the occupation chosen without training, they would be prepared to accept a lower wage (obviously a higher wage is necessary where there are non-pecuniary disadvantages). Similarly the education or training itself could be regarded as a consumption good such that the value of the benefits derived from the education imply the necessity of a lower monetary rate of return than if it were ignored. In practice, this discussion relates to the theory of compensating wage differentials (Hammermesh and Rees, 1993, p. 431).

Firm decision making

Specific versus general training

This section draws heavily on an earlier paper on firm training decisions (Bosworth and Warren, 1990). One focus of this earlier paper is Becker's (1964) suggestion that the age-earnings profile of the individuals concerned, would depend on whether the training in question was specific or general. Specific training increases productivity in firms providing the training, but not in other firms; by contrast, general training increases the worker's productivity by an equivalent amount in all firms. The more specific the training, the more inclined the employing firm is to pay for the training. However, in the case of general training, individuals pay the costs, which will be reimbursed in future years through higher earnings associated with their increased skills.

In other words, the specific-general dichotomy provides a mechanism for dividing the costs and benefits of training between the two main parties:

1. the employer is more willing to pay the costs of specific training because the 'irrelevance' of the training to other potential employers implies that market forces do not pressure them into paying a premium for the worker's higher skill and increased output - the training firm pays the whole of the training costs and reaps the whole

83

of the benefits in terms of higher productivity, with no necessity of paying a higher wage;

2. the individual is willing (and the employer unwilling) to pay the costs of general training because the skills can be used by any company and all other employers would be willing to pay the higher wage commensurate with the increased level of skill - thus if the employer paid for the training, market forces would never allow it to recoup its costs by depressing the individual's post-training wage below the value of their marginal product.

The precise allocation between the two cases depends crucially on the existence of market forces that put training firms at a competitive disadvantage unless they can recoup the costs of training. One of the aims of this section is to demonstrate that tenure is not exogenous to the firm's decision making process; the firm can influence the duration of the employment spell by manipulating relative wages and this, in turn, has an impact on the firm's optimal training expenditure. A second aim is to emphasise that other social or institutional factors also influence the expected tenure of the individual within the enterprise. Thus, while relative wages are a determinant of individual mobility, they are far from being the only or, perhaps, even the most important influence. Whatever the causes, while tenure of employment with a given employer is often much shorter than the individual's lifetime, even so it is around 10 or 12 years in the U.K. (Bosworth and Warren, 1990). Thus, while the distinction between specific and general training remains important, it is no longer able to provide a clear-cut answer to the question of who funds and who receives the benefits of training. In other words, the individual may stay in the firm for a sufficient period for the employer to reap some of the benefits from general training.

Supply of training

In this paper, the firm is envisaged as a potential supplier of training. Equation (28) can be respecified to define the price of training. In the simple world envisaged in the standard dynamic supply model, the total cost of training to the individual can be written,

$$PR(t) - (M(t)/H(t))PR(t) = (T(t)/H(t))PR(t) \qquad (43)$$

where M/H is the proportion of the individual's time within the company spent in paid, market work, PR is the productivity of the individual and T=H-M is the amount of time spent training. Developing equation (43), however, we can define the underlying price of training paid by the individual as,

$$p(t) = p(T(t)/H(t)) \qquad (44)$$

where p is the price of training set by the firm. If, for example, the price set increased with T/H at an increasing rate, then $p' > 0$ and $p'' > 0$. Thus, the linear cost to the individual shown in equation (43) can be rewritten,

$$p(T(t)/H(t))PR(t) = p(t)PR(t) \qquad (45)$$

which, in our example, increases disproportionately with T/H.

Thus, if the firm is a monopoly supplier of training to the individual, in principle, it can set p( ) to a level at which the net present value of the training in each period is just positive, thereby inducing the individual to undertake training, but ensuring that the net benefits of training accrue largely to the firm. Clearly, if there are a large number of potential suppliers of training, this will not be the case. If, for example, it attempts to charge above the market price, p( )*, for training, p( ) > p( )*, while offering the going post-training market wage, w=w*, the firm will find that its employees move to less expensive training employers. Exactly the same argument applies to an employer charging the 'market' price for training, but attempting to offer a lower wage than the market.

Having introduced p() as a price, it is immediately apparent that firms may differ in the quality of their training and therefore in the effective amount of training offered per unit p(). This is most clearly apparent from equation (29), as long as Z contains innate ability and effort, which allow the firm's efficiency to be isolated. Firms which are lower quality trainers must offer lower prices (or higher wages) in compensation. Further, training may be subject to economies of scale and many of the arguments that have been applied to research and development may be equally applicable to training activities (Reeve, et al. 1988). Thus, we would anticipate that firm size would be an important factor in the cost and efficiency of the delivery of training. There may also be a similarity between the economics of training and R&D in the distinction between economies of scale linked to company size and economies of scale linked to the size of the training unit (Fisher and Temin, 1973). The analogy between R&D and human capital is further explored below.

The demand for training by employers

Production and training: joint activities
Production and training can be thought of as joint outputs of the firm; training is a form of investment which increases the future capacity of the firm. There are two essential themes of this section. First, the tenure of employment of the individual within the company is determined by many factors and not just by relative wages. Thus, if duration is, in part, socially or institutionally determined, the crucial role of market forces which underpins the role of specific versus general training as the allocative mechanism to some degree breaks down. Second, insofar as relative wages are important in determining duration of stay, tenure is both stochastic and partially endogenous. Thus, this section goes on to argue that the economics of training from the firm's point of view is both intimately tied up with the determinants of the (remaining) tenure of the individual and that the associated hazard rate is the outcome of some form of bargaining between the individual and their employer.

Model with exogenous wages and tenure
In order to emphasise the durational aspects, the net present value of training to the firm can be written as PV, where,

$$PV = \int_0^D e^{-rt}H(t)\{R(t)[1-c(\ )]-w(t)\}dt \tag{46}$$

where $c(\ )=c(T(t)/H(t))$ denotes the hourly cost of training, such that $c(0)=0$, $c'(\ )>0$ and $c''(\ )>$ or <0. The sign of the second derivative is determined by the nature of economies of scale in training. Alternatively, we can express the problem in terms of the probability in each period that the individual will leave the company. Writing the instantaneous hazard rate as ß, then the expected duration of employment can be written,

$$\epsilon(D) = ß(1) + ß(1-ß)(2) + ß(1-ß)^2(3) + \ldots. = 1/ß \tag{47}$$

and equation (46) can be rewritten,

$$\epsilon(PV) = \int_0^\infty e^{-(rt+ßt)}H(t)\{R(t)[1-c(\ )]-w(t)\}dt \tag{48}$$

Equation (46) indicates that, in a system of lifetime employment, where the link between the employee and employer is exogenously given, the firm's investment problem looks very similar to that of the individual. There are, however, a number of differences. Most importantly perhaps, in the firm's problem, $PR(t)$ is endogenised (through the acquisition of human capital), but, given the way in which the problem is specified to date, $w(t)$ is not. In the simplest training models, $w(t)$ is generally assumed to be set at (or just above) the corresponding wage that the individual can obtain from another employer, $w(t) > m(t)$. At least two further considerations may also be relevant in determining $w(t)$: first, the search and mobility costs that would be borne by the individual in moving; second, the individual's 'reservation wage', which is formed as the maximum of the alternative wage offers obtained by optimal search behaviour and the benefits they can obtain in unemployment. The issue of $w(t)$ appears crucial, and we return to it in detail below.

Movements in $PR(t)$ over time are determined by investments in human capital, where the knowledge acquired is embodied in the individual worker. The main relationships are summarised by equations (1), (26) and (29) above. These equations help to emphasize the joint production process being undertaken: as the firm provides training it adds to the individual's human capital, making the worker more productive. This raises two further issues relevant to the economics of training for the firm. First, equation (29) indicates that the efficiency of the transformation process depends crucially on the individual's ability to absorb and use new knowledge (Solo, 1966) and, thereby, the 'trainability' of the individual (as in the Thurow, 1975, 'job queue' model): incremental knowledge acquired depends not only on the existing human capital, Q(t-1), and the time spent in training, T(t), but also the personal characteristics of the individual, Z(t). Second, equation (26) shows that the efficiency of the process depends on the efficiency with which the firm can exploit the potential of the more highly qualified workers (ie. translating human capital into higher output or product prices).

Endogenous wages and tenure

The joint determination of training, wages and tenure is suggested in a number of earlier papers (Mincer and Jovanovic, 1981; Mincer and Higuchi, 1988). The underlying hypothesis put forward by Mincer is that, the more training a worker receives, the more it tends to be firm specific and, consequently, the steeper is the wage profile and the lower is turnover (Mincer, 1989, p. 2). There is no explanation in the Mincer (1989) or Mincer and Jovanovic (1981) models as to why the firm is willing to pay higher wages to workers who receive specific training. The most obvious reason, put forward in this section, is that this raises the duration of tenure of the individual within the firm, raising the period over which the returns to training are collected. Whether this raises the rate of return to training depends on the precise parameters of the model, as outlined below. The essential feature of this type of model, therefore, is that training, wage offers and duration are all simultaneously determined.

In order to illustrate the joint determination of wages, training and employment, for the moment, we continue to assume that the location of individuals is highly sensitive to relative wages. Under these conditions, if the firm sets $w(t) > m(t)$ in all periods, then, in a deterministic world, the individual would never leave because of wage considerations (although, clearly, there could be instances where, because of changing economic fortunes, the firm might find it impossible to match m(t) or the individual might leave on non-economic grounds). In practice, however, duration of spell, D is a stochastic variable determined by the search behaviour of the individual and, thereby, dependent on the wage, w(t), and the distribution of offers, f(m(t)). Thus, search theory yields a different perspective on D and enables w(t) to be endogenised; the hazard rate from employment, ß(t), becomes a function of the wage rate, w(t).

Assume that the wage offers across alternative employers are independently and identically distributed in each period and that employers are risk neutral, profit maximisers. Again, for simplicity, it is possible to assume an exogenously given arrival rate, $\Theta(t)$, reflecting the probability that the individual will receive an offer during period t. In the real world, Θ will depend on the extent of the individual's search activity and this may be taken as a signal about their likely (remaining) tenure within the job. The wage, w(t), now acts like a reservation wage, and thus, in this fairly simplified world, generates a job-change rule,

$$w(t) \geq m(t) \quad <--> \quad \text{stay with existing employer}$$
$$\tag{49}$$
$$w(t) < m(t) \quad <--> \quad \text{move to new employer}$$

where w(t) is assumed to be the wage currently paid to the individual. Thus, the probability of the individual locating an alternative wage offer which is more acceptable is $\Theta(t)[1-F(m(t))]$.

For any given iid wage offer distribution, which is constant over time, w(t) determines the probability of receiving an acceptable offer in each period, then the firm's problem is to maximise,

$$\epsilon(PV) = \int_0^\infty e^{-(rt+\beta)(w(t))t)} H(t) \, \{R(t) \, [1-c(\ )]-w(t)\} \, dt \tag{50}$$

where $\beta(w(t))$ is the instantaneous hazard rate, given a wage offer by the existing employer of w(t). Equations (1), (26) and (29) still hold. It can be seen that, in effect, writing $\beta=\beta(w)$ endogenises the wage, because the firm can affect the returns to training by altering either $F(t)=T(t)/H(t)$ (the index of training) or w. We can imagine using equation (50) to search across w and F to maximise either the net present value, PV, given r, or the rate of return, r, given PV=0. This problem is illustrated both graphically and by means of a simulation experiment elsewhere (Bosworth and Warren, 1990).

Market for training

Joint nature of training decisions

The training supplier was viewed above as entirely passive (ie. there was a perfectly elastic supply of training at the going market price). We then considered what happens when the individual was passive, reacting to market forces, encapsulated in the wage-offer distribution. In this section we want to develop the idea of an (implicit) market for training. Such a 'market' is likely to exist because both the individual and the firm have some power over the distribution of the benefits of training and this creates incentives for both to share in the costs of training. As a consequence, therefore, there are reasons for both parties to want the individual to jointly invest in specific training.

Training as signalling and screening devices

As noted above, it is generally argued that the likely wage offers in alternative employment are based on some notional market wage, bearing in mind that any earlier bouts of specific training are not relevant to other, potential future employers. In practice, this is unlikely to be true, not because one firm's specific training is relevant to another employer, but because the individual's successful completion of training may act as an indication that the individual can be trained in a new firm. This kind of indicator takes on particular importance because some of the vector of personal characteristics, $Z(t)$ (see equation 29), are likely to be unobservable (such as the amount of effort the individual puts into the process), although extensive and costly selection and interview procedures may reveal some of them. These unobservables may be proxied by information about $Q(t-1)$, $T(t)$ and $q(t)$, which may be deduced from information about the formal training they have undertaken and their 'tested performance' on these courses. From the individual's point of view, some kind of certification linked to training is an aid to making desirable career moves, acting as a signal to other potential employers that the individual would efficiently and successfully assimilate their own training. Thus, other firms can use this signal to reduce their own training costs; past performance in training is an indicator of the individual's 'trainability'. If the new firm has lower wastage in training and a greater proportion of successful trainees, they can offer higher wages or more training to their potential new recruits.

If the current employer is to reduce their wastage rates and reap the benefits of training, they must take some kind of evasive action. There are a number of alternatives. The most obvious is that they will share the potential surplus from training with the more successful trainees. This suggests that,

$$w(t) = m(m(t)) = m(Z(t)) \qquad (51)$$

Alternatively, however, they may try and cloak the true abilities of their employees and offer lower wages. One reason for this is that, while the wage offered is a deterrent to other employers, it is also an unambiguous signal. Again, however, if the employer is going to use the higher wage strategy, it pays them to share both the costs as well as the benefits of the training. In effect, specific training that acts as a signal to other employers is directly analogous to general training. One prediction of the traditional view of specific training is that individual's wages should jump down as they move from one employer to another for non-wage reasons. However, insofar as past specific training is an indicator of future productivity with another employer, wages may nevertheless show a smooth increase over time.

Asymmetric information and risk aversion

A situation of asymmetric information exists, in which the employee has more information about expected tenure than the employer. Risk aversion on the part of employers would be reflected in attempts to reduce the probability of an individual leaving before the investment is recouped. Thus, one possibility is that the employer pushes up the wage profile above the level suggested by the profit maximising (risk neutral) level, $w^*(t) > w(t)$. The effect of this will be to reduce the volume of training undertaken. If the employer is seen by the individual to be risk averse, then the employee perceives some profitable (specific) training investments which are not being made. Thus, the individual may be able to agree with the employer to undertake payment for some part of the training, in return for some share of the higher future wages. This signal by the employee, however, may produce a revision of the firm's degree of risk aversion, resulting in some intermediate outcome. This suggests that there will be situations in which both individuals and firms share the costs and benefits of training. Thus, the firm can distinguish between potential 'stayers' (to whom, other things being equal, they would offer more training) and potential 'leavers' (to whom, other things being equal, they would offer less training) by constructing a contract in which both the costs and (future) benefits of training are both shared.

Bosworth and Warren (1990) explore the possibility that individuals may attempt to capture a disproportionate part of the training surplus by 'cheating', that is, by sending misleading signals to their employer about their likely duration of stay. It pays individuals to disguise themselves as 'stayers' rather than 'movers' because their employer will be induced to finance more training for them. In practice, it may cost something for movers to disguise their true intentions. Bosworth and Warren develop a simple 'mover-stayer' model which attempts to answer the question, 'how much would an individual who knows himself to be a mover be willing to pay to represent himself as a stayer?' In our context, 'How much of the cost of specific training would an individual be prepared to pay?'. The answer is any amount thought necessary to 'deceive' the employer, up to the value equal to the difference in the net present value of the income stream which the individual will appropriate from the additional training, as long as the individual is certain this will convince the employer. Clearly, this kind of potential behaviour will bring reactions from both employers and 'stayers' (whose future job security may be adversely affected by such behaviour). It is possible to think of employers designing 'screening contracts' to make misrepresentation unattractive to individuals thought likely to behave in this way.

Joint training models

While, at first sight, the firm appears to hold the upper hand in terms of specific training, more detailed consideration shows that the individual is in a position to undermine the investment in a number of ways, causing the firm financial loss on its investment. Assume that the firm has committed itself to the investment. The individual could threaten to leave unless their wages are raised to reflect some part of the training surplus (this has many similarities to a 'strike threat'). Alternatively, they might under-perform in the learning process, increasing the costs of training or reducing the returns from training (a 'go-slow' threat), if the firm fails to share the training surplus. These issues appear to have direct analogies with the union literature (Farber, 1986; Ulph and Ulph, 1990). Firms are likely to anticipate such behaviour, forming a view of credible threats and lowering the probability that they will occur to acceptable levels by sharing some part of both the training costs and surplus, which effectively help to lock the individual into the firm.

There are a number of other problems of this type where consistent solutions for the two parties are isolated (see, for example, male and female household labour supply Grift and Siegers, 1989, 1990; Barmby, 1990). The two decision makers affect the outcome in two principal ways: first, by influencing the overall surplus available to both participants; second, by affecting the shares which go to each. Bosworth and Warren (1990) illustrate this using a more general version of equation (50); in this instance, the returns to the firm are made conditional on the amount of training funded by the individual and vice versa,

$$\epsilon(PV)_f = f(F_f, w \mid F_i) \tag{52}$$

$$\epsilon(PV)_i = g(F_i, w \mid F_f) \tag{53}$$

where F is the index of training (F=T/H), comprised of individual F_i and firm funded F_f components. For the moment, the model is simplified by assuming that wages are fixed, in order to illustrate the main features of the training equilibrium. In a 'who-pays-benefits' situation, the profit and cost curves of each player are not independent; as the firm reduces their training expenditure, their profit from training is also reduced; at the same time, the cost and profit curves of the individual shift upwards. The precise relationship between PV_f and PV_i for any given reallocation of the costs of training, depends on the relative bargaining strengths of the two parties over the training surplus.

The outcome of the non-cooperative game is derived from the reaction curves of the individual and the firm. For any given choice of training by the individual, the firm maximises its profits on the highest isoprofit curve it can reach. The locus of such points form the reaction curve of the firm. An identical argument applies in the construction of the individual's reaction curve. Thus, in a non-cooperative model, any given choice of F by one party results in the other player choosing the appropriate point on their reaction curve. The only time that these two decisions are consistent is where the two reaction curves cross. This is a simplified version of the overall solution, however, as the problem is three dimensional. In essence, there is a set of isoprofit curves of this type for each possible value of the wage; thus, the Nash solution determines both F* and w*.

Two principal cases were explored by the authors. In the first, the shift in the iso-profit curves for each actor was relatively insensitive to the reallocation of costs between the two parties; in the second, the iso-profit curves were sensitive to the reallocation of costs. In essence, the difference in the assumptions determines the relative slopes of the two reaction curves. This distinction was shown to be important for the nature of the cooperative outcome (ie. where the firm and the individual collude about the optimal w* and F*). Cooperative solutions were shown to be Pareto superior to the Nash outcome in both cases, however, where the profit curves PV are relatively invariant as training effort is reallocated, the Pareto optimal training outcomes are associated with higher levels of training than non-cooperative outcomes; the reverse is true where the PV curves are relatively sensitive to the reallocation. Certainly, a priori, it seems likely that unionised firms are more likely to reach a cooperative solution than firms with fragmented, non-unionised workforces. It also seems likely that the allocation of the training surplus may be less sensitive under unionised conditions. This is consistent with the general finding that individuals in unionised firms receive greater amounts of training; unions realise that their (and their members') long term interests are served by higher levels of training.

The model developed above is entirely market driven and does not require the existence of sociological or institutional factors to reach these conclusions. Nevertheless, there are many parallels with the training models of the implicit contract literature. This literature suggests that employee mobility will be low; individuals remain linked to their previous employer even when they are laid off. Under an implicit contract regime, the resulting long term relationships between employers and employees should prove a positive influence on the training of existing employees, giving both sets of actors sufficient time to recoup any investments. This corresponds broadly to an efficiency wage, labour turnover model. In the main, such models have been rationalised in terms of reducing costly labour turnover (Akerlof and Yellen, 1986, p. 7; Bosworth and Warren, 1990; Salop, 1979; Schlicht, 1978; Stiglitz, 1974). Such effects are reinforced by the fact that firms which offer higher wages are also likely to attract more able candidates for the vacancies they offer (Malcolmson, 1981; Stiglitz, 1976; Weiss, 1980).

Private versus social aspects

Sources of divergence of private and social returns

Perhaps the most contentious, but also potentially the most major contribution of human capital theory arises from the distinction between private and social rates of return, linking the micro and macro levels. There are at least two areas of interest. First, concerning tenure of employment with the training provider. Second, concerning externalities of training.

Mobility and tenure of employment: static versus dynamic efficiency

We have demonstrated that, once the assumption of perfect mobility of labour in search of the highest wages is relaxed in favour of a model in which the hazard rate from a given job is determined by other, socio-economic and institutional factors, then there is an incentive for both the firm and the individual to invest in both specific and general training and to share in the returns to that investment. The first point, therefore, is that labour markets which generate greater stability of employment may be less efficient in a static sense (ie. as greater individual mobility improves market clearing), but may be dynamically more efficient insofar as longer tenure encourages training. There is an almost direct analogy here with Schumpeterian theories of static versus dynamic efficiency (Schumpeter, 1928). Clearly, the theory suggests that, insofar as there is a system, for example, of life-long employment, we can expect investment in training to be higher. On the other hand, the movement of individuals between companies is a mechanism for the diffusion of both codified and uncodified knowledge (Bosworth, et al. 1993). Thus, dynamic efficiency is likely to be positively related to tenure up to some point, but negatively related after that point.

The 'poaching' debate is a very old one, but still one of considerable importance to understanding the economics of training. In a system where all employers train to given, high standards, then mobility of employees has less fundamental implications insofar as general training is passed on from one employer to another. On the other hand, there is still an efficiency loss associated from the redundancy of specific knowledge as an individual transfers between employers. Thus, in countries with well established and high levels of training amongst the vast majority of companies, such as West Germany, we might expect the maintenance of at general training even in the face of employee mobility. However, if for some reason the proportion of firms funding training begins to decline, then this rapidly erodes the returns to training (as firms funding the training will increasingly lose employees to those who do not pay for training, which gives them an economic advantage in the payment of wages). This debate provides at least part of the rationale for the introduction of the old ITBs and, more recently, the TECs.

Individual and firm training decisions take place against a given economic background, which is going to influence the returns to training. There are a number of key features which appear to distinguish the U.K. economy from some of its major competitors. In particular, it is probably fair to say that the UK economy has exhibited greater amplitude in its business cycles and these have taken place against slower longer term growth of economic activity. Indeed, while most industries have exhibited a growth in output, fewer have shown a growth in employment, as productivity improvements have driven a wedge between output and employment. Manufacturing has been hit hard by a series of recessions, including the one centered on 1980/81 but also the downturn of 1991/92. In addition, taken overall, manufacturing has seen a growth in output, but a contraction of employment. This economic background seems far from ideal in the development of implicit training contracts. While service industries have, by and large, been associated with a growth in both output and employment, many of the associated jobs have been part time and there has been a considerable growth of self employment (Wilson, 1991, Chapter 4). The associated jobs have often been casual or temporary in nature. All of these features seem unlikely to be conducive to high returns to training investments.

Here there are considerable analogies between the treatment of research and development and the treatment of human capital (Reeve, et al. 1988). Indeed, there are grounds for arguing that R&D can be treated as a special case of human capital formation and that theories that focus on formal R&D alone (ie. based on the Frascati definition, OECD, 1976) can only, by definition, provide a partial explanation. Recent work points to the fact that R&D (at least as perceived by employees who believe that they are working in this functional area) is a much broader activity than the one suggested by the Frascati definition. Thus, for a variety of reasons, the existing theories of R&D do not translate directly to human capital, although the new growth theories seem likely to provide a potential bridge (Romer, 1990a and 1990b). Nevertheless, in the following discussion, we reinterpret the notation as a theory of human capital.

Before commenting on some of the areas of potential development, we begin by outlining a well established result of the R&D literature using simple, illustrative model of 'within-industry spillover effects' developed by Griliches. Following Griliches (1991, p. 10), the production function is defined as,

$$Y_i = AX_i^{1-\alpha}K_i^{\alpha}K_a^{\mu} \qquad (54)$$

where Y_i is the output of the ith firm, which depends on the level of conventional inputs, X_i, its specific knowledge capital K_i and the aggregate knowledge base of the industry, K_a; α and μ are constants, $1 > \alpha > 0$ and $\mu > 0$. A major simplifying assumption is that the firm's own inputs, X_i and K_i, exhibit constant returns to scale. In this simple example, the aggregate level of industry knowledge can be illustrated by, $K_a = \Sigma_i K_i$. Finally, it is assumed that all firms face the same factor prices and allocate their own resources optimally. Under these conditions, the input ratios can be written,

$$K_i/X_i = \alpha \ P_x/(1-\alpha)P_k = \Omega \qquad (55)$$

where P_x and P_k are the prices of X and K and the input ratio, Ω, is independent of i.   Aggregation of the individual production functions yields,

$$\Sigma_i Y_i = \Sigma_i A X_i (K_i / X_i)^\alpha K_a{}^\mu = \Sigma_i A X_i r^\alpha K_a{}^\mu = A_r{}^\alpha K_a{}^\mu \Sigma_i X_i \qquad (56)$$

As $K_i / X_i = \Omega$ for all i, then $\Sigma K_i / \Sigma X_i = \Omega$.   Substituting the latter expression for Ω back into equation (56) yields,

$$\Sigma_i Y_i = A(\Sigma_i K_i / \Sigma_i X_i) K_a{}^\mu \Sigma_i X_i = A X_a{}^{1-\alpha} K_a{}^{\mu+\alpha} \qquad (57)$$

where $X_a = \Sigma_i X_i$ and $K_a = \Sigma_i K_i$.

The key result is that the coefficient of aggregate knowledge capital, $\alpha + \mu$, is greater than the corresponding coefficient at the firm level, α. Thus, aggregate (social) returns to investment in new knowledge (human capital) exceed micro (private) returns.

Conclusions

This paper draws on the growing empirical evidence of a link between training and wages and between training and turnover.   It indicates a number of alternative reasons why such relationships should be anticipated.   In particular, the paper suggests that wages and turnover can be endogenised in the firm-side model, using the wage-offer distribution of search theory.   In addition, it shows that the traditional distinction between the funding of specific and general training begins to break down in such a model.   It is argued that individuals also have considerable power over the profitability of any training investment and, if firms take this into account ex ante, then they will tend to adopt a strategy of sharing the benefits of training.   It is argued that there are several ways in which the firm can share the benefits which help to 'lock' the individual into the firm, for example, by raising wages to levels that make it increasingly improbable that the individual will find a more acceptable offer and by allowing individuals to jointly invest in specific training.   In essence, raising wages lengthens the tenure of the individual within the firm and, under certain assumptions about the underlying parameters of the model, raises the rate of return to training. The increased wage can be viewed as a return to the individual for complying with an employment/training contract of given duration. The important feature about this post-training wage is that it is, in part, market determined. The resulting wage-employment-training contract may be the subject of various forms of self-selection in a market comprised of heterogeneous individuals. Such selection processes will influence the final training wage differential.

The distinction between firm funded, specific training, and individual funded, general training, is further undermined by individuals sending signals about their commitment to stay with the firm, and firms sending signals about their commitment to maintaining the contracts of individuals. The individual's training record in one company also acts as a signal to other, potential employers about their trainability, influencing the wage the individual can command in the external labour market; specific training with formal accreditation may therefore be analogous to general training. The important feature about signalling processes is that they are not necessarily passive: the individual and the firm can, in principle, send a variety of signals to their respective partner in an employment/training contract.

Finally, the discussion introduces the concept of a 'market for training'. Dynamic, though myopic wealth maximising behaviour on the part of individuals and firms leads to an internal labour market solution determining wages and the training investments of individuals and firms. Training investments of this type, however, are not Pareto efficient; competition between the two parties in attempting to maximise their part of the training surplus can lead to either an under- or over-investment in training. The precise result depends on the rate at which the training surplus is redistributed amongst the players as the burden of the training effort is shifted from one to the other. Thus, Pareto efficient outcomes, which require joint training decisions by individuals and firms, result in either higher or lower levels of training activity. One unambiguous result, however, is that if unions focus on wages alone, rather than seeking the optimal wage-training contract, this can be detrimental to the volume of training activity; equally, if management depresses the wage and increases the use of temporary and casual labour, reducing the tenure of employment, the result is again likely to be a sub-optimal level of training.

The paper argues that there are strong grounds for believing that the social returns to R&D are higher than the private returns. In considering the social returns to training, it is the paper develops the analogy between R&D and training with regard to both mobility and externalities. It argues that, up to a certain point, the dynamism of the economy is encouraged by increased tenure as this encourages both general and specific training, after that point, however, the benefits are off-set by the gains from increased mobility caused by individuals diffusing knowledge as they move between firms. In addition, it is argued that the government would have improved the supply and demand for training simply by providing a more stable economic climate, avoiding the excesses of the business cycle. Finally, it is shown that where productivity depends not only on the knowledge base of the firm but also of the industry, then there are spillover effects which automatically increase the social returns over the private returns.

In conclusion, therefore, the shift in emphasis of human capital theory from education to training has resulted in a number of improvements in the understanding of age-earnings profiles and the interrelationship between life-cycle education, training and economic performance. Nevertheless, there are still many gaps in our current state of knowledge. Although it is outside the scope of the present study, we believe that a vintage approach would yield useful insights about the relationship between productivity and human capital. In addition, we note that some dynamic form of the production function may be necessary, as more qualified labour may affect future outputs, prices and input levels rather than current levels. Attempts to develop more dynamic counterparts can be found in the literature (Schott, 1978), often in the context of endogenising technical change (often R&D), which we argue has many analogies with human capital. There are many examples where the social and institutional context are not given sufficient emphasis within the human capital literature. Equally, however, it would be wrong to think of this context as fixed and immutable; a recurring theme of this paper which requires further development is that economic forces gradually reshape the social and institutional context. It is clear from the empirical results that human capital variables are often significant but not sufficient, in isolation, to explain the whole age, education, training and earnings relationship. One implication of this approach is that the human capital, social and institutional views of training are all special cases. It is taken as given that each of these approaches has something to offer, but it will not be possible to judge their relative contributions to the understanding of the causes and consequences of training until a more general model is constructed which subsumes the various alternatives. This paper sketches an outline of such a model, although it is recognised from the outset that further research is required to develop this idea.

References

Akerlof, G.A. and Yellen, J.L. (1986), *Efficiency Wage Models of the Labour Market*. Cambridge: Cambridge U.P.

Arrow, K.J. (1962), 'The economic implications of learning by doing', *Review of Economic Studies*, 29, pp. 609-625

Ashton, D. (1988), 'Educational institutions, youth and the labour market', in Gallie, D. (Ed.) *Employment in Britain*. Oxford: Basil Blackwell, pp. 406-433.

Barmby, T. (1990), 'Pareto household labour supply', Paper presented to the EMRU Labour Economics Study Group Workshop, University of Loughborough, Loughborough.

Becker, G.S. (1964), *Human Capital*. New York: Columbia U.P. 2nd edition.

Blinder, A.S. and Weiss, Y. (1976), 'Human capital and labour supply: a synthesis', *Journal of Political Economy*, 84, pp. 449-472.

Bosworth, D.L. and Ford, J. (1985a), 'Income expectations and the decision to enter higher education', *Studies in Higher Education*, 10, pp. 21-32.

Bosworth, D.L. and Ford, J. (1985b), 'Perceptions of higher education by university entrants: an exploratory analysis', *Studies in Higher Education*, 10, pp. 257-267.

Bosworth, D.L. and Warren, P. (1990), 'The market for training', Discussion Paper No. 45. IER. Coventry: Warwick University. Paper presented to EALE, University of Lund.

Bosworth, D.L., Wilson, R.A. and Hogarth, T. (1993), *Competition and Collaboration in the European Research and Development*, Research Report to the European Commission. Management School. Manchester: UMIST.

Bover, O. (1989), 'Estimating intertemporal labour supply elasticities using structural models', *Economic Journal*, 99, pp. 1026-1040.

Deaton, A. (1974), 'A reconsideration of the empirical implications of additive preferences', *Economic Journal*, 84, pp. 338-348.

Denison, E.F. (1962), *Sources of Economic Growth in the United States and the Alternatives Before Us*, New York: Committee for Economic Development.

Elias, P. and Blanchflower, D. (1988), *The Occupations, Earnings and Work Histories of Young Adults - Who Gets the Good Jobs?*, Research Paper No. 68. London: Department of Employment.

Fisher, F.M. and Temin, P. (1973), 'Returns to scale in research and development: what does the schumpetorian hypothesis imply?', *Journal of Political Economy*, 81. pp. 56-70.

Flueckiger, G.E. (1976), 'Specialisation, learning by doing and the optimal amount of learning', *Economic Inquiry*, 14, pp. 389-409.

Freeman, R.B. (1986), 'Demand for education', In O.C. Ashenfelter and R. Layard (eds.). *Handbook of Labour Economics,* Vol 1. Amsterdam: North Holland, pp. 357-386.

Grift, Y.K. and Siegers, J.J. (1989), 'Estimating and individual utility labour supply model with a family budget constraint and with pareto optimal outcomes', Paper presented to the Third Annual Meeting of ESPE, University of Utrecht, Utrecht.

Grift, Y.K. and Siegers, J.J. (1990), 'An individual utility - household budget constraint model for dutch couples', Paper presented to the EMRU Labour Economics Study Group Workshop, University of Loughborough, Loughborough.

Griliches, Z. (1991), The search for R&D spillovers', *Proceedings of the Uppsala Conference on Welfare, Quality and Productivity in the Service Industries.* Department of Economics, Uppsala, 21-23.

Hammermesh, D.S. and Rees, A. (1993), *The Economics of Work and Pay*, New York: Harper Collins.

Heckman, J. and Polacheck, S. (1974), 'Empirical evidence on the functional form of the earnings-schooling relationship', *Journal of the American Statistical Association*, 69, pp. 350-4.

Heckman, J.J. (1976a), 'Estimates of a human capital production function embedded in a life cycle model of labour supply', in Terleckyj, N. (ed.), *Household Production and Consumption.* New York: Columbia U.P. pp. 227-58.

Heckman, J.J. (1976b), 'A life cycle model of earnings, learning and consumption', *Journal of Political Economy*, 84, pp. S11-44.

Heckman, J.J. (1987), 'Selection bias and the economics of self-selection', *The New Palgrave.* London: Macmillan, pp. 287-297.

Jenkins, R. and Troyna, B. (1983), 'Educational myths and labour market realities', in B. Troyna and D. Smiths (eds), *Racism, School and the Labour Market.* Studies in Research, Book 2. Leicester: National Youth Bureau.

Jorgenson, D.W. and Fraumeni, B.M. (1991), 'Investment in education and U.S. growth', *Proceedings of the Uppsala Conference on Welfare, Quality and Productivity in the Service Industries.* Department of Economics, Uppsala, pp. 21-23.

Jorgenson, D.W. and Griliches, Z. (1967), 'The explanation of productivity change', *Review of Economic Studies*, 34, pp. 249-283.

Killingsworth, M. (1983), *Labour Supply.* Cambridge, Mass: Cambridge U.P.

Malcolmson, J. (1981), 'Unemployment and the efficiency wage hypothesis', *Economic Journal*, 91, pp. 848-866.

MaCurdy, T.E. (1981), 'An empirical model of labour supply in a life-cycle setting', *Journal of Political Economy*, 89, pp. 1059-1085.

MaCurdy, T.E. (1985), 'Interpreting empirical models of labour supply, in an intertemporal framework with uncertainty', in J.J. Heckman and B. Singer (eds.), *Longitudinal Analysis of Labour Market Data.* Cambridge, Mass: Cambridge U.P.

Manning, A. (1990), 'Implicit contract theory', in Sapsford, D. and Tzannatoz (eds.), *Current Issues in Labour Economics.* London: Macmillan. Chapter 4.

Mincer, J. (1974), *Schooling, Experience and Earnings.* New York: NBER.

Mincer, J. (1989), 'Job training: costs, returns and wage profiles', *NBER Working Paper Series No. 3208.* National Bureau of Economic Research. Mass: Cambridge.

Mincer, J. and Higuchi, Y. (1988), Wage structures and labour turnover in the U.S. and in Japan', *Journal of the Japanese and International Economics.*

Mincer, J. and Jovanovic, B. (1981), 'Labour mobility and wages', in S. Rosen (ed.), *Studies in Labour Markets.* Chicago: University of Chicago Press.

OECD (1976), *The Measurement of Scientific and Technological Activities. Proposed Standard Practice for Surveys of Research and Experimental Development*, ('Frascati Manual'). Paris: OECD.

Reeve, N., Metcalf, J.S. and Georghiou, L. (1988), *The Benefits of Training*, A Report Prepared for the Manpower Services Commission. PREST. Manchester: University of Manchester.

Romer, P.M. (1990a), 'Endogenous technical change', *Journal of Political Economy*, 98, pp. S71-S102.

Romer, P.M. (1990a), 'Capital, labour and productivity', *Brookings Papers on Economic Activity. Microeconomics 1990*, pp. 337-367.

Rosen, S. (1972), Learning and experience in the labour market', *Journal of Human Resources*, 7, pp. 336-42.

Ryder, H.E., Stafford F.P. and Stephan P. (1976), Labour, leisure and training over the life cycle', *International Economic Review*, 17, pp. 651-74.

Salop, S. (1979), 'A model of the natural rate of unemployment', *American Economic Review*, 69, pp. 117-125.

Schlict, E. (1978), 'Labour turnover, wage structure and natural unemployment', *Zeitschrift für die Gesamte Staatswissenschaft*, 134, pp. 337-346.

Schott, K. (1978), 'The relations between industrial research and development and factor demands', *Economic Journal*, 88, pp.

Schumpeter, J. (1928), 'The instability of capitalism', *Economic Journal*, 38, pp. 361-386.

Silberberg, E. (1978), *The Structure of Economics: a Mathematical Analysis*, New York: McGraw Hill.

Solo, R. (1966), 'The capacity to assimilate an advanced technology', *American Economic Review*, pp. 91-97.

Stiglitz, J. (1974), 'Wage determination and unemployment in LDCs: the labour turnover model', *Quarterly Journal of Economics*, 88, pp. 194-227.

Stiglitz, J. (1976), 'Prices and queues as screening devices in competitive markets', *IMSSS Technical Report No. 212*. Stanford University. August.

Thurow, L. (1975), *Generating Inequality: Mechanisms of Inequality in the U.S. Economy*. London: Macmillan.

Ulph, A. and Ulph, D. (1990), 'Union bargaining: a survey of recent evidence', in D. Sapsford and Z Tzannatos (eds), *Current Issues in Labour Economics*. London: Macmillan. pp. 86-125.

Weiss, Y. (1972), 'On the optimal pattern of labour supply', *Economic Journal*, 82, pp. 1293-1315.

Weiss, A. (1980), 'Job queues and layoffs in labour markets with flexible wages', *Journal of Political Economy*, 88, pp. 526-538.

Williams, G. and A. Gordon (1981). Perceived earnings functions and ex ante rates of return to post-compulsory education in England, *Higher Education Review*. 10. 2. 199-227.

Wilson, R.A. (1980). The rate of return to becoming a qualified scientist or engineer in Great Britain 1966-1976, *Scottish Journal of Political Economy*. 21. 1. 41-62.

Wilson, R.A. (1991). *Review of the Economy and Employment, Occupational Assessment, 1991*, Institute for Employment Research. Coventry: University of Warwick.

4 Training, productivity and underemployment in institutional labor markets

Clair Brown

An institutional framework

In an institutional model, underemployment is assumed to be a basic characteristic[1], so that capital is more scarce than labor (see Table 4.1.) A worker's productivity is determined by access to capital, training, and protected markets as well as by own effort, already-acquired skills, and innate ability. For a given level of skill and effort, a worker's productivity depends on his or her job, since the job determines the worker's access to resources (including capital and market rents) and training. Job placement thus determines the worker's long-run productivity, bargaining power, and earnings. The productivity of a firm's job structure reflects the firm's past investment decisions, which determine the technology used in the product design and capital stock, and the demand for the firm's product, which reflects macroeconomic conditions.

This is in contrast to a neoclassical labor market, where prices allocate labor so that competitive forces produce full employment in the long run. A worker's productivity is a result of individual human capital decisions, both in investing in education and on-the-job training. Observed differences in lifetime earnings primarily reflect differences in preferences and abilities. On-the-job training is an investment made on the basis of profit maximization, with the costs and returns rationally assigned to the firm or employee. The firm's investment decisions will not influence workers' productivity, since the firm will locate its capital globally to equalize wages and marginal products. Training in an institutional world reflects three important economic structures. The first is the labor market structure that simultaneously forms and rations workers' skills. The second is the firm's organizational structure, including the training process, that shape the demand for and use of labor. The third is the macroeconomic structure, especially the institutions shaping unemployment and investment, that governs the economy. The first two structures are interrelated, and they function within the context of the third. These structures are discussed in turn.

Labor market structures

The assumption of underemployment, or the inability of workers to use their full capabilities or to develop fully their potential productivity, is essential to the institutional model. Since the labor market presents unequal opportunities, institutions (i.e., social rules and customs) are used to ration people into and through the labor market. These institutions form segmented or non-competing markets, which each function as internal labor markets.[2] The institutions for rationing must be accepted as fair in order for the labor market to function effectively.

The need for job rationing reflects two phenomena--more than the needed number of available workers possess the required skills and competence and are willing to make the required effort for any given job; and most workers' talents are not fully utilized or developed by their jobs. Although it is true that most well-paying jobs require competent workers who work hard, the converse that all people who are competent and hardworking are well paid is *not* true. The rationing process is responsible for this distinction, which cannot exist in competitive labor markets. Although individuals do have innate differences in personality and abilities, these are small relative to the differences that are formed and rewarded, first, by the educational system and, then, by the labor market. The socialization and education of children, both within the family and in the school system, teach children the appropriate rules and customs that govern their behaviour and thinking.[3] The rationing process requires this socialization process in order for the rationing to occur and be accepted automatically.

The role of training in forming underemployment

The training that is acquired while employed is an essential part of the dynamic process that both creates the structure of underemployment and rations workers within it. The job itself determines the development of the worker as it provides the acquisition of new skills (through on-the-job and off-the-job training) and networks as well as the honing of these skills (especially through experience or learning-by-doing) and the development of appropriate behaviour. This process occurs both informally (i.e., without any explicit training) and formally (i.e., with a specific training plan) on the job. The results are both observable and valuable in terms of the worker's performance in the current job and the worker's ability to gain access to higher paying jobs. This development of the worker, especially in creating networks, developing behaviour or personality, and learning job tasks, takes place within the workplace, so initial access to employment is a required first step in a chain of potential job development. The consequences of the developmental process are irreversible since the steps are incremental in creating a more productive worker. Since some job chains are very short and do not provide much opportunity (if any) for worker development, while other job chains are long and provide extensive development, how workers are rationed into the various job chains determines their lifetime chances in the labor market.[4]

The training process within the firm

The training process is one part of the production system created by the employer. This paper focuses on four major instruments chosen by the firm in setting up an production system--the process of training, the organization of work, the design of the product, and the use of capital. The technology used by the firm is embedded in the last two instruments, which dictate the skills of the work force, which are produced and practiced with the first two instruments.

This section analyzes the training process within the firm. First, the nature of skills used and developed on the job, and how these skills have been changing with the computerization of work, are discussed. Then the costs of and returns to training, and how training must be evaluated as part of the production system, are examined.

The nature of skills

The skills used on the job include a wide array of workers' attributes, including basic literacy, physical skills, specific craft know-how, communication and interpersonal skills, ability to train others, technical knowledge, and problem-solving skills. In addition, a worker's attitude affects performance on the job. Attitude, which is shaped by one's experience on the job[5], includes obeying orders or following directions, being punctual, being honest, being willing to work overtime, being eager to learn, having good attendance, being pleasant under trying circumstances, and generally assisting in meeting goals as defined by one's supervisor.

Formal education, family background, and innate abilities determine a new entrants' skills and attitude, which define their potential in the workplace. A worker's potential is constrained and shaped by job placement, which determines how much her or his potential is actually used and how much the potential will be expanded through experience on the job. Over time, workers' skills and attitudes are determined by their job experiences. A well-functioning employment system can improve skills and attitudes. A badly managed workplace or deadening, low skill jobs can have the opposite effect, so that skills learned in school and desirable work attitudes will deteriorate if they are not used, rewarded, and expanded on the job.

Changing skill demands

As the production process has become designed and controlled by computers, and as work has become robotized, the nature of skills required by production workers has changed from being based in a physical process to being based in an information system. For this reason, the skills of white collar, blue collar, and pink collar workers have been converging as work requires the operation of robots and computers. Many skills once based on mechanical knowledge and/or the manipulation of physical components have been replaced by the use of knowledge to operate computers, which requires a more abstract approach both to performing routine tasks and to solving problems. As production work becomes based on computer knowledge, including problem-solving or trouble-shooting skills, the nature of the job and the embedded skills transform from being physically based to being information based.[6] The amount of (re)training required increases, so job tasks require longer training periods. Although some tasks may temporarily become more routinized, these tasks will eventually be computerized. As blue and pink collar job hierarchies require more internal training, employers will organize work to train workers efficiently and to reduce turnover in order to protect their investment. This process has been termed the 'white collarization of blue collar workers.'[7] Although this process is evident, firms are also incorporating new technology into computerized equipment that replaces some of the judgment required by workers in making adjustments and solving problems.

The costs of and returns to training

Although the idea of selecting applicants on the basis of ability to train, which would reduce the employer's training costs, is an appealing one,[8] employers are limited in selecting new hires by their training costs because the relationship between employees' ability to be trained and training costs is not a unique one. This partially results from 'skill' being a complex variable that encompasses a wide array of attributes with each worker possessing a different mix of these attributes. In addition, for a given product and capital stock, the relationship depends on the process of training and work organization chosen by management. For example, work can be organized so that testing equipment is run by operators who perform only routine tasks with problem-solving, change-over, and maintenance tasks performed by engineers. Alternatively, operators can be trained as technicians to perform some of the problem-solving, change-over, and maintenance tasks under engineering supervision. Another example can be used to show how work can be organized in various ways even within a team system. Although team members can be required to perform all tasks and rotate jobs frequently, teams can also function effectively by having members perform different tasks and not rotate. For example, one operator who is illiterate but has excellent job-related skills could train co-workers, but she would not be trained in statistical process control (SPC). Another worker with good math skills, but who performs assembly tasks slowly, would be trained in SPC to be in charge of making graphs for analyzing and solving problems; he would not be used for assisting co-workers with job tasks.

Technological innovation in the product or in the production process will provide the employer with long-run options that change the implicit short-run training function. In general, technological innovation in the production process are labor saving and require additional training (or retraining) for some workers, so that the innovations reinforce the rationing process already in place. The presence of underemployment does not mean that the employer does not attempt to minimize training and other labor costs, given the labor market and product market structures within which the company operates. The rationing process allows employers some leeway in assigning similarly qualified workers within the hierarchy, so that the costs associated with mistakes are small. This does not imply that the costs of mistakes associated with other instruments (e.g., the training process, the organization of work, the product design, the capital stock) are small.

In order for training to be analyzed as an investment, the training process must satisfy several requirements - the amount of training must be optional (i.e., chosen by the firm), and training costs and returns must exist and be measurable. These strict requirements are seldom met because of information and control problems resulting form the fact that training is embedded in the job structure. Some training, especially improvements in speed and quality of work, occurs with experience at no cost to the employer. Although formal on-the-job training can be varied, within bounds, by the employer, the cost of training depends on the intensity of training along with the relative number being trained, since part of the cost is borne by experienced workers, who assist the learners. The company can incur costs in terms of lowered output or increased defects if the trainee is not performing well, is not supervised properly, or is not assisted by co-workers. These costs are likely to increases when more than one employee is being trained in a work group at the same time. For this reason, the total turnover/hiring rate is not as important as whether or not turnover/hiring occurs in a smooth and orderly fashion. In a world with fast-changing technology, the longevity of skills becomes questionable. In this situation, a company's commitment to retrain becomes important to employees. Even if a worker could transfer skills to another employer for a higher wage in the short run, a worker will remain with the company promising continual (re)training, which translates into higher lifetime earnings. In this way, employment security functions to lower turnover at the same time that it increases (re)training and ensures that the company will recoup its long-run training costs.

Although most scholars differentiate between general (or transferable) skills and specific skills for theoretically allocating training costs and returns between the company and the employee, this differentiation often loses meaning in practice. This is especially true in an institutional labor market where the job structure is established to train workers internally, where there are queues to better-paying jobs, and where the employer seldom knows the transferability of applicants' job skills. In general, the skills acquired cannot be accurately measured and the costs cannot be accurately measured and allocated between the company, the trainee, and the co-workers.

Because the costs and amounts of training are difficult to calculate, because the costs can be borne in varying combinations by the learners, experienced co-workers, and employer, and because past costs are fixed costs, training results in a monetary cost and return that must be negotiated either individually (non-union) or collectively (union). Training also represents an investment that must be carefully guarded since it is embodied in the workers.

Training as part of a production system

Since training is only one part of a production system, how it functions must be evaluated within the context of the company's overall production system, especially its employment or human resource system that includes the organization of work, the structure of compensation, and the provision of security.[9]

Seniority security provides incentives for employees to retrain, since they are laid off without replacement income if their jobs become obsolete. Workers will be willing to train less senior workers provided that seniority is plant-wide by job classification. With income security, however, an employee's willingness to retrain depends on how much income replacement is received if laid off. With employment security, employees will be willing to train co-workers since their jobs cannot be threatened. Employment security may not contain incentives to retrain unless training is required to retain employment. However, if pay is based on relative performance, workers may not be willing to share ways

113

of doing the job better or more efficiently if they view co-workers as competing for relative job evaluation points or promotion.

Companies with a commitment to income or employment security must also have a commitment to training, since security creates an incentive to retrain experienced employees as technological innovation requires new job skills and makes old job skills obsolete. The fixed costs associated with security arrangements makes the retraining costs minimal. Training and compensation are determined by the promotional process up a job ladder. Firms often want to tie promotion and pay to performance and the willingness to learn new skills in order to motivate workers. Performance-based promotion or pay, which theoretically relates performance and compensation, faces difficulties in practice because of the problems involved in accurately evaluating workers on the basis of objective criteria rather than on the basis of subjective evaluations by supervisors. For example, perceived or real favoritism becomes a problem in the situation where a large number of workers can perform the next or 'better' job approximately the same, but only one person is needed. In this case, the use of seniority for allocating job assignments is probably not inefficient and is usually accepted as fair. Performance-based pay or promotion may be more effective in the situation where a person has control over his or her productivity and variation among workers is observable.

An example of how training must be evaluated within the context of the company's production system is provided by analyzing the goal of providing flexibility in response to changes in market demand. This goal has many components, and the firm chooses among different strategies to improve flexibility (along with its other goals). Overall, the firm's main focus is its return to investment in an production process that integrates capital (embodying technology) and labor (embodying training) in an organization of work.

Flexibility in using workers' skills can be improved in two basic ways: (1) by broadening skills so that each worker can do multiple tasks with the combination easily altered as needed; (2) by breaking down complex tasks into simple components so that a worker can quickly learn any one task and workers can be easily switched among tasks as needed. Both approaches to the organization of work can provide flexibility in the labor input. The former way has the advantage of reducing the managerial time required to plan work assignments. In addition, broadly-skilled workers will have more job-based knowledge, which they can use to make improvements in the production process. The latter way has the advantage of using specialization of skills to attain high productivity and with few defects. Which approach is chosen by a firm depends on the relative costs and benefits associated with each. A firm will tend to train broadly-skilled workers if the returns to specialization are not great, if job tasks are not quickly learned, if product innovations are made often, if a system for employee involvement that utilizes workers' job-based knowledge in making suggestions or in solving problems is functioning, if labor is scarce so that the firm wants to reduce turnover, if quality problems are rooted in the work process rather than in workers' sloppiness, and if the higher training costs are warranted by higher productivity and quality.[10]

Alternatively, flexibility can also be built into the production process by designing flexible programmable machines rather than dedicated machines. Flexible programmable machines, like broadly-skilled workers, may result in loss of productivity that accompanies specialization. The company's choice between dedicated machines with the use of standardized and interchangeable products parts or flexible programmable machines must be made simultaneously with its choice of work organization and training process.

The macroeconomic environment

The company's performance is heavily influenced by macroeconomic policies that affect the level of unemployment and the variability in product demand. The macroeconomic environment in which the firm operates affects the costs of and returns to its production system, including the training process, work organization, product design, and capital stock. For example, the firm's net cost of providing security or training is directly related to long-run product demand and the short-run variations in demand. The firm's quit and hiring functions depend on the unemployment rate and the overall attractiveness of its jobs relative to alternative jobs. Firms benefit from providing security, which lowers quits, during periods of strong demand, and workers benefit more from security provisions, which reduce the probability of lay-off or income loss, during periods of weak demand.

115

Over time, macroeconomic policy affects the composition of the jobs being formed. This determines the skills and attitudes that are created at the workplace as well as the rate at which education embodied in new entrants is put to use in the labor market. The educational requirements of entrants into the labor force must rise over time and experienced employees must continually be acquiring new skills if a country is to achieve continual growth in productivity and wages.

Supply of labor does not create its own demand in an institutional world, and workers who are unable to find a suitable job for their skill level will experience skill deterioration rather than skill enhancement on the job. Companies will teach employees the skills that are required to meet a robust market demand. Companies would, of course, prefer that employees (especially new hires) obtain any required formal training through the public school system, since this would reduce the company's training costs. However, when companies can rely on strong and growing product demand, their internal training programs are cost efficient. Companies would also prefer that their employees have basic math, English, and problem-solving skills, since this would make training and managing in a traditional fashion easier. However, many companies have techniques for conducting on-the-job and classroom training for employees lacking basic skills.

In a high pressure economy, higher skill jobs are created, and the less skilled jobs are not filled.[11] Companies are willing to train and upgrade employees because they are reasonably certain they can sell their output. Unfortunately, countries have been deterred from pursuing full employment policies because of the problems of price inflation and deficit balance of payments.[12]

Policy issues

Since institutional theory assumes that government plays a necessary role in creating the structure within which the economy functions, government is largely responsible for shaping labor market outcomes. In particular, the government helps create and preserve the social rules and mechanisms by which people are prepared for and accept their social and work roles, without which an economy cannot function. The institutional structure exists to ensure social order, to ensure social reproduction, and to provide a system of value through the creation and enforcement of rule and custom. The daily conduct of business requires this institutional structure.

In creating labor market structures, policy makers would like to assume that future jobs will require increased skills and will pay accordingly. However, this assumption cannot necessarily be made since scholars disagree over what skill and education will be required for jobs in the future.[13] In addition, they disagree if current employees lack the basic skills required by their employers. An important study by the Commission on the Skills of the American Workforce (1990) reported on the skill needs and training plans of over 400 U.S. companies. In general, few companies reported concerns about skill shortages. Most companies, however, were concerned about workers' attitudes. Fewer than 10 per cent of the companies surveyed are reorganizing work for a 'high performance' workplace. Other companies are using automation to create very simple work tasks with little training, low wages, and no employment security.

The lack of understanding about the role of training in forming a high performance production system may lead to focusing on training as the cause of low productivity or quality problems when the actual cause may be insufficient investment to develop superior products, the insufficient use of engineers on the shop floor to develop well-functioning equipment, or the lack of coordination with suppliers to develop high quality parts. Large investments in training employees to solve problems or make suggestions cannot compensate for an inferior product, defective parts, or malfunctioning equipment. Although production workers can assist in making suggestions for product improvements, can identify inferior parts, and can do some routine maintenance or simple repairs of equipment, these activities can only be used to make marginal improvements to a production process that is already functioning well.

Policy debates about the role of training in raising productivity should distinguish among the several different dimensions of skill formation. One dimension is the job skills desired for high school graduates; a second is the job skills required for college graduates; a third is the required supply of college versus high school graduates; a fourth is the need for employers to supply and employees to accept continual learning as part of the job. These dimensions tend to become confused during recessionary periods because employers are forced to decrease costs in the short run, although their production system and its cost structure may be efficient in the long run. Financial pressures may lead employers to have unrealistic expectations of high school graduates performing engineering tasks, or of suppliers improving quality while decreasing prices. Policy makers, discouraged by a long recessionary period and pressured to revive the upward trend in living standards, may unrealistically expect increased education to decrease unemployment and increase productivity. Although increasing education for the individual can increase that person's productivity and ability to find a job, we cannot extend the results for the individual to the labor force as a whole, which is constrained by the total demand for labor and the job composition this demand represents.

The educational requirements of new entrants into service, clerical, and production jobs are very different from the educational requirements of new entrants into professional, managerial, and technical jobs. These two non-competing groups hold very different positions in the labor market, and their on-the-job training reflects the differences in their job tasks. Policy makers should be more concerned with the types of jobs being created over time than with the educational preparedness of new entrants since a powerful incentive for young people to acquire skills or education is the lure of a well-paying job that uses the skills. A labor market with high unemployment or an economy that is creating low wage jobs will not produce the needed educational incentives, and this in turn will hamper the economy's long-run ability to create a high productivity/high wage labor market.

As computerization of work decreases the need for jobs in the low end of the labor market, we need to ask if there will be sufficient jobs available to high school graduates and if these jobs will provide on-the-job training that increases employees' skills over time. A full employment economy with a high level of investment is a policy that can ensure this outcome. Policies that limit immigration while allowing export of labor-intensive capital would be a part of a high wage, full employment macroeconomic policy.

Even if we adopt an expansionary macroeconomic policy to improve productivity growth and decrease unemployment, we would still have important training policies to consider. We need to identify the desired skills for specific types of workers and the most efficient way to obtain these skills. For example, what is the most effective and least costly way to provide the skills needed in the various occupations in the workplace? Which skills are efficiently provided by the school system? What is the most effective way for students to acquire these skills? Similarly, which skills are most efficiently provided by the firm? What is the most effective way for employees to acquire these skills? Is there a reason (e.g., a public good is being provided) for the government to subsidize these training activities by firms? These are important questions that need to be answered in order for us to provide training and educational efficiently. However, answering these questions alone will not provide us with the solution to improving productivity and income growth, since training and education programs can only function properly in a full-employment economy.

Notes

I am indebted to my colleagues Michael Reich, David Stern, and Lloyd Ulman, from whom I have learned during our joint research project on training and employment systems in the U.S. and Japan. This research was supported by the Institute of Industrial Relations at the University of California, Berkeley, the Bureau of Labor-Management Cooperation at the U.S. Department of Labor, and the Pacific Rim Foundation of the University of California. This paper does not necessarily represent the position of the sponsoring agencies.

1. See Brown (1988) for a comparison of the assumptions made in the neoclassical and institutional models. Both Brown (1988) and this paper are in the tradition of American institutional labor economics and draw on literature about internal labor markets. See, for example, Commons (1934), Doeringer and Piore (1971), Dunlop (1958), Kerr (1977), Osterman (1988), Piore (1979b), and Slichter (1941).
2. The division of the labor market into non-competing markets dates back to at least Cairnes. See also Gordon, Reich, and Edwards (1975) for analyses of segmented labor markets. The internal labor market, which is the operation of one labor market segment, is analyzed in Doeringer and Piore (1971). Piore (1979b) has argued

that even minimum wage labor markets have internal labor market characteristics, so that all labor market segments function by institutional rules.

3. See Bowles and Gintis (1976), Piore (1979a).

4. Michael J. Piore discusses how automatic, incidental learning on the job explains the construction of 'mobility chains'. (Edwards, Reich, and Gordon, 1975, ch. 5)

5. See, for example, Piore (1979b) and Kanter (1977).

6. Zuboff (1988)

7. Koike (1988).

8. Thurow (1975).

9. See Brown, Reich, and Stern (1992) for an analysis of the role of security, employee participation, training, and compensation in a well-functioning employment system.

10. This approach is consistent with Bailey (1991b), who develops a 'managerial cost theory' of skills, where the relationship between technology and required skills depends on the managerial effort (or cost) involved in producing skills.

11. See Okun (1973).

12. This is a large topic that cannot be pursued here. However, many economists have written on this subject. See, for example, David Soskice (1989).

13. See a summary and critique of BLS occupational forecasts in Bailey (1991A).

References

Aoki, M. (1988), *Information, Incentives, and Bargaining in the Japanese Economy*. New York: Cambridge University Press.

Aoki, M. (1990), 'Toward an economic model of the japanese firm', *Journal of Economic Literature*, 28, pp. 1-27.

Bailey, T. (1991a), 'Jobs of the future and the education they will require: evidence from occupational forecasts', *Educational Research*, March, pp. 11-20.

Bailey, T. (1991b), *A Managerial Cost Theory of Skills,* Mimeo Columbia University.

Berger, S. and Piore, M., eds. (1980), *Dualism and Discontinuity in Industrial Societies*. Cambridge: Cambridge University Press.

Bowles, S. and Gintis, H. (1976), *Schooling in Capitalist America*. New York: Basic Books.

Brown, C. (1988), 'Income distribution in an institutional world', In Mangum, G. and Philips, P., (eds.), *Three Worlds of Labor Economics*. Armonk, N.Y.: M. E. Sharpe.

Brown, C. and Reich, M. (1989), 'When does union-management cooperation work?', *California Management Review*, 31, no. 4, Summer.

Brown, C., Reich, M. and Stern, D. (1991), *Skills and Security in Evolving Employment Systems*, Mimeo. University of California, Berkeley.

Commission on the skills of the american workforce (1990), *America's Choice: High Skills or Low Wages*, Rochester, N.Y.: National Center on Education and the Economy.

Commons, J. R. (1934), *Institutional Economics*. New York: Macmillan.

Cutcher-Gershenfeld, J. (1988), *Tracing a Transformation in Industrial Relations: The Case of Xerox Corporation and the Amalgamated Clothing and Textile Workers Union*, Washington, D.C.: U. S. Department of Labor.

Dertouzos, M. L., Lester, R. K., and Solow, R. M. (1989), *Made in America: Regaining the Productive Edge*. Cambridge, MA: MIT Press.

Doeringer, P. B. and Piore, M. J. (1971), *Internal Labor Markets and Manpower Analysis*. Lexington, MA: D. C. Heath.

Dore, R. P. (1973), *British Factory, Japanese Factory*. Berkeley: University of California Press.

Dore, R. P. and Sako, M. (1989), *How the Japanese Learn to Work*. New York: Routledge.

Dunlop, John T. (1958), *Industrial Relations Systems*. New York: Holt.

Endo, K. (1990), *Satei (Personal Assessment) and Inter-Worker Competition in Japanese Firms*, Working Paper.

Edwards, R., Reich, M. and Gordon, D., eds. (1975), *Labor Market Segmentation*. Lexington, MA: D.C. Heath & Co.

Foulkes, F. K. (1980), *Personnel Policies in Large Nonunion Companies*. Englewood Cliffs, N.J.: Prentice-Hall.

Foulkes, F. K. (1989), *Human Resources Management*. Englewood Cliffs, N.J.: Prentice-Hall.

Friedhan, S. and Fischer, L. (1988), 'Collective bargaining and employment security', In *Proceedings of the Forty-First Annual Meeting*. Industrial Relations Research Association, December.

Ishida, M. (1990), *The Social Foundation of Wage Systems: A Comparative Study of Japan and the U.K.* Tokyo: Chuo Keizai Sha. (In Japanese).

Jacoby, S. (1985), *Employing Bureaucracy*. New York: Columbia University Press.

Jacoby, S. (1990), 'The New Institutionalism: What Can It Learn from the Old?', *Industrial Relations*, no. 2.

Kanter, R. M. (1977), *Men and Women of the Corporation*. New York: Basic Books.

Katz, H. C. (1985), *Shifting Gears: Changing Labor Relations in the U.S. Automobile Industry*. Cambridge, MA: MIT Press.

Kerr, C. (1977), 'The balkanization of labor markets', Reprinted in Kerr, C., *Labor Markets and Wage Determination*. Berkeley, CA: University of California Press.

Kerr, C. and others (1960), *Industrialism and Industrial Man*. Cambridge, MA: Harvard University Press.

Kochan, T. A., Katz, H. C. and McKersie, R. B. (1986), *The Transformation of American Industrial Relations*. New York: Basic Books.

Koike, K. (1988), *Understanding Industrial Relations in Modern Japan*. New York: St. Martin's Press.

Koike, K. and Inoki, T. (1990), *Skill Formation in Japan and Southeast Asia*. University of Tokyo Press.

Lave, J. (1988), *Cognition in Practice: Mind, Mathematics, and Culture in Everyday Life*. New York: Cambridge University Press.

Lazear, E. (1991), *Labor Economics and the Psychology of Organizations*, Journal of Economic Perspectives, 5, no. 2, Spring.

Lincoln, J. R. and Kalleberg, A. L. (1990), *Culture, Control, and Commitment*. New York: Cambridge University Press.

Okun, A. (1973), *Upward Mobility in a High Pressure Economy*, Brookings Paper on Economic Activity. 1, pp. 207-252.

Osterman, P. (1988), *Employment Futures*. New York: Oxford University Press.

Osterman, P. (1990), *Processes and Prospects for Employment Security in the United States*, Mimeo, Massachusetts Institute of Technology.

Piore, M. J. (1979a), *Birds of Passage*. Cambridge University Press.

Piore, M. J. (ed.) (1979b), *Unemployment and Inflation*. White Plains, N.Y.: M. E. Sharpe, Inc.

Piore, M. J. and Sabel, C. F. (1984), *The Second Industrial Divide*. New York: Basic Books.

Slichter, S. H. (1941), *Union Policies and Industrial Management*. Washington, D.C.: Brookings Institution.

Soskice, D. (1989), 'Reinterpreting corporatism and explaining unemployment' In Brunetta, R. and della Ringa, C. (eds.). *Markets, Institutions, and Cooperation: Labour Relations and Economic Performance*. Macmillan.

Stern, D. (forthcoming). *Institutions and Incentives for Developing Work-Related Knowledge and Skill*, In Adler, P. (ed.): *Technology and the Future of Work*, Oxford University Press.

Streeck, W. (1989), *Skills and the Limits of Neo-Liberalism, Work, Employment, and Society*.

Thurow, L.C. (1975), *Generating Inequality*. New York: Basic Books.

Turner, L. (1990), *The Politics of Work Reorganization*. Unpublished Ph.D. Dissertation, Berkeley: University of California.

Zuboff, S. (1988), *In the Age of the Smart Machine*. New York: Basic Books.

Table 4.1
Assumptions in institutional and neoclassical models

I. Institutional Model

A. Labor market is characterized by underemployment.

B. Allocation of workers within unequal job and training structures is by institutions (i.e. rule and custom).

C. Workers' productivity is a result of command over resources, which includes on-the-job and off-the-job training.

D. Although workers can influence their access to training through their effort, their options are constrained by institutions.

E. Training produces job-related skills as well as networks and the correct behavior and value system.

F. On-the job training increases the value of workers to the firm, and this training is embedded in the work process as well as taught by co-workers.

G. Productivity of workers is primarily dependent upon the technology used, which reflects firm's investment. decisions, and upon demand conditions, which reflect macro-economic conditions.

II Neoclassical Model

A. Labor market functions as a competitive market, which produces full employment

B. Allocation of labor is by price (wages)

C. Workers' productivity is a result of individual human capital decisions, which determine education and on-the-job training.

D. Workers choose their training to maximize their lifetime utility, given their preferences and their ability.

E. Training produces job-related skills. Behavior and value systems, which are exogenous to the skill formation process, are initial conditions for making the training decisions.

F. Training is differentiated by type of skill (specific versus general), which determines who (the firm or worker) pays for the investment and receives the return.

G. Investment decisions will influence location of capital rather than workers' productivity, and macroeconomic policies will not affect long-run unemployment rate.

5 Training policy and economic theory: A policy maker's perspective

Judith Marquand

Introduction

This paper examines the relevance of economics to the development and implementation of training policy, drawing on my own experience as an economist with what was once the Manpower Services Commission but which, through a series of (non-trivial) metamorphoses, became part of the Employment Department.

When I arrived at the MSC some ten years ago, there was virtually no analysis, economic or sociological, of the British training scene. There were virtually no training statistics or training-related data sets. Even management information was scant. Training policy activity was composed, for the most part, of relations with Industrial Training Boards, the management of Skillcentres, and the administration of the TOPS scheme for unemployed adults. The New Training Initiative had just been announced. Development of training offerings for young people and schemes to match them had just started.

The conceptual and language gap between training practitioners and economists attempting to inform training policy decisions appeared almost unbridgeable. Learning to bridge that gap has been - and continues to be - an exciting activity, with implications as least as much for the types of analysis which are chosen as for the policy decisions which are made.

Some definitions

What, then, is special about training? Investment in training is unlike investment in physical capital. It is also unlike most other investment in human beings, such as investment in health care or in providing support services of various kinds for the disadvantaged. It *is* like investment in education, in that both are deliberate interventions to enable the individual to understand and act competently in a wider range of circumstances than before.

Training relates to the individual, and the individual's learning processes. Education and training enhance the capacity of the individual to understand a wide range of situations and to act competently on the basis of that understanding. The boundaries between education and training are dissolving in official policy; the only logical distinction that anyone seems able to draw is that training is concerned with competences relevant to the world of work. But that can include most things, when you come to think about it - flower-arranging for florists, for example, or ancient Egyptian for archaeologists. So the public policy lines are blurring, while the medley of views derived from tradition (such as 'training is apprenticeship', or 'my workers need no training; what would they do with it?') changes rather more slowly.

If training is a deliberate intervention to enhance the acquisition of knowledge and competence, training *policy* in turn may be defined as deliberate intervention to change the quantity, nature, composition, or incidence, of training.

Where, then, does the economic dimension enter into training policy? I take the subject matter of economics to be the production and allocation of goods and services, just as there is to any other set of decision and actions. But, of course, the economic dimension is only one of several, in training policy as in everything else.

Policy problems do not come in disciplines. Thus, there are several steps between acknowledging the importance of the economic dimension in training policy and elucidating the use of economic theory in training policy decision making.

I confess to a certain difficulty at this point. What is meant by 'economic theory?' Is it to be regarded as theory about economic questions, or is it to be restricted to one, or two, or n of the particular well-defined traditions of economic thought? The former view includes the latter as a series of special cases. Thus, I shall take it as my starting point and turn to the well-defined tradition at a later stage.

Policy making and the role of theory

In any society, it is always appropriate to ask who is the policy maker and what is the policy maker's area of competence? Even if we restrict ourselves to governmental policies, there are important questions regarding the delegation of powers. Other bodies act on behalf of government, or by negotiation with government, to deliver the policies which the government wishes to implement. Their decisions are part of the policy process too.

For policy is never made in a vacuum. It is set at a particular point in history, with particular institutions and particular actors. The actors have particular views shaped by particular cultural traditions. There will be a particular allocation of powers of various kinds, including economic resources, as well as legal powers and the more elusive powers of influence. These are the given factors from which any policy making has to start. Apart from time, all of them are socially constructed. No primacy need attach to one aspect rather than another.

In every policy, there are many stakeholders. In the field of training, decisions are made by individuals, by firms, by training providers, by intermediary bodies of various kinds (more of these later), as well as by government. All of these have a direct stake in training policies. All of them have views, and powers and rights. They all need to be considered when policy is developed and implemented.

There is also a range of policy tools. There is legislation and regulation. There are modes of encouraging institutional change without changes in legislation - through persuasion or through negotiation with institutions. Change may sometimes be helped by incentives of various kinds, or induce d by disincentives. Institutional change and cultural change are closely interwoven: lasting institutional change usually brings cultural change, whilst cultural change is the most effective catalyst of changed institutional behaviours and structures. Individuals also may be endowed with changed rights, persuaded, bribed, or deterred.

To *frame* the policy decision adequately, we need to take account of all these factors. For a good policy - good in the sense of *effective* - is a policy which achieves the desired results, which gives rise only to pressures which can be accommodated, and which manages to become embedded in the way that people and institutions behave. The achievement of such a policy is a highly skilled art, requiring negotiation and rhetoric (in the traditional sense of 'argument' or 'persuasive utterance') as well as such instruments as legislation and allocation of economic resources, if the many stakeholders are to respond as the policy makers would like. And the whole exercises needs to be set realistically within the constraints given by the context.

Of course, we often make policy without having addressed all these questions. Policies are often ill designed, quite apart from the risk of being overtaken by unforeseen events. Indeed, we have no choice but to make policy with *selected* knowledge of the context. Complete knowledge is a physical and logical impossibility. The human brain has limited working capacity; we have to *select* the matters we think salient. Moreover, large volumes of knowledge can only be used if they are digested and carefully presented.

It is here then that theory enters. Theory (of all kinds, not just 'economic' theory) is used to structure decision makers' views of the context in which their decisions are made, and the options available to them. It also pervades the rhetoric which they use in negotiating to gain acceptance for their policies. Economic analysis of various kinds is part of that rhetoric. So are various economic theories. The parties to a negotiation do not necessarily share the same theories or the same judgements about the analyses.

There is nothing sinister in any of this; theory is the means by which we reduce our welter of experience to something which we are able to comprehend. Theory develops, and is modified continually, to take account of new experience or to reinterpret old. Moreover, a multiplicity of theories is part of the human condition. It is implicit in the need to select. To take a simple example, the table at which I sit is legitimately regarded as a piece of oak furniture, combustible material, a collection of atoms, *ein Tafel* and *una tavola*, depending on the concepts in the observer's repertoire and the context in which the observer is operating.

What we must ask of our theories, however, is that they be *good* theories. They should be internally consistent, and they should be well rooted in appropriate observation of the phenomena which they purport to explain. As we all now, these in fact are stringent criteria.

Theory, then is used to structure people's views of context and options, and to build arguments which are used to persuade and negotiate. In the context of training policy, the relevant people are the many stakeholders in the training system. Economic theory I interpret broadly at fist, as theories about economic phenomena. Against this background I briefly examine two major areas of policy associated with training: TECs and public expenditure survey decisions.

Economic analysis and training policy: the case of TECs

The ten years since the announcement of the New Training Initiative, in 1981, have seen unprecedented change in almost every aspect of British training policy. Of the many innovations, one of the most important of all is the introduction of TECs (Training and Enterprise Councils). The new standards and qualifications system is potentially just as important. If both innovations succeed, Britain should enter the twenty-first century with a training system well on the way to becoming a national asset. But the success of neither is yet assured; a great deal of painstaking work by a great many people is needed if either is to become successfully embedded.

To consider both innovations is beyond the scope of one article. Thus, I shall confine myself to TECs; what the initiative comprises; how it emerged as the solution to what perceived problems; what it is supposed to achieve; the nature of its theoretical underpinnings and the relevance of economic analysis within them and to the continuing development of the policy towards TECs.

Training and Enterprise Councils were first announced in the White Paper, *Employment for the 1990s* (Employment Department, 1988), in December 1988. There were to be 82 TECs in England and Wales, 'to contract with Government to plan and deliver training and to promote and support the development of small businesses and self-employment in their area' (p. 40). All 82 TECs were in operation by Autumn 1991.

TECs replace the previous Training Agency Area Offices, but they are new organizations with new boards and new powers. They are private sector companies limited by guarantee, but overwhelmingly dependent on public sector funding. Their boards have 10 to 15 members, of whom at least two-thirds must be employers at top management level, drawn from the private sector within the TEC area.

TEC funds comprise some £2.5 billion (in a full financial year, with all TECs up and running). These are drawn from what used to be Training Agency expenditure on programmes for training young people and adults, for supporting self-employment, and for stimulating training and improved management by small and medium-sized firms. TECs are also expected to raise further funding for themselves; the expenditure of such funds is at the TECs' own discretion, subject to the annual agreement of their plans. The assignment of funds to TECs takes place against a detailed contract signed by the TEC with one of the nine Employment Department Regional Offices.

TEC expenditure can be set in the context of total national expenditure on training which, in 1986-87, was estimated at £33 billion (Training Agency, 1989). TECs are thus responsible for less than ten per cent of this, but they are the only substantial source of funding for training the unemployed, and for a wide range of catalytic and developmental activities. The Government has increasingly been involving them in relations with education, as well as the industry; they are seen as co-ordinating bodies for virtually all the vocational education and training activity in their areas.

How and why were TECs seen as appropriate institutions for delivering the Secretary of State's training policies? Two influential reports were commissioned in the mid-1980s. (It might be held that their influence was out of all proportion to their quality. That is germane to my general thesis of the relevance of context to argument). The first report was *Competence and Competition*, published in August 1984 (NEDO, 1984). It argued the inadequacy of Britain's training effort in relation to its main competitors. The second report, *Challenge to Complacency*, set out to demonstrate the need to change employers' attitudes if this was to be remedied, and made suggestions as to how this might be done. An awareness campaign followed and, in 1987, a scheme of national training awards. But the Manpower Services Commission itself regarded such measures as being too blunt for the effective catalysis of change.

Some small experiments took place to foster local training networks. first, Local Collaborative Projects (LCPs) were set up on 1984 and 1985, in conjunction with the Department of Education. Grants were given to enable local consortia of employers and training providers to investigate local training needs of various kinds, and to develop provision to meet them. LCPs were favourably evaluated, but were discounted when resources were tight. Second, the Responsive College Project was designed to demonstrate in a pilot sample of areas how further education collages and local education authorities could better meet the vocational education and training (VET) needs of the labour market, and to disseminate the results. Third, from 1986, the Association of British Chambers of Commerce and the CBI worked together to set up Local Employer Networks intended 'to ensure employer participation in the VET system in a structured way' (UK Network, 1987). Local Employer Networks were given no clear objectives, no clear powers, and little funding. Many of them were poorly organized. They were not a great success. But, meanwhile, the MSC was studying the operation of the German Chambers of Commerce with some care.

In 1988, the then Secretary of State, Norman Fowler, visited PICs (Private Industry Councils) in the United States. He was particularly impressed by the Boston Compact. The time was ripe to pull the strands together. TECs were the result. Broadly, they resemble PICs in their composition and legal status, but they have far grater funding and powers. Some of their functions are more akin to a German Chamber of Commerce than to anything on the other side of the Atlantic.

Thus, TECs were not born of ignorance. Nor were they born of any rigourous analysis, and certainly of no *economic* analysis beyond the Hayes' Tour recorded in *Competence and Competition* (Nedo, 1984). A significant part of their function is economic - influencing the quantity, quality, composition, and distribution of training. Could economic analyses have played a useful role in advising on their formation?

To try to answer this, let us see what it is that TECs are expected to do. It is the characteristic TEC contribution to these functions that lies under the microscope. Retrospective analysis of this contribution should throw light on the theoretical constructs which might have been relevant to analysing it in advance.

The Secretary of State's remit for TECs has developed slightly since the initial White Paper (Employment Department). The changes were made, in large part, through discussion with the TECs themselves. Collation of statements in the White Paper with later statements in the TEC Prospectus (Training Agency, 1989) and the Secretary of State's Strategic Guidance for TECs (Training Agency, 1990) has produced ten objectives, against which the Employment Department has started to evaluate TECs. TECs are expected to:

1. Influence employers' attitudes and increase their commitment (financial and practical) to training.

2.	Change individuals' attitudes to training and enterprise.
3.	Improve access and opportunities for *all* who enter the labour market, including young people and the disadvantaged (e.g. the long-term unemployed).
4.	Tailor provision to meet local needs and ensure that training and education are relevant to the economy.
5.	Improve the quality and cost effectiveness of training, education and enterprise.
6.	Promote and support small businesses, self-employment, and enterprise.
7.	Enhance the community's involvement in local economic development.
8.	Have the expertise to influence others.
9.	Act as a catalyst and agent for change.
10.	Break down barriers between education, training and industry, and co-ordinate initiatives.

The evaluation strategy around TECs' activities in pursuit of these objectives is complex, for training policy itself is complex. All of the studies will contribute to understanding how far, and by what means, TECs are influencing and implementating decisions about quantity, quality, composition and incidence of training.

Many of the questions which the evaluation should answer have economic dimensions. For the activities of a particular TEC (and the collectivity of TECs), as indeed for any decision-making organization, some major economic questions are:

1.	Who decides what? (what is the allocation of powers?).
2.	On what are the decisions based? (what is the availability and use made of information?).
3.	How are the decisions implemented? This leads to: Who gets what? (what are the benefits and how are they distributed?) Who pays what? (what are the costs and their distribution?).
The evaluation should provide some answers to all these questions. Thus it is, at least in part, an economic evaluation, intended to inform decision making by all the stakeholders in the system. Their needs have implications for methodology.

TECs, although they are the delivery mechanism for the Secretary of State's policies and programmes, can exercise considerable discretion. This has a crucial influence on design. For TECs are an intervening variable in a whole wide range of training decisions in their areas. Thus, they need to enter explicitly - and individually - into any strategy for evaluating the policies and programmes themselves. Examination of the TECs' own decisions and actions is relevant, even for such programmes as Youth Training or the Enterprise Allowance Scheme. Indeed, since one of the Department's main policy instruments is the definition of guidelines, flexibilities, and management information systems to be incorporated in the TEC contracts, an understanding of TEC behaviours is essential. (An example is a recent qualitative study of the operation of output-related funding in a sample of TECs).

Moreover, because the whole territory of England and Wales is covered by TECs, there is no counterfactual today for the TEC initiative as a whole. Instead, comparison can be made between different TECs, with different contexts, different organizational characteristics, and different priorities. Such comparison is at least as important for TECs themselves as it is for the Secretary of State. The whole TEC initiative can appropriately be viewed as a giant development programme, where the detection, dissection and dissemination of good practice are essential to the success of individual TECs and the initiative as a whole. Thus, the structure for TEC evaluation work is very different to that for the programmes which preceded them. The balance has shifted from the uniform to the particular.

A crucial part of the work has to be the continuing development of broad framework studies such as the Youth Cohort Study, a portfolio of studies on individual's training behaviour, the Employers' Manpower and Skills Practices Survey and its companion Skills Monitoring Survey, and the proposed new Qualifications Survey. These allow the Employment Department to judge how each TEC lies in relation to the average, in terms of its client groups as well as in terms of some of its outputs.

Within this framework, for each TEC, the Employment Department has some regular management information. It has their labour market assessments, their plans, and their annual reports. It will have some of the results of their self-evaluations. It is investigating the feasibility of a Local Economy Index, to characterize and monitor relevant dimensions of their contexts more systematically than their labour market assessments require. It has reports from training standards inspectors and careers service inspectors, and knowledge of the individual TECs in regional offices and from the system of regional evaluation advisers.

Beyond this, for particular questions, the Employment Department is developing case studies in collaboration with samples of TECs. The most developed example, so far, comes from the evaluation of pilot Training Credit schemes for young people. Here, the Youth Cohort Study allows before and after comparisons, and comparisons between training credit TECs and others. Within this frame, case studies in all the pilot TECs allows understanding - useful for TECs and the Department alike - of what modes of training credit work well, and in what contexts.

Note that methodologies, like problems, need not come in disciplines. The full range of social science methodologies is available for tackling policy problems. Methodologies are selected according to the context (including timing) and the role of the study. To give a trivial but true example, you cannot place much reliance on a postal survey of illiteracy.

Within the research spectrum - running from experiment at its most structured end, through structured survey, semi-structured and unstructured surveys to naturalistic observation - the main differences lie in the way in which the observer enters as a research instrument. At the most structured end, the researcher enters late, but needs substantial confidence in constructs already developed if the research is to demonstrate anything at all. Ungrounded theories (Glaser and Straus, 1967) and unvalidated indicators make nonsense of structured research. At the less structured end, the observer enters earlier and theories can be developed to be well grounded, but are harder to generalize.

The need to capture the flavour of the particular, in much TEC evaluation, pushes the chosen methodologies towards the unstructured end of the spectrum. There is still a place for the structured survey, but it needs to be rooted in careful preparatory work to be sure that its implicit behavioural assumptions apply. *A fortiori*, manipulations of structured survey data stand or fall by the relevance of those data as well as by their own validity.

I started by asking whether economic theory was to be regarded as theory about economic questions. If it is regarded as such, *grounded* economic theory clearly has a major role in the evaluation and subsequent policy recommendations concerning TECs, and the other aspects of training policy. But that is too broad a definition of economic theory to satisfy everybody.

A further possibility is that economics is defined by its methodologies in tackling economic questions. This account of 'the discipline' has some plausibility. Much economic work lies right at the structured end of the spectrum of methodologies. Economists are great consumers of other people's data. Data collected for administrative purposes, sociologists' and psychologist's grounded concepts embodied in statisticians' survey data, or data designed as well as collected by statisticians - all can be grist to the economists' mill. This implies either a remarkable degree of confidence by the economist in the relevance of the theoretical constructs, or a considerable degree of foolhardiness. Such a degree of confidence would often by misplaced in cases where TECs are intervening variables. (But there is a growing body of well-documented data sets, relating to other aspects of training policy, where the types of analysis which economists like to do have at last become relevant).

I also asked what advice could have been given beforehand in deciding to set up TECs, if advice had been sought. Lessons from organizational studies, particularly studies relating to decentralized decision making, would have been highly relevant. So would sociological work on the operation of networks. So might work from political studies on the behaviour of elites. I find it hard to see much that the more traditional economics literature would have contributed, largely because such economics has tended to neglect empirical studies of what goes on inside the black box of the individual's mind, and the translucent box of the organization's decision-making structures. Economics is now starting to develop theories in these broad areas (Aoki et al, 1990) but they are still far from operational. Yet these areas are the stuff of policy advice when decisions are made to change the nature of institutions.

My discussion has been conducted in terms of TECs. With a few small changes, it would also apply to policy on standards and qualifications, and to any other area of training policy where policies and programmes are delivered through intermediaries and where the intermediaries' own decisions and actions are able to affect the outcomes. Economic questions are important, but the methodologies characteristic of economics have only a minor role in answering them and economic analysis, so far, has few behaviourally-relevant insights to offer.

TECs are an area of training policy decision making which is far removed from the traditional stamping-grounds of economists.

Public expenditure decisions about training policy

The Public Expenditure Survey is the means by which the Treasury controls expenditure by departments. The present system has its origins in the Plowden Report of 1961. There had been concern that the Treasury had no coherent view of how departments were spending their money; there was almost no forward planning. Over the three decades since then, the system has expanded and matured.

Each spring, the Treasury tells departments what their baseline expenditure for each of the next three years should be. The figure is simply a rolling forward of the previous year's baseline, with an inflation allowance. Sometimes adjustments agreed during the course of the year are incorporated, but this does not necessarily happen. The baselines are set out in great detail, line by line, in the departmental accounts. Training policy expenditure is in no way exceptional in its treatment.

During the summer, departments prepared arguments to support increases in their expenditure and changes in its composition. In early autumn, the Treasury holds a bilateral discussion with each department. Finally, usually in November, the Cabinet approves the outcomes of the Chief Secretary to the Treasury's discussions with departmental ministers (Pliatzky, 1989, ch. 5).

It is indubitable that the Treasury needs to control the total of public expenditure and its allocation between departments. It is indubitable that it needs heuristics to guide its proposals. It is inevitable that departments will put forward counterproposals, supported by arguments which they think the Treasury will find convincing and which their ministers, each defending their corner with their own and their department's arguments. The questions which interest us here are the role and nature of the arguments.

Some of the more technical aspects of the negotiating process apply, whosoever the players. For example, the Treasury is always faced with choices between expenditures where the outcomes are incommensurable. Thus the discussion has to be conducted in money terms (whether real or financial). Problems inevitably arise in valuing outcomes. The negotiations are complex; there is pressure to use simple indicators of 'performance' or 'value for money'. Such simple indicators fail to do justice to the complex phenomena they are intended to indicate. Moreover, in a negotiating situation, any figure is usually better than none. Theres is also inevitable pressure to use low-quality indicators where high-quality ones are not available.

If the effects of these inevitable pressures were random, we would not need to worry much about them. But they are not. The outputs or benefits which it is particularly difficult to indicate, tend to be of certain kinds. Improvements in quality and the valuation of new goods - innovations - have always caused measurement problems. Benefits which are widely diffused are hard to measure. Benefits which may be confounded with the effects of other variables will be downplayed. Benefits which take time to arise will be underestimated. Benefits which produce cash savings to the Exchequer will be preferred to ones which do not. Moreover, these figures are used in negotiations where there is no shortage of candidates for the use of public money.

So the unintended by-products from these technical difficulties will tend to be a preference for cure rather than prevention, for well-tried paths rather than innovation, for short-term gains rather than long-term strategies. In short, the technical problems alone provide a recipe for conservatism masquerading as prudence. And yet, no one should doubt that the public expenditure exercise needs figures to support the judgements made.

Now consider the arguments which are used. The crucial point is that the Public Expenditure Survey is the means by which the Cabinet relates its use of public money to its *political* priorities. The economic arguments are mustered in support of a *political* case. Thus, there are inevitably translation problems. It is only if the reductions inherent in the economic language used happen to coincide with the political priorities that the technical problems inherent in the negotiating figures cease to be important.

Training policy is no exception to this. Decisions about training policy expenditure are not the same as decisions about training policy. The expenditure decisions constrain the training policies which can be implemented, but *their* policy basis is different. It concerns the allocation of *economic* resources only, but to serve much broader policy needs.

Economic theory can be viewed as a subset of political theory. In the broadest of terms, neoclassical economics, in particular, depends heavily on utilitarian assumptions; Marxian economics relates to the broad Marxian tradition; institutional economics to forms of communitarianism; socio-economics to the current concern of politician-theorists in marrying strands from the liberal tradition with the communitarian approach. Unless we are simple nineteenth century utilitarians, propositions derived from neoclassical economics are going to need considerable massaging if they are to fit our more complex views of the world. Yet, in essence, our public expenditure measurement systems derive from the neoclassical tradition. Attempts at weighing costs and benefits certainly spring from there. We are back with our technical measurement problems again, but now they need to be viewed as something far more important - as the indicators of a mismatch between utilitarianism and other views of the world.

Public expenditure negotiations are political in every sense. They take place between powerful political figures with different immediate interests, but with common longer-term interests, and sharing, to a major degree, a common culture. The economic arguments which will find favour are these which are expressed in terms of that common culture.

In the 1980s, 'a belief in the market economy and competition and in rolling back the frontiers of the state provide(d) the dominant ideas in the government's economic philosophy' (Pliatzky, 1989, p.48]. Thus, it is not surprising that arguments for public expenditure carried more conviction if they were couched in the neoclassical language of market failure.

The Employment Department has tried to do this for training policy. For each of the detailed objectives of the TEC initiative, there is a translation into 'market failure' rationales. This is a useful discipline. 'Market failure' is, in fact, a broad church. If you try to use an argument which cannot be brought within it, there is probably something wrong with the argument. It is useful, given the negotiating context, to be able to put the different measures into their appropriate market failure pigeon-holes and, later, to try to translate the evaluation results the same way.

But there are technical problems in relying heavily on 'market failure' concepts, once it is recognized that policy is broader than its economic dimension. There is an enormous process of reduction implicit in forcing policies into a 'market failure' mode. The fact that in logic, there are few policies which need to be excluded *ex ante* should alert us to the risk that we may be achieving generality by thinning the concepts to the point where their content is negligible. For the concepts are impossible to operationalize directly. We cannot evaluate training policies in terms of the degree of perfection of markets; we have to evaluate them in terms of more concrete objectives - many of which are not plausibly reducible to economic terms alone. The broader political agenda enters legitimately again.

What, then is the role of economic theory in public expenditure decision making? Developing the measures needed for public expenditure decisions provides a wide scope for economists. Developing ways of handling the biases implicit in easy measures can provide a useful professional challenge. These biases are crucially important - they are the points where the living, changing, challenging world breaks in to the thin, reduced systems - which inevitably have to be used, if the complexity of decisions is to be presented in a manner sufficiently simple to be grasped. They are the only points where policy priorities which do not fit comfortably with the measurement system have a chance to show through. But let no economists deceive themselves that improved technical measures can necessarily be derived which will carry conviction within the Treasury's conceptual framework.

Uncritical acceptance by economists of the reduction inherent in any simple economic theory is a betrayal of their professional status. For the task of economists as advisers is to help administrative policy makers and politicians to confront the consequences of their own assumptions. It is good economics, using theories well grounded in behaviour, which is needed. We all need to be aware of the consequences of the political assumptions built into our measuring rods. We all need to be aware of the limits which are inherent in the application of any simple system.

Simplification is an inevitable part of the human condition, but any simplified system uncritically applied is an ideology. In Havel's words, 'Ideology.... pretends that the requirements of the system derive from the requirements of life. It is a world of appearances trying to pass for reality' (Havel, 1986, 11, p.44).

Conclusions

So we return to the role of economic theory in policy. There is no doubt of the importance of the economic dimension in decisions about training policy. Like almost all policy areas, training policy is concerned with production and distribution - the quantities and qualities of training produced, who provides them, who receives them, who pays for them. Like almost all policy areas, a wide range of methodologies drawn from social science is relevant to setting policy questions in an appropriate form, to planning their implementation, and to analysing their operation and impact. Some of the methodologies are commonly used by economist.

But note that many of the instruments of policy are not directly concerned with quantities. Legislation, regulation, and negotiation about institutions and processes are at least as important. Persuasion plays a role too. And it must be recognized that the neoclassical brand of economic theory has little to say about organizational and institutional behaviour, and less with behavioural roots.

Analysis is only one small part of policy making. Policy makers make decisions. They will have no choice but to use implicit models and hunches if they do not have evidence. For policy makers are busy people and have to juggle all the dimensions of a problem. Like all of us, they tend to develop heuristics from within their own cultural tradition and use them to cut their way through the jungle.

The problem for the analyst therefore is when and how to inject messages, in such a form that they can get through. It is particularly difficult to change basic assumptions of any kind. And the basic assumptions themselves constrain heavily what messages can be received. These comments hold for all kinds of policy making.

In modern democracies, the characteristic mode of most policy making is negotiation. Training policy is no exception. In negotiation, the parties use arguments and they need to find a language which they all can share. Every administration has its simplified model. Civil servants need to learn to use it. But external parties do not necessarily see the world in this way. In negotiation, the model becomes elaborated. Bargains are struck. Justifications are developed. Economic theory has a role here, but economics in only one of several dimensions.

As social scientists, we need to use the most appropriate methodologies to develop well-rooted views of how the world (of training policy interest) works. As policy-linked social scientists, we need to convince our policy colleagues that our view *is* well rooted, that it matches their concerns, and that it yields practical lessons for their decisions and actions. If we want our decisions to be robust, this is done by building relations of trust and working in close consultation. Training policy tries to fit this model.

But this does not really apply to negotiations with the Treasury. Strictly speaking such negotiations are not about training policy. They are about obtaining the resources to carry through training policy. The arguments at root are political, but they are cast in a formal mode within a well-structured procedural ritual. They need to pass the test of the Treasury's concepts. Arguments which cannot carry this form of conviction tend to fail. All models are simplifications, and all models have technical biases. But particular models become deeply embedded.

For 'practical men, who believe themselves to be quite exempt from any intellectual influences, are usually the slaves of some defunct economist' (Keynes, ch. 24).

References

Aoki, M., Gustafsson, B. and Williamson, O. E. (Eds), (1990), *The Firm as a Nexus of Treaties,* Sage, Beverly Hills, CA.

Coopers & Lybrand Associates for MSC and NEDO, (1985), *Challenge to Complacency*, NEDO, London.

Employment Department, (1988), *Employment of the 1990s*, Cmnd 540, HMSO, London.

Glaser, B. G. and Strauss, A. L. (1967), *The Discovery of Grounded Theory*, De Gruyter, Aldine, NY.

Havel, V. (1986), *Living in Truth,* Faber & Faber, London.

IMS and NEDO and MSC, (1984), *Competence and Competition: Training and Education in the Federal Republic of Germany, the United States and Japan,* National Economic Development Office, London.

Keynes, J. M. (1936), *The General Theory of Employment, Interest and Money,* Macmillan, London.

Pliatzky, L. (1989), *The Treasury under Mrs Thatcher,* Blackwell, Oxford.

Training Agency. (1989a), *Training in Britain*, HMSO, London.

Training Agency. *1990s: The Skills Decade,* Employment Department Group, 1990.

Training Agency. (1989b), *TEC Prospectus*, Employment Department Group.

UK Network Head Office. (1987), *Local Employer Networks: the Foundation for the Future,* Sheffield.

6 A review of data available for research on training issues in the UK

Peter Elias

Introduction

This paper reviews the major sources of information which are currently available, or will soon become available, to inform research on the extent and consequences of vocational education and training in the UK. The paper divides into two main sections based upon the availability of data which address these areas of research. A division is made between those data sources which have collected training information from the perspective of the individual and those which relate to data provided by employers or their representatives.

The focus of this review paper is not so much on the *quantity* of data on training, other sources already provide useful summaries of the nature, coverage and availability of different sources[1], but on the *quality* of information, a subjective evaluation of the potential of the data under consideration to inform research in the above mentioned areas. The sources are restricted to those which have national coverage, thereby excluding specific local area surveys.

The individual's perspective

Sources of information on training from the perspective of the individual fall into two categories; those which provide a longitudinal view, placing training events within the work and educational history of the individual, and those which are essentially cross-sectional, relating to the most recent training event in the work history of the individual or derived from a sample of (ex)trainees.

Longitudinal sources of information on training can be further classified into those which derive from a *cross-sectional panel of respondents*, a group of individuals, selected to be representative of the working population, who are subjected to repeated re-interview at regular periods, those which derive from a *birth-cohort panel of respondents*, a group of individuals who are selected for panel inclusion on the basis of their birth dates and again re-interviewed at regular periods and those which are obtained by *retrospective enquiry of a cross-section of respondents*. Each type of source has its advantages and disadvantages in terms of the quality and quantity of information obtained and the extent to which such data can be used to explore causal processes in the relationships between training, employment, career mobility and income.

Information from cross-sectional panels

Information from cross-sectional panels of respondents was, until fairly recently, virtually non-existent in the UK. This situation has changed dramatically in the last few years with the development of the New Earnings Survey Cohort, the establishment of the British Household Panel Study and the decision to add 1991 Census of Population information to the Census Longitudinal Study.

New earnings survey cohort study
The New Earnings Survey (NES) is an annual enquiry of the earnings and hours of, in general, a 1 per cent sample of persons within the 'Pay-as-You-Earn' (PAYE) system for the collection of income tax from employees. Within the sampling frame, the sample is drawn on the basis of the last two digits of an individual's National Insurance (NI) number. The qualification 'in general' is added because some larger organisations return information on all employees with the relevant NI number regardless of whether or not those individuals are earning above the PAYE thresholds. For statistical reasons, information is required from employers for the *same* 1 per cent of persons each year. New additions to the cohort consist of those people with the requisite NI number who become employees and, in general, earn over the PAYE threshold. The linked data set, containing pay, hours and employment details for approximately 450,000 individuals for the period 1975-92, has recently been made available to researchers outside the Department of

Employment under access arrangements which guarantee that the confidentiality of these data are maintained.

Training information contained within the NES cohort is limited. In 1984 a special question was asked of employers, concerning whether or not the stated employee was currently receiving training in one of four categories: 'YTS apprentice', 'non-YTS apprentice', 'YTS other formal vocational training' and 'non-YTS other formal vocational training'. Although limited, this information will be an important source for the proposed initiative for three reasons. First, the size of the sample is such that the potential exists for detailed analysis of the 1984 training provision for specific occupation/industry/age/sex groups. Second, the data are such that previous and subsequent job tenure and labour mobility can be investigated. Finally, the cohort data set facilitates a long-term investigation of the link between training and earnings.

British Household Panel Study
The British Household Panel Study (BHPS) is an annual survey of each adult member of a national representative panel of about 5,000 households, initially yielding information from about 10,000 individuals. These same individuals will be reinterviewed in annual successive waves over the 10 year funding horizon for the study, including as new respondents the household members of any new households formed by wave 1 respondents. The questionnaire will contain a 'core' section repeated each year plus supplementary topics which may vary with each interview. The first wave was conducted in the Autumn of 1991. Data from the first wave are now available from the ESRC Data Archive.

In wave 1 the following issues were covered:
(i)   participation in education/training provided by an employer;
(ii)   the nature of training provided under (i) (eg induction, skill
        improvement, skill updating, general skill development);
(iii)   number of days of training provided by current employer in year
        preceding interview.

In addition, three similar questions were asked about education or training other than that provided by an employer.

The BHPS will not provide much information on training in the short run. Due to resource limitations, questions on attitudes towards training, perceptions of training outcomes and motivation for training have not been included as 'core' questions. By the mid 1990s, this situation will

145

have improved somewhat through the replication of these core questions, the availability of related material on the employment and income of respondents and the possibility of a 'training history' in wave 3.

Census Longitudinal Study

The Census Longitudinal Study (LS) is similar in size to the New Earnings Survey cohort panel. It is derived by linking the 1971, 1981 and 1991 Census of Population records of all persons born on one of four key dates spread throughout the year. Because it links the records of *all* persons born on these dates it provides a cross-section of the population rather than a specific age cohort. Additional information matched into the LS includes vital registration statistics, certain medical statistics and geographical mobility as recorded by the National Health Service Central Register.

Despite its size and potential to record long term transitions through the labour market, the LS is not particularly useful as a source of information which can be used to address training issues. The relationships between high-level vocational qualifications and occupational mobility can be investigated, as can some limited analysis of the occupational histories of persons who have been classified as 'apprentices', but the general decline in the apprenticeship system has reduced the relevance of this method of training provision as an important dimension of the training process. The 1991 linked data will not be available until late in 1993. For further details, contact the Social Statistics Research Unit at City University.

Information from birth Cohort Panels

There are three major national sources of information on training which derive from birth cohort panels of respondents. Two such sources are multi-purpose studies which relate to groups of persons all born in a specific period, the third defines its cohorts in terms of the school-leaving age, yielding repeated observation on single year cohorts, with the study itself being repeated annually.

National Child Development Study

The National Child Development Study (NCDS) has followed the progress of all persons born in Great Britain in one week in 1958, augmented in later sweeps with immigrants born outside Great Britain in the same week. Apart from the initial perinatal study, four sweeps of the birth cohort have since been conducted, in 1965 (NCDS1), 1969 (NCDS2), 1974 (NCDS3) and 1981/2 (NCDS4). A further sweep was conducted in 1991 (NCDS5), providing detailed information on the birth cohort at age 33 years.

The study combines the technique of retrospective enquiry with detailed questioning about an individual's current status. By these means, a full account of each individual's work history is obtained. Training and educational information is 'overlaid' on the work history via questions which relate to the most recent, second most recent and third most recent training event. Training events are defined as 'work-related training courses lasting at least three days in total'. Details are obtained about the name of the course, location, whether or not it led to qualifications, nature of qualifications so obtained, reasons for starting the course, the course provider, financial provision, whether or not a course of training was completed, use of skills gained from training, satisfaction with training and an appraisal of whether or not the training assisted a subsequent job change. Apart from such training information, details are also collected of all educational courses and qualifications obtained since leaving school.

NCDS is one of the most detailed and useful sources of information on education and training in Great Britain. Its importance derives not only from the detail which will be available in the seventeen year work/training/educational histories and the information on earnings at ages 23 and 33 years but also from the vast amount of information on the educational, social and psychological development of respondents in their early years. Its main disadvantage is the narrow definition of its population. In terms of recent changes in access to, and provision of, job-related training, it could be argued that 33 year olds in 1991 'missed out' on much of these current developments. Countering these arguments, it is possible that the focus of research on youth training over the last decade has ignored the impact of training provided to 20-30 years olds. Information from the Labour Force Surveys for the period 1984-90 (see next section) indicates that twice as many 25-35 year olds in 1990 experienced training over a four week reference period than was the situation six years earlier and that, on average 25-34 years are exposed to training to about the same extent as 16-24 year olds. It seems likely, therefore that data from the fourth and fifth sweeps of NCDS in particular, and from the study in general, will play important role in assessing the factors underlying the training of young adults in Great Britain.

NCDS5 data and relevant information from earlier sweeps are held at the ESRC Data Archive.

British Cohort Study '70

The Child Health and Education Study (CHES), now renamed the British Cohort Study '70 (BCS'70), is similar to NCDS in that it has recorded the progress of a (smaller) cohort of children born in 1970. Last interviewed in 1986, recontact has been made with study members in a pilot survey in 1991, preparing for a full sweep of the cohort in 1993. Information collected replicates with some of the questions asked of NCDS respondents at their age of 23 years in 1981 (NCDS4), providing for a comparison across the cohorts with detailed control for social and educational background factors in each cohort. The fact that such a comparison with NCDS will be possible lends weight to the importance of NCDS as a source of information for the investigation of training related issues.

Further information about BCS 70 can be obtained from the Social Statistics Research Unit at City University.

Youth Cohort Study

The Youth Cohort Study is a programme of research based upon a series of surveys of cohorts of young people defined in terms of their school-leaving age. Five cohorts have been studied since the programme commenced in 1983 and a sixth may be undertaken in 1992. A feasibility study has been conducted to test the possibility of recontacting cohorts as they reach the age of 22/23 years. On the basis of this feasibility study it has been concluded that a further sweep at this age should be undertaken.

Figure 6.1 below describes the timing of the surveys and the definition of each cohort in terms of the year in which cohort members attained the minimum school leaving age:

Figure 6.1:   Cohorts and cohort sweeps in the Youth Cohort Study

	Attaining min. school leaving age in	Surveys conducted, planned or envisaged										
		'85	'86	'87	'88	'89	'90	'91	'92	'93	'94	'95
Cohort I	1983-4	1	2	3								
Cohort II	1984-5		1	2	3							
Cohort III	1985-6			1	2	3				4		
Cohort IV	1987-8					1	2	3				
Cohort V	1988-9							1	2	3		
Cohort VI	1989-90								1	2	3	

Note

Table entries refer to sweep number of indicated cohort
Plans for all sweeps beyond 1992 are tentative.

Each 'sweep' of a cohort collects information by postal questionnaire from a sample of the relevant age group of young people, regardless of whether or not respondents have completed their full-time education.

Apart from Cohort I, the first sweep provides information on approximately 14,000 young people (response rates average about 70 per cent from a target population of 20,000 young people). About 10-15 per cent of the sample is lost through attrition at each subsequent sweep.

Through its eight-year history, the YCS postal questionnaire has not changed radically. A key feature of the study is the month-by-month diary in which a respondent indicates his/her main economic/education status in each month of the year preceding the survey date. The study collects information on school qualifications, sources of career advice, details of unemployment, government-provided training (YTS), training provided in current employment (type, location, duration), continuing education (courses, qualifications) and future plans.

YCS is an important source of information on the provision of training for young people and the position of such training within their work histories. Together with the longitudinal information generated within each cohort on earnings growth, job tenure and occupational mobility, this source will prove invaluable for research on the evolution of youth training (both employer and government provided). Additionally, the ability to compare analyses across different cohorts, thereby monitoring change within a dynamic framework, will undoubtedly shed new light on the impact of demographic change, the integration of GCE 'O' level with CSE qualifications, changes in the social security regulations affecting 16/17 year olds and the impact of a general upward trend in the educational background of parents. Where YCS is at its weakest is in its ability to monitor changes in attitudes and motivation underlying decisions by young people to seek and obtain job-related training.

YCS data for the three sweeps of Cohorts I to IV are available via the ESRC Data Archive.

Information from cross-sectional retrospective enquiries

This section examines the availability of data which can inform research on training issues within the UK and which contains retrospective training information. At the level of the individual, such data are collected by work history techniques, asking respondents to recall the sequence and (possibly) the duration of particular training events in their work histories.

The National Training Survey

The National Training Survey (NTS) was conducted in 1975/6. Planning for this survey took place immediately after the Manpower Services Commission was established in 1974. The survey was intended as a 'benchmark' study, providing information on the availability of skills and trained labour in the British labour force, and the extent of training activities (see Claydon, 1980).

The NTS has never been fully exploited, nor did it serve its original purpose as a benchmark study. The size of the study (54,000 16-60 year olds) and its scope (full occupational history and complete training history for each individual) rapidly exhausted the budgets for this project. The sheer complexity of the data proved to be a major obstacle in its analysis, given the lack of good database management software in the late 1970s. Not all of the available information was placed in machine-readable format. In particular, occupational histories only cover the period 1965-75.

As a detailed historical record of training in Britain in the late 1960s and early 1970s, the NTS is unsurpassed. Given the improvements in database management software, there may well be a case for resurrecting this survey to obtain comparison groups for the study of changes in the nature and delivery of training.

The NTS is available from the ESRC Data Archive.

Women and Employment Survey

The Women and Employment Survey (WES) was a national study of women aged 16-59, conducted in 1980. Over 5,000 women provided details of their life and work histories, educational qualifications, current employment, work aspirations and details of their domestic lives. Included in the questionnaire was a set of questions relating to the incidence and duration of formal and informal training in their current (1980) job, reasons for not receiving training, opportunities for further training and the potential demand for further training. Additionally, information on participation in training courses and plans to participate in such courses was also included.

A major weakness with these data is the lack of comparable information for men. A small sample of the husbands of respondents was interviewed, but no questions on training were asked of this group. For this reason, it is not possible to pursue the issue of whether men and women perceive and evaluate the benefits from training along different dimensions.

WES data are available at the ESRC Data Archive.

Adult Off-the-Job Skills Training Survey

Most of the data arising from the evaluation of publicly-provided vocational training schemes has been excluded from this review, because of the selective nature of the information so obtained. An exception is the 1986-9 study of adult off-the-job skills training (Payne, 1990), which compared the post-training experience of a group of programme participants with that of a matched sample of non-participants, matched in terms of age, location, gender, and economic activity status at, and prior to, the time that participants commenced their training. For participants, 785 persons were interviewed in the Autumn of 1987, about one year after completion of adult off-the-job training in 1986. Approximately two thirds of this sample were recontacted by postal questionnaire in the Spring of 1989. For the matched sample of non-participants, interviews were conducted in the Summer and Autumn of 1988 with a group of persons identified via an omnibus survey conducted approximately one year earlier. Data collected include administrative information from the application forms of participants, detailed work histories for participants and non-participants covering the ten years prior to the interview, earnings, general attitudes towards work and training, satisfaction with training, use of skills learnt, participation in further training and information on the personal characteristics of respondents.

Data from this study are available through the ESRC Data Archive.

Working Lives Survey
The Department of Employment is currently investigating the feasibility of conducting a survey which will be similar in nature to the Women and Employment Survey, but which will document the working lives of both women and men. It is highly likely that considerable emphasis will be placed upon the collection of information on training aspirations, access and uptake.

If these plans come to fruition, data from such a survey will not be available before 1994 at the earliest.

Employment in Britain
This survey, carried out in the Spring and Summer of 1992, examines the motivation and commitment of individuals to work and to their employers and will provide information for a study of variations in work attitudes between individuals. The survey is based upon a national random sample of approximately 6,000 persons aged 20-60. Integral to the design is the collection of information on the work and training history of the individual. A particular focus of the study is an examination of the relationships between work commitment, training (formal and informal), personal development, opportunities for job enlargement or enrichment, technical change and skill transferability. Data from the survey, which is partially financially supported by the ESRC is available via the ESRC Data Archive.

Information from cross-sectional surveys

This section focuses specifically on those sources which are essentially cross-section in nature and which contain little by way of any historical information on the experience of training for the individual.

Labour Force Survey

The Labour Force Survey (LFS) is a household-based survey which, from 1973 to 1983, provided information from 60-80 thousand households biennially. The survey has been conducted annually since 1984, incorporating a five-quarter longitudinal element in its structure. From 1992 the survey became fully continuous and the sample size was boosted to facilitate the production of quarterly reports.

Training information contained within the LFS is broken down into vocational qualifications obtained (or being sought) and training received in the four weeks prior to the survey. Details are obtained on the time spent on such training activities in the week preceding the survey, the location of training, the nature of financial provision, the duration of training and the occupational group for which training was received. Prior to 1993, a major weakness of these data derived from the lack of information on earnings. This has been addressed via a question on household earnings.

Because of its size and the fact that it is conducted on a regular basis, LFS training data provide scope for detailed analyses of the incidence and duration of training, examining for differences by industry sector, occupation, job tenure, external mobility and for regional effects.

LFS data from 1979 to 1991 and the first five quarterly surveys (1992-3) are available via the ESRC Data Archive.

General Household Survey

The General Household Survey is a multi-purpose continuous survey which has been running since 1971. It is based each year on a sample of the general population resident in private households in Great Britain. The survey covers nearly 20,000 persons, resident in 10,000 households.

The 1987 and 1988 GHS provided training information which, particularly for 1987, complements the information available from the Labour Force Survey. A major disadvantage of the LFS is the lack of any information on earnings and on the motivations underlying training. The GHS provides such details, albeit for a sample which is only one sixth of the size of the LFS.

Information on training in the 1988 GHS covers the following: incidence of on-the-job training in 4 weeks prior to survey; incidence of training other than 'on-the-job' training in 4 weeks prior to survey; nature of training received; time spent in training activities.

In the 1987 GHS, details were also collected about the financial arrangements made for training, and the reasons for engaging in training. GHS data are available through the ESRC Data Archive.

British Social Attitudes Survey
Since 1983, Social and Community Planning Research has organised and conducted an annual survey of a cross-section of the population aged 18 years and over. In the first three years, the survey covered 1,700 - 1,800 respondents. From 1986 the sample size was increased to over 2,800 respondents.

The 1987 and 1991 surveys contained a significant amount of information on training, including: occupation, industry, size of workplace; perceived degree of control over nature of respondent's work; performance related pay; incidence of training in last 2 years; number of days spent in job-related training; introduction of new technologies at workplace; extent to which respondent uses new technology; union coverage; income from employment.

The importance of the BSA stems not only from these data, but from the wealth of attitudinal information which can be related to the uptake of training.

BSA data from 1983 to 1989 are available through the ESRC Data Archive.

PSI Survey of Individuals' Training Activities
The PSI Survey of Individuals' Training Activities, conducted by the Policy Studies Institute (PSI) in 1987 as part of the Training Funding Study, covered more than 2,500 adults aged 19 to 59 years. The report on survey findings (Rigg, 1989), lists the variety of topics addressed in the study; how individuals fund their training, evidence of unmet demand, long term expectations of training outcomes and perceived obstacles to participation in training.

The survey contains much interesting information on the opportunities for training and promotion in the respondent's current employment, attitudes to education and training, qualifications, job tenure, experience of training in three years preceding the survey, satisfaction with training, financial aspects of training (costs, methods of financing training, subjective evaluation of effect of financing training, subjective evaluation of effect of training on living standards whilst undertaking training), evaluation of post-training benefits (job prospects, promotion, long term earning ability).

The sample selection rules governing the choice of respondents to the survey were exceedingly complex and, to a large degree, weaken the extent to which the information contained in the survey can assist in an investigation of the relationship between motivational factors and training.

Notwithstanding the above comment, the information contained in this survey is most important, particularly in terms of the extent to which it provides details of the methods through which individuals financed their training and their subjective evaluations of the effect of training. For detailed analytical research, enquiring into the relationship between motivation, training uptake and training outcomes, the survey must be interpreted with caution.

The PSI Survey of Individuals' Training Activities is available through the ESRC Data Archive (*Training in Britain - Individual Perspectives*).

The Employer's perspective

Information provided by employers on training, uptake, structure, budgets and plans is limited, on a national basis, to a few studies. In part, this stems from the methodological problems associated with employer surveys (inadequate sampling frames, problems stemming from the choice of an appropriate respondent, the choice of organisational level at which to collect data, poor response rates, etc). Apart from these problems, there has been a deliberate attempt throughout the 1980s to reduce the burden of 'form-filling' on employers. This has restricted the number and scope of official employer-based surveys.

Longitudinal sources of information

Workplace Industrial/Employee Relations Surveys.
The Workplace Employee Relations Survey (WERS) covers about 2,000 employing establishments in all sectors of the economy. The latest survey in this series was the third survey, conducted in 1990. A longitudinal element was included in the design of the second survey, the Workplace Industrial Relations Survey (WIRS2), conducted in 1984, in

that a significant number of establishments contacted were also respondents to the first Workplace Industrial Relations Survey (WIRS1) conducted in 1980.

Training data collected in this series of surveys are fairly limited. In the 1980 survey (WIRS1), the only relevant question related to the management responsibility for training policy. In 1984 (WIRS2), broad questions were asked about the extent of training associated with internal mobility. The WIRS/WERS series of surveys do not contain a significant amount of information on training, but they do provide much contextual material for the follow-up to the third survey, known as the Employers' Manpower and Skill Practices Survey (EMSPS). Data from WIRS1 and WIRS2 are available through the ESRC Data Archive. WERS3 data are available via the ESRC Data Archive.

Employers' Manpower and Skill Practices Survey.

Conducted in 1990/91, this survey was designed as a follow-up to the Third Workplace Employee Relations Survey. About 94 per cent of WERS respondents make up the EMSPS sample. The interview was conducted, where possible, with the key respondent who provided information for the WERS interview, the 'Main Management Respondent' (usually the most senior personnel officer in the establishment). Information collected in the EMSPS interview includes details of the structure of the workforce by Standard Occupational Classification (SOC) major groups, processes of change within the organisation, turnover, recruitment, training, a detailed study of two occupational groups within the organisation and information about the external environment in which the organisation operates.

In terms of interview time devoted to particular subjects, questions on training collected in EMSPS account for about one quarter of all the information obtained from respondents. Subjects covered include induction training, initial instruction, reasons why training may not be provided, apprentice training, training which is not induction or initial training, type of training, external utilisation of training services, training for multi-skilling, trends in training provision over the last three years, reasons for such trends, training evaluation and assessment and a series of general questions about the reasons for training, training budgets and links with the organisation's objectives.

WERS3/EMSPS data will soon be available from the ESRC Data Archive.

Cross-sectional sources of information

Cross-sectional sources of information on training, provided by employers or their representatives, are not uncommon. However, as stated earlier, the ability to compare between sources or to generalise from a particular source is hampered by sampling problems and the variety of definitions of training and workforce classification that have been used.

IFF Survey of Employers' Training Activities
This survey was conducted by Industrial Facts and Forecasting Ltd in 1986/7. The intention of the survey was to gather 'nationally representative material on how much training was undertaken by employers in Great Britain in 1986/7, how much was spent by them on that training, what influenced them and what employers' general attitudes were towards training.' (Deloitte, Haskins and Sells *et al*, 1989; p.9).

The survey excluded establishments with less than 10 employees and the agricultural, forecasting and fishing sector. Approximately 1,600 establishments were interviewed in both the public and private sectors. Of these, nearly 1,500 completed a *Training Activities Record* detailing the establishment's workforce structure and recruitment in six broad occupational categories. Other topics covered in detail include the amount of off-the-job training, off-site training costs, on-the-job training and costs. Interviews were conducted with these organisations to collect additional information on the nature of training, to assist with the estimation of training costs and to enquire into the establishment's recent performance.

Survey work associated with this enquiry was conducted in 1985/6. The data were not adequately documented for subsequent secondary analysis at the time the data set was created. Data editing and processing of these complex data proved problematic. Consequently, the data derived from this survey are not currently accessible. A project to clean and validate the data and to provide suitable documentation was undertaken at the Institute for Employment Research. A clean data set was deposited with the ESRC Data Archive during 1992.

Skills Monitoring Survey

The Skills Monitoring Survey (SMS) is an annual survey of employers' recruitment difficulties, as a proxy for skill shortages. Although this has been undertaken by a variety of methods in the past (eg CBI Quarterly Industrial Trends Survey, CALLMI interviews, etc), the skills monitoring surveys represent a wider and more detailed investigation than these other sources permitted. Fieldwork on the first such survey was conducted in Winter 1989/90; fieldwork on the latest survey commenced in February 1991.

The surveys are conducted by telephone interview with over 4,000 establishments per annum each, employing 25 or more employees. It asks for details of hard-to-fill vacancies, together with information on qualification/experience requirements, the current workforce, recruitment and turnover for this occupational category. Questions are asked about responses to both *existing* difficulties and *recently resolved* difficulties. Respondents also supply information on the perceived calibre of applicants, steps taken in response to skill shortages (including retraining), perceptions of future shortages, the 'skills gap' within the organisation and brief details of the extent of training within the organisation (existence of training plans, budgets and the volume of off-the-job training provided).

These surveys are not longitudinal. However, the size of the samples obtained, together with the fact that they are repeated surveys, offers some scope for examination of research issues focussing upon the skill shortage/training response relationship.

Data from the first and second Skills Monitoring Surveys are to be deposited at the ESRC Data Archive.

PSI/IER Survey of Demand for Graduates

In 1989 the Policy Studies Institute and Institute for Employment Research combined to conduct a national survey of the recruitment, employment and training of new graduates. The survey, commissioned by an Interdepartmental Committee, covered a random sample of approximately 1,200 employers of over 20 employees in the private sector. Information collected by a combination of postal questionnaire and telephone interview included the structure of the workforce and recruitment by broad occupational groups, graduate recruitment (if any), the nature of training offered to graduates (type, duration), costs of training, reasons for employing graduates and non-graduates. Particular emphasis was placed in this survey on the impact of technological and organisational change as factors in graduate recruitment and training and on the estimated length of time before graduates 'become effective'.

These data have not been deposited at the ESRC Data Archive due to undertakings of confidentiality given to respondents. With a suitable approach to the anonymisation of these records, and subject to the agreement of an intergovernmental department group which 'owns' these data, there is no reason why such data should not be made available through the Archive.

Summary

This review of data available to inform UK-based research on training issues is necessarily selective. Two criteria guide such selectivity. First, information sources should be sufficiently comprehensive in scale and detailed in nature to facilitate major projects based upon secondary analyses of these sources. Thus, for example, an employer-based survey conducted in five local labour markets and London has been excluded on the grounds that poor response rates, as low as 16 per cent in one locality, (Burgess, 1989) would undoubtedly lead to difficulties in the interpretation of further research based on such a sample. The second criterion relates to the accessibility of data. This criterion effectively eliminates most existing case study material (eg. Centre for Corporate Strategy and Change, 1989). For information collected under statutory provision (Census of Population, New Earnings Survey) which is included in this review, availability of data will be subject to stringent conditions.

Selecting data on the basis of their ability to inform research on key training issues and their accessibility still leaves a considerable list of sources, reviewed in the two main sections of this report. Other issues which may be relevant in narrowing this list, assuming that some further sharpening of the focus of the initiative is required, could involve consideration of factors such as the date upon which data were collected. Research on training issues can become out of date very quickly in a period of rapid change. The reshaping of the Department of Employment and the evolving role of TECs are generating pressures for change which must be taken into consideration in future research proposals. Additionally, account must be taken of the quality, breadth and richness of available data. Secondary analysis can do little to 'repair' data which are fundamentally deficient in some way.

A number of sources stand out in terms of their ability to inform new research in the area of training, their up-to-date nature, the quality and depth of information. At the individual level, NCDS5 will be a most important source. The link with NCDS4 and NCDS3 will be required to facilitate best use of this information, as will local labour market indicators. The criticism often levelled at this source, that it has a narrow focus on a single year age cohort, is of less importance given the developing role of BCS'70 to replicate such work with a 12 year interval and the need to generate understanding of the growing importance of training among young adults. NCDS5 information on training needs to be contextualised given the narrow focus on a particular year group of individuals. The LFS is the most appropriate source for such contextualisation.

The linked WERS3/EMSPS data will be the most important source of employer-based training data in the early 1990s. Employer-based surveys suffer from notoriously low response rates. WERS3/EMPS have the advantage of a good response rate, 'stability' in terms of the respondent and high quality interviewing.

In terms of young entrants to the labour market, the Youth Cohort Studies are rapidly evolving into a major resource. Some channelling of additional research resources into this area seems appropriate, provided that good coordination can be attained between those currently researching in this area and any proposed research.

Notes

I am indebted to many individuals who provided me with detailed information about sources of training data at very short notice. Judith Marquand and Alan Davies were particularly helpful in establishing contacts. Alison Booth, Derek Bosworth, Hilary Cooper, Angela Dale, Gareth Dent, Clare Elliot, John Elliot, Duncan Gallie, Christine

Greenhalgh, Jane Mark-Lawson, Stephanie Morgan, Iain Noble and Jill Robson offered valuable assistance in preparing this review paper.

1. For example *Training Statistics, 1993* (Employment Department, 1993) provides a useful summary of such sources.

References

Burgess, C. (1989), (In conjunction with others), *Training in Britain. A Study of Funding, Activity and Attitudes. Market Perspectives*, London: HMSO.

Centre for Corporate Strategy and Change. (1989), (In conjunction with Coopers and Lybrand Associates), *Training in Britain. A Study of Funding, Activity and Attitudes. Employers Perspectives on Human Resources*, London: HMSO.

Claydon, S. (1980), 'Counting our Skills: the National Training Survey', *Employment Gazette*, pp. 1150-1154 (November).

Deloitte, Haskins and Sells with IFF Research Ltd (1989), *Training in Britain. A Study of Funding, Activity and Attitudes: Employers' Activities*, London: HMSO.

Department of Employment (1991), *Employment Gazette*, April, London: HMSO.

Employment Department Group (1993), *Training Statistics 1993*, London: HMSO.

Payne, J. (1990), *Adult Off-the-Job Skills Training. An Evaluation Study*. Research and Development Report No. 57, Sheffield: Training Agency.

Rigg, M (1989), *Training in Britain. A Study of Funding, Activity and Attitudes: Individuals' Perspectives*, London: HMSO.

7 Evaluating training at the company level

Jaap de Koning

Introduction

Why is it important to assess the effects of company training on the company level, how can it be done, and what has research brought to light? Those are, briefly formulated, the questions that are central to this paper.

In the Netherlands the interest in company training started in the early 1980s when there was a widespread feeling that the Netherlands were lagging behind in that respect. The fact was pointed out that the number of apprentices - the only statistic available at the time - was dropping. Moreover, companies were complaining about the poor match between regular vocational education and professional practice. There was a general feeling that in the Netherlands training and vocational education were seriously failing and that this was a major cause of the poor performance of the Dutch economy at the time. From that time onward there has been a lively interest in the association of education and economic growth, and in particular the role of vocational and company training in that respect. Policy makers have since actively tried to restructure their educational and training policy. In general, the tendency is to grant private companies a greater share in training and education and to offer them more opportunities for training subsidies. This explains - at least in part - the growth of company training between 1986 and 1991. According to two surveys held by the Central Bureau of Statistics (CBS) (1988, 1992), the number of courses per worker amounted to 0,25 in 1986 and 0,34 in 1991.

The government appears to have high hopes of stimulating economic growth through - among other things - company training, on the premise that the direct involvement of companies ensures a fair economic profitability. That premise is not founded on research outcomes, however. Hardly anything is known (at least in the Netherlands) about the economic effects of company training. In view of this fact and the high priority company training is given by the government, research in the field is of the utmost importance.

This paper is organised as follows. In the next section the definition of company training is discussed, because so far different surveys have used different definitions. We then examine the question of why research on company training should preferably be done at the micro-level and why on the company level. Next we consider some theoretical aspects of research into the economic effects of company training. These aspects are: the matter of causality, general versus specific training, and evaluation by the companies themselves. Finally, we present some experiences with micro-research into company training based on two recent studies.

Definition of company training

The various surveys held in the Netherlands so far have used different definitions of 'company training'; moreover other forms of training and education have not been clearly delimited. For that reason we will look somewhat closer at the definition of company training. So far, the following surveys have been held in the Netherlands: - the CBS surveys of 1986 and 1991, that were mentioned above;

- a survey carried out by the Agency for Strategy Labour-Market Research (OSA) in 1988;
- a small survey among 50 companies we carried out ourselves in 1991.

The CBS defines company training as training exclusively accessible to persons employed by the company, and regards all other forms as external training. The OSA has adopted another definition: by company training it understands both internal and external training courses. Internal training by the OSA definition also comprises training within the company that is open to outsiders, and to that extent does not coincide with company training by the CBS definition. CBS and OSA both consider exclusively formal training; (informal) on-the-job training does not come under either definition.

We have joined the OSA in understanding by company training both internal and external courses. Our argument is that internal and external training may have exactly the same contents. There is no essential difference with other services (advertising, computer services, etc.) which can either be carried out internally or farmed out. We differ from the OSA in that we understand by internal training only those courses that are open exclusively to the company's own employees. Not unfrequently, schools run by large companies fulfil a regional function; there is no obvious reason to regard courses given at such schools as internal training.

Both the CBS and the OSA are vague about the dividing line between company training and other forms of training and education. Obviously the term 'company training' presupposes a certain involvement of the company, but that involvement has not been clearly defined. Our definition is that company training is financed in part or entirely by the company. Mostly, but not invariably, financing means that the company actually bears the costs or a portion of them. Sometimes, the expenses are as it were balanced with the wages: the employee need not actually pay the fees, but receives a relatively low wage during the period of training or gets only a moderate wage increase after the training.

The definition also encompasses those cases where an employee attends regular classes for the account of the company (evening classes, for instance). To speak of company training in such cases may not seem immediately logical, but the fact is that recruiting companies more and more find available candidates lacking in basic education, and in need of extra schooling in such subjects as the Dutch language and arithmetics. Some companies include such general subjects in their internal training classes.

We exclude from company training both (informal) on-the-job training and courses which employees attend on their own initiative, in their leisure time, and entirely for their own account. The reason not to count on-the-job training as company training is that it largely escapes control. The reason to exclude from the concept of company training any classes which employees attend without intervention of the company is obvious. Nevertheless, there is a 'grey area' even there. Indeed, the company may induce an employee to take a course by holding out to him the hope of promotion. In that case the company is involved after all.

Micro versus macro research

Limitations of research on meso- and macro-level

In the Netherlands, little research has been done so far into the economic effects of company training, for the simple reason that there were hardly any data to go on. As mentioned above, the Central Bureau of Statistics conducted in 1986 and in 1991 surveys of company training courses in the Netherlands.

Both surveys are oriented entirely to company courses and give no information about, for instance, production volume and other performance indicators. Consequently, these surveys provide no basis for micro-economic analyses of the effects of company courses. The survey data thus permit only analyses on the level of sectors, the level on which production data and the like are of course known from other statistics. Obviously, this is but a poor basis for a reliable assessment of effects.

But even if sufficient data were available on the aggregate level, the question remains whether aggregate analysis can give a proper insight into the economic effects of company training. In that respect the literature on measuring the effect of education on productivity and economic growth is illuminative. From an inventory of studies in which production functions with different educational categories have been estimated, the results appear to diverge widely[1].

Although this is no proof that analyses on the aggregate level with respect to company training would also fail to produce convincing results, we do believe that research on the basis of micro-economic data opens better prospects. We realise, of course, that if training increases productivity and growth on the company level, that does not necessarily mean that training is also beneficial to the economy as a whole.

Measurement on the level of individual employees versus that of companies

The micro-economic effects of company training courses can be measured on two levels:
- individual employees;
- companies.

What we want to assess is how far company training increases productivity. Measurement on the level of individual employees is hampered by the near impossibility of measuring individual productivity. That is why most studies following the individual approach use wage income as indicator on the assumption that productivity and wage income are more or less equal. There are strong indications, however, of productivity and wage income not necessarily being closely related on the individual level[2]. In the Netherlands the currently dominating idea is that the discrepancy between wages and productivity is the very reason for employers to expel the older employees, reducing them to the ranks of the unemployed and the unfit-for-work.

To measure the effects on the company level seems more promising. The result of training seems easier to assess on that level, the same on which such performance indicators as productivity, production growth and profit tend to be measured. Moreover, as we will argue in the next section, the incidence of company training is largely a matter of company behaviour. But measurement on the company level has its own drawbacks. For one thing, the only training courses on which companies can give a reliable report are those which they themselves finance or co-finance; they cannot tell much about courses which their employees may enrol in at their own expense and in their leisure time. Nevertheless, the latter courses may also have their effect on company performance. The optimum but hard-to-practise procedure would be to analyse simultaneously both forms of training on the basis of measurements collected from the companies as well as from the people in their employ.

Theoretical aspects

Causality

An interesting point to clear up in the relation between company training and company performance is the matter of causality: does company training cause the company to improve its performance, or, inversely, does a better company performance foster expenditure on training? Or are both influences at work simultaneously? The theory of human capital simply postulates that education and training increase productivity. Later theoretical contributions have suggested that while people may take part in education and training from economic motives, there may be no productivity-boosting effect at all[3].

It is quite possible that the improvement of the company's performance is not the primary object of company training, and that company training has no (clear) effect on productivity and output growth. The following possibilities come to mind:
- company training is a tool for selecting employees for more responsible jobs;
- the training is a form of (tax-free) reward, intended to bind present or recruit new staff;
- employers are compelled to stage training courses because of the poor quality of the labour available.

In those circumstances the training may still have an indirect favourable effect on the position of the company, but that will be hard to assess.

On the other hand, company performance may be a determining factor for the company's training efforts. One suggestion is that profitable companies will be more than others inclined to invest in training for their employees because they can well afford it.

For empirical research we have to consider the possibility of a two-way relationship between company training and company performance. Simultaneity in this relation is indeed a factor to reckon with, because most company training courses are of limited duration[4] so that only a short time elapses between the moment of the company's decision to invest in training and the moment its effect becomes noticeable. Consequently, appropriate (so-called simultaneous) estimation methods have to be applied, which is by no means common practice in empirical research in the economics of training and education[5].

Becker (1964) made a distinction between general and specific training, the former being useful in several companies and specific training only in one. Arguably, a company would leave it to the employee to pay for his general training, lest a rival should profit from the company's investment by 'buying' its trained employee. Inversely, the logical assumption is for company-specific training to be paid for at least in part by the company.

As has already been observed by other authors[6], actual practice does not confirm the arguments.

Company training is mostly of a general nature, and companies bear a considerable part of the training costs. Companies may have several reasons to pay for, or contribute to, the general training of their employees.

1. Employees will be inclined to pay for general training only if they are free to capitalise on it elsewhere. A move to another company may involve expenses, such as removal costs. Unless the return on the training compensate for such expenses, employees will not be inclined to put up money for their training (Bishop, 1988).
2. General and specific training may be complementary. General training may be more profitable if going hand in hand with specific training (Feuer, Glick and Desai, 1987).
3. Uncertainty about the profitability of training and risk aversion may make employees inclined to underinvestment in general training[7]. Kodde (1986) has developed a two-period model, featuring a worker enroling for general training in the first period in the uncertain hope of receiving higher wages in the second period. Maximising his expected utility (on the assumption of diminishing marginal utility) that worker will invest less than he would in a situation without risk. Companies are in that context considered risk-neutral. Ritzen reasons that they are able to enhance their employees' propensity to train by a kind of inverse-insurance scheme: supporting their employees by a study compensation in the first period, but taking a corresponding amount out of their expected wages in the second period. In that way, every employee would reach his expected return. Actually, in consideration of the moral hazard involved, the company will take care not to remove all uncertainty. Beside, risk aversion may still be

a major consideration for smaller companies. That is why, in sectors with many small companies, such a scheme will have to be organised on the level of the sector. It is also conceivable that the government is involved in it. The point Ritzen makes is that the proposed scheme leads to a more efficient allocation.

Now the uncertainty that Kodde and Ritzen have in mind is in fact a specific type, namely the possibility of employees not successfully completing the training, or, through sickness or otherwise, failing to capitalise on it. It is a risk which in particular major companies must be considered able to calculate. Things are different with the uncertainties associated with economic fluctuations and structural change. People may lose their job and be unable to find a new one in their own profession. The company cannot remove that kind of uncertainty. Therefore, financing training expenses may not be enough to persuade workers to participate in general training; companies will have to bear at least some of the costs.

4. For some companies, certain types of labour may be very important. They will try to select the best workers and bind them to the company. For that reason, companies will want to have some influence on the quality of the training and the admittance requirements, and try to recruit the best students.

5. There is by no means always clarity about how "general" general training is, in particular if organised entirely or in part within the company and not leading to a generally recognised certificate. If employees doubt the general validity of the training, they will be reticent to invest in it themselves.

On the whole, the above considerations lead us to expect that workers will tend to underinvest in general training and that companies will take over at least some of the costs. However, the extent to which companies will pay for general training will vary in time and between sectors. The strongly procyclical development of the number of participants in apprentice arrangements indicates that companies are less willing to invest in training during recession periods. Sectors with many small companies, great fluctuations in production, many part-timers and very mobile manpower (such as the building trade, the hotel and catering sector and the retail trade) will probably invest less in general training. This is confirmed by the results of the surveys mentioned before.

Evaluation by the companies themselves

The effectiveness of training at the level of companies probably depends not only on the percentage of employees participating in training or the expenditure on training as a percentage of the wage sum, but also, or perhaps mostly, on the quality of the training. Quality in that connection implies two things:

a. a proper adjustment of the training to the requirements of the company. Within the company a training strategy has to be designed that fits in the overall recruitment policy and matches corporate strategy;
b. good training results. An analysis has to be made of the supply of training courses (if necessary including the possibility of internal organisation). Beside, the results of the training have to be evaluated.

So, it seems important for companies to evaluate their own training efforts.

Evaluation by companies may imply:

- ex-ante evaluation: why is training important; which employees have to be trained and which training courses chosen; what costs are involved and what benefits can be expected; which is more efficient, internal or external training;
- monitoring: keeping an eye on the training results;
- ex-post evaluation: assessment afterwards whether or not the results come up to expectations, and if not, why not; if necessary, adjustment of the training.

In principal it is possible to compare the performance of workers before and after training, or to compare the performances of workers who followed a training course and those who did not. However, the fact remains that in most cases individual productivity can be assessed only in a qualitative sense.

Two examples of studies into company training using company data

In this section two recent studies will be discussed that have examined company training on the company level[8]. We will focus on the design of the studies and only briefly discuss the results.

A large-scale survey among companies

We referred above to a survey carried out by the OSA among some 2,000 companies and agencies. This survey covered a wide range of aspects, among which participation in company training, technology, internal organisation, production volume, composition of the staff by such characteristics as age, educational level and sex, wage structure, work conditions, workhours, flexible labour, and financial data. We have used the data yielded by that survey to carry out analyses, primarily intended to explain the productivity and the wage level of companies[9]. The explanatory variables that interested us most were the education, training and age of the staff, in view of the massive expulsion of workers in the older age brackets from the labour market in the Netherlands. Presumably, the philosophy underlying that phenomenon is that ultimately productivity decreases with age while the wage level remains stable. The question is to what extent training can enhance the productivity of the older employees and put off the moment of their expulsion.

The survey has given a fair idea of the possibilities and impossibilities of data collection from companies. On the one hand, data could be obtained on a wide range of aspects. On the other hand, precisely because of the wide variety of subjects, only few questions could be asked about each of them if the survey was to remain acceptable to the companies. Even then, there was a considerable non-response on a number of questions. The conclusion is that, in terms of available data, measurement on the level of companies does by no means offer only advantages.

The results of the study are as follows[10]:

1. External training has a significant positive effect on productivity; internal training has a positive effect too, but is not significant.

172

2. The effect of training on productivity is relatively small: a doubling of the training effort increases productivity by about 10 percent.
3. Productivity is much more affected by both training and age then wages. That is why training can improve the position of older workers.

Indicators of company performance are not significant in the equation for participation rates in internal and external training. Company size is the dominant explanatory variable in both equations. On average, small companies are growing faster than large companies, but show much lower participation rates in company training.

In-depth interviews with 50 companies

This investigation[11] was undertaken to collect from a limited number of companies - 50, to be exact - data on various aspects of company training. The main questions the study had to answer was to what extent underinvestment in company training occurs and, if so, what effect this has on the companies' performance. The questionnaire concentrated on the following aspects of company training courses: composition of the participant group, nature of the courses, bottlenecks, costs and subsidies, and organisation.

The drawback of the detailed questioning on these five aspects was that only a limited number of questions could be asked about other aspects. One consequence is a sub-optimum measurement of indicators of company performance (for instance, turnover has been taken instead of value added).

We already referred to this study in the previous sections. In this section we will take some topics somewhat further. First, we will go into the evaluation of training by companies themselves. It appears that evaluation by the companies themselves is the exception rather than the rule. We were surprised to find that companies, even those with full-time training officials, knew so little about their own training efforts. Hardly any company used a computerised information system for the registration of company training. We often got the impression that companies took the interview as an opportunity to make the first overall picture of their training efforts. Information about the costs of training was extremely rare, especially about the worktime spent on company training. In fact, companies lack the basic information needed to make a proper evaluation of their training efforts.

Our tentative conclusion is that the training provided for by companies is often based on rather vague notions about the expected returns. Training is fashionable. To improve productivity is still the primary motive for most companies to train their staff, but company training is increasingly used for newly hired workers who lack basic education. Nevertheless, the lower educated workers are still under-represented among the participants in company training. According to the companies the lower educated are more difficult to convince of the necessity of training.

Underinvestment in training is observed not only among specific groups of workers, but also among specific types of company. The survey indicates that most bottlenecks are highly dependent on the type of industry. However, even after correcting for the type of company the training efforts appear to be significantly related to the way training is organised within a company (is there a training manager, a training scheme, etc.?).

The study set out to estimate a two-equation model with company performance and training efforts as the two dependent variables. The training variable has a positive, but insignificant effect on company performance. This may have something to do with the size of the sample. The size of the effect of training on company performance is very similar to the results based on the OSA survey.

Final remarks

We think that in further investigations into the economic effects of company training, research on the micro-level should have priority. The most appropriate level to measure the effects of company training is that of companies, for only on this level can performance indicators such as productivity be adequately measured. Indeed, from our findings, substitution of wages for productivity, as is common practice in research based on employee data, may give misleading results, for education and training affect productivity much more than wages. So, a survey among companies is necessary. On the other hand, most companies appear unable to unearth sufficient data about the age, sex, and educational patterns of their staff, characteristics which are important determinants of productivity. Such information is best gathered from employees. So, ideally, companies as well as their employees would have to be surveyed. To combine in one dataset all the relevant information needed to assess the effects of company training, seems illusory.

Our plea for micro-economic analysis of the economic effects of company training does by no means imply that meso- and macro-economic analyses should be superfluous. In fact, displacement phenomena may cause the effects on an aggregate level to differ from those on the micro level. However, the current data constraints prohibit aggregate analyses. And even if the necessary data were available, to draw definitive conclusions from aggregate data would probably be very difficult.

A last remark is due about the way companies plan their training efforts. Surprisingly, companies seem to know very little about the training they pay for, especially about the costs. This makes it very hard to believe that the money spent on training is spent in the most efficient and effective way. Perhaps, that explains why we have found that the effect of company training on company performance is relatively small. On the other hand, it could mean that there is room for improvement.

Notes

1. See De Koning et al. (1990). For instance, estimates of the substitution elasticity between higher and lower educated workers varies between almost zero and ten!
2. See, for instance, Bishop (1987)·
3. By the screening hypothesis (Spence, 1973; Arrow, 1973) school certificates may serve exclusively as a selection tool for employers and have no connection whatsoever with labour productivity.
4. According to the CBS-survey 87 per cent of the company training has a duration of less than 10 days.
5. An exception is an article by Razin (1977), who tried to determine by means of a cross-section analysis across countries the nature of the causal relation between education and economic growth.
6. See Ritzen (1989) for an overview.

7. Courses are expensive and opportunities to borrow limited, for financial agencies will take into account that the returns on training are of study is uncertain and students may be unable to pay off their study debts.
8. Both studies were carried out by the Netherlands Economic Institute. Thanks are due to Arie Gelderblom and Robert Olieman of the Institute who participated in these studies.
9. This research was commissioned by the OSA.
10. See Gelderblom and De Koning (1992).
11. See De Koning et al, 1991 (Commissioned by the RVE (the advisory council for adult education)).

References

Arrow, K.J. (1973), 'Higher education as a filter', *Journal of Public Economics*, 2, pp. 193-216.

Becker, G.S. (1964), *Human Capital*, New York.

Bishop, J.H. (1988), *Do Employers share the Costs and Benefits of General Training?*, Cornell University.

Bishop, J.H. (1987), 'The recognition and reward of employee performance', *Journal of Labour Economics*, 1987, 5, no. 4.

CBS, (1988), *Bedrijfsopleidingen in Nederland in 1986* (Vocational training financed by the private sector in the Netherlands in 1986).

CBS, (1992), idem, Provisional results.

Feuer, M., Glick, H. and Desai, A. (1987), 'Is firm-sponsored education viable?', *Journal of Economic Behaviour and Organization*, 8, pp. 121-136.

Gelderblom, A. and de Koning, J. (1992), *Can company training improve older workers' productivity-wage ratio? A summary*, Netherlands Economic Institute, Rotterdam.

Kodde, D.A. (1987), 'Uncertainty and the demand for education', *The Review of Economics and Statistics*, pp. 460-467.

De Koning, J., Gelderblom, A., Koss M. and Olieman, R. (1990), *Soorten onderwijs en economische groei* ('Types of education and economic growth'), Netherlands Economic Institute, Rotterdam.

De Koning, J., Gelderblom, A., Hammink, A. and Olieman, R. (1991), *Bedrijfsopleidingen: omvang, aard, verdeling en effecten* ('Company training: size, nature, distribution and effects'), published by the RVE and the Ministry of Education and Science, Utrecht.

Razin, A. (1977), 'Economic growth and education: new evidence', *Economic Development and Cultural Change*, 25, pp. 317-325.

Ritzen, J.M.M. (1989), *Market Failure for General Training and Remedies*, paper for the Robert M. La Follette Symposium on Market Failure for Training, May.

Spence, M.A. (1973), 'Job market signalling', *Quarterly Journal of Economics*, 87, pp. 355-375.

8 Methods for evaluating employment and training programs: Lessons from the US experience

Rebecca A. Maynard

Introduction

Rigourous experimental evaluations are commonplace in US studies of employment and training programs, and they have been gaining popularity in evaluations of health policy reforms, education programs, and other social service arenas. At their best, experimental evaluations are the most powerful method for estimating program effectiveness. However, generating reliable results from experimental evaluations requires clear specification of the research questions and careful implementation of the operational aspects of the experiment. The past 30 years of program and evaluation experiences in the United States have led to an emerging consensus about what constitutes a rigourous evaluation design.

Thirty years of US employment and training policies

The first major US job training resulted from the passage of the Manpower Development Training Act (MDTA) in 1962. MDTA was designed to address problems of structural unemployment, and thus emphasized job training and placement assistance services for disadvantaged workers. There was no research basis for the program. Moreover, there were few attempts - and no rigourous attempt - to evaluate this initiative (see O'Neill, 1973; and Perry et al, 1975).

In the early 1970s, the focus of US employment and training policy broadened to encompass concerns over cyclical, as well as structural, unemployment. This shift led to the passage of the Comprehensive Employment Training Act (CETA) of 1973, which replaced the MDTA programs with programs that focused increasingly on job creation through public service employment. For the first time, there was a major focus on the systematic monitoring of program services and outcomes. A major national data base - the Current Population Survey (CPS) - was used as the basis for creating a comparison group of CETA eligibles that formed the basis for measuring what the employment prospects of CETA participants would have been had they not had access to program services.[1]

By the mid-1970s there was growing concern about the economic and social well-being of populations with limited or no attachment to the labor market, who tended to have a high incidence of welfare dependence, criminal life styles, and drug abuse. Much of this concern was focused on youth, leading to the investment of over $600 million in numerous small-scale and poorly evaluated demonstration programs.

Concurrent with this massive expansion of small-scale projects focused on youth, we also witnessed the design and field testing of the first major social experiment in the employment and training field - the National Supported Work Demonstration. This demonstration implemented graduated stress work experience programs for welfare recipients, ex-addicts, ex-offenders, and young school dropouts and an experimental (random-assignment) evaluation to measure program impacts on a variety of economic and social outcomes (Hollister, Kemper and Maynard, 1984). The Supported Work Demonstration, as well as numerous smaller and less rigourous evaluations of other similarly timed intensive, targeted demonstrations, resulted in mixed messages: impacts on earnings were modest for those groups who benefited and were largely offset by reductions in welfare benefits.

Despite the mixed messages from prior research, the high unemployment rates of the late 1970s and early 1980s led to increased national emphasis on broadly focused programs to promote the employment of unemployed workers and 'work-ready' welfare recipients. Political forces led to the replacement of CETA with the Job Training Partnership Act (JTPA) fo 1982, which eliminated public service employment and stressed job placement and training services. These forces also led to the first large-scale demonstration of closely linked employment and welfare policies, the Employment Opportunity Pilot Project. This demonstration tested sequenced employment services - job-search assistance followed by job training for those not securing a job

179

during the mandatory job search period - and was similar to smaller state-initiated tests of variations on this concept (Brown et al, 1983; Burstein, 1980 and Goldman, 1981).

As a result of econometric developments that promised to address the methodological limitations of non-experimental evaluation designs (Heckman, 1976 and 1979) and due to rising concerns over the ethics of using random assignment in social evaluations (Burtless and Orr, 1986; and Boruch, 1976), many of these demonstrations relied on non-experimental evaluation designs. Moreover, evaluation cost considerations led to increased reliance on administrative data, which significantly restricted the background data on the population under study. The pattern of evaluation results from this wave of demonstrations was qualitatively similar to that from the previous wave. Programs targeted at women tended to have consistently positive (albeit modest in size)impacts, and there was no consistent evidence of program effectiveness for males.

By the mid- to late-1980s, federal policy makers, troubled by the lack of solid evidence about the effectiveness of the JTPA program, implemented improved longitudinal tracking of program participants through the Job Training Longitudinal Survey and a rigourous national impact evaluation that relied on an experimental design (Doolittle and Traeger, 1990). Moreover, in response to the dearth of evidence on how to mitigate problems of long-term welfare dependency, we witnessed a number of major federal, state, and private-sector initiatives to test policies that required able-bodied welfare recipients who had low basic-skills to participate in education as a condition of their welfare eligibility, mandated work or training requirements on welfare recipients with preschool-age children, and provided employment services to welfare recipients in two-parent households in addition to those in single-parent families (Gueron and Pauly, 1992; Maynard and Hershey, 1992; and Burghardt and Gordon, 1990).

The experience from these demonstration and evaluation efforts, together with increasing pressure for national welfare reform, culminated in the passage of the Family Support Act of 1988. This legislation institutionalized some of the state-piloted policies. There is a major effort underway to conduct a large-scale experimental evaluation of the employment and training services provided under the Job Opportunities and Basic Skills Training (JOBS) program, which was created under the Family Support Act.[2]

The influence of evaluations in policy and program development

The US is now in its third era of employment and training evaluation efforts. In this era, we are systematically experimenting with numerous programs, and nearly all of our major national programs are being subjected to evaluation using experimental methods. This focus emerged from two earlier eras of program evaluation, each of which consisted of two quite different strands of research.

The first era of evaluation began in the mid-1970s and lasted into the early 1980s. One strand of this research involved rigourous evaluations of highly specialized and targeted programs, such as the Supported Work Demonstration, a costly intervention implemented on a fairly small scale and with a significant level of technical assistance. Moreover, these programs tended to be targeted at relatively small numbers of volunteers, who were not characteristic of the population meeting the program eligibility criteria.

The other strand of studies during this first era consisted of those with serious methodological flaws. For example, virtually all of the 400 evaluations of our youth programs during the mid-1970s lacked a good comparison group, many had very small samples, and many relied on limited and poor-quality data (Betsey et al, 1985). Similarly, our large-scale evaluations of the National CETA programs, which relied on comparison group methods, generated widely varying and often qualitatively inconsistent results (Barnow, 1987).

For quite different reasons, both of these strands of research yielded primarily new programmatic ideas and stimuli for additional testing. The rigourous evaluations, in particular, also provided a model for the design and collection of high-quality longitudinal data.

The second era of evaluation, conducted in the mid-1980s, was also characterized by two general types of studies. One relied on detailed longitudinal data and large samples, but adopted comparison group strategies rather than rigourous experimental designs. The rationale for this type of design was twofold: (1) advances in econometric procedures were thought to allow statistical adjustments for unmeasured differences between the program participant group and the nonparticipant group; and (2) random assignment studies did not permit measurement of the community-wide effects of policy changes - specially, such policies as job creation strategies where it was believed to be necessary to implement the program 'to scale' in order to test its true effectiveness (Garfinkel et al, 1992).

The other type of study in this second wave adhered to the rigourous experimental design, but tended to rely on a highly restricted data sets (due largely to cost considerations). The most notable examples of this cluster of evaluations are the state work-welfare demonstrations (Gueron and Friedlander, 1992). These studies relied primarily on welfare and unemployment insurance administrate data and thus had limited ability to investigate such issues as effective targeting strategies.

Limitations of past evaluation efforts

The US experience with employment and training evaluations embodies more lessons about how to conduct solid program evaluations than lessons about effective program design or targeting. The most general lesson is that there is no perfect evaluation design. It simply is not possible to design a study that *faultlessly* addresses all the key policy questions: Are the programs effective? Which types of programs are most effective? For which types of participants are programs most effective? Which types of programs are most cost-effective? And how are programs best implemented?

Knowledge of whether a program is effective requires that we have reliable estimates of both the outcomes for those who participated in the program and what the outcomes for participants would have been had they not participated in the program. Prompted by the inconsistent results of studies relying on comparison group methods and state-of-the-art econometric techniques, the US Department of Labor funded a methodological evaluation of the reliability of comparison group estimates of program impacts.

In this evaluation, the researchers used the National Supported Work Sample, which had a randomly assigned control group, to determine whether any of the alternative comparison group evaluation methods that had gained popularity during the mid-1980s would yield reliable estimates of program impacts. The results of this study indicated that nonexperimental designs *cannot* be relied on to estimate the effectiveness of employment programs. Impact estimates tended to be sensitive both to the comparison group construction methods and to the analytic models used (Franker and Maynard, 1987). Using their "best" comparison group (generated by statistically matching the Supported Work participant sample with the sample in the Current Population Survey) and their most comprehensive analytic model, the researchers obtained impact estimates that were qualitatively similar to the experimental results only for one of the two subgroups studied - welfare recipients. For the youth sample, the impact estimates generated using the randomly selected control group differed vastly from those generated based on the comparison groups (Table 1). The authors concluded that 'currently there is no way *a priori* to ensure that the results of the comparison group studies will be valid indicators of the program effects'.[3]

Table 8.1
Experimental versus nonexperimental estimates of
program-induced annual earnings effects

Year	Youth		Welfare Recipients	
	Control Group	Comparison Group	Control Group	Comparison Group
1977	313	-668*	1,423**	1,560*
1978	-28	-1,191***	505*	537*
1979	-18	-1,179**	351*	257*
Number of Observations				
Experimentals	566	566	800	800
Controls/ Comparisons	678	2368	802	909

Source: Fraker and Maynard (1987), Table 1. Data are based on the National Supported Work Demonstration and the Current Population Survey.

*	Statistically significant at the 90 percent confidence level, two-tailed test.
**	Statistically significant at the 95 percent confidence level, two-tailed test.
***	Statistically significant at the 99 percent confidence level, two-tailed test.

More recent econometric work has identified some promising specification tests that can limit the range of errors in impact estimates based on comparison group methods (Heckman and Hotz, 1989). However, the tests developed thus far still leave considerable uncertainty about the accuracy of impact estimates based on comparison group methods, particularly if it is not possible to identify a comparison group that is closely matched to the participant group (Friedlander and Robins, 1991).

Current knowledge regarding program effectiveness

The experience of the past 20 years of research has left policy makers and researchers in general agreement about the serious shortcomings of evaluations based on comparison group designs and small samples and about the dearth of solid research to guide policy debates. For example, there are only 18 rigorous studies of adult-oriented employment and training initiatives focused heavily on welfare recipients - including separate evaluations of programs for adult males and for different population subgroups. These studies cover six different types of interventions: job-search assistance only; work experience/workface only; job-search assistance and work experience/workfare; basic education and other services; job training and other services; and supported work. The findings from these studies can be summarized as follows:

- A broad range of programs are generally effective at promoting employment and increasing earnings for adult females. But there is no statistically reliable evidence of earnings gains among disadvantaged adult males (Table 2).

- The average earnings gains of these types of interventions are generally modest (up to $1,500 per year) and not sufficient to lift families out of poverty

- There is substantial variability across programs (especially the job training programs) in the estimated size of the earnings impacts - a result that could arise due to differences in the programs or to imprecision in the estimates of their effectiveness.

The weight of the evidence from these studies also suggests that employment and training programs are most effective from prime-age women (for example, women age 30 to 45), for those who have limited prior work experience (and thus the lowest prospects of gaining employment in the absence of an intervention), and for those who have some history of welfare dependence. The more intensive services, such as job training, tend to be relatively more effective for those with the most limited employment skills - those with low levels of education and limited work experience - while job-search assistance is relatively more effective for disadvantaged women who are most job ready.

Program costs range from a low to a few hundred dollars for the low-intensity job search and work experience/workfare programs to several thousand dollars for job training, education and supported work programs (Table 2). But it is important to note that the significance of these cost differences depends on their relationship to program impacts. Looking at the female target populations, we observe that the less expensive programs tended to generate smaller average earnings. From the perspective of the program operator who is trying to get the greatest program impacts for a limited program budget, resources should be targeted so as to achieve the largest earnings gain per dollar of expenditure. Yet research to date offers no clear guidance on this issue (Figure 1). Research needs to be directed to informing the development of policies that may involve multi-service programs and effective screening and targeting policies to improve cost-effectiveness.

A somewhat broader perspective on the cost-effectiveness of the various types of interventions relates to the net benefit (or cost) to society. Are we more productive and better off as a result of adopting the intervention? Are the social benefits from one type of intervention or targeting strategy greater than from another? The weight of the evidence from studies to date is that most programs targeted at women are beneficial from the perspective of society, yielding estimated net benefits ranging from $400 to nearly $9,000 over a five-year period. Moreover, the more intensive programs (particularly supported work) tend to have especially high net present values (Maxfield, 1990, Table 3).

Table 8.2
Summary of the estimated earnings impacts and costs from experimental program evaluations

Type of Program/ Intervention	Females Annual Earnings	Females Costs per Participant	Males Annual Earnings	Males Costs per Participant
Job-Search Assistance Only				
San Diego WIN	$201	$563	$307	$590
Louisville WIN	$399 ***	$376		
Work Experience/Workfare Only				
West Virginia WIN	$0	$170	-$162	$170
Job-Search Assistance and Work Experience/Workfare				
Chicago WIN	$45	$157	-	-
Arkansas WIN	$156*	$158	-	-
San Diego WIN	$560***	$640	-	-
Basic Education and Other Services				
Washington, DC MFSP	-$219	$2,679	-	-
Atlanta, GA MFSP	$15	$3,816	-	-
Providence, RI MFSP	$99	$4,824	-	-
Job Training and Other Services				
Virginia WIN	$108	$430	-	-
San Diego SWIM applicants	$287	$1,545	$506	$1,292
Baltimore WIN	$511**	$958	-	-
Maine WIN	$698***	$2,251	-	-
San Diego SWIM recipients	$889***	$1,545	$383	$1,292
San Jose MFSP	$1,594***	$3,573	-	-
Supported Work				
Ex-Offenders	-	-	$37	$8,214
Ex-Addicts	-	-	$326	$8,214
Long-term AFDC recipients	$967**	$8,214	-	-

Figure 8.1
Average earnings gains per dollar of program costs for various types of services: results from studies with rigorous evaluations

Program Type

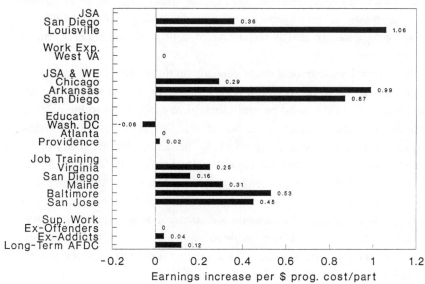

Source: Based on data provided in Maxfield (1990), Table 1.

JSA	=	Job-Search Assistance Programs
Work Exp	=	Work Experience Programs
JSA & WE	=	Programs Focusing on Job Search and Work Experience
Education	=	Programs with Education as the Primary Focus
Job Train	=	Programs with a Job Training Focus
Sup Work	=	Supported Work

Designing effective evaluations of employment and training programs

Thirty years of program experience and 20 years of research have left us with more knowledge gains about effective and efficient evaluation strategies than about program designs and policies. Most policy makers and researchers agree that the most critical factor in reliable evaluation designs relate to the internal and external validity of the findings. Developing a design that is responsive to both of these concerns can be thorny.

The external validity of a study depends on three factors: (1) the policy being tested must be relevant; (2) it must be tested on a relevant population; and (3) it must be replicable. The main threat to the external validity of a study relates to issues of scale of operation and possible saturation or sample selectivity effects. The demonstration nature of the program should not distort the environment significantly from that which would occur in a fully implemented program. Moreover, the intervention itself should not be distorted in order to meet evaluation requirements or in response to its special demonstration status. For an evaluation to have policy relevance, it must be possible to replicate it on a larger scale, and the program must be evaluated in a manner that accounts for macro-economic or community feedback effects.

The internal validity of evaluation results can be assured through the use of a well-designed randomized experiment. With random assignment, one can compare outcomes for two statistically identical populations, only one of which received the intervention of interest (or received an entitlement to the services).[4] Under this type of an evaluation strategy, we can estimate the differences in outcomes that are attributable to the intervention, and we can compute the range of error in those estimates. Moreover, on average, the estimates will not systematically over- or under- estimate program impacts.

There are two potential limitations of this methodology. One is that either the randomization process or the method of delivering the intervention could contaminate the experiences of the control group. If this occurs, the effects of the intervention could be masked or exaggerated, threatening the internal validity of the impact estimates. The second possible limitation is that implementing an experimental design requires that the intervention be operated at less than full-scale. The smaller-scale program may not induce the same effects on participants (or on the environment) that would result from a universal implementation, threatening the external validity of the findings.

In both cases, the temptation is to consider comparison group alternatives to the experimental design. However, comparison group methods are plagued by the necessary assumptions about the effectiveness of statistical methods to control for unmeasured differences between the treatment and comparison groups other than those resulting from the intervention. It is precisely the validity of these underlying assumptions that have been challenged by the recent methodological work (Fraker and Maynard, 1987; LaLonde, 1986; LaLonde and Maynard, 1987; and Friedlander and Robins, 1991). Moreover, it is generally the case that a comparison group study design will require significantly larger samples to generate statistically reliable estimates of program impacts, even if the possible selection bias issues can be dealt with through statistical modeling.[5]

The most serious limitation of comparison group methods is that there is no way to know *a priori* whether there will be significant selection bias. After the fact, we may find ourselves in one of three undesirable situations: first, we may determine that we have selection bias, but not be able to find a way to correct for it; second, we may find evidence of selection bias and be reasonably confident that we can correct for it, but can do so with confidence only if we have significantly larger sample sizes; or, finally, and most likely, we may find no evidence of selection bias and be left with the uncertainty about whether selection bias exists and we failed to detect it because of data limitations or the limited power of the analysis.[6]

Recommendations

The 20-year history of employment-training evaluation experience leads to the following five specific recommendations for planning and evaluation strategy. First, it is important to define the specific policy questions to be addressed by the evaluation in advance of defining the program design and the evaluation strategy. Second, the intervention strategy should be shaped so as to maximize the external and internal validity of the results. Third, the evaluation strategy should complement the impact analysis with a detailed examination of program implementation, operational and contextual factors. Fourth, the evaluation plan should include a rigourous impact evaluation that pays close attention to the comparison or control group strategy used. Wherever feasible, the impact analysis should use an experimental design. However, it may also be prudent in some cases to have 'saturation' sites.

. The sample sizes for the impact analysis should be large enough to support independent analyses of important subgroups.

. Moreover, the design should include a sound, longitudinal data collection plan.

Finally, when a random-assignment evaluation is not feasible, it is important to invest heavily in the development of the best possible comparison group strategy. (One possible alternative is randomized or paired site designs). Any time one must rely on a comparison group design, it is important to collect comprehensive background information on sample members to support state-of art statistical controls for pre-existing differences between participant and control group members. One should also pay close attention to the sample size requirements for achieving the desired level of statistical power for the impact estimates.

Both researchers and funders need to continue to support studies that can improve our ability to evaluate programs using nonexperimental methods. We have one major methodological evaluation being conducted in conjunction with the national JTPA evaluation (Hotz, 1992). Others need to be initiated. Finding reliable nonexperimental evaluation methods could substantially enhance our ability to provide timely evaluations of ongoing programs and would relieve some of the natural tensions between the internal validity and external validity concerns of study designs.

Notes

This paper was prepared for the International Conference on the Economics of Training: Differing Perspectives on Theory, Methodology, and Policy, Cardiff Business School, 23-24 September 1991. Helpful comments on an earlier draft of the paper were provided by Walter Corson, Mark Dynarski, Paul Decker and Myles Maxfield.

1. For reasons that are discussed below, the analyses of program effectiveness based on the use of the CPS comparison sample yielded inconsistent results (Barnow, 1987).
2. Case management services are the cornerstone of the JOBS program. The program provides child care assistance and other support services, and some employment-directed services. But it generally contracts directly with or relies on our public education and JTPA training services to provide skill-upgrading and job placement services.
3. In another, similar methodological study, LaLonde (1986) found qualitatively similar results.
4. A variation on this design is to compare groups assigned randomly to alternative treatments.
5. Evaluators must not handle participant and comparison group samples as if they were samples drawn from the same population, since there will undoubtedly be both systematic differences in the outcomes for the two groups that are due to selection into the program and local factors that contribute to the variability in the impact estimates.
6. Frequently, researchers apply tests of statistical precision to comparison group designs, ignoring the fact that the participant and control samples are not statistically identical. In such cases, they may be lulled into a false sense of security about the absence of selection bias. They may not have found it because their sample size is too small to detect it.

References

Barnow, B. (1987), 'The impact of CETA programs on earnings: a review of the literature', *Journal of Human Resources,* 22, pp. 2.

Betsey, C. L., Hollister, R. G. and Papageorgio, M. R. (eds.), (1985), *Youth Employment and Training Programs: The YEDPA Years.* Washington, DC: National Academy Press.

Boruch, R. (1976), 'On common contentions about randomized field tests', in G.V. Glass (ed.), *Evaluation Studies Review Annual.* Beverly Hills, CA: Sage Publications.

Brown, R. et al. (1983), 'The employment opportunities pilot project: analysis of program impacts', Princeton, NJ: Mathematica Policy Research, Inc.

Burghardt, J. and Gordon, A. (1990), *More Jobs, Higher Pay.* New York, NY: The Rockfeller Foundation.

Burstein, P. (1980), *The Estimated Effects of the Work Equity Project on Welfare Caseload.* Cambridge, MA: Abt Associates.

Burtless, G. and Larry L. O. (1986), 'Are classical experiments needed for manpower policy?', *Journal of Human Resources,* 21, pp.

Doolittle, F. and Traeger, L. (1990), 'Implementing the national JTPA study', New York, NY: the Manpower Demonstration Research Corporation.

Fraker, T. and Maynard, R. (1987), 'The adequacy of comparison group designs for evaluations of employment-related programs'. In *Journal of Human Resources,* 22, pp.

Friedlander, D. and Gueron, J.M. (1992), *Are High Cost Services More effective than Low Cost Services: Evidence from Experimental Evaluations of Welfare-to-Work Programs*, Cambridge, MA: Harvard University Press.

Friedlander, D. and Robins, P. (1991), *Estimating the Effects of Employment and Training programs: Assessment of Some Nonexperimental Techniques.* New York, NY: Manpower Demonstration Research Corporation.

Garfinkel, I., Manski, C. and Michalopoulos, C. (1992), 'Are micro-experiments always best? Randomization of individuals or sites', In Cambridge, MA: Harvard University Press. Madison, WI: Institute for Research on Poverty Conference Paper. April.

Goldman, B. (1981), 'Impacts of the immediate job search assistance experiment', New York, NY: The Manpower Demonstration Research Corporation.

Greenberg, D. and Robins, P.K. (1984), *Trends in Social Experiments*. College Park, MD: University of Maryland, April.

Gueron, J.M. and Pauley, E. (1991), *From Welfare to Work*. New York, NY: Russell Sage Foundation.

Heckman, J. (1976), 'The common structure of statistical models of truncation, sample selection, and limited dependent variables and a simpler estimator for such models', *Annals of Economic and Social Measurement*.

Heckman, J. (1979), 'Sample selection bias as a specification error', *Econometrica, 47*.

Heckman, J.J. and Hotz, V.J. (1989), 'Choosing among alternative nonexperimental methods for estimating the impact of social programs: the case of manpower training', *Journal of the American Statistical Association 1989*, pp. 862-874.

Hershey, A.M. and Maynard, R.A. (1992), *Designing and Implementing Services for Welfare Dependent Teenage parents: Lessons from the DHHS/OFA-Sponsored Teenage Parent Demonstration*. Written statement for the Committee on Ways and Means, Subcommittee on Human Resources, US House or Representatives, Hearing on Education, Training and Service Programs for Disadvantaged Teens.

Hollister, R., Kemper, P. and Maynard, R.A. (1984), *The National Supported Work Demonstration*. Madison, WI: University of Wisconsin Press.

Hotz, J.V. (1992), 'Designing and evaluation of the job training partnership act', in C. F. Manski and I. Garfinkel (eds.), *Welfare and Training Programs,* . Cambridge, MA: Harvard University Press.

LaLonde, R. and Maynard, R.A. (1987), 'How precise are evaluations of employment and training programs: evidence from a field experiment', in *Evaluation Review*, 2, number 4.

LaLonde, R. (1986), 'Evaluating the econometric evaluations of training programs with experimental data', *American Economic Review*, 76.

Maxfield, M. (1990), *Planning Employment Services for the Disadvantaged*. New York, NY: The Rockfeller Foundation.

Maynard, R. and Polit, D. (1987), *Overview of the DHHS/OFA-Sponsored Teenage Parent Demonstration*. Princeton, NJ: Mathematica Policy Research, Inc.

O'Neill, D. (1973), *The Federal Government and Manpower*. Washington, DC: American Enterprise Institute.

Perry, C., et al. (1975), *The Impact of Government Manpower Programs*. Philadelphia, PA: University of Pennsylvania.

9 Measuring the effects of training in the Youth Cohort Study

Peter J. Dolton, Gerry H. Makepeace and John G. Treble

Introduction

The measurement of the effects of training on the subsequent careers of trainees has been the subject of a large quantity of literature in recent years (see, for example, Main and Shelly, 1990 and Whitfield and Bourlakis, 1991). This literature is dependent on two main types of data source: general purpose surveys of individuals, and data generated by randomised experiments. In Britain, we have shied away from the challenge of evaluating public programmes by means of randomised experiment, so that our only sources of data are of the first type.

In this paper, we describe our attempts to use the Youth Cohort Study's third cohort (YCS3) responses to examine the impact of various sorts of training on the earnings of trainees. The particular focus of our study has been the issue of whether privately provided (or employer-led) training has different consequences for trainees than government-sponsored training. This question is clearly an interesting one, and on the answer may well depend important issues of policy. Having wrestled with it for some time, we now have doubts as to whether the question is meaningful, and part of this paper is an attempt to make clear the basis of these doubts. We also undertake the task of analysing the data in a manner that is feasible, in the belief that some light is shed by what we have done on the main question at issue.

To a great extent, our problems are dependent on the nature of the data with which we are working, and it is sometimes difficult to distinguish a truly conceptual issue from one that arises simply from the structure of YCS3. The difference is that a problem that arises from YCS3 can presumably be solved by redesign of the survey or its questionnaire, conceptual problems may be impossible to solve by such simple means.

The YCS is intended to be the primary source of information on the school to work transition. It has been running since 1983-84. Cohort 3 respondents completed their compulsory schooling during the school year 1985-6. The earliest information they are asked to report relates to September 1986. A sample of about 20,000 of these 16 year olds was sent a questionnaire asking for details of their educational achievements and their experiences of the labour market or of post-compulsory schooling. Respondents to this first sweep were sent a further questionnaire one year later, and second sweep respondents were contacted two years after the initial mailing to give the Sweep 3 information.

The paper begins by summarising the main movements between different possible states of the respondents during a 30 month period beginning in September 1986. It is clear from this discussion that there is a wide diversity of experience. This diversity implies that there are many routes that one might take in analysing the data, and we have necessarily had to select a particular way of viewing the YCS3 data. We intend to adopt some different approaches in future work.

Our approach here is to consider the respondents' position at Sweep 3 of the survey, and to use information from previous sweeps largely as explanatory variables in our analysis. This is open to the objection that many decisions are made in the expectation of an outcome at a time fairly remote in the future, so that the whole of an individual's progress from one labour market or educational state may be conditioned by some future, possibly unobserved, objective. For instance, some of our respondents will have stayed at school in order to obtain A-levels with a view to entering the banking profession immediately after. Thus the whole sequence of states from leaving school until job entry are part of a single career plan.

The paper goes on to consider the different types of training that can be distinguished within YCS3, and their adequacy for illuminating the issues with which we are concerned. We also touch on some more general issues concerning the usefulness of YCS3 in its present stage of development.

Finally, we present a summary of the results of our estimation of two different models of the determinants of earnings. The first is motivated by the work of Lynch (1989), which attempts to measure the benefits accruing to trainees from privately provided training, by estimating a set of earnings equations. We then note that Lynch's methodology does not readily transfer to the British context, because of difficulties in the identification of purely privately funded training. Our second model attempts to tackle the problem in a different way, by modelling the selection of individuals into alternative training regimes, and comparing the earnings of typical individuals in each regime.

The brief description of the data given above shows that there may be a problem of non-random attrition in our sample. While we have plans to model this attrition using the full data from all three sweeps, the results reported below are based on a balanced dataset of Sweep 3 respondents, and no corrections for attrition have been made.

Work and education profiles from YCS3

An individual's position in the labour market at any point in time is conditioned by their past history. Thus an understanding of labour market data on individuals requires some perspective on how people progress through the labour market over time. In this section we summarise what YCS3 tells us about the activities of young people in the 30 months following the end of their compulsory education. The survey asks respondents to complete a diary at each sweep, recording their main activity each month during the previous 12 months (6 months at Sweep 1).

Diary responses distinguish the following activities: (i) out of work and registered at the Unemployment Benefit Office, (ii) out of work but not registered, (iii) on a government training scheme, (iv) in a full time job, (v) in full time education and (vi) something else. We call each of these possibilities a state. Since there are a very large number of possible sequences of states, presentation of what the diary data contain is not easy. We present the data in four ways as (i) state-proportions for each diary month, (ii) state-transitions between diary dates (iii) work history profiles and (iv) empirical hazards of leaving each state. These methods are widely used; for an example and further references, see Dolton and Makepeace (1991) Chapter 3. We discuss the structure of the data using each of these approaches in turn.

At any point in time most respondents are in one of: government training schemes, employment and education. There is a fall in the proportion on government training schemes from 30% in September 1986 to 4% in February 1989 for men and from 25% to 3% for women while the proportion in employment grows from 20% to 64% for men and from 16% to 60% for women. The proportion in education falls from 40% to 21% for men and from 49% to 19% for women. The presumption is that individuals are entering work over time either directly or following spells in full time education and on government training schemes, as in the three main routes to work identified in YCS2 by Sime, Pattie and Gray (1990).

Employment grows more or less continuously over the whole period for both men and women (one exception for men is September to October 1988). Closer inspection reveals certain 'jumps' in the figures at various times. These may reflect the ending of courses or training periods, or they may be a reflection of the reporting bias described below. For instance, there are falls in the proportion on government training schemes from February to March in each year. Employment trends are more obviously correlated with the numbers leaving full time education in each summer although the proportions in full time education follow an interesting pattern from June to September. Large numbers of students move from education into employment, unemployment and something else. The proportion in education in September never returns to its June value as some people move permanently into the labour market. There is clearly a substantial number of individuals who are de facto in full time education during the summer but who regard their vacation activities as different. This causes some problems for the analysis of work histories which we will discuss further below.

Larger proportions of women continue with full time education than men initially although by October 1988 relatively more men than women are still in full time education. By contrast larger proportions of men enter work or participate in government training schemes than women although the fractions of men and women on government training schemes at the end of the period are both small. By December 1989, the percentage of the women declaring that they are doing something else

(8.1%) is much larger than that for men (2.5%). We attribute this to the different family roles adopted by men and women.

State transitions and empirical hazards

Summarising the full set of state transitions is not straightforward, since there is a very large quantity of data to be considered. There are two striking characteristics of the data showing month to month transitions. The first is that there is a substantial degree of month-to-month inertia in the system. The second feature is that the transition matrices representing the join between questionnaires (February-March each year) are the major exception to this. This implies that there is a reporting bias introduced by the structure of the questionnaire. For the Sweep 2/Sweep 3 join, the bias takes the form that people who claimed to be in the residual category at the end of S2, report themselves in one of the other categories (especially full time employment) at the start of S3. There seems to be no reason to expect a genuine movement of this sort at the start of March, and it could probably be convincingly interpreted as a consequence of poor memory of events 12 months in the past.

The main unanticipated feature of the empirical hazards analysis for each state is that in each series there are large spikes at month 6 and every ensuing 6th month. This is true for both males and females. The spikes are a further consequence of the phenomenon noted above. There is a tendency for people to change their reported state between sweeps in greater numbers than one would expect from the evidence of the frequency of within-sweep changes. In the comments that follow we assume that these spikes are an artifact of the data collection method, and make no further comment. The general features of the hazards are much the same for males and females, except where noted below.

The hazard of leaving unemployment falls rapidly after the first six months, levelling out thereafter to somewhere between 0.1 and 0.2. This is consistent with the usual picture of youth unemployment consisting predominantly of short spells. Some evidence of short periods of employment is also apparent.

The hazard of leaving a government scheme is consistently small, until the two year YTS period is approached. At month 21, the hazard starts to rise, reaches a peak at month 24 (this is probably exaggerated by the reporting bias noted earlier), and then falls off again rapidly.

To produce our work history profiles, we classify the individual responses for each month of the diary into (i) unemployed (out of work whether receiving benefit or not), (ii) government training scheme, (iii) full time employment, (iv) full time education and (v) other (something else or do not know).

There are a large number of individual work and education profiles, revealing the diversity of experience in the early careers of young people. The 4318 men in our sample have 529 distinct profiles and the 5010 women have 602 profiles. One woman reports a profile with 10 distinct spells including at least one example of all five possible states. The diversity, although great, is, perhaps, overstated by these figures, since there is considerable bunching of respondents on a few profiles. The most common ten profiles for each sex include 57% of the men and 56% of the women while the most common twenty profiles cover 67% of the men and 65% of the women. Many of the profiles contain small numbers of individuals, for example, 324 of the men's and 369 of the women's profiles only have a single individual.

One further complication concerns the length of spells. The mean length is often small, suggesting that the change of activity might not be important in economic terms although it may be sufficient to define a new profile. This appears to be common for profiles where full time education is involved because it is perfectly reasonable to answer that one is undertaking some other activity during the vacations. This is a practical problem for our analysis because there are several profiles which might reasonably be described as full time education for the whole period amongst the most frequently occurring profiles. For example, four of the ten most common profiles for each sex have spells of full time education interspersed with short spells in another state.

Short spells may be important for subsequent labour market histories; for instance, if an individual in full time education spends the summer vacation in employment, it may indicate that the individual is better motivated or has better access to job information than a similar individual who spends the vacation unemployed. In our present study we are not emphasising the activities while in full time education and to retain the present level of detail complicates the analysis. We have therefore treated all individuals who appear to have temporary breaks from full time education as in full time education. This considerably reduces the number of profiles with 'large' numbers of individuals.

We define the period from June to September as being full time education if the states in May and October are full time education. Consider a person with the profile (education, unemployed, education, other, employment, education) with length of spells (in months) respectively (11,1,10,1,1,6). This profile is classified as continuous full time education because the spells out of education occur in the summer months. There are 106 profiles for men and 105 profiles for women which are reclassified by this rule to leave 423 profiles for men and 497 for women. Adding the people who reported education for the whole period, full time education then becomes the most frequently reported single profile for each sex with 1097 males and 1131 females or 25.4% of the males and 22.6% of the females.

The definition has certain shortcomings. Short spells out of education occur at other times than the summer and are not taken into account. There are profiles where a short period in another state occurs at the beginning or the end of a profile which would, otherwise, be defined as full time education. Nonetheless given the objectives of the present study, this definition is not pursued further.

The work profiles can be used to describe different ways of reaching full time employment by the end of the sample period. The twenty most common profiles are shown in Table 9.1. The most common way is a spell on a government training scheme followed immediately by work. About 13% of both men and women arrive in work by this route, with women spending a slightly shorter period of time, on average, in government training schemes. Full time employment for the whole 30 months is the second most frequent profile for men and the third for women and accounts for 10.5% of the men and over 7.5% of the women.

Three of the five most frequently reported profiles record ways of moving from education to work either directly (profile 3 for men and profile 2 for women), with a short intervening spell out of work (profile 4 for men and for women) or with a short intervening spell doing something else (profile 5 for men and for women). Given the short length of the intervening spells, there is a case for aggregating these together; in which case education followed by work would include 679 (15.7%) of the men and 1076 (21.5%) of the women and become the most frequent profile. Education followed by government training and employment (profile 8 for men and profile 7 for women) has a similar structure to these profiles but is clearly different because of the longer time spent in the training spell and the different nature of the intermediate spell.

Two more of the ten most frequent profiles involve an initial spell in education. These are a spell in education followed by something else (profile 9 for men and profile 6 for women) and a spell in education followed by unemployment (profile 10 for men and profile 8 for women). In each case the initial spell in education is much longer than the following spell (over 21 months compared with under 9 months). Both are probably heavily influenced by the length of the standard A-level course.

The results for men are in many ways similar to those for women. Although the rankings are slightly different, the same nine profiles appear amongst the most frequent ten profiles for men and women, the exceptions being Un, G, Em (profile 6) for men and G, O, Em (profile 9) for women. There are differences in the mean lengths of time spent in particular spells but these are not particularly large compared with the standard deviations.

Differences do occur in the proportions in each profile. Rather more men than women enter employment directly at age 16 or following a spell on a government training scheme. Amongst the most common profiles, more women than men enter employment following an initial period of education.

Training and YCS3

Our particular objective is to examine the extent to which YCS can throw light on employer-led training. We would like to be able to compute the returns to this kind of training, relative to those of other types, and we would like to know if the client groups for various sorts of training are different. This complex of issues involves the theory of the evaluation of training programmes, what is meant by employer-led training, and the practical difficulties imposed by the structure of YCS3 data.

In human capital theory, training imposes immediate costs, including the opportunity cost of foregone earnings, but offers higher returns in the future. The costs and benefits may, in principle, be non-pecuniary but, in practice, we have to restrict ourselves to monetary rewards in terms of earnings. In simple terms the more training an individual has completed, the higher is his marginal productivity. The first problem that we encounter is that of measuring this marginal productivity. In many applications, earnings can be taken to be a reasonably good indicator of marginal productivity, but this is a little dubious in the present context. This is because there are good reasons for believing that some of the costs of training may be borne by the trainee, and that the mechanism by which they are extracted is by means of structuring the earnings profile. Effectively, an employer may only be prepared to offer training to a worker, if the worker bears some part of the cost. The earnings profile can be used as a device by which the worker can 'borrow' the necessary funding. A worker in this situation may have a low wage for some time, because initially he will be spending time training, so that his marginal productivity is low. As his skills improve, we may expect his wage to continue to be low as his contribution to the cost of training is amortised. A trainee may be prepared to take a job for low current remuneration, in the expectation that his earnings will be enhanced in the future.

The question of what the information content of earnings observed early in a person's career is further complicated in two other ways. Firstly, the extent to which the costs of training are shared, and hence the amount of repayment that has to be accommodated depends on a little understood mechanism, by which employers and trainees implicitly arrive at a bargain over the division. In a static model, Hashimoto (1981) has clarified some of the issues here. Secondly, the management of training costs is not the only cause of wage profile structuring. The existence of salary scales, of promotion ladders and competition for promotion all are believed to have incentive effects, and all have implications for the lifetime earnings profile.

An important issue in the implicit bargain mentioned above is the degree of specificity of training. This concept envisages that types of training can be ranked by the number of firms in which a person's marginal productivity is enhanced on completion of the training. The more general the training, the more firms in which the trained individual's skills are improved. The more firms that are willing to hire the worker, the more closely will the market for his skills approximate a competitive market. It has been argued that, because of potential poaching of trained personnel, the more general the training the less will the employer be prepared to contribute to the cost of training, and hence the lower will be the observed earnings of a trainee (since these incorporate a deduction covering the training cost). Thus comparing the earnings of the no training group with those of various groups with different kinds of uncompleted training, the larger are the earnings differences the more general is the type of training.

While this may be generally true, we have a further problem arising from the specific nature of the YCS3 data. YCS3 at the moment only includes data for the first three years in the labour market. This is a period of heavy human capital investment and most individuals will not have completed their training and will not be obtaining the long term benefits of their training. To take an extreme example, we cannot say anything about the benefits obtained by individuals undertaking full time education. However the problem is more pervasive than this. Many working individuals who are undertaking training courses will not have completed their training by Sweep 3 of YCS3. Not only do we not observe the long term benefits of training but the earnings of trainees may actually be lower than those of individuals with no training, not because their expected earnings stream is generally lower, but because we only observe that part of it which happens to be lower. This is almost certainly the case for the apprentices in our sample.

We have one further conceptual issue to discuss before moving on to a description of our methods and results. This is the question of what is meant by 'employer-led'. In some institutional contexts, this may be clearly defined, but we have been unable to construct a satisfactory definition within the context of the British training system. When we come to consider whether we can make a definition operational when using data from YCS3, our problems are multiplied.

The first problem with the notion of employer-led is that the term does not make clear what the alternative is. Is it government-led, provider-led, employee-led, union-led or something else? The second is that it is not clear that any single agent can be identified as the 'leader' of a particular spell of training or training programme. If we conceive of training being provided within some sort of market, then provision will reflect the mutual interests of both employer and employee, and presumably any other agent who may be involved. Some may set these remarks aside as mere semantics. Perhaps the point can be made more clearly with an example. Suppose that the relevant distinction being made is between training that is financed by government and training that is financed by the employer. Set aside the possibility that the trainees themselves will contribute to provision, and suppose that an employer runs an apprenticeship scheme which uses company facilities, pays a negotiated apprenticeship wage and is part of the YTS scheme. Who is the leader? One could argue that the employer is clearly the leader, since at least part of the human capital created is specific to his firm. On the other hand one could argue that the government is the leader, because the scheme relies on the YTS subsidy. Ultimately, the issue is not one of leadership at all, but whether the training would have been provided in the absence of government intervention.

One way out of this sort of difficulty is to break the set of training spells up into a number of subsets determined by the nature and financing of the training. This essentially enables some analysis to be done while maintaining a degree of agnosticism as to whether a particular spell is employer-led or not. This approach has the characteristic that a critic who does not agree with one particular aggregation of these subsets being treated as 'employer-led' can always choose a more appealing aggregation.

We base our analysis below on the familiar earnings equation formulation that was introduced by Mincer, and has been used widely ever since. The earnings equation proposes that, for each individual, the natural logarithm of earnings depends systematically on the amount and type of training, personal characteristics and, for completeness, other factors such as conditions in the industry or locality in which the individual works. Thus:

$$\ln w = f(\text{training, personal factors, other factors})$$

Our basic methodology identifies different training types and compares the 'typical' earnings of different training types after adjusting for differences due to personal and other factors. Thus, to simplify, assume that we have three groups of individuals who, respectively, have had no training, have completed a government training scheme and have completed an apprenticeship. The earnings equation enables us to compare the earnings of individuals with no training with the earnings of otherwise identical individuals who have completed a government training scheme or an apprenticeship.

The earnings equation analyses earnings at a particular point in time: in the present case, at Sweep 3. The previous section established the many different experiences individuals have in the labour market over time. Individuals enter the labour market at different times with different education levels. The timing of vocational training varies across individuals as does the sequence of states over time. To some extent, we can compensate for different backgrounds by including variables such as number of employers, completion of a particular type of training, and length of time employed and unemployed in the earnings equation. This approach can only be taken so far and can at best only approximate the wide diversity we reported in the labour market histories. We must recognise that, by its construction, the earnings equation can only give a limited appreciation of the dynamics of the labour market and the role played by training in determining the history of the individual.

Our purpose is to uncover the relative effects of different kinds of training on the earnings of workers. An important issue here is that workers who undertake a particular kind of training may not be a random selection from the group of all workers. It then becomes difficult to disentangle the effect on earnings of training *per se* from that of the different attributes of the group. This problem is known to econometricians as sample selectivity. The problem arises if the training groups consist of different types of individual. Suppose, for example, that our analysis is based on a sample of YTS graduates and a sample of other workers, and that the earnings of individuals who have been on YTS are lower than the earnings of other individuals. It apparently follows that YTS training is of limited value because YTS graduates are more poorly paid. However this presumes that YTS trainees are directly comparable to other individuals in the sense that they would have received the same earnings if they had not participated in YTS. Suppose, to the contrary, that YTS trainees are less able (in some sense relevant to productivity) than other young people. Clearly, a direct comparison of earnings is not relevant because it confounds the two effects of ability and training. To compute the effects of training, we require an estimate of the earnings of less able individuals assuming they had not been on YTS or an estimate of high ability individuals assuming they had been on YTS.

The earnings equation provides a method for controlling for different ability levels provided that not all YTS graduates have low ability and not all non-YTS workers have high ability. The estimates for the sample of YTS graduates can be used to predict the earnings of non-YTS graduates assuming they are paid as YTS graduates and the estimates for the sample of non-YTS graduates can be used to predict the earnings of YTS graduates assuming they are paid as non-YTS graduates. We can therefore control for ability by comparing the earnings of, for instance, a low ability individual assuming they are and they are not a YTS graduate (so ability is held constant and training varies). At this point the technical problems posed by sample selection arise.

Sample selection is likely to arise if the sample of YTS graduates is systematically different from the sample of other young people[2]. The earnings predictions described in the previous paragraph assume reliable estimates of the effect of ability on the earnings of the two groups concerned. If there is sample selection, the Ordinary Least Squares method no longer provides appropriate estimates of the earnings equation. There do exist, however, estimation techniques designed to generate estimates with good properties.

At the heart of sample selection is the problem of controlling adequately for individual variation in the variables determining selection and earnings. In our example, ability determines which training group an individual is in. We can observe certain dimensions of ability such as examination performance but many dimensions such as interest, motivation and adaptability are not recorded. For example, suppose that there are two types of individual, one type which is highly motivated and 'loves' work and the other which does not. To simplify further, suppose each type is equally well qualified in terms of measured ability so, for example, they graduate from school with similar qualifications. Assume, perhaps not unreasonably, that all the 'love work' individuals obtain employment because of their high level of motivation and the others go onto YTS because they require more encouragement or preparation before work.

Sample selection techniques introduce what we shall call a 'selector equation' which determines whether an individual undertakes a particular type of training. Let P* be a continuous variable showing the propensity of an individual not to undertake YTS. The more ability (whether measured or not) that an individual has the more likely it is that the individual will be in the non-YTS group. The selector equation is then:

P* = effect of observed ability + effect of unobserved ability (motivation?)

$$P^* = A\alpha + u$$

(where $\alpha > 0$ and A is a variable which increases with measured ability).

The probability of working as a non-YTS graduate is:

$$Pr(\text{being non-YTS}) = Pr(P^* > 0) = Pr(u > -A\alpha)$$

If the data are generated by this structure, then the earnings of the YTS graduates will reflect their poor motivation and the earnings of other workers will reflect their high motivation. The effect of ability on earnings in each earnings equation will not indicate the returns available to the other group. The argument suggests that the mean earnings potential for each ability level (over both training groups) will be underestimated for the YTS group and overestimated for the other group. In fact, the effect of changes in ability is also affected (that is the slope of the earnings function is affected as well as the intercept) because the selection rule also implies that individuals with high earnings potential are less likely to be YTS graduates.

From the selector equation, as measured ability (A) increases for a given level of unmeasured ability (u), an individual is more likely to avoid YTS ($-A\alpha$ is more likely to be less than u). At the same time, increases in measured ability, holding motivation constant, increase earnings. Thus the sample of non-YTS participants will contain more individuals with high earnings potential (given their motivation) as well as more motivated individuals. The sample of non-YTS participants is therefore selected in such a way as to contain more motivated and more able individuals. This is sufficient to cause estimation problems. (For a graphical interpretation, see Main and Shelly (1990), Figure I)

The key policy issue is the value of government intervention in training, compared to that of other sorts of provision. This requires some evaluation of the extent to which employers support training and the specificity of that training. We therefore wish to make inferences about the effects of employers' involvement in training. YCS3 provides what is essentially supply side data which should facilitate comparisons of individuals with different backgrounds but which is contaminated by the operation of government training schemes; in our case, mainly YTS. It gives no information on how employers view their commitments or detailed data about the extent of their commitments. Nor is there information about the extent to which YTS has affected the aggregate provision of training by employers[3]. These problems are bound to lead to ambiguities about what is meant by employer-led training.

Finally, we should mention two further issues:

1. One non-pecuniary benefit of training which is often stressed is security of employment. The likelihood of employment, appropriately defined, increases with the amount of training. Typically this question has been investigated by examining the effect of training on the probability of unemployment at a particular point in time. We merely note that the YCS3 data does not allow us to say much about this issue. For example, individuals undertaking most types of work related training, such as apprenticeships, are in employment at the time of the Survey. By definition, there is no unemployment amongst many important training types.

2. As we mentioned above, an important issue is the long term benefits to training. On an individual level, we would like discover whether there are clearly defined incentives to undertake training and, if so, to quantify them. For policy purposes, it is important to examine the influence of market conditions on individuals' choices. This requires measures of the long term returns to various training decisions. We are currently attempting to supplement the YCS3 data with estimates of long run earnings obtained from the New Earnings Survey but, as yet, are unable to comment on this work.

Modelling the impact of employer-led training

We use changes in earnings as a measure of the impact of training and the earnings equation to provide a context for assessing such changes. In a recent paper, Lynch (1990) attempts to distinguish between general and specific training by estimating an earnings equation including among the regressors measures of previous and current exposure to on-the-job and off-the-job training. She argues that the estimated coefficients of these variables enable us to assess the degree of specificity of the training provided and the returns to completed training. In our work, we use

Lynch's basic premise, but since our data come from a different institutional context, we are forced to attempt rather more complex estimation methods.

In essence Lynch's approach assumes that the effect of different training types is limited to changing the intercept term, so that the earnings function for a person who has received one particular type of training is a simple upward or downward shift of the earnings function for another person. While we have attempted as close a replication of Lynch's method as is possible given the different institutional background and the limitations of our data, we also have generalised her technique to allow the earnings functions to differ in their slopes as well as their intercepts, while also taking account of the fact that workers choose which regime they are in. In section I, we described the structure of our data. It should be clear from that description that there may be bias due to non-random attrition in the sample. While we have future plans to model this attrition and introduce appropriate corrections, no such attempt is made in the present paper.

The individuals in our data undertake different types of training which are distinguished by three sets of training variables. The first two sets, T1 and T2, are derived from questions in the YCS identifying whether the respondent is or has been on a government training scheme (almost always Youth Training Scheme) or whether the respondent has either of two basic types of employer led training. The third set, T3, contains a YCS form of the training variables used by Lynch (1990). The third set, T3, contains a YCS form of the training variables used by Lynch (1990). The sets are defined more precisely as:

T1   (TRG41, TRG42, TRG43),

T2   (TRG61, TRG62, TRG63, TRG64, TRG65) and

T3   (YTS, APRNT, OJT, OFJT, POJT, POFJT, PAPRNT, OJTYTS).

Variables are defined in the Data Appendix.

We make a distinction in the determination of earnings between training type (one set of variables selected from T1, T2 or T3) and other 'standard' variables which affect earnings such as work experience and schooling. We estimate two models of earnings determination which we call the fixed earnings equation model and the training choice model.

Following Lynch (1990), the fixed earnings equation model assumes that the standard regressors have the same effect on earnings across training types. The earnings equation is estimated for all individuals in work and the effects of training are captured by including one set of training variables in the list of regressors. An equation explaining labour force participation is added to the earnings equation to deal with the familiar selection problem.

As in Lynch's paper, the earnings equations include work experience and work experience in the current job to capture the traditional Mincer approach to on-the-job training. The individual variables entering the definitions of T1, T2 and T3 are all binary variables measuring the explicit contribution, over and above that measured by work experience, of specific types of training. Thus the coefficient on the apprenticeship variable should enable us to compare the effects of being an apprentice on earnings for a given level of work experience. For each individual, the model is:

$$\ln Y \; = \; X\beta \; + \; T\alpha \; + \; u \tag{1}$$

$$\Pr(P = 1) \; = \; \Pr(\, v \, > \, -Z\delta\,) \tag{2}$$

where P is a binary variable taking the value 1 if the individual works and zero otherwise and $\ln Y$ is only observed if $P = 1$ and $\Pr(x)$ is the probability of x.

Equation (1) is the earnings equation with the regressors divided into standard human capital variables, X, and a set of training variables, T. We assume u and v have a bivariate normal distribution with non zero covariance. With these assumptions, the participation equation is a probit model and the earnings equation can be estimated by the Heckman Two Step method.

Supply and demand side interpretations can be given to the participation equation. An individual works if the market wage, given by the earnings equation, exceeds the reservation wage. In which case Z shows the difference between the market wage and the reservation wage (see Maddala (1983) p.228 for a discussion of this model) and includes variables determining both the market and the reservation wage. The reservation wage reflects preferences which are a function of social background, demographic variables and education. Alternatively we can view employment as demand determined so that the participation equation shows the likelihood of an individual being employed in the market place. Thus training affects the probability of employment in two ways: (i) by raising the market wage relative to the reservation wage and (ii) by moving an individual into a different segment of the labour market with different probabilities of employment.

The second model proposes that each type of training constitutes a distinct regime with its own earnings equation and that there is systematic selection into training regimes. Thus one type of training differs from another because the coefficients in the earnings equations are different and because the individuals working in each sector are different. We estimate this model for the classification of training given by the sets T1 and T2. Indexing the training type by t, the model, for each individual, is:

$$\ln Y_t = X\beta_t + u \qquad t = 0,..,m \qquad (3)$$

$$\Pr(I_t = 1) = \exp (Z\delta_t)/ \sum_{t=1}^{m} \exp (Z\delta_t)t = 0,..,m \qquad (4)$$

where $m+1$ is the number of alternatives ($m = 3$ for T1 and $m = 5$ for T2), It is an indicator function for t, and $d0 = 0$ is imposed as the identifying restriction. Y_t is only observed if $I_t = 1$.

Our model and estimation methods follow Lee (1983). Each of the types of training examined has a specific earnings equation given by equation (3) and the choice of training type is determined by the multinomial selector equation given by equation (4). Individuals are only observed in one type of training regime so account has to be taken of potential selection biases. This achieved by including Lee's sample selection term amongst the regressors in the earnings equation.

Results

Fixed earnings equation model

We estimated several specifications of the fixed earnings equation model in order to obtain a feel for the important determinants of earnings. The

212

sample selection effects were normally significant[4] for men but not for women. We interpret the sample selection term as a diagnostic statistic. All the results reported are for estimates corrected for sample selection.

Our baseline or reference specification is the set, BASE, defined as:

BASE = (HSE, FSIZE1, FSIZE2, MOBIL, MEOL, EDUCAT, TOTEMP, TUNEMP, VOCATQ, EMPLOYS, MARD3, SCHOOL, LITR, NUM, BLOCK, REGW, OJTEVER)

(N.B. Definitions of all variables in the Data Appendix).
We define the following sets of variables of interest:
SOC occupation dummines for SOC major group 1 to 9.
   The reference group is 4 - Clerical and Secretarial Occupations.
SIC industry dummies for SIC codes 1 to 9.
   The reference group is 8 - Banking, Finance and Insurance.
REGION regional dummies for standard regions 1 to 10.
   The reference group is 2 - Yorkshire and Humberside.

We estimate the models separately for each sex and for each set of training variables T1, T2 and T3 (these are defined in Section III above) for the following specifications:

   Spec. a) BASE+SIC;
   Spec. b) BASE+SIC+SOC;
   Spec. c) BASE+SIC+SOC+REGION.

Specifications using T3 omit OJTEVER from BASE and specifications using REGION omit REGW. In addition, we estimate each specification with separate variables for tenure in current job (TENR) and its square (TENR2). In practise, neither of these variables were ever significant and we do not therefore discuss any results for this specification.

We tested the joint significance of the industry dummies (against BASE), the occupational dummies (against BASE+SIC) and the regional dummies (against BASE+SIC+SOC [minus REGW]). In each case, the set of dummies is jointly significant. The sets of training variables, T1 and T3, are jointly significant in tests for their inclusion in the specificatins BASE, BASE+SIC, BASE+SIC+SOC. Tests of T2 against T1 for these specifications leads to the rejection of T2 for men but its acceptance for women.

The following discussion of the results focuses on the effect of training variables. We begin with the fixed earnings equation model which consists of a probit equation determining whether an individual participates in the model and an earnings equation, augmented by the sample selection term, determining earnings given individual characteristics.

In this model there is strong evidence that the attainment of a vocational qualification increases the probability of an individual working at Sweep 3 regardless of their sex. There is also evidence that individuals who have been on YTS are less likely to be in work but individuals with on-the-job training before Sweep 3 are more likely to be in work. These findings illustrate some of the problems of interpreting training effects with these data. In technical terms, the values of these variables may be simultaneously determined with whether or not the individual is working.

For example, given the short period covered, the attainment of a qualification may only be possible if the individual has a good work record (although not all individuals of this type will have such a qualification) so the result is not surprising in itself. Vocational qualifications are closely linked to the choice of training type and occupation so there are implicitly several selection effects which should, ideally, be modelled. Indeed, firms may explicitly chose individuals who can take vocational qualifications. Another issue is whether it is the attainment which is important rather the training. Many individuals may still be studying, but those individuals who have qualified are more highly motivated than the typical individual so the effect we are observing is an individual effect. Similar comments can be made about the remaining two types of training.

Point estimates of the coefficients of different training variables are presented in Tables 9.2 and 9.3. Only significant coefficients are reported although the sign of insignificant values is given in parenthesis. The percentage increases in earnings associated with a one unit increase in the value of each variable are given in Tables VI and VII. These tables report estimates from a wide range of models. The R^2 are high given that the data is for a cohort of young people of more or less the same age although the explanatory power of the earnings equation is much higher for women ($0.32 < R^2 < 0.42$) than for men ($0.20 < R^2 < 0.26$).

The training variables, T1 and T3, are jointly significant supporting their inclusion as determinants of earnings on statistical grounds. T2 is a less restricted form of T1 in which off-the-job training and apprenticeships are divided into those backed by some experience of YTS and those which are not. Statistical tests show that the two types of off-the-job training and the two types of apprenticeships have the same effect on earnings for men but different effects for women. It is therefore appropriate to make distinctions between these training types in the earnings equation for women but not for men.

Our basic premise is that completed training raises earnings compared with the no training group but that uncompleted training lowers earnings. The two variables, previous on-the-job training and previous block release, provide two measures of completed training (in the first three specifications). Previous on-the-job training gives a boost to earnings of around 5% for men and, less consistently, about 3% for women. Previous block release leads to a rather substantial loss of earnings for men but, at least in the preferred specifications, there is no statistically significant effect for women although the effect is negative. The results for men apparently contradict our hypothesis about completed training. One difficulty about the interpretation of this result is that previous block release may be highly correlated with current training in this sample. If, for example, individuals with previous block release are by and large individuals who are currently apprentices, then the coefficient on block release may be picking up part of the effect of being an apprentice.

The results for the training sets, T1 and T2, are quite different for men and women. The tests discussed above indicate that we can ignore the results for T2 for men though not for women. For men, there is a small differential paid to individuals on YTS although the statistical robustness of this result may be questioned. This is somewhat surprising but it appears to be sensitive to the specification and disappears when other sets of training variables are considered. In any case, an individual on YTS at Sweep 3 may be atypical of YTS trainees given his age and, possibly, background. Current off-the-job training is associated with rise in earnings of over 3% while a current apprenticeship leads to a fall in earnings of 4% or more.

These results illustrate how important it is to separate the *ceteris paribus* interpretation of the regression coefficients given above from the typical experience of individuals. Most individuals undertaking current off-the-job training may have previous block release. For these individuals the effect on earnings can be approximated by adding the two effects together so the overall effect is a fall in earnings of 4%.

By contrast to the men, previous and current YTS experience plays an important role in the determination of earnings for women. A woman on YTS receives lower earnings but previous YTS experience also affects earnings because the results for T2 are preferred to those for T1 on statistical grounds. In general, previous YTS experience lowers earnings. A current apprenticeship without YTS experience has no statistically significant effect (although, if anything, it lowers earnings) while an apprenticeship with YTS experience lowers earnings by up to 11%. Current off-the-job training without YTS experience raises earnings by about 6% but current off-the-job training with YTS experience lowers earnings by about 4%.

Multinomial logit selection model

In a full model of training selection, the individual's choice of training regime would depend on the earnings in each regime and individual preferences as proxied by various social and educational variables. We intend in future work to address the role of earnings in the selection of training type by simulating lifetime earnings profiles for various training choices using data from another source. This should provide estimates of expected earnings which are exogenous and which extend beyond the period covered by the present data. It would in principle be possible to estimate a model of training choice using the present data (see, for example, Dolton, Makepeace and Van Der Klaauw (1989)) but the restricted duration of the observation period and the predictive power of the earnings equations militate against such an exercise. To avoid problems with earnings, we estimate multinomial logit models which make the choice of training regime depend on social and educational variables only. The models have been estimated for the sets of training variables given by T1 and T2.

In the fixed equation model, we are able to measure the effects of different types of training by examining the coefficients of the training variables in the earnings equation. This option is not available in the training choice model. We propose to compare the predicted hourly earnings of 'typical' men or women in each of the training regimes and use this as our measure of the impact of various types of training.

The results of the multinomial logit estimations are presented in Tables 9.4 and 9.5. Because the results reported above suggested that there is no significant impact of YTS on the earnings of male apprentices, and males who are receiving off-the-job training, we report estimates using the fourfold classification of males. The results for females use the full sixfold classification. One cost of using the sixfold classification is that the computation of correct standard errors is beyond the capabilities of our present software. Consequently, the female results are presented with uncorrected t-statistics. Experience indicates that the corrections required are usually small.

We look first at the results for men. The reference group is the subset of men who report that they are receiving no training at all. In comparison with this group, respondents with YTS only (i.e. those with training who are neither apprentices nor receiving formal off-the-job training) have significantly lower educational attainment and come from regions with significantly higher unemployment. The only significant variable in the regression describing selection into the off-the-job training category is, rather oddly, school type. Those who did not attend an independent school are more likely to be included in this group. The apprenticeship category is characterised by respondents with a higher than average rate of access to motorised transport, who are less likely to have attended an independent school, and are in a region with a high unemployment rate. In the earnings equations only this category has a significant sample selection term.

Turning now to the estimates of the earnings equations themselves. the results for YTS make much sense, since the majority of YTS participants receive an allowance determined centrally by the government. One would expect, therefore, to find little explanatory power in the variables that we have included here. It appears that those firms who pay more than the standard allowance are large ones and there is some weak evidence that pay of YTS participants is correlated with regional wages.

The remaining results show a marked degree of consistency across the three categories. In all cases, earnings rise significantly with firm size. Access to motorised transport, the length of previous employment experience, and the regional wage rate, are also significant determinants of wage rates in all categories. Two further effects are present: i) workers reporting the receipt of no training appear to receive higher earnings if they have had longer experience of unemployment and ii) the only group of workers who appear earn a return for a higher level of educational attainment are those who report receiving off-the-job training, but are not apprentices.

We now comment on the results for women. Here there are six separate regimes. As with the men, respondents with YTS only have significantly lower educational attainment, and come from regions with significantly higher unemployment. This is also true for selection into the other YTS regimes. The significant variables in the selector equations are not easily interpreted. Disability apparently makes it easier for women to get a YTS place, but not in conjunction with an apprenticeship. There is no similar effect for men. Attendance at an independent school reduces women's chances of reporting off-the-job training in a college or training centre. There is evidence that father's labour market status and access to motorised transport are important, although these variables do not enter in any easily interpretable way.

Now we turn to the earnings equations for women. The first point to make is that the selection term is of manifest importance in the women's results. It enters into four of the six earnings equations. The earnings themselves are influenced, as expected, by regional wage levels and by firm size. There is evidence that employment experience increases wages. Educational attainment is of little importance, except for those on YTS without an apprenticeship or off-the-job training, and except insofar as it enters via the selection term.

Finally, using the estimated earnings equations, we can compute predictions of earnings within the various regimes. There are many ways in which this might be done. We have chosen to do it in a relatively easily interpretable fashion, by predicting earnings in each regime for an individual who has average values of all characteristics included in the earnings equations. Among the men, the hypothetical average person would earn 35% more if assigned to YTS than he would with no training, 26% less if assigned to the off-the-job training regime and 8.5% less if assigned to an apprenticeship. The observed earnings differentials are much smaller than this, thus indicating the importance of the selection effects. For instance, the differential of 35% quoted above does not feature in the observed data, because the average YTS participant does not have the same characteristics as the average member of the whole sample. For women the results are perhaps less striking, although they do show a marked effect of YTS in reducing earnings of women apprentices and boosting those of women undertaking off-the-job training. YTS seems to have small positive impact on earnings of women compared to those with no training, but a negative impact on earnings of men.

Conclusion

In this paper we have attempted to devise and put into use a technique by which it is possible to compare the earnings of individual young workers in a variety of training regimes. It is worth reiterating that the results that we report here are subject to a number of caveats , which are described in full in the paper.

Primary amongst these is the fact that when we observe an earnings stream for an individual who has undergone training, there are good reasons to suppose that this is net of some contribution to the cost of training. It is not possible to argue that this is likely to be the same for all individuals because the share of the cost borne by the trainee will depend, among other things, on the degree of specificity of training.

In addition to this conceptual problem we also have to take account of the fact that in YCS3 we are observing only a small segment of the respondents' earnings streams. Furthermore it is a segment that is particularly prone to the kind of problem described in the previous paragraph. There is little that we can do to correct this in the short term.

Notes

1. The respondents were asked 'Do you get any on-the-job training from a supervisor, trainer or experienced colleague?'. We use the answers to this question in the various sweeps to define the dummy variable OJTEVER measuring whether the respondent has ever had any

explicit on-the-job training. In an earnings equation containing work experience, this would measure the additional impact of explicit on-the-job training. One problem is how respondents interpret such a question. It is hard to think of situations where an experienced colleague does not give advice and guidance or lead by example, albeit mostly in an informal manner (OJTEVER should equal one for everyone). It seems likely that respondents think of training as a formal activity and are only responding positively if explicit training sessions have been held.

2. The term 'sample selection' refers to the fact that the 'sample' of YTS graduates is "selected" from the sample of all workers and the 'sample' of other workers is 'selected' from the sample of all workers.

3. For instance, Deakin and Pratten (1987) report that about a third of the YTS trainees in their sample are either replacing other workers (substitution effect) or taking jobs that would have existed anyway (deadweight effect).

4. In this paper we use the term significant to mean significantly different from zero at the 5% level on a two tailed test (an absolute value for the tstatistic greater than 1.96) and the term significant at the 10% level to mean significantly different from zero at the 10% level on a two tailed test (an absolute value for the tstatistic greater than 1.64)

Table 9.1
Work history profiles (excluding full time education)

	Men				Woman		
Profile Number	n	%	State Sequence	Profile Number	n	%	State Sequence
1	603	13.96	G, Em	1	630	12.50	G,Em
2	454	10.51	Em	2	609	12.16	Ed,Em
3	390	9.03	Ed, Em	3	376	7.50	Em
4	166	3.84	Ed, Un, Em	4	234	4.67	Ed,Un,Em
5	123	2.85	Ed,O,Em	5	233	4.65	Ed,O,Em
6	52	1.20	Un,G,Em	6	61	1.22	Ed,O
7	48	1.11	Un, Em	7	54	1.08	Ed,G,Em
8	47	1.09	Ed, G, Em	8	48	0.96	Ed,Un
9	35	0.81	Ed, O	9	42	0.84	G,O,Em
10	35	0.81	Ed,U	10	40	0.80	Un,Em
11	34	0.79	Em,Un,Em	11	39	0.78	Ed,Em,Un,Em
12	32	0.74	G,Em,Un,Em	12	35	0.70	G,Un,Em
13	26	0.60	G,Un,Em	13	30	0.60	Un,G,Em
14	25	0.58	G,O,Em	14	30	0.60	G,Un
15	24	0.55	G,Un	15	30	0.60	G,O
16	23	0.53	Em,G,Em	16	30	0.60	Em,Un,Em
17	23	0.53	Ed,Un,G,Em	17	28	0.56	G,Em,Un,Em
18	22	0.51	O,Em	18	28	0.56	O,Em
19	21	0.49	G,Em,G,Em	19	27	0.54	Ed,O,Un,Em
20	21	0.49	Ed,Em,Un,Em	20	26	0.52	Ed,Un,G,Em

Key

n   number of individuals with the profile
%   percentage of the total sample, for each sex, with the profile
Un out of the labour force
G   government training scheme
Em employment
Ed full time education
O   other

Table 9.2
Coefficients of training variables in earnings equations (men)

Training Variables	Base	Spec (a)	Spec (b)	Spec (c)
N	2202	2202	2202	2202
Excluding T1,T2,T3 R^2	0.202	0.220	0.236	0.248
Previous OnJT	0.0494	0.0486	0.488	0.0583
Previous Block Release	-0.0843	-0.894	-0.0810	-0.0665
Including T1 R^2	0.214	0.234	0.246	0.257
YTS only	[0.0555]	0.0475	[0.0476]	ns[+]
Current OffJT	[0.0315]	0.0313	0.0364	0.0363
Current Apprentice	-0.0471	-0.0579	-0.0396	[-0.0374]
Previous OnJT	0.0493	0.0486	0.0452	0.0539
Previous Block Release	-0.0746	-0.0794	-0.0806	-0.0675
Including T2 R^2	0.215	0.234	0.246	0.258
YTS only	[0.0501]	ns[+]	ns(+)	ns[+]
Current OffJT Not YTS	ns[+]	ns[+]	[0.0367]	[0.0357]
Current OffJT YTS	ns[+]	ns[+]	ns (+)	ns[+]
Current Apprentice Not YTS	[-0.0401]	-0.0503	ns(-)	ns[-]
Current Apprentice YTS	-0.0666	-0.0772	-0.0643	-0.0646
Previous OnJT	0.0521	0.0514	0.0490	0.0582
Previous Block Release	-0.0673	-0.0726	-0.0703	-0.0566
Including T3 R^2	0.221	0.242	0.253	0.264
YTS Only	ns[-]	ns[-]	ns[-]	[-0.0380]
Current Apprentice	-0.0940	-0.1038	-0.0952	-0.0923
Current OnJT	0.0330	0.0322	0.0322	0.0322
Current OffJT	ns[-]	[0.0251]	ns[-]	ns[-]
Previous OnJT	ns[+]	ns[-]	ns[-]	ns[+]
Previous OffJT	0.0502	0.0498	0.0516	ns[+]
Previous Apprentice	ns[+]	ns[-]	ns[-]	ns[-]
Previous OnJT YTS	0.0340	0.0349	0.0323	0.0346
Previous Block Release	-0.0747	-0.0759	-0.0762	-0.0420

Note

Estimates which are significant at the 5% level are shown normally
Estimates which are significant at the 10% level are shown in brackets
Estimates not significant at the 10% level as 'ns' with the sign of the coefficient in brackets

Table 9.3
Coefficients of training variables in earnings equations (women)

Training Variables	Base	Spec (a)	Spec (b)	Spec (c)
N	2560	2560	2560	2560
Excluding T1,T2,T3 R^2	0.325	0.376	0.397	0.410
Previous OnJT	0.0450	0.0393	0.0245	0.0268
Previous Block Release	-0.0464	-0.0456	-0.0476	-0.0385
Including T1 R^2	0.336	0.382	0.402	0.414
YTS only	-0.0470	-0.0557	-0.0582	-0.0497
Current OffJT	0.0393	0.0305	0.0270	0.0310
Current Apprentice	-0.0482	[-0.0277]	ns[-]	ns[-]
Previous OnJT	0.0456	0.0381	0.0232	[0.0250]
Previous Block Release	-0.0628	-0.0609	-0.0624	-0.0548
Including T2 R^2	0.342	0.389	0.409	0.421
YTS only	-0.0537	-0.0630	-0.0666	-0.0581
Current OffJT Not YTS	0.0623	0.0550	0.0567	0.0587
Current OffJT YTS	ns[-]	-0.0355	-0.0448	-0.0369
Current Apprentice Not YTS	ns[-]	ns[-]	ns[-]	ns[-]
Current Apprentice YTS	-0.1181	-0.0950	-0.0759	-0.0707
Previous OnJT	0.0534	0.0546	0.0307	0.0318
Previous Block Release	ns[-]	ns[-]	ns[-]	ns[-]
Including T3 R^2	0.343	0.388	0.409	0.422
YTS Only	-0.0588	-0.0658	-0.0715	-0.0671
Current Apprentice	-0.1136	-0.0793	-0.0672	-0.0678
Current OnJT	0.0377	0.0293	[0.0212]	[0.0198]
Current OffJT	ns[+]	ns[+]	ns[+]	ns[+]
Previous OnJT	ns[-]	ns[+]	ns[-]	ns[+]
Previous OffJT	0.0581	0.0469	0.0428	0.0435
Previous Apprentice	ns[-]	ns[-]	ns[+]	ns[+]
Previous OnJT YTS	ns[+]	ns[+]	ns[+]	ns[+]
Previous Block Release	ns[-]	ns[-]	ns[-]	ns[-]

Note

Estimates which are significant at the 5% level are shown normally
Estimates which are significant at the 10% level are shown in brackets
Estimates not significant at the 10% level as 'ns' with the sign of the coefficient in brackets

Table 9.4
Multinomial logit selection results (Men)

| | EARNINGS EQUATIONS | | | |
	T4=0	T4=1	T4=2	T4=3
ONE	-1.812	-1.051	-2.334	-0.960
	(-4.212)*	(-1.030)	(-5.924)	(-2.354)*
HSE	0.031	0.068	-0.013	-0.022
	(1.181)	(1.229)	(-0.556)	(-0.857)
FSIZE1	0.192	-0.089	-0.205	-0.134
	(-7.259)*	(-1.460)	(-8.429)*	(-5.083)*
FSIZE2	-0.116	-0.206	-0.096	-0.102
	(-3.838)*	(-3.549)*	(-3.845)*	(-3.680)*
MOBIL	0.103	0.063	0.061	0.103
	(4.215)*	(0.808)	(2.795)*	(3.314)*
MEOL	-0.003	0.091	-0.026	-0.036
	(-0.077)	(0.846)	(-0.802)	(-1.152)
EDUCAT	0.002	0.008	0.003	0.002
	(0.891)	(0.846)	(-0.802)	(-1.152)
TOTEMP	0.003	0.002	0.004	0.009
	(2.307)*	(0.750)	(3.699)*	(7.781)*
TUNEMP	0.007	-0.006	-0.002	0.009
	(2.031)*	(-1.055)	(-0.428)	(1.565)
VOCATQ	-0.223	-0.038	-0.015	-0.008
	(-0.719)	(-0.554)	(0.770)	(-0.399)
EMPLOYS	0.010	0.023	0.011	0.004
	(1.175)	(1.212)	(1.263)	(0.490)
MARD3	0.075	0.028	0.077	-0.009
	(0.892)	(0.233)	(1.110)	(-0.112)
LITR	-0.077	-0.005	-0.034	0.004
	(-1.882)	(0.062)	(-0.935)	(0.108)
NUM	-0.136	0.027	-0.016	-0.026
	(-1.983)	(0.299)	(-0.322)	(-0.475)
REGW	1.670	1.327	1.999	0.827
	(6.682)*	(1.942)	(8.519)*	(2.985)*
λ	-0.062	-0.166	-0.049	0.223
	(-0.996)	(-0.798)	(-0.325)	(2.448)*
R^2	0.222	0.220	0.227	0.190
N	597	113	772	720

* indicates significantly different from zero at 5%

Table 9.5
Multinomial logit selection results (Women)

	EARNINGS EQUATIONS					
	T6=0	T6=1	T6=2	T6=3	T6=4	T6=5
ONE	-2.444	-1.260	-1.890	-2.445	-3.095	-1.958
	(-8.038)*	(-1.182)	(-3.586)*	(-4.545)*	(-3.983)*	(-2.195)
HSE	0.035	0.093	0.013	0.019	-0.015	-0.061
	(1.877)	(1.931)	(0.381)	(0.825)	(-0.316)	(-1.238)
FSIZE1	-0.216	-0.165	-0.216	-0.190	-0.267	-0.231
	(-10.738)*	(-2.440)*	(-6.814)*	(-8.361)*	(-5.143)*	(-4.763)*
FSIZE2	-0.041	-0.159	-0.059	-0.545	-0.028	-0.148
	(-1.958)*	(-2.960)*	(-2.090)*	(-2.078)*	(-0.549)	(-2.418)*
MOBIL	0.738	0.010	-0.005	0.043	0.043	0.016
	(4.471)*	(0.186)	(-0.144)	(2.085)*	(1.006)	(0.291)
MEOL	0.012	-0.142	-0.030	-0.011	-0.013	0.081
	(0.520)	(-2.089)*	(-1/027)	(-0.384)	(-0.265)	(1.193)
EDUCAT	-0.000	0.011	0.000	0.001	0.005	-0.009
	(-0.085)	(2.322)*	(0.044)	(0.383)	(1.925)	(-1.358)
TOTEMP	0.004	0.003	0.006	0.006	0.003	0.018
	(3.470)*	(1.029)	(5.169)*	(4.363)*	(1.332)	(5.377)*
TUNEMP	-0.006	-0.009	-0.021	0.009	0.003	0.009
	(-2.056)*	(-1.624)	(-2.444)*	(1.461)	(0.208)	(0.549)
VOCATQ	0.017	-0.048	-0.021	-0.027	-0.021	-0.012
	(0.954)	(-0.913)	(-0.934)	(-1.296)	(-0563)	(-0.264)
EMPLOYS	0.008	0.008	0.310	0.008	-0.013	-0.011
	(1.210)	(0.532)	(2.349)*	(-0.804)	(-0.947)	(-0.517)
MARD3	0.017	0.123	-0.000	0.114	0.137	-0.108
	(0.552)	(1.538)	(-0.006)	(2.776)*	(1.800)	(-1.007)
LITR	-0.536	0.158	-0.054	-0.062	0.046	-0.028
	(-1.472)	(1.867)	(-1.039)	(-1.549)	(-0.611)	(0.338)
NUM	0.002	0.005	0.034	0=0.001	-0.028	-0.038
	(0.068)	(0.052)	(0.536)	(-0.028)	(-0.339)	(-0.364)
REGW	2.130	1.078	1.953	1.875	2.283	0.979
	(11.835)*	(1.543)	(7.848)*	(5.327)*	(5.405)*	(1.658)
λ	-0.203	0.071	-0.261	0.144	0.119	0.552
	(-3.766)*	(0.547)	(-2.036)*	(2.245)*	(0.836)	(2.693)*
R^2	0.293	0.294	0.384	0.229	0.349	0.438
N	1015	128	442	642	167	166

* indicates significantly different from zero at 5%

DATA APPENDIX

LW	logarithm of hourly earnings at Sweep 3

EDUCAT   Educational attainment. Total points score for examination results at end of fifth year at school. points are assigned to grades accoring to the following schedule:

Qualification	Grade	Points
CSE	1	3
	2	2
	3	1
GCE O-level	A	5
	B	4
	C	3
	D	2
	E	1
16+	A	5
	B	4
	C	3
	D	2
	E	1
	1	5
	2	4
	3	3
	4	2
	5	1
All other grades	0	

TENR	job tenure in months
BS	number of siblings
TOTEMP	total number of months in full time employment, Sept 1986 - Feb 1989
TUNEMP	total number of months in unemployment, Sept 1986 - Feb 1989

ALEDUCAT   Post-16 education. Total points score for all sixth form examinations taken before Sweep 3

Qualification	Grade	Points
GCE A-Level	A	5
or AS-Level	B	4
	C	3
	D	2
	E	1
GCE S-Level	Distinction	7
	Pass/Merit	6
All other grades	0	

OLEDUCAT   Post-16 education. Total points score for all other academic qualifications taken after fifth form.

Qualification	Grade	Points
CSE	1	3
	2	2
	3	1
GCE O-Level	A	5
or O/A or A/O	B	4
	C	3
	D	2
	E	1
GCSE	A	5
or CEE	B	4
	C	3
	D	2
	E	1
	1	5
	2	4
	3	3
	4	2
	5	1
16+	1	5
	2	4
	3	3
	4	2
	5	1
	A	5
	B	4
	C	3
All other grades	0	

EMPLOYS   number of employers to Sweep 3

BLOCK   1 if on block release in Sweep 1
2 if on block release in Sweep 2
3 if on block release in both Sweep 1 and Sweep 2

Dummy variables. Alternative value is zero.

LAH	1 if living at home with both parents at Sweep 1
OP	1 if living at home with one parent at Sweep 1
FS	1 if father in a job at Sweep 1
MS	1 if mother in a job at Sweep 1
DISAB	1 if has disability or handicap
HSE	1 if current residence owner-occupied (Sweep 1)
YTS	1 if ever on YTS or other government training scheme
UNEMP	1 if every unemployed
OJT	1 if does, or did, get any on-the-job training (Sweep 3)
OFJT	1 if attends, or has attended a course at a college, or tainingcentre as part ofjob (Sweep 3)
FSIZE1	1 if works at place with 1 to 9 workers (Sweep 3)
FSIZE2	1 if works at place with 10 to 24 workers (Sweep 3)
MOBIL	1 if has access to motorised transport (Sweep 3)
APRNT	1 if doing a recognised apprenticeship (Sweep 3)
PDEG	1 if either parent has a degree
ENGOL	1 if holds GCE O-Level in English or equivalent
MATHOL	1 if holds GCE O-Level in Mathematics or equivalent
POJT	1 if on-the-job training received before Sweep 3
POFJT	1 if training at a college or training centre received as part of job before Sweep 3
PAPPRNT	1 if on a recognised apprenticeship before Sweep 3
VOCATQ	1 if vocational qualification obtained
MARD3	1 if married at Sweep 3
SCHOOL	1 if attended independent school
LITR	1 if difficulty reading or writing
NUM	1 if difficulty with number work
SOCi	1 if SOC90 equals i
SICi	1 if SIC equals i
Ri	1 if region equals i
TRG41	1 if YTS only (Sweep 3)
TRG42	1 if receiving off-the-job training (Sweep 3)
TRG43	1 if apprentice (Sweep 3)
TRG61	1 if YTS only (Sweep 3)
TRG62	1 if receiving off-the-job training (not YTS) (Sweep 3)

TRG63	1 if receiving off-the-job training (YTS) (Sweep 3)
TRG64	1 if apprentice (notYTS) (Sweep 3)
TRG65	1 if apprentice (YTS) (Sweep 3)
OJTYTS	1 if received on-the-job training during YTS

References

Dolton, P.J. and Makepeace, G.H. (1991), 'The early careers of 1980 graduates. Work histories, occupational choice and job tenure', Department of Employment *Research Paper*.

Dolton, P.J., Makepeace, G.H. and van der Klaauw, W. (1989), 'Occupational choice and earnings determination: The role of sample selection and non-pecuniary factors', *Oxford Economic Papers*, pp. 573-594

Hashimoto, M. (1981), 'Firm-specific human capital as a shared investment', *American Economic Review*, 71, pp. 475-82.

Lee, L.F. (1983), 'Generalized econometric models with selectivity', *Econometrica*, pp. 507-512

Lynch, L.M. (1990), 'Private sector training and the earnings of young workers', NBER, mimeo.

Maddala, G.S. (1983), *Limited Dependent- and Qualitative Variables in Econometrics*, CUP.

Main, B. and M. Shelly (1990), 'The effectiveness of the YTS as a manpower policy', *Economica*, 57, pp. 495-514.

Sime, N., Pattie, C. and Gray, J. (1990), 'England and Wales youth cohort study. What now? - The transition from school to the labour market amongst 16-19 year olds', Training Agency Research and Development No. 62 - *Youth Cohort Series* No. 14.

Whitfield, K. and C. Bourlakis (1991), 'An Empirical Analysis of YTS, Employment and Earnings', *Journal of Economic Studies*, 18, pp. 42-56.

10   Looking into the black box: Using experimental data to find out how training works

John Ham and Robert J. LaLonde

Introduction

During the last two decades in the United States, program evaluations that employ experimental designs have become increasingly common. Many of these evaluations have examined the impact of government sponsored employment and training programs on economically disadvantaged persons or on redundant workers. These experimental evaluations have substantially increased policymakers' and researchers' understanding of the extent to which training successfully raises earnings and employment rates and reduces participation in public assistance programs.

One of the most appealing features of these experimental evaluations is their comparative simplicity. For example, we may obtain unbiased estimates of training's impact on earnings by comparing the trainees' and controls' mean earnings. But the success of such evaluations has not eliminated or reduced policymakers' and researchers' dependence on more complicated nonexperimental evaluations. One reason for our continued reliance on nonexperimental methods is that many training schemes can not be feasibly evaluated with an experimental design. Another reason is that even in experimental settings, we require those methods in order to address many important questions about the impact of training.

In this paper we show that even in experimental settings, we must often rely on nonexperimental methods when we turn from examining whether training works to how it works. Accordingly, even when we randomly assign eligible participants to a training or control group, in order to address questions such as the effect of training on wages or on employment durations, we must rely on the same nonexperimental methods used to evaluate large public sector programs in the United States. Our reliance on such methods does not reflect a shortcoming of the experimental designs. Indeed, we show that without such designs, it is much more difficult to address these questions.

When public sector training works

Nearly three decades of experience indicate that the economic benefits of government sponsored employment and training programs exceed their costs when they are targeted toward either economically disadvantaged adult women or older redundant workers. Among these groups who have benefited from training, economically disadvantaged adult women have benefited from both expensive on-the-job and work experience programs and from inexpensive job search assistance programs. Redundant workers have benefited primarily from job search assistance programs and have gained little from the more expensive programs. In contrast, training programs' benefits are usually too small to outweigh the costs for economically disadvantaged adult males and youths. Some studies even suggest that for these participants public sector programs lead to reduced earnings and employment rates.

Accordingly, for economically disadvantaged adult women and redundant workers, it is appropriate to ask how these government sponsored programs achieved their earnings gains. One possibility is that when trainees found jobs they earned higher wages than they would have otherwise. A second possibility is that training may have helped unemployed trainees find jobs sooner than they would have otherwise. A third, but related, possibility is that when trainees found jobs they held onto their jobs longer.

The foregoing list of reasons for why training raised earnings is by no means exhaustive. Our purpose for listing them is that they generally must be addressed using nonexperimental methods even when the data are generated by an experimental design. In the remainder of the paper we provide a nontechnical explanation for the problems that arise when addressing these questions with experimental data. We also show that an analysis of these issues is much more difficult in nonexperimental settings.

Effects of training on wages

Among the foregoing questions, the most straightforward to address is the effect of training on wage rates. Interest in this questions stems from the human capital literature which suggests that if training raises individuals' skills, their wages should rise to reflect their increased productivity. In a standard experimental evaluation, the difference between trainees' and controls' mean wages yields an unbiased estimate of the training effect. In practice, however, that estimate is biased because training influences both wage levels and employment rates. If training raises employment rates, we observe some trainees with jobs who would not be employed if they were a control group member. In other words, we do not observe wage rates for the same types of individuals in both experimental groups. As a consequence, the observed and unobserved characteristics of the employed trainees differ from those of the employed controls.

To see how these differences in characteristics arise, consider an experimental evaluation of individuals who have only two characteristics: their training status and whether or not they are high school dropouts. Further, we assume that dropouts have lower earnings and wages than high school graduates. If training raises the likelihood that trainees find jobs, a larger fraction of trainees who are high school dropouts will find jobs than similarly educated controls. As a result there will be more high school dropouts among the employed trainees than among the employed controls. Since, the employed trainees are less educated, the difference between their mean wages and those of the controls' underestimates the effect of training on wages. This bias arises because workers' training status is correlated with individuals' dropout status. That correlation violates the underlying premise behind experimental evaluations: that individuals' training status is independent of their other characteristics.

Because a person's training status is likely to be correlated with their characteristics, an analysis of training on wages should explicitly account for this correlation. In the example above, we should compare the treatments' and controls' regression adjusted wages, in which we explicitly control for whether a person is a high school dropout. More generally, an analysis of training's effect on wages requires a formal statistical model like those used in the nonexperimental literature that simultaneously accounts for how individuals characteristics determine wage levels and the probability that they are employed.

When we turn to a nonexperimental setting, the question of how training affects wage rates becomes more complex. In such a setting, we must compare the trainees' wages to the wages of individuals in a comparison group. That comparison group is made up of individuals who did not participate in training. That distinction creates an additional problem, because the characteristics that make a person likely to participate in training are also likely to be associated with their wage levels. Thus differences in trainees' and comparisons' wages may reflect not only the likelihood of being employed but also the likelihood of participating in training. For example, we may find that the trainees' wages are systematically lower than those of the comparisons not because training is counterproductive, but because persons with low wages are likely to participate in training. Thus, besides accounting for differences in trainees and comparisons characteristics, and the probability that they are employed, in a nonexperimental setting, we also must account for the selection process into training. In an experimental setting, we may avoid this latter problem because the programs' administrators used random assignment to determine training participation.

The effect of training on durations

Prior program evaluations suggest that the earnings gains from training result largely from higher employment rates rather than higher wages. Since training raises employment rates, the next question to ask is whether training helped their participants hold on to their jobs longer or leave unemployment sooner than they would have otherwise. There are several reasons why this particular question might interest policymakers or researchers. First, if we find that one training scheme worked because it reduced unemployment durations, while another scheme worked because it raised employment durations, we could achieve additional gains by combining the two programs. Second, suppose two programs raise short-term employment rates, but one works by raising employment durations, while the other works by lowering unemployment durations. We would probably prefer to fund the program that raises employment durations, because longer employment spells are more likely to lead to the accumulation of human capital and higher wages in the future. Third, in short sampling frames, which are common in program evaluations, we can use this information about training's effects on durations to predict the likely long-term impact of training. In particular we may estimate the long-run employment rate from the expected durations of employment and unemployment spells.

Unfortunately, in a nonexperimental setting, it is extremely difficult to address these issues. In that setting, we must compare the durations of trainees' employment (or unemployment) spells to the corresponding durations of a comparison group. That comparison group is made up of individuals who did not participate in training. The problem that arises when constructing a comparison group is that those comparisons' characteristics ■ many of which we do not observe ■ are related to their decision to volunteer and to be admitted into training. Thus, differences between trainees' and comparisons' durations may reflect either differences in their training status or differences in their observed characteristics. Attempts to disentangle those effects have not been very successful.

When we turn to an experimental design, the foregoing sample selection problem is eliminated. If eligible program volunteers are randomly assigned into a treatment or control group, the two experimental groups' average characteristics should be the same. Yet as with the evaluation of wages, several problems remain, because in general, the difference between the trainees' or controls' durations or transition rates out of employment or unemployment spells yield biased estimates of the effect of training.

The biases associated with treatments' and controls' durations arise from two common features of job training programs and their evaluations. First, job training takes time. It is common for on-the-job training or subsidized work experience to last for one year. While the trainees are in training, the controls remain in the labor market. Second, budget limitations usually require limitations on the sampling frame, so that trainees and controls are followed only for a short period before and after training. Indeed one reason for studying how training affects durations is that we can potentially learn something from the short sampling frame about the likely long-term effect of training.

As a result of the foregoing features of job training programs, several problems arise when comparing treatments' and controls' durations or transition rates in experimental settings. First, the timing of treatments' and controls' spells differ because we observe spells for the controls while the treatments are still in training. Consequently, at the very least we need to account for differences in demand conditions facing the two experimental groups. Second, even when a person's training status is independent of her other characteristics, the difference between the treatments' and controls' transition rates out of either employment and unemployment are biased estimates of the effect of training. Thus, in addition to demand conditions, we need to account for differences in individual characteristics such as their age, schooling, race, and marital status. These two problems may be addressed using standard statistical models in the event history literature.

The next two problems are more difficult to address with standard duration models. The first of these more difficult issues reflects the eligibility criteria required for admission into a training program. Eligible program volunteers often must be unemployed and to have had poor labor market histories. When eligible program volunteers are randomly assigned into either a treatment or a control group, the treatments' current unemployment spell ends as they are placed into training. Their subsequent employment and unemployment spells are all new spells. In contrast, the controls' unemployment spells continues until they find a job. If as is likely, the transition rate out of a spell depends the current length of that spell, comparisons between the trainees' new spells and the controls continuing spells overestimate the impact of training. If we were to observe those same controls in a new spell rather than a continuing spell, they would find that they leave unemployment more quickly when in the new spell.

The second difficult issue arises when we try to address the first issue using standard empirical practice. This practice consists of discarding the continuing spells and using only new spells in the analysis. But when studying economically disadvantaged persons that procedure creates a sample selection problem. Many of the controls will never find a job during the relatively short sampling frame. As a result, we never observe them leaving their continuing unemployment spell. Because controls who find jobs are likely to have better labor market skills than the controls who remain jobless, they are also likely to leave unemployment faster than the rate we would observe for the full sample of controls. Therefore comparisons between the durations of trainees' spells and controls' new spells underestimates the effect of training on durations.

In addition to the problems associated with the controls' spells, similar problems arise with the treatments' training spells. Treatments leave training when their program terms expire or they may leave early to become employed or to become unemployed. In a short sampling frame we may never observe some trainees in an employment spell or others in an unemployment spell. In particular, we may never observe an unemployment spell for some trainees who move directly from training into a regular job. Because those trainees are likely to have above-average labor market skills, the skills of the trainees with unemployment spells is likely to be below that of the typical trainee. That difference may be another source of bias when comparing the durations of trainees' and controls' employment and unemployment spells. In order to address these problems surrounding the controls' continuing spells and the treatments' training spells we must develop a statistical model that accounts for these biases.

To examine the importance of these issues and to find out in practice how training raises employment rates, Ham and LaLonde (1991) reevaluated the National Supported Work (NSW) Demonstration. This employment and training demonstration was among the first to use an experimental design. The NSW program provided subsidized work experience in clerical and services occupations to economically disadvantaged adult women. The eligible participants had long histories on public assistance and had poor employment histories. Their average age was 33 years and nearly 75 percent were high school dropouts. The experimental evaluation indicated that 13 months after the typical treatment had left the program, the trainees' employment rate was 9 percentage points higher than the controls' employment rate.

In light of this evidence that training had been effective, Ham and LaLonde examined whether those higher employment rates resulted from longer employment spells or shorter unemployment spells. As shown in Table 10.1, when they followed standard empirical practice and used only new spells, they found the treatments had both longer employment and unemployment spells. As indicated in the first two columns of the table, among those that had found employment, 64 percent of the trainees as opposed to 56 percent of the controls were still employed after 6 months. But surprisingly, as indicated in the last two columns of the table, among those who were unemployed, 72 percent of the trainees compared with 62 percent of the controls remained unemployed after 6 months. Further analysis using standard statistical practices indicated that training appeared to increase employment durations by 11 months, but to increase unemployment durations by nearly 40 months.

Table 10.1
Empirical survivor functions for new spells
of employment and unemployment.
[percentage remaining employed or unemployed]

Months since Spell Began Treatments	Employment Treatments	Controls	Unemployment Treatments	Controls
1	91%	85%	89%	89%
3	76%	69%	81%	75%
6	64%	56%	72%	62%

Source: See Ham and LaLonde (1990), Table 3.

As a result of the foregoing findings, Ham and LaLonde (1991) concluded that the estimated effect of training potentially reflected the biases associated with using only new spells in their analysis and with excluding the controls' continuing spells and the treatments' training spells, Indeed, when they accounted for those spells, the effect of training on unemployment durations was close to zero, while the training effect on employment durations was unchanged. Consequently, they concluded that the NSW program raised employment rates because it increased employment durations. The program did not help trainees leave unemployment sooner than they would have otherwise.

Conclusion

This paper makes two basic points. First, many interesting questions concerning the effect of training on earnings or employment rates cannot be answered using simple estimators even in the presence of experimental data. Second, the first point does not imply that experimental data are unnecessary, because addressing these issues in a nonexperimental setting raises a whole host of new problems in addition to those that arise with experimental data. For example, when we analyze the effect of training on employment and unemployment durations with experimental data, we know that the only difference between the treatments and the controls is how they entered new employment and unemployment spells. With nonexperimental data, a researcher must also model the process by which individuals enter training as well as deal with the selection process into new spells.

References

Ashenfelter, O. (1978), 'Estimating the effect of training programs on earnings', *Review of Economics and Statistics*, 60, pp. 47-57.

Ashenfelter, O. and Card, D. (1985), 'Using the longitudinal structure of earnings to estimate the effect of training programs', *Review of Economics and Statistics*, 67, pp. 648-60.

Barnow, B. (1987), 'The impact of CETA programs on earnings: A review of the literature', *Journal of Human Resources* 22, pp. 157-93.

Björklund, A. 'Evaluations of labor market policy in Sweden', this volume.

Björklund, A. (1988), 'What experiments Are needed for manpower policy?', *Journal of Human Resources*, 23, pp. 267-77.

Gritz, M. (1989), 'The impact of training on the frequency and duration of employment. University of Washington.

Ham, J. and LaLonde, R. (1990), 'Using social experiments to estimate the effect of training on transition rates', In *Panel Data and Labor Market Studies*, ed. J. Hartog, J. Theeuwes, and G. Ridder. Amsterdam: North Holland.

Ham, J. and LaLonde, R. (1991), Estimating the effect of training on the duration of employment and unemployment spells, evidence from experimental data, University of Chicago, mimeo.

Heckman, J. (1991), 'Randomization and social policy evaluation', National Bureau of Economic Research, *Technical Working Paper* No. 107.

Heckman, J. (1979), 'Sample selection bias as a specification error', *Econometrica*, 47, pp. 153-61.

Heckman, J, and Flinn, C. (1982), 'Models for the analysis of labor force dynamics', in *Advances in Econometrics*, 1, JAI Press, pp. 35-95.

Heckman, J. and Robb, R. (1985), 'Alternative methods for evaluating the impact of interventions', in J. Heckman and B. Singer (eds.), *Longitudinal Analysis of Labor Market Data*, Cambridge University Press.

Heckman, James J. and Singer, B. (1984a), 'Econometric duration analysis', *Journal of Econometrics*, 24, pp. 63-132.

Hollister, R G., Kemper, P. and Maynard, R. eds. (1984), *The National Supported Work Demonstration*. Madison: University of Wisconsin Press.

Keifer, N. (1979), 'Population heterogeneity and inference from panel data on the effects of vocational training', *Journal of Political Economy*, 87, pp. S213-126.

Lancaster, T. (1990), *The Econometric Analysis of Transition Data*, Cambridge: Cambridge University Press.

Lancaster, T. and Nickell, S. (1980), 'The analysis of re-employment probabilities for the unemployed', *Journal of the Royal Statistical Society* 143, Series A, 143, pp. 141-165.

Leigh, D. (1990), 'Does training work for displaced workers: A survey of existing evidence', W.E. Upjohn Institute for Employment Research, Kalamazoo, MI.

Maynard, R. (1991), 'Evaluating employment and training programs: Lessons from the U.S. experience', Princeton, NJ: Mathematica Policy Research, Inc.

241

11 The determinants of training of male and female employees, and some measures of discrimination

Francis Green

Introduction

For some time now, the reform and expansion of training and education in Britain has been placed high on the political agenda. This imperative derives from the recognition that training and education levels are relatively low overall in the British workforce, particularly among 16 to 18 year olds, and the realisation that this is a probable contributory factor to Britain's poor long-term economic performance. There is, accordingly, increasing interest in knowing who gains access to training and education, and in estimating how much is their and society's economic reward. Where large amounts of public funding are at stake, it is more than useful to know where it should best be spent.

We have at hand, in human capital theory, a ready-made model of who is likely to demand and to be provided with training. This model suggests that training decisions are like other investments: they respond to economic incentives. Training would thus be expanded up until the point where the net present value of training projects is zero. Hence it is predicted that, ceteris paribus, training is more likely to occur a) where an individual is young (since this gives a greater expected post-training period of working life); b) where the individual already has good educational qualifications (this may be interpreted plausibly as raising 'trainability' or, alternatively, as lowering the 'psychic' costs of training); c) in expanding industries or industries with greater technological change; d) where the individual is regarded, rightly or wrongly, as more committed to paid labour (bereft, for example, of family caring responsibilities); e) in larger firms, where the company can both reap economies of scale in training provision and be more certain of retaining the trainee; f) in occupations where the labour process is more subject to change, mainly higher-level occupations; g) in the public sector, since private profit-maiximising firms are more likely than public employers to be inhibited by the fear of poaching; h) for individuals who have been recently recruited to a new job.

Earlier empirical studies have thrown some light on some of these matters (see Table 11.1). There is, to start with, a consensus that training decreases, ceteris paribus, with age. Other predictions of the human capital model also receive support, with the exception that the independent effect of industry shows little consistency in its pattern. While the Construction Industry tends to have a negative impact on training, only one study (this of the unemployed) claimed to find a pattern predicted by the human capital theory model.

There can be little pretence, however, that training decisions are taken solely, as human capital theory suggests, on the basis of a rational individualistic calculus. For example, that the bulk of training activity is concentrated in the first years of working life is an institutional feature with historical origins in the apprenticeship system and in traditional sluggish attitudes to re-training for older workers, rather than an implicit or explicit cost-benefit calculation. Another institutional factor of considerable importance, given the changing composition of the workforce, is the differential stance taken by and towards men and women as regards training. The presence of sex discrimination, thought to be especially irrational in these days of growing female employment, has already been explicitly or implicitly detected to some degree in some previous studies. As a third example, it is widely thought that British companies under-invest in training activities due to underestimating their value (Ashton, Green and Hoskins, 1989), which may be why considerable governmental effort has gone into highlighting the benefits of training through the conferring by the Training Agency of awards for good practice.

The main aim of the present chapter is to investigate the determinants of 'job-related' training, using a new source of training data, the 1987 General Household Survey, paying particular attention to the different exposures of men and women to training and to developing quantitative measures of employer discrimination. This survey is nationally representative, and identifies any 'education, training or self-instruction that would help with (your job or) a job that you might do in the future' that happened in the four weeks prior to interview. The survey also has the advantage of including motivational data that helps to distinguish between specific and general training. The survey includes, too, comprehensive information about participation in educational programmes. There is a blurred boundary between activities normally regarded as 'education' and those seen as 'training' so it is useful to set the participation figures alongside each other. A subsidiary objective, therefore, is to present a picture which dovetails the stylised facts of training with those of education.

Training and education

In the 1987 General Household Survey, each individual is classified as either at school, or at some other form of education (stretching from college-based YTS courses to university students) termed for these purposes 'other education', or in training at some stage in the previous four weeks, or as doing none of these. Two-thirds of people aged 16-59 acquiring human capital are doing so through training, by virtue evidently of the fact that most are in the labour force. 'Other education' is important only for the economically inactive. The most notable aspect of the data is that the proportions of males exceeds that of females in each category, though schooling is broadly equal. The disparity between males and females in human capital acquisition shows up for every age group. The only areas in which female participation exceeds that of males are amongst 16-18 year olds at college (reflecting the preponderance of females in FE colleges), and amongst 19-24 year olds in nursing or related medical fields, evidently a consequence of sex segregation.

It is also striking how low is the overall participation in human capital acquisition, most alarmingly for 16-18 year old females amongst whom almost one in two are not gaining any form of education or training. This picture confirms the widely held disturbing perception of a low qualified and poorly skilled young British workforce.

The data for 'training only' also indicates a preponderance of males over females participation for every age group. However, among those under 25 females have a wider exposure to training that is exclusively 'off-the-job'; where males do consistently better is in training that

Table 11.1
British studies of the determinants of training

	Hypothesis	Studies Confirming It
(a)	Training decreases with age	For males or for both sexes together: all For females: (1) and (4) confirm; (3) and (5) show insignificant effect.
(b)	Higher-level qualifications raise training probability	(1), (2), (4), (5) and (6).
(c)	Growing or changing technology industries raise training	(6). Others show no consistent pattern
(d)	Caring for children reduces training probability	(1), (4), (5). (3) shows no effect
(e)	Larger establishments do more training	(2), (3), (4) and (5)
(f)	Higher-level occupations require more retraining	(1), (2) and (5)
(g)	Training is greater in the public sector	(4)
(h)	Recent recruits to new jobs need training	(2) and (5)
(i)	Sex discrimination over training access	(1), (3), (4) and (5)

	Studies	Data Set
(1)	Greenhalgh and Stewart (1987)	National Training Survey (1975)
(2)	Rigg (1989)	Training in Britain, Survey of Individuals, Summer (1987)
(3)	Booth (1990)	Survey of Graduates and Diplomats (1980)
(4)	Booth (1991)	British Social Attitudes Survey (1987)
(5)	Green (1991a)	Labour Force Survey (1984)
(6)	Allen, McCormick and O'Brien (1991)	Sample of unemployed in Sunderland (1986)

involves 'on-the-job' skill acquisition. The male/female imbalance is reinforced by the length of the training episodes reported by trainees.

The survey also contains information about the form and funding of training and its motivation. The most widely used form of training is 'following a course of instruction or teaching one's self'. Female trainees are less likely than males to be doing this, or using audio-visual aids, but more likely to be involved in formal classroom teaching or working in small informal groups. These differences, however, are not substantial. More than three-fifths of males' training took place in normal working hours compared to less than half for females. It is also of some note that 42 per cent of females had to find fee contributions from their friends or relatives or themselves, compared to 37 per cent of males. While this disparity is not great, it reinforces the observation of Clarke (1991) that an aspect of the overall social discrimination between young women and men is that the latter's training costs are on average lower: the typically male 17 year old apprentice receives wages while the female 17 year old college student tends to receive neither grant nor wages. The General Household survey data on income confirm this observation. While 16-18 year old females gained but a few educational grants, the males were more likely to receive YTS allowances or wages. The males' gross weekly income averaged £52, compared to £36 for females[1]. In about three-quarters of cases, training was entered into voluntarily, in the sense that participation was neither compulsory nor undergone simply because 'it was expected'. The most widely quoted reason for wanting to do training was for the satisfaction it provided or for general interest: as many as four in five females gave this reason, and 70 per cent of males. More telling, though, is that many more males than females saw training as a route to increased earnings or promotion. Finally, it is possible to infer approximately from observations on trainee motivation whether the training is of the job-specific or transferable (general) kind. Where the motive is not specially concerned with the trainee's present job, we may judge the training to be more likely to be at least partly general. In the case of compulsory training, this would seem more likely to be regarded by employers as in effect specific for, as theory suggests, employers are unlikely to require and fund employees to undertake training unless they are fairly sure of keeping them. On the basis of this admittedly approximate method of classification, about 52 per cent of trainees were found to be involved in training that is to some extent transferable.

The determinants of employee training

In this section multivariate analyis of the extent and form of training is developed. Attention is concentrated on employees, which is by far the largest group of workers[2].

It should first be emphasised that the observation that an employee is being trained is the joint outcome of two decisions, those of employer and employee. It is possible for either party to be frustrated. Some 43 per cent of individuals from the Training in Britain survey recalled occasions when they wanted to but were unable to get some training. Not all of these would have been employees, but the figure suggests a considerable unmet training demand. Conversely, the General Household Survey data shows a quarter of individuals doing training that was a compulsory part of a job: presumably some of these individuals might have preferred not to train. Employers may also, at times, have difficulty in finding employees for training, as for example when YTS schemes became more difficult to fill in the South during the 1988/9 boom years. Since we cannot separately analyse employer and employee demands for training in individual cross-section data, the ensuing models must be regarded as reduced form equations.

In order to focus also on the different training determinants for males and females separate analyses were performed for each sex. 'Market discrimination' is defined as occurring when male and female employees, having identical personal characteristics, have an unequal chance of receiving training. This, of course, is only a limited measure of the extent to which the societal opportunities for males and females to acquire skills are differently circumscribed. It excludes forms of 'pre-market discrimination' and, by concentrating on the extent of training, sets aside the widely recognised problem that much existing training reinforces the existing segregation of labour into male and female jobs, thereby reproducing pay differentials[3]. The definition also cannot be taken unequivocally to mean 'involuntary' discrimination, in the sense that women who apply for training are more likely than men to be denied it by discriminatory employers. It may well be the case that the attitudes

247

of men and women towards training differ, as a result of pre-market experiences. Yet this distinction between voluntary and involuntary is not ultimately helpful, because the attitudes and choices of people are liable to be affected by the opportunities they perceive. If women see less opportunity for training and career advancement, they will be less likely than men to apply to their employers for training.

Finally, the definition makes no reference to the motivation for employers' discrimination, whether it be sheer prejudice, or whether it be related to a possibly rational fear that women are more likely than men to quit their jobs than men. Such 'statistical discrimination' may or may not be a profit-maximising strategy. To the extent, therefore, that discrimination is revealed, the conclusion points to the gains to be had from a policy of state intervention to internalise the externality associated with high turnover of female labour, and from better enforcement of anti-discriminatory legislation.

The determinants of participation in training

Let $Y*$ be the net unobserved present value of training, to be shared by employee and employer. Assuming an efficient bargain is struck, training will take place if $Y*$ is positive. Hence our model is:

$$Y*^F = a^F X^F + u^F \tag{1}$$
$$Y*^M = a^M X^M + u^M \tag{2}$$
$$Y^k = 1 \quad \text{iff} \quad Y*^k > 0 \qquad)$$
$$\qquad\qquad\qquad\qquad\qquad) \text{ for } k = M, F$$
$$Y^k = 0 \quad \text{iff} \quad Y*^k \leq 0 \qquad)$$

where Y is a dummy variable indicating training participation, X a vector of firm and individual characteristics, u the error term, and superscripts M and F refer to males and females respectively. I assume the error terms have a logistic distribution, and hence (1) and (2) may be estimated by a standard logit procedure.

Separate estimation for the male and female samples allows the impact of independent variables to differ from males to females, but it also means there is no single measure of discrimination. Four possible measures may be obtained. Let $P(X^k, \alpha^j)$ (where k, j = M or F) be the predicted probability of training for an individual with characteristics X^k. The first definition considers an individual with average female characteristics $\overline{X}^F$, and contrasts the probabilities of training using female and male coefficients:

$$D_{F1} = P(\overline{X}^F, \alpha^M)/P(\overline{X}^F, \alpha^F) - 1$$

Inserting the logistic distribution, this gives:

$$D_{F1} = (e^{-\alpha^F \overline{X}^M} + 1)/(e^{-\alpha^M \overline{X}^F} + 1) - 1 \qquad (3)$$

Alternatively, we may calculate the mean probability of training obtained by applying the male coefficients to the female sample, and compare this to the mean probability of training by applying the female coefficients to the female sample:

$$D_{F2} = P(\overline{X}^F, \alpha^M)/P(\overline{X}^F, \alpha^F) - 1 \qquad (4)$$

By virtue of the maximum likelihood first order conditions[4], the denominator of the first term is simply the sample frequency for females training (this assumes X includes an intercept term). Owing to the non-linearity of the logistic function, in general $D_{F1} \neq D_{F2}$.

We may, of course, equally choose the male sample as the base for comparisons and ask what happens if their training is determined according to the female coefficients. This produces two more discrimination measures:

$$D_{M1} = 1 - (e^{-\alpha^F \overline{X}^M} + 1)/(e^{-\alpha^M \overline{X}^M} + 1) \qquad (5)$$

and

$$D_{M2} = 1 - \{P(\overline{X}^M, \alpha^F)/(P(\overline{X}^M, \alpha^M)\} \qquad (6)$$

That $D_{M1} = D_{F1}$, $D_{M2} = D_{F2}$ is the familiar index number problem.

Unfortunately, none of these measures lend themselves to an interpretation analogous to the Oaxaca method of separating pay differentials into a component due to discrimination and a component due to differences in characteristics (Oaxaca, 1973). To see this, we may write the difference in actual training participation rates of males and females as:

$$P(\overline{X}M, \alpha M) - P(\overline{X}F, \alpha F) = [P(\overline{X}M, \alpha M) - (P(\overline{X}M, \alpha F)] + [P(\overline{X}M, \alpha F) -$$

$$P(\overline{X}F, \alpha F)] \tag{7}$$

While the first term in square brackets relates to definition DM2, the second term cannot be expressed in terms of the differences between male and female characteristics, again due to the non-linear nature of the logistic function. An additional reason is that the second term could just as likely be negative as positive, there being no reason to expect male characteristics necessarily to favour higher training - in which case discrimination could 'account for' more than 100 per cent of the difference in training.

The results of the maximum likelihood estimates of equations (1) and (2) from samples of all male and female employees aged 16 to 59 reveal some notable differences between the processes determining male and female training participation.

There are different age profiles, in that for males the probability of training declines with age till a minimum at 68 (beyond the sample span), while for females there is but a gentle and statistically insignificant decline with age. This finding is consistent with Green (1991) based on the 1984 Labour Force Survey, which concluded that discrimination occurred but mainly for younger age groups. There are also differences in the impact of previous qualifications and of occupation: being in a higher level occupation and having higher qualifications raises the chances of training, as previous work has found, but the effects are notably more pronounced for females. There is, also, a large and significant negative impact for females of being part-time.

There is also, as expected from theory, an impact from size of establishment: ceteris paribus, smaller establishments are likely to find unit training costs higher and to be less sure of reaping the benefits of training. Training also tends to decrease with job tenure, more sharply so in the case of females. The explanation for this is that training is more likely for those relatively new to a job. Training may be particularly important for women returning to jobs after spending time out of the labour force. As expected, too, family caring responsibilities tended to decrease the likelihood of training, significantly for women. Among the included industry dummies, only 'Energy and Water Supplies' and 'Other Services' showed a significant (positive) effect on training compared to the Construction Industry, and this only for males: there is, therefore, little support for the thesis that training is especially important in certain faster-growing industries, but it should be added that the data were only disaggregated at the level of division. There was also no significant effect of being in the public sector, contrary to Booth (1990b). Finally, hourly pay was included, principally for comparison with earlier work which found that higher pay raised the probability of training (Rigg, 1989). There is no a priori reason for entering this variable, since what is relevant for the individual is the future pay deriving from current training. Current pay has no clear relation to future pay, nor to current training costs. In the event the coefficient is small and insignificant, which suggests that Rigg's conclusion derives from the omission of key variables from his analysis (of which the full-time/part-time dummy seems an obvious candidate).

These results indicate a considerable degree of discrimination[5]. For example, they suggest that the females in the sample would have had 26.4 per cent greater training participation if they had all been treated as or acted as males; the average female would have had been 45 per cent more likely to participate in training if she had been treated like a male. As to which measure is the 'correct' one there is no single answer: it depends, of course, on the question asked.

The measure appears to be heavily dependent on whether a female or male base is used. The chief reason is that males and females differ considerably in the proportions working part-time (three percent compared to 44 per cent) and this variable has a substantial negative impact for females, while not for males. This suggests that, taking only full-timers, the extent of discrimination will be lower. To investigate this, further estimates were obtained that compared males with full-time females. Two resulting discrimination coefficients were obtained; giving D_{F1} = 14.7 per cent and D_{M1} = 13.3 per cent. These being close to the estimate for the whole sample based on the male data as base, it is confirmed that the higher discrimination coefficients calculated from the whole female data base derive from the substantial impact of the 44 per cent part-time females being treated like part-time males[6].

Before concluding the discussion of this model, a caveat needs briefly to be mentioned. Where coefficients are estimated for special samples, there is often a possibility of sample selectivity which can bias coefficient estimates. It is perhaps plausible that attitudes towards and aptitude for training could affect individuals' decisions to seek employment, or of firms to employ them. This effect may be different for males and females. By restricting the above analyses to samples of employees, there may be an unobserved missing variable causing $E(u_F) = 0$. Taking, first, older women, it is possible that their employment, and hence inclusion in the sample, would be promoted by any unobserved positive attitudes towards training or by employers' perceptions of their 'trainability'. To this extent the measure of discrimination is likely to be understated, since the above argument is far less likely to affect males, and so the conclusion earlier, that discrimination against older women is reduced or removed, must be qualified. On the other hand, for young people aged 16 to 18 there is a major choice to be made between schooling and college education and employment. For this group, participation in employment could reflect a negative attitude to the acquisition of human capital. This may differ for males and females, and it is possible that those young women in employment may have greater unobserved negative attitudes towards training: if so, the measure of discrimination would be an overstatement.

This argument suggests that the analysis might be improved by incorporating a sample selection correction procedure, which estimates the training probabilities conditioned on individuals' employment. There are, however, two difficulties with such a course of action, one practical the other theoretical. First, the employment decision would need to be modelled in a sophisticated manner, taking into account the various alternative states which include unemployment, full-time education and other forms of being 'economically inactive'; the determinants of which state the individual rests in, will vary with age. But second, it is doubtful whether such a modelling procedure would improve further the reliability of the interpretation we may place upon the estimates of discrimination, because the employment decision itself may be subject to the very discriminatory process herein examined. Discrimination against females for jobs with training associated amounts also, of course, to discrimination over the training.

The determinants of on-the-job and off-the-job training
While the previous analysis has examined all training for employees, it is of some interest to split the experience of training according to whether it involved at least some on-the-job training ('learning by practice and

example while actually doing the job') or whether it involved exclusively off-the-job training. Nearly three-fifths of trainees (male or female) were involved in on-the-job training.

Table 11.2
The determinants of training for male and female employees:
independent variable means

		M	F
AGE		36.6	36.7
AGE^2		1475	1484
MARRIED		0.73	0.70
DEPCHLD	Under 5 Child present	0.19	0.10
PAY	Gross Hourly Pay (£)	5.43	3.57
PT	Part-Time = 1; Full Time = 0	0.03	0.44
PUB	Public Sector dummy	0.27	0.33
Establishment Size (No. of Employees):			
SIZE1	1 - 2	0.03	0.06
SIZE3	100-999	0.34	0.27
SIZE4	1,000 and over	0.14	0.09
Job Tenure:			
JOBTEN1	Less than 3 months	0.05	0.07
JOBTEN3	6 months but less than 12 months	0.09	0.10
JOBTEN4	12 months but less than 5 years	0.26	0.36
JOBTEN5	5 years or more	0.56	0.41
MAN_PROF	Managers and Professionals	0.27	0.10
INTNONMA	Intermediate Non-Manual	0.11	0.21
JUNNONMA	Junior Non-Manual	0.10	0.46
SKMA	Skilled and Semi-Skilled Manual	0.45	0.15
Highest Qualifications:			
HIGH_DEG	Degree and other higher qualifications	0.25	0.12
VOCAT	Nursing, Commercial, Apprenticeships	0.07	0.15
A_LEVEL	At least one GCE A-level	0.13	0.07
O_LEVEL	CSE and GCE 0-levels	0.23	0.28
OTH_QUAL	Other and Foreign Qualifications	0.03	0.02

Table 11.3
The determinants of training for male and female employees: logit estimates

	Males		Females	
AGE	-0.079	(-2.73)	0.01	(0.33)
AGE^2	0.00058	(1.58)	-0.00031	(-0.76)
MARRIED	0.10	(0.86)	-0.28	(-2.55)
DEPCHLD	-0.18	(1.60)	-0.45	(-2.65)
PAY	0.0023	(0.19)	0.0082	(1.17)
PT	0.09	(0.37)	-0.49	(-4.23)
PUB	0.11	(0.88)	0.02	(0.14)
SIZE1	-0.11	(-0.4)	0.13	(-0.57)
SIZE3	0.25	(2.71)	0.05	(0.44)
SIZE4	0.12	(0.96)	0.21	(1.35)
JOBTEN1	0.12	(0.54)	0.28	(1.26)
JOBTEN3	-0.54	(-2.58)	-0.38	(-1.77)
JOBTEN4	-0.57	(-3.10)	-0.84	(-4.56)
JOBTEN5	-0.63	(-3.38)	-0.88	(-4.57)
MAN_PROF	1.16	(5.04)	1.81	(4.54)
INTNONMA	1.24	(5.23)	1.86	(4.83)
JUNNONMA	0.82	(3.40)	1.44	(3.82)
SKMA	0.44	(2.00)	0.76	(1.86)
HIGH_DEG	0.96	(7.10)	1.21	(7.13)
VOCAT	0.33	(1.60)	0.59	(3.65)
A_LEVEL	0.70	(4.71)	0.80	(4.17)
O_LEVEL	0.52	(3.99)	0.54	(3.69)
OTH_QUAL	0.44	(1.53)	0.82	(2.66)
CONSTANT	-0.45	(-0.82)	-2.28	(-3.09)
INDUSTRY DUMMIES	Included		Included	
Mean of Dependent Variables	0.219		0.185	
Likelihood Ratio Index	0.10		0.14	
Sample Size	4,125		3,844	

These outcomes are analysed by a straightforward generalisation of the previous section using a tri-nomial logit procedure. The fairly remarkable finding is that for the most part the conclusions with regard to training determinants, discussed in the previous analysis, apply to both types of training separately. They will not therefore be repeated here. There are two main exceptions. First, for women, the estimated probability of receiving off-the-job training actually increases to a peak at age 35 then falls off. This is no less consistent, however, with human capital theory, owing to the common practice of leaving the workforce and returning later, in need of some re-training. Second, the effect of size is important and significant only where the training involves on-the-job learning. Since on-the-job learning is more likely to be job-specific than off-the-job training, this suggests that the main reason for large establishments doing more training is that they are better able to retain the trained labour that they want. If economies of scale were also an important reason, this would have showed up as a size effect on off-the-job training as well.

Table 11.4
Predicted probabilities for employees of receiving training

	Male	Female
Basic Case* : Single childless person on £3 an hour, full-time, unskilled, private-sector manual worker with no qualifications, 3 to 12 months in establishment of 100 to 999 workers, in financial and business services	23.0	10.5
As basic, but part-time*	26.5	5.2
As basic, but aged 40, on £4 an hour	11.1	9.1
As basic, but a junior non-manual worker with O-levels	48.0	48.7
Person with average female characteristics *	20.1	13.8
Person with average male characteristics *	18.8	16.0

Source : Estimates from Table 3
* : Male/Female difference significant at the 5% level

Table 11.5
Discrimination coefficients

Female Data as base	D_{F1}	45.5
	D_{F2}	26.4
Male Data as Base	D_{M1}	15.3
	D_{M2}	8.4

Source : Estimates from Table 3
For definitions, see text

Coefficients of discrimination are calculated by predicting, with each type of training, the average probability of training with male or female coefficients, for the members of the female (or male) data set[7]. The conclusion is that, using the female data as the base, there is much more discrimination over on-the-job training than over off-the-job training. However, this is not observed where males are used as the base.

The determinants of the length of training
Survey respondents who answered that they had received training were also asked how long each training 'episode' in the previous four weeks had lasted. It is possible to aggregate multiple episodes, where they occurred, by adding the mid-points of the hours' bands, and allocating each trainee to a band of total hours received. This method being somewhat approximate it was thought more reliable to regard these bands as an ordinal rather than a cardinal ranking. Unfortunately, only 57 per cent of trainees gave information about how many hours and episodes of training they had received. Ideally one would want to include those with no training in the analysis. In view of the missing information, it was decided to examine only those who had responded on training hours, but to regard the results with considerable caution.

Given the ordinal ranking of training hours, an ordered probit analysis was considered appropriate,[8] and the resulting estimates, using the same independent variables as in the earlier analysis reveals that the estimates are on the whole poorly determined, and the equations do not give a good fit to the data. Nonetheless, the x^2 statistics indicate some of the variance is being explained. Of particular note is the finding that whereas for

256

females the higher-level occupations tend to involve longer hours of training, for males the reverse is the case : the male unskilled manual worker has significantly longer training than all other groups. The effect of qualifications is also uneven. The male with A-levels seems to be the one who has the longest hours of training, other things equal. Also of note is that female workers in the public sector have shorter training spells than those in the private sector. It is also worth recording that being part-time which, as the earlier analysis showed, substantial effect on participation in training, has no significant effect on the hours spent training by trainees.

An appropriate analogous measure of discrimination, in this context, is the difference between the predicted length of training according to whether male or female coefficients are used. This shows that (whether an average male or an average female base is used) the predicted training length is five to nine hours for female coefficients and 10 to 14 hours for male coefficients[9]. However, since the estimates are poorly determined, the difference between the two was not highly significant[10].

The determinants of 'general' or 'specific' training
Finally, the motives and the nature of the training may also be subjected to a multi-variate analysis. As noted above, roughly half of trainees were involved in training which appeared to contain at least some element of transferable skill acquisition. Human capital theory readily provides us with the hypothesis that the cost of 'general' training will tend to be born by trainees, whereas the costs and benefits of job-specific training may both be shared between firm and employee, or even born wholly by the firm. The GHS data allow the construction of a 1/0 dummy variable which equals one if either the trainee (or friend or relative) contributes towards the fees, or the employer does not pay basic wages in full during training, or both. The hypothesis of human capital theory is that training is more likely to be of a general kind if the trainee is paying.

This hypothesis is tested with a simple logit model amongst trainees. As with the above analysis, only a proportion of respondents recorded answers to both the motivational questions and the funding questions, so the results must be taken with a great deal of caution. Nevertheless, the

Table 11.6
The determinants of on-the-job or off-the job training for male and female employees: multinominal logit estimates

	On-the-Job Training Involved				Only Off-the-Job Training			
	M		F		M		F	
AGE	-0.113	(-3.15)	-0.041	(-1.1)	0.021	(0.47)	0.104	(2.30)
AGE^2	0.00094	(1.99)	0.00028	(0.57)	-0.00053	(-0.97)	-0.00143	(-2.39)
MARRIED	0.07	(0.52)	-0.26	(-1.9)	0.16	(0.97)	-0.29	(-1.92)
DEPCHLD	-0.12	(-0.85)	-0.40	(-1.84)	-0.22	(-1.41)	-0.50	(-2.09)
PAY	-0.00026	(-1.25)	0.00008	(0.96)	0.00015	(1.01)	0.00008	(0.82)
PT	-0.02	(-0.08)	-0.55	(-3.70)	0.31	(0.80)	-0.41	(-2.5)
PUB	0.06	(0.39)	0.16	(0.87)	0.18	(1.00)	-0.16	(-0.85)
SIZE1	-0.24	(-0.7)	-0.19	(-0.6)	0.05	(0.14)	-0.05	(-0.14)
SIZE3	0.37	(3.2)	0.03	(0.24)	0.11	(0.86)	0.09	(0.59)
SIZE4	0.19	(1.2)	0.33	(1.8)	0.05	(0.32)	0.05	(0.24)
JOBTEN1	0.22	(0.92)	0.53	(2.09)	-0.47	(-0.98)	-0.28	(-0.83)
JOBTEN3	-0.62	(-2.66)	-0.24	(-0.94)	-0.30	(-0.81)	-0.62	(-1.98)
JOBTEN4	-0.81	(-3.94)	-0.88	(-4.0)	-0.004	(-0.17)	-0.79	(-3.07)
JOBTEN5	-0.91	(-4.33)	-0.94	(-4.0)	-0.05	(-0.17)	-0.82	(-3.1)
MAN_PROF	1.09	(3.87)	1.91	(3.50)	1.21	(3.38)	1.74	(3.08)
INTNONMA	1.34	(4.65)	1.83	(3.44)	1.12	(3.05)	1.92	(3.51)
JUNNONMA	0.96	(3.36)	1.53	(2.94)	0.52	(1.33)	1.33	(2.47)
SKMA	0.49	(1.86)	0.70	(1.26)	0.37	(1.05)	0.86	(1.46)
HIGH_DEG	0.82	(4.72)	0.91	(4.11)	1.16	(5.81)	1.49	(6.31)
VOCAT	0.25	(0.92)	0.64	(3.15)	0.45	(1.55)	0.52	(2.20)
A_LEVEL	0.69	(3.77)	0.62	(2.60)	0.75	(3.32)	1.06	(3.89)
O_LEVEL	0.49	(3.05)	0.58	(3.20)	0.60	(2.90)	0.43	(1.93)
OTH_LEVEL	0.41	(1.13)	0.71	(1.73)	0.48	(1.17)	0.92	(2.22)
CONSTANT	0.17	(0.26)	-1.84	(-1.99)	-4.09	(-4.64)	-5.0	(-4.5)
INDUSTRY DUMMIES	Included				Included			
Mean of Dependent Variable	0.125		0.109		0.094		0.078	
Likelihood Ratio Index			Males : 0.10		Females : 0.13			

analysis produced some plausible estimates. In particular the hypothesis that those who pay towards their training are more likely to be investing in general skills is strongly confirmed. Of interest also are the findings that those on lower pay, in the public sector and/or working part-time are more likely to be receiving job-specific training. There is, however, no significant difference, ceteris paribus, between males and females.

Table 11.7
Discrimination coefficients: types of training

	Predicted Probabilities (%)		
	Male Coefficient Estimates	Female Coefficient Estimates	Discrimination Coefficient
Female Data Set as Base:			
Involving On-the-Job Training	14.73	10.89	35.2
Off-the-Job Training Only	8.96	7.79	15.1
Male Data Set As Base:			
Involving On-the-Job Training	12.51	11.57	7.5
Off-the-Job Training Only	9.41	8.36	11.1

Table 11.8
The length of training: ordered probit estimates

	Male		Female	
AGE	-0.02	(-0.62)	0.02	(0.48)
AGE^2	0.00016	(0.34)	-0.00027	(-0.46)
MARRIED	-0.18	(-1.3)	-0.23	(-1.78)
DEPCHLD	-0.01	(-0.12)	0.02	(0.1)
PAY	-0.00022	(-1.09)	-0.00021	(-1.05)
PT	0.06	(0.26)	-0.09	(-0.65)
PUB	0.15	(0.96)	-0.27	(-1.52)
SIZE1	0.09	(0.27)	0.18	(0.64)
SIZE3	0.17	(1.51)	0.18	(1.29)
SIZE4	0.13	(0.88)	0.32	(1.80)
JOBTEN1	0.54	(1.76)	0.33	(1.19)
JOBTEN3	0.30	(1.08)	0.42	(1.36)
JOBTEN4	0.29	(1.22)	0.08	(0.34)
JOBTEN5	0.45	(1.88)	0.21	(0.92)
MAN_PROF	-0.79	(-2.47)	1.15	(1.91)
INTNONMA	-1.02	(-3.13)	0.89	(1.50)
JUNNONMA	-1.07	(-3.09)	0.87	(1.48)
SKMA	-0.98	(-2.96)	0.18	(0.28)
HIGH_DEG	0.26	(1.51)	-0.33	(-1.37)
VOCAT	-0.03	(-0.12)	-0.40	(-1.59)
A_LEVEL	0.50	(2.55)	0.16	(0.59)
O_LEVEL	0.23	(1.25)	0.01	(0.06)
OTH_QUAL	0.21	(0.57)	-0.32	(-0.78)
CONSTANT	1.71	(2.29)	-0.41	(-0.41)
INDUSTRY DUMMIES	Included		Included	

Likelihood Ratio Index	0.029	0.035
$X^2(32)$	56.4	49.1
Sample Size	539	398

Table 11.9
The determinants of 'general' or 'specific' training:
logit estimates

AGE	-0.07	(1.0)
AGE^2	0.00083	(0.9)
PAY_TRNG	1.34	(6.06)
SEX	-0.002	(-0.01)
MARRIED	0.28	(-1.28)
DEPCHLD	0.18	(0.71)
PAY	-0.00097	(3.01)
PT	0.41	(1.36)
PUB	0.43	(1.59)
CONSTANT	13.9	(0.16)
SIZE DUMMIES		Included
JOB TENURE DUMMIES		Included
Occupation Dummies		Included
Industry Dummies		Included
Mean of Dependent Variable	0.52	
Likelihood Ratio Index	0.13	
Sample Size	656	

Conclusion

The analyses in this chapter have confirmed a number of features of training incidence consistent with the human capital approach. The main findings which confirm the consensus of earlier studies comprise the following:

(i)   At least for males, training (especially on-the-job-training) declines significantly with age.

(ii) Those with higher qualifications are more likely to receive training. The explanation may be either that they are likely to

261

benefit more from the training or that the psychic costs may be lower.

(iii)   Those, especially women, with family responsibilities, are less likely to receive training.

(iv)   Those working in larger establishments are more likely to receive on-the-job training.

(v)   Certain occupations, particularly the higher status ones, require more participation in training.

(vi)   Those who have recently started a new job tend to need and receive training.

The main new findings that go beyond the earlier consensus are as follows:

(vii)   This analysis has added support to those previous studies which showed a substantially different training-age relationship for females, in that the decline of training of females with age is but gentle and significant; moreover it has revealed that, for females, off-the-job training increases with age to a peak in the mid 30s.

(vii)   A new finding is that the receipt of off-the-job training is not affected by establishment size and, accordingly, that all the establishment size effect works through on-the-job training.

(ix)   As a qualification of (v) it appears that, for males, trainees in unskilled manual occupations have relatively long training hours.

(x)   Where training is paid for at least in part by the trainee or friends and relatives, it is less likely to be job-specific.

(xi)   Finally, a result which contradicts earlier evidence is that training is not significantly greater, ceteris paribus, for employees working in the public sector.

None of these findings, however, can lend any support to the proposition that human capital acquisition is best left to individuals, and firms, given market incentives. They cannot deny, for example, the generally-held perception that more training would be welfare-improving, because the data simply do not allow either the economist or the company manager to make a precise calculation of the benefits and costs of training.

The argument that levels of human capital acquisition in Britain are 'too low' has been touched on here by examining a snapshot of different forms of education and training that are taking place at a point in time. The abominably low participation in human capital acquisition of 16 to 18 year old female is perhaps the most dramatic feature of this snapshot.

The chapter has focussed more closely on a particular institutional determinant of training, by developing and measuring the concept of discrimination over training, in that through a complex of institutional mechanisms employers systematically provide less training for female than for male employees. The 1987 General Household Survey was divided into males and females and separate analyses carried out. If, then, it is asked 'by how much would the females in the sample have raised their training frequency if they had been treated as males' the answer is 26 per cent. Other measures of discrimination, equally plausible, range from 8 per cent to 45 per cent, depending on the precise question asked.

The policy implications of these findings depend first upon accepting the proposition that more training should be encouraged. Given that, the findings support measures to raise the contribution of small establishments to training, and measures to provide childcare facilities which would enable women to participate more in training. They also call for greater efforts generally to resist discrimination, particularly against younger women. In so far as some of this discrimination is not plain prejudice but is based on the perceived risk of losing women employees, there is a strong case both for a campaign to change employers' perceptions (in this age of continually growing female participation in the labour force), and for state intervention to fund the training of women who may otherwise suffer from moving into and out of the labour force. A recent evaluation study of the 'Training Opportunity Scheme', later the 'Old Job Training Scheme' has shown how they provided a wide range of skills training, some at high levels, and that these schemes were relatively beneficial for women, especially women returners (Payne, 1991). It is a matter of regret that these schemes were subsumed and disappeared within the cheaper Employment Training Scheme, which provides very little high-level skill training and is far less use for women. On the other hand, the general expansion of training participation during the expansion period of the mid and late 1980s, as highlighted by successive Labour Force Surveys, has raised the numbers of women participating in training (Greenhalgh and Mavrotas, 1991). Only further work will reveal whether the collapse of government-provided adult training opportunities for women has been counter-balanced if at all by the growth of job-related training amongst employees.

Notes

This research was supported by ESRC Grant Number R000232636. The author is extremely grateful to Johnny Sung for his excellent research assistance. Material from the 1987 General Household Survey made available through the OPCS and the ESRC Data Archive has been used by permission of the Controller of H.M. Stationery Office. A shorter version of this paper appeared under the title 'The determinants of training of male and female employees in Great Britain' in *Oxford Bulletin of Economics and Statistics*, vol 55, no1, February, pp.103-122.

1. There were several missing observations on incomes for this age group, so the mean is no doubt subject to a substantial margin of error.
2. It was felt that numbers precluded satisfactory analysis of the self-employed for whom, as also with those not in employment, the forces determining training were likely to be different from those relevant to employees.
3. For discussion of wider discriminatory processes over training in society, see Green (1991), Mallier and Roser (1987), Benett and Carter (1983), Cockburn (1987) or the overview by Clarke (1991).
4. Maddala (1983), p.26.
5. DFI and DMI were both significantly above zero at the 5% level; it was not possible, using LIMDEP, to obtain standard errors for DF2 and DM2.
6. A further comparison was made by separating males and part-time females. Unsurprisingly, the discrimination coefficients were much higher (DF1 = 154%, DM1 = 69%). However, the part-timer sample was relatively small, and the equation was not very well defined; consequently the variance of the predicted logit for an average part-time female was high, and the resulting estimate of

discrimination subject to such a large margin of error that it was not significantly different from zero.

7. For example, for any individual the predicted probability of receiving on-the-job (j = 1) or only off-the-job training (j = 2) is given by $P_j = e^{\alpha j x}/(1 + e^{\alpha lx} + e^{\alpha lx})$ j = 1,2.

    These probabilities are then averaged over the females or males in the sample to give the predicted probabilities and hence the discriminations coefficients in Table 11.7.

8. See, e.g. Maddala (1983) pp46-9.

9. The predicted outcome is defined as the range containing bX where b is the vector of estimated coefficients and X is the characteristics vector.

10. For both the average male and average female bases, the t-statistic was 1.0.

Table A1
Proportions of the population aged 16 to 59 acquiring human capital according to working status (%)

	Working	Unemployed	Economically Inactive	Total
a) *Males*				
Total acquiring human capital	23.5	14.5	26.2	23.9
of which:				
At school	1.0	0.8	2.5	2.2
Further Education _	5.3	5.4	21.2	6.4
Training —	17.2	8.3	2.5	15.3
(Base)	(6193)	(725)	(523)	
b) *Females:*				
Total acquiring human capital	22.5	11.7	11.5	19.6
of which :				
At school	1.0	1.0	4.4	2.0
Further Education _	5.4	1.7	5.2	5.2
Training —	16.1	9.0	1.9	11.4
(Base)	(4921)	(412)	(2323)	
c) *All:*				
Total acquiring human capital	23.1	13.3	17.2	21.0
of which :				
At school	1.0	0.8	7.0	2.1
Further Education _	5.4	4.0	8.2	5.5
Training—	16.7	8.5	2.0	13.4
(Base)	(11114)	(1137)	(2846)	

Source: GHS 1987

‒ Includes: At college or university full-time; on a sandwich course; on a Youth Training Scheme which involves studying at a college; training for a qualification in nursing, physiotherapy or similar medical subject; studying at college part-time or on day or block release; doing an Open University or other correspondence course not regarded as training.

‒ Having had education, training or self-instruction (apart from above categories defined as Further Education) that would help with present or future jobs, during four weeks prior to interviews

Table A2
Proportions of the population acquiring human capital by age group

		16-18	19-24	25-34	35-44	45-59
Total acquiring human	M	57.3	28.6	21.9	16.0	9.4
capital	F	53.1	23.3	14.4	13.2	7.2
of which:						
At School	M	23.1	0.2	0.0	0.0	0.0
	F	23.5	0.2	0.0	0.0	0.0
Further Education*	M	24.0	13.9	4.2	1.6	0.3
	F	20.5	10.1	2.9	2.4	0.5
Training**	M	10.2	14.5	17.7	14.4	9.1
	F	9.1	13.0	11.5	10.8	6.7
(Base)	M	705	1320	2056	2029	2457
	F	650	1350	2207	2050	2500

Source : GHS 1987
*,** : See Table A1

Table A3
Proportions of those in young age groups in various types of non-school education (%)

	Ages 1 - 18		Ages 19 - 24	
	M	F	M	F
On a Youth Training Scheme involving college study	7.7	5.1	0.1	0.1
Full-time college or University	6.5	10.5	6.1	4.2
Sandwich course	0.2	0.0	1.0	0.6
Nursing, Physiotherapy or similar medical subject	0.0	0.1	0.1	1.1
Part-time or day or block release at college	9.5	4.8	6.4	3.8
Open University or other correspondence course	0.0	0.0	0.6	0.7

Source : GHS 1987

Table A4
Proportions of the population in work who participated in training (%)

		16-18	19-24	25-34	35-44	45-59
Participated in	M	37.0	26.1	26.0	21.3	14.3
Training	F	31.3	24.8	21.4	16.9	12.2
of which :						
Participated in	M	34.6	20.6	14.2	9.7	6.4
On-the-Job	F	24.7	18.6	11.9	8.2	6.0
Training						
Participated	M	2.5	5.5	11.7	11.6	7.9
only in Off-the-	F	6.6	6.3	9.7	8.7	6.1
Job Training						

Source: GHS 1987

Table A5
The length of training

	% of Males	% of Females
Proportions of training workers who receive over 4 weeks :		
Less than 5 hours	20.4	25.6
5 to 9 hours	23.3	25.6
10 to 14 hours	11.0	12.3
15 to 19 hours	11.2	9.8
20 to 29 hours	12.3	11.0
30 to 39 hours	7.4	6.0
40 hours and over	14.4	9.6

Source : GHS 87

Note

In a minority of cases, workers had more than one training spell in the 4-week reference period. In such cases, the mid-point of the training hours category was used to aggregate spell lengths, and allocate each case to the appropriate band. If one spell was of 40 hours or over the aggregate spell length was automatically also allocated to 40 hours or over.

Table A6
The form of training

	M	F
% when training involved :		
a) formal classroom teaching	37.3	42.1
b) working in small informal groups	46.7	51.4
c) following a course of instruction or teaching oneself	63.2	55.7
d) watching videos, TV programmes or listening to tapes	35.8	29.6

Source: GHS 1987

Note

In each case the base is made up of those working and training who responded to these questions

Table A7
The payment for and timing of training

	M	F
Proportion where trainee or friends or relatives contributed to fees (%)	37.3	42.1
Proportion where training took place in normal working hours (%)	61.5	48.9

Source: GHS 1987

Note

In each case the base is made up of those working and training who responded to these questions

Table A8
The motivation for training

	M	F
Proportion of employees where training was compulsory	22.9	22.7
Proportion of population for whom training was not compulsory but took place 'only because it was expected'	7.9	6.8
Proportion of population for whom training neither compulsory nor 'expected' : reasons for wanting to do the training *		
a) To improve prospects of increased earnings	35.2	20.4
b) To improve promotion prospects	29.5	18.9
c) General interest/own satisfaction	69.5	78.7
d) To learn something necessary for present job	56.0	53.0
e) To help you in some other way to do your present job	43.6	45.4
f) To be able to do a different kind of job	21.7	22.6
g) To help to do a future job that will be taken up	19.4	17.1
h) To improve the chances of getting a job	14.1	16.8
i) To prepare for self-employment	8.2	5.8
j) To give confidence in applying for jobs	4.6	9.5

* Base = 475 males, 328 females

References

Allen, H. J., McCormick, B. and O'Brien, R. J. (1991), 'Unemployment and the demand for retraining: an econometric analysis', *Economic Journal*, 101, pp. 190 - 201.

Ashton, D., Green, F. and Hoskins, M. (1989), *Training in Britain: An Overview of the Evaluation of the Net Benefits of Training*, Training Agency.

Bennett, Y. and Carter, D. (1983), *Day Release For Girls*, Manchester: Equal Opportunities Commission.

Booth, A. (1990a), 'Earning and learning: what price firm specific training?', Birkbeck College, mimeo.

Booth, A. (1990b), 'Job-related formal training: who receives it and what is it worth?', Birkbeck College, mimeo.

Clarke, K. (1991), *Women and Training: A Review of Recent Research and Policy,* Manchester: Equal Opportunities Commission.

Cockburn, C. (1987), *Two-Track Training: Sex Inequalities and the YTS*, London: Macmillan.

Green, F. (1991), 'Sex discrimination in job-related training', *British Journal of Industrial Relations,* 29, pp. 295-304.

Greenhalgh, C. and Mavrotas, G. (1991), 'Workforce training in the Thatcher era - market forces and market failures', paper presented to The International Conference on the Economics of Training, Cardiff Business School.

Greenhalgh, C. and Stewart, M. (1987), 'The effects and determinants of training', *Oxford Bulletin of Economics and Statistics,* 49, pp. 171-190.

Maddala, G.S. (1983), *Limited-dependent and Qualitative Variables in Econometrics,* Cambridge: Cambridge University Press.

Mallier, A.T. and Rosser, M.J. (1987), *Women and the Economy*, London: Macmillan.

Oaxaca, R. (1973), 'Male-female wage differentials in urban labor market', *International Economic Review,* 14, pp. 693-709.

Payne, J. (1991), *Women, Training and the Skills Shortage: The Case for Public Investment,* Policy Studies Institute.

Rigg, M. (1989), *Training in Britain: Individuals' Perspectives,* London: HMSO.

12 Women's training needs: The British policy gap

Joan Payne

Introduction

In adult vocational training, the rolling back of the frontiers of the state has been accomplished with relatively little public comment. The growth of Youth Training and of schemes for the long-term unemployed has drawn attention away from the fact that public funds for vocational training for other groups have been severely cut. Adult training has not been merely an unfortunate victim of the squeeze on public spending; on the contrary, the cuts have been part of an explicit policy to push vocational training further into the market-place. Thus the 1988 White Paper 'Employment for the 1990s' stated,

> 'Developing training through life is not primarily a Government responsibility. Employers must take the lead' (Employment Dept. 1988.

Private individuals as well as employers were encouraged in the White Paper to take responsibility for their own training, and personal responsibility for self-development was stressed even more strongly in the Department's 'Strategic Guidance' to the Training and Enterprise Councils:

> 'Perhaps our most formidable challenge is the need to increase motivation among our people, to change antiquated attitudes and values, to instill a philosophy of self-development and self-investment in every worker....Individuals need to be motivated to invest some of their own time and, where appropriate, money in training' (Employment Dept. 1990a).

According to this view of adult vocational training, the state has two main duties. First, it must provide a 'framework' for training activities. To this end the government has set up a network of employer-led Training and Enterprise Councils (TECs) in England and Wales and Local Enterprise Companies (LECs) in Scotland, and has developed the system of National Vocational Qualifications. Second, it must put in place a safety-net for people whom employers are reluctant to train and who cannot fund training for themselves, which is interpreted as meaning primarily the long-term unemployed. This has been accomplished through the establishment in 1988 of Employment Training, recently incorporated into a new programme, 'Training for Work', but referred to in what follows by its popular name 'ET'.

With the skill level of the British workforce lagging behind our industrial competitors (Dept. of Education and Science 1990, National Institute of Economic and Social Research 1989), clearly it is essential for a national skills policy to mobilise all possible resources. The 'low-skill equilibrium' which Finegold and Soskice (1988) claim lies at the root of Britain's training problems has to be attacked on many fronts, and it would be foolish to deny that both employers and individuals have a big part to play. While accepting this, the thesis of this paper is that the responsibility for adult vocational training above the ET safety-net should not be carried by employers and individuals alone. In particular, it is argued that restricting public spending primarily to training for the long-term unemployed disadvantages women. In view of the inadequacy of Britain's skills base and the proven effectiveness of adult training, including training for women, there is a strong case for public investment to create opportunities for adult training which are open to all who have the motivation to succeed.

In numerical terms women are an increasingly important part of Britain's workforce, and by Autumn 1992 they held 45 per cent of all paid jobs[1]. However, in terms of the skills they bring to the workforce, their potential contribution is grossly under-used. In 1991, of all female full-time employees aged 16 to 59 in GB who had qualifications of A Level standard or higher, only 27 per cent worked in professional jobs or as managers in large establishments, compared to 47 per cent of male employees with equivalent qualifications. For female part-time employees, the under-use of skills was even greater, with only 12 per cent of those with qualifications of A Level standard or higher in top level jobs. Furthermore, more than a fifth of women of working age with this level of qualifications were not in the labour force at all; that is, they were neither working nor seeking work.[2]

There are many reasons why women work at levels below their full potential, or do no paid work at all. Metcalf and Leighton (1989) propose a range of policies needed to redress the situation, and providing access to training is just one element amongst these. Nevertheless, training is important. There is firm evidence that high quality adult training can enable women to move into jobs which are better matched to their abilities than the jobs that they otherwise would be able to obtain. This evidence comes from a formal evaluation study of the now closed Training Opportunities Programme, which was popularly known as TOPS.

Policy background

As Sheldrake and Vickerstaff recount (1987), the Labour governments of the sixties and seventies pursued strongly interventionist policies in the field of vocational training. The Industrial Training Act of 1964 established the Industry Training Boards (ITBs), with the power to raise compulsory levies on firms falling within their constituency. In the early seventies, the Manpower Services Commission was created. One of the Commission's most important tasks was to expand the government's role as a direct provider of skills training for adults. Despite the work of the ITBs, there was concern that industry alone was unable to produce all the skilled labour that a technological economy needed. In particular, employers tended to cut spending on training during periods of recession, and the consequent skills shortages were believed to have held back economic recovery during the 'stop-go' years. It was hoped to alleviate this problem by providing publicly funded training 'for stock' - that is, for the general needs of the economy rather than for particular jobs with particular employers - and by training counter-cyclically, at times when industry was retrenching. This was to be achieved primarily through the TOPS programme.

Though it built on the foundations of the Vocational Training Scheme which had survived from the Second World War, TOPS was in many ways a new departure. Courses were open to all adult men or women whether they were in work or not, as long as they were prepared to give up their job in order to train. They enabled adults who were out of work to refresh, update or upgrade their skills or to retrain in a field where it was easier to find jobs, and they also gave a chance to people in work either to pursue their chosen occupation at a higher level or to change career. TOPS offered intensive off-the-job training in a very wide range of subjects, at all skill levels from the operative to the professional. TOPS courses lasted anything from a month to a year, and were held in government skills centres, in colleges, and in private training institutions; in certain circumstances, places on other courses could also be financed through the programme. Training allowances, at rates above unemployment benefit, were payable to all full-time trainees and were not means-tested. Under the wide TOPS umbrella there were also special part-time courses for women returners, which, in addition to providing skills training, aimed to rebuild confidence and to train women in job search and interview techniques. TOPS was a popular programme, and by the late 1970s around 90,000 adults were completing courses each year.

The coming to power of the Thatcher government in 1979 brought with it a change of ideology. Interventionist policies were rejected in favour of market solutions, and it was not long before the dismantling of the Industry Training Boards was underway. Meanwhile, the deep recession starting in autumn 1979 diverted attention away from the skills needs of the economy, and training began to be seen as a way of cushioning the impact of record levels of unemployment rather than providing for the needs of an expanding economy. Initially most of the government's efforts were directed into training for school leavers, but as the number of adults who were long-term unemployed grew and proved relatively unresponsive to improvements in the economic climate, their needs claimed more attention. A variety of initiatives culminated in 1988 with the launch of ET.

In order to fund the new programmes, resources had been gradually withdrawn from TOPS. By the mid-eighties there were only half as many TOPS trainees as when the Conservative government came to power. In 1985 the programme was repackaged and relaunched as the Job Training Scheme, with a greater emphasis on market responsiveness, and was almost immediately renamed the Old Job Training Scheme (OJTS), to distinguish it from the short-lived New Job Training Scheme,

276

the direct precursor of ET. It survived under its new name, though with a declining number of trainees, until 1988, when its final demise went unnoticed by the media. Within ET a small corner of high quality training embodying some of the principles of TOPS/OJTS was retained for a while under the programme High Technology National Training (Wilson 1990), but this was effectively terminated in 1992.

In 1987, the year before TOPS/OJTS was closed down, the Training Agency (which the Manpower Services Commission had by this time become) commissioned an evaluation study of TOPS/OJTS, reported in Payne (1990). Though the findings regarding both sexes were of interest, recent policy developments made the results relating to women particularly important. The experiences of women on TOPS/OJTS, and their implications for public training policy, were discussed in Payne (1991), on which the present paper is based[3].

Research design

The Evaluation Study was designed to assess the contribution that training made to the subsequent employment prospects, earnings and job satisfaction of trainees. It was based on 785 trainees who formed a representative sample of all men and women in Great Britain completing TOPS/OJTS courses during the last two quarters of 1986. These people were interviewed in person in autumn 1987, and were contacted a second time by post in the spring of 1988, when they were also invited to comment freely on their experience of training. In addition, administrative data were obtained for a nationally representative sample of 2710 trainees (from which the interview sample had been drawn).

The research design also included a matched comparison sample consisting of 760 men and women who had experienced similar patterns of employment to trainees up until 1986 but who had not had any recent training. This sample was located through screening interviews conducted via a commercial national 'omnibus' survey, followed by a second interview with individuals who satisfied the criteria for matching.

For both the interview and comparison samples, complete work histories were collected from January 1980 up until the time of interview. These histories proved invaluable in understanding the role that adult training played in women's lives.

Women's need for training

The research showed that while both men and women seek adult training in very diverse circumstances, there are certain typically female experiences which can make the need for training particularly acute. Prominent here are the needs of women returners. Because of the scarcity of public childcare in Britain, many women have little option but to give up paid employment while their children are small; others make a positive choice to look after their own children full-time. Some women are forced to leave their jobs to care for sick or elderly relatives. Women who have been kept out of the labour market by domestic commitments sometimes lack the confidence even to try to go back to paid employment, and this is especially true if they have been away from work for many years. Those that do return can often find only low-skill work. Martin and Roberts (1984) showed that 37 per cent of all women who had done paid work both before and after the birth of their first child returned to work at a level below that of the last job they had held before the birth, and for those who returned only part-time the figure was 45 per cent. More than three quarters of those returning part-time had stayed in part-time work, and of these only three in ten had moved to a more skilled job even after they had been back at work for over ten years.

In the Evaluation Study there were many women who, before training, had been working in jobs that were less skilled than the jobs they had held before their children were born. Former clerks, typists and secretaries had become canteen assistants, cleaners and check-out operators. They were obliged to take such jobs by a combination of factors. Some had skills which were rusty with disuse or had been overtaken by new technologies and needed updating. Others still had good skills, but had lost confidence. Often women had taken a low skill job as a short-term expedient because the hours or location fitted in with family commitments, but this strategy set a trap from which it could prove difficult to escape. Working at a low skill level made the problem of decaying skills and failing confidence even worse, and low wages meant that women could not afford childcare or the domestic equipment or help that they needed if they were to give more of their time to paid employment.

It was, of course, not only women returners who needed training. There were also women who had lost their jobs, often through redundancy, and women who had left school with no qualifications and whose jobs had always been low skilled. In other cases the catalyst for seeking training was a crisis of some kind: divorce or widowhood, leaving the woman as the sole breadwinner; leaving a job in order to move house in response to the demands of a husband's career; illness or injury leading to the enforced abandonment of a chosen occupation. There were also a few women in the study who had been in relatively well paid jobs, but who wanted to change career and take up work which they felt would be more fulfilling.

The squeeze on training for women

Recent policy developments have led to a disproportionate squeeze on publicly funded training places for women. In the mid-1980s 45 per cent of trainees on TOPS/OJTS were women; in 1992, the proportion of women trainees on ET, which absorbs the large bulk of government funding for adult training outside of the education system, was around 30 per cent. This has come about because eligibility for ET is tied primarily to long-term unemployment, which in turn is a consequence of its role as safety-net rather than mainstream provision.

The eligibility criteria for ET discriminate against women in several ways. In the first place, fewer unemployed women than unemployed men register at Job Centres or Employment Offices, because they are less likely to be entitled to unemployment benefit. Furthermore, the criteria favour young people, giving priority to 18-24 year olds who have been unemployed for six months, but priority to 25-49 year olds only if they have been unemployed for more than two years, and no priority at all to those aged 50 or more. Here as elsewhere, albeit unintentionally, ageism entails sexism, for women's demand for training is greatest in their thirties and forties. In the third place, the priority given to the long-term unemployed has meant that there have been very few places on ET for women returners, and these places have been vulnerable to budget cuts. To be defined as a 'returner' for the purposes of ET, women have to have been away from work for at least two years. This means that women who gave up good jobs to have children and who have since gone back to less skilled jobs where the hours fit in with family demands are not eligible for a training place on ET. Nevertheless their need for refresher courses to enable them to move back to the kind of jobs they held before is as great as the need of women who have not yet returned to work at all. There is no way in which the current employers of such women can be expected to pay for courses whose purpose is to enable their employees to quit.

The increased flexibility now possessed by the TECs and LECs makes it difficult to foresee future trends in training provision. Unfortunately there is no reason to suppose that they will give a high priority to women's needs. Because of the rule that most directors have to be drawn from the senior levels of large local companies, there are very few women on TEC/LEC boards, and hardly any are chaired by a woman.

If there are fewer publicly funded training places for women, we need to ask whether employers are making up the shortfall. In the past, the record of British employers as providers of training has not been good. Even in the fastest growing sector of the economy, banking and finance, expenditure on training per employee (excluding wages) increased by only 0.4 per cent between 1984 and 1988, and this followed a drop in spending in 1981 to 1984. In construction and manufacturing industry, spending on training did not grow at all. Meanwhile our major European competitors were maintaining or increasing their expenditure (McLeish 1990). Nevertheless, between 1984 and 1990 there was a very encouraging rise from 9.2 per cent to 15.4 per cent in the proportion of employees who had received some job-related training during a four week reference period. Unfortunately, this was brought to an abrupt halt by the recession of the early 1990s, and by autumn 1992 the proportion had fallen back to 13.7 per cent (Employment Department 1993).

The increase in job-related training during the second half of the 1980s undoubtedly benefited women, and by spring 1989 the proportion of women employees receiving job-related training very slightly exceeded the proportion of men (ibid). However a closer examination of the figures reveals that a number of problems remain. Most of the growth in job-related training during the 1980s was in short courses, and much of it can probably be accounted for by an increased volume of induction training as employers began once more to recruit labour after a period when recruitment rates had plummeted (Greenhalgh and Mavrotas 1991). Moreover, employers remain very reluctant to train workers in part-time jobs, and part-time workers are, of course, overwhelmingly female. Green (1991) demonstrates, on the basis of 1987 General Household

Survey data, that, after taking account of a wide range of factors including qualifications, age, occupational level and length of time in the job, women have a substantially lower chance than men of receiving job-specific training which is paid for by an employer, with young women, part-timers and mothers of young children at a particular disadvantage compared to men. Thus employer-funded training, though discriminating less against women than it did a decade ago, still fails to provide equal opportunities for both sexes.

What, then, of the government's view that individuals should bear a greater share of the costs themselves? With average hourly earnings in full-time jobs around three-quarters those of men, women are less likely than men to have the financial resources to be able to do this; still less so if their work is only part-time. Recent government moves to make it easier for people to pay the fees for training courses have included Career Development Loans (CDLs) and tax relief on fees for courses leading to approved vocational qualifications, but both of these measures benefit men more than women. Taking out a CDL represents a considerable risk for a woman returner, who may well be far from confident of her ability either to obtain or hold down a job, and the low level of the earnings that women can expect even after training makes repayment difficult. It is not surprising, therefore, that only 30 per cent of CDLs have gone to women (Employment Department 1992a), and that most CDLs are taken out for training in a narrow range of well paid occupations in which there are good prospects of either employment or self-employment (Employment Department 1992b). Indeed, in the financial year 1991/92, more than half of the CDLs taken out by women were for courses at further and higher education colleges and universities/polytechnics *(ibid.)* - presumably including courses for which, in the days when local authority spending was less tightly squeezed than now, discretionary grants were available. CDLs are thus of benefit only to a minority of women. Tax relief on course fees is of benefit to people who have a taxable earned income, and is unlikely to be of much help to women returners or women on very low wages.

Public versus private funding

The government's preference for private funding for adult training rests on the conviction that centrally funded training is wasteful and unresponsive to the needs of industry. Public funding is however completely compatible with local planning and delivery. The MSC/Training Agency's own regular monitoring of the employment position of trainees three months after completing TOPS/OJTS courses gives evidence of the effectiveness of the programme. As Figure 12.1 shows, though placement rates slumped in 1980/81, they recovered very quickly to their pre-recession levels, well before unemployment nationally began to fall in 1987. In order to achieve these results, the MSC must have had some success in identifying the nature and location of skills shortages that persisted in the recession, and in planning provision to match.

Another strand in the argument between public and private funding concerns the viability of the policy of 'training for stock'. Training for stock cannot be done if the primary responsibility for adult training lies with employers, for their efforts, as the White Paper pointed out, 'must be directed primarily at the people they already employ' (Employment Dept. 1988, para. 8.4). Training for stock also sat unhappily with the government's rejection of the planned economy and its espousal of market principles, though its validity was not questioned in the case of Youth Training. It was therefore a finding of particular significance in the evaluation study that the policy of training for stock through TOPS/OJTS appeared to be vindicated, with substantial proportions of trainees succeeding in getting jobs in the long term. Three months after finishing their training 62 per cent of trainees were in work, a figure which rose to 75 per cent ten months after finishing training, and 83 per cent more than two years afterwards. Well over two thirds of these were in work which directly used the skills in which they had been trained.

The effectiveness of adult skills training for women

The Evaluation Study examined a range of measures of the effectiveness of TOPS/OJTS. The results were favourable for both sexes; this paper focuses specifically on the outcomes for women.

In terms of expressed satisfaction the courses rated very highly. More than four fifths of women were satisfied with the content of the training, support from teachers, relevance to employment prospects and the value to their personal development, and on all of these counts those who said

282

they were 'very satisfied' easily outnumbered those who were only 'fairly satisfied'. When given the opportunity to write freely about their training, many women described personal gains from their course, and in particular they stressed the growth of confidence in themselves. This was a key factor for women who had spent several years at home with children, and the following comment was typical:

> I would not have easily faced returning to work without without the knowledge it gave me, confidence in former abilities, skills it refreshed, stimulus it provided, update and practical application of modern technological equipment...

In 1987 employment in Britain was growing more quickly for women than for men, and as a result women trainees found work more quickly than men did. Three months after their course 67 per cent of women trainees were in a job compared to 58 per cent of men, though when the trainees were last contacted in spring 1989 there was very little difference between the sexes. However, women were also more likely than men to find work which directly used the skills in which they had trained (around four fifths of women trainees in work), and in this respect their relative advantage over men remained constant over time. This was due partly to the fact that they both trained and worked in a narrower range of occupations than men did. Training also led to an increase in the number of hours that women contributed to the labour force. Sixty-two per cent of jobs taken by women after training were full-time, and 45 per cent of women who had been working part-time immediately before their course moved into full-time work afterwards.

The Evaluation Study also compared the jobs that women got after their course with the jobs that they had been doing previously. Overall, the proportion in clerical and related work increased from 46 to 85 per cent, while the proportion in sales occupations or low-skill personal service jobs fell from 38 per cent to five per cent. The transition matrix given in Table 12.1 shows the pattern of movements between jobs. The most striking feature of this table is the large number of women whose training enabled them to exchange less skilled service jobs for clerical and secretarial occupations. Many of these women had done clerical or secretarial work some years previously, but had been downwardly mobile on their return to work after having children.

Table 12.1 also shows that 102 of the 112 women who were last employed in clerical and related jobs before their course took the same kind of work afterwards. What had been the benefit of training for them? Their work histories give the answer. About a third had been economically inactive for a period before their course, and a further third had been unemployed seeking work. For both these groups training was a step towards securing a job. The remaining third had been working immediately before their course but had wanted to upgrade their skills so they could get a better job. The gains they made were not large and do not show up in the very crude classification of occupations used in the table, but they were nonetheless real; typical among them was the switch from routine clerical work to a job involving modern office technology, or from the typing pool to a secretarial post.

Most of the women who had been working in manufacturing jobs before their course did not return to this type of work afterwards, but took office jobs instead. They were balanced by a similar number of women previously working in less skilled service jobs who moved into manufacturing after training. However, whilst most of the women who left manufacturing had been doing repetitive semi-skilled or unskilled work as assemblers or packers, those who went into manufacturing after training took jobs requiring a higher level of skill.

Overall women's mean earnings after training were 11 pence per hour higher in real terms than in their last job before their course, and as Table 12.2 shows, this modest gain contrasted with a mean loss of 27 pence per hour experienced by male trainees. Mean gains and losses, however, give a very incomplete picture of the changes that took place. Table 12.2 also shows that there was much less variability in the earnings of both sexes after their courses than there was before. This was because after training there were far fewer men and women with either very low or very high earnings. The women who increased their earnings the most after training typically exchanged a low-skill job in the service sector for a clerical or secretarial post. In fact mean earnings gains would have been much greater were it not for a small number of trainees previously in well paid jobs who had retrained for a new career, taking a substantial cut in pay, at least in the short term. In the case of men this was usually prompted by redundancy; in the case of women, the motives were more varied.

In terms of earnings gains and losses for individuals, these changes meant that 50 per cent of male trainees made losses and 46 per cent made gains while 37 per cent of female trainees made losses and 58 per cent made gains. For most women, the gains and losses were fairly modest, and smaller than those experienced by men, but changes which were small in absolute terms were important in relative terms when initial earnings were very low.

Modelling the training effect

While the work history data made it possible to understand the part that training played in women's lives, the comparison sample allowd this to be set against the situations of women with similar histories but no recent training. Thus the effectiveness of training can be assessed from a different angle. This analysis does not claim to give a definitive answer to the question of what was the 'training effect'. In many circumstances social experiments give a better indication of the effectiveness of a programme than do econometric analyses (see, for example, LaLonde 1986). Even so, as all approaches to evaluating social programmes present some methodological difficulties, it is wisest to base conclusions on the broadest range of evidence that can be obtained, and to probe further if inconsistencies emerge. In the Evaluation Study the experimental method was not feasible, either practically or politically. Nevertheless the comparative analysis complements the evidence of the work histories and of women's own opinions of their training, and the composite picture is consistent.

The matching of the trainee and comparison samples met with a considerable degree of success, though it presented some difficulties for women which are detailed in Payne (1990). The matching was intended only to reduce the between-sample variance, and the models that were fitted to the data also included among the predictor variables measures of all the characteristics on which the two samples were matched. Table 12.3 shows that women who went on TOPS/OJTS had a significantly greater chance of finding employment than women in the comparison sample, though this finding is partly explained by selection effects which it was not possible to eliminate by the matching process. The model for men, however, where a more successful matching process had ensured that selection effects were much less marked, showed an even greater training effect, which suggests that some part at least of the effect for women was real. Table 12.4 shows that women trainees were significantly more satisfied with the jobs they held when they were interviewed than were women in the comparison sample, though only if they were working in jobs which used the skills in which they had trained - a qualification which again suggests that the effect was real, and not an artefact either of selection effects or the questionnaire design.

Turning finally to earnings, Table 12.5 indicates that, other things being equal, women trainees were considerably better off than women who had not had recent training, though once again, only if they found a job using the skills in which they had trained. There were strong interaction effects in this model, with qualifications of A Level standard or better entirely eliminating the earnings premium attributable to training. This is explained by the pattern of movements between jobs before and after training that was described in the previous section, and represents a complication in the evaluation of training programmes that has not always been taken into account in previous studies.

One of the most important reasons why the earnings of women trainees were higher than those of similar women in the comparison sample was that, as long as they found work in the field in which they had trained, training considerably mitigated the detrimental effect of a career break on hourly earnings. Table 12.6 shows that in the comparison sample, women who had recently returned to work after a career break earned substantially less than women who had worked continuously in recent years. In contrast, for women who had trained on TOPS/OJTS during 1986, there was very little difference between the earnings of returners and the earnings of women who had been in employment before their course. As has been argued above, a very important function of training for women was to enable returners to get work at a skill level close to that of the job they held before their career break. In effect, training can establish a virtuous circle. Improved skills, qualifications and confidence increase the chances of getting a job with good pay and conditions, and these improved rewards in turn increase the chances of the return to work being permanent, and of the employer being prepared to invest in the woman's training.

Costs and returns

The demise of TOPS/OJTS was brought about not only by the shift towards voluntarism, but also by the expense of the programme. The direct costs were in fact lower for women than for men, for their courses were on average shorter and more often part-time. Nevertheless, the cost per place was considerably higher than on ET.

In training, however, there is a trade-off between costs and returns. Compared to TOPS/OJTS, ET is a low skill programme. Higher level training in the new technologies formed a substantial element in TOPS/OJTS, but represents only a minute proportion of training on ET. Training for low skill occupations, for example in personal services, is much more prominent on the latter scheme. As Tables 12.7 and 12.8 show, the number of ET trainees gaining qualifications is about a third of the figure on TOPS/OJTS, and placement rates in jobs are substantially lower.

If the focus is on enhancing the country's skills base rather than securing a temporary reduction in the unemployment count, then the current restriction of government training schemes primarily to the long-term unemployed is not helpful. It tends to devalue and stigmatise training in the eyes of trainees and employers alike, and when programmes are chasing the monthly unemployment count, a pace of change is induced which is not compatible with carefully planned and monitored development. The country's skills needs would be better served by long-term programmes that give high quality training, are relevant to industrial needs, and open to all who want to make a serious commitment to learning new skills, whether unemployed or not. This cannot be achieved without accepting higher costs.

Sexual segregation

Though TOPS/OJTS was undoubtedly of great benefit to women, it had little impact on another fundamental problem which plagues attempts to improve the position of women in the workforce in Britain, namely their clustering within a narrow range of occupations traditionally regarded as 'woman's work'. These occupations are typically less well paid than the jobs done by men, and carry fewer opportunities for advancement.

Training on TOPS/OJTS mirrored these divisions: women were heavily concentrated on clerical and secretarial courses and courses for 'women's' jobs in manufacturing (such as sewing machining or printed circuit board assembly), and they were extremely sparsely represented on courses in engineering science and technology and the traditional manual crafts. Though training enabled many women to move to more skilled and better paid jobs, they achieved this through traditional female career paths and not by breaking into male strongholds.

Sexual segregation in work, and the consequent sexual segregation of training, will not be overcome without a vigorously pursued equal opportunities programme. The fact that there are skills shortages in the newer technologies should encourage employers to increase their efforts to recruit women in these fields, but the history of the 1980s has proved that skills shortages alone are not a sufficient catalyst for change. Adult training programmes can play a part, through targeted recruitment drives, 'taster' courses, special arrangements to support women training in male-dominated fields, and efforts to increase the awareness of employers of the possibility of employing women in non-traditional ways. Before TOPS/OJTS was closed down, the Manpower Services Commission with the help of European funds had been developing initiatives like these under the programme 'Wider Opportunities for Women', but the programme was never introduced on a large scale. Similar courses can still be found, but they are scattered and unco-ordinated, and offer only a small number of places (see Clarke 1991).

Conclusion

Compared to current government policy on training, TOPS/OJTS had three main merits: it opened the door to training to everyone who wanted it, the training it offered was of high quality and focused on the country's emerging skills needs, and a much higher proportion of the training places went to women. The squeeze on publicly funded training for women is almost certainly an unplanned and unforeseen consequence of the preference for market rather than interventionist solutions in training; it is nonetheless real. If the country relies primarily on employers and private individuals to provide the funds for adult training, the current recession will inevitably reduce women's opportunities still further.

The argument of the 1988 White Paper was that those who benefit most from training must take the major share of the costs. Though the major responsibility for training people in employment was said to lie with employers,

> 'Individuals too have a crucial part to play...For individuals, investment in training is the best way to ensure both greater job security and enhanced earnings over the course of their working lives' (Employment Dept. 1988, para. 8.6).

The Evaluation Study gave evidence of the truth of this claim; however it is a logically separate proposition that all the costs of training outside of current employment should be borne by the individual being trained, with publicly funded places provided only as a safety-net for the long-term unemployed. The relationship between the public and the private good is the subject of an ancient debate; it is nevertheless entirely clear that the benefits of training do not accrue solely to the individual trained. If they did, the Secretary of State for Employment would not trouble to exhort individuals to invest in training. As far as women are concerned, current policy fails to take into account both their unequal access to the money with which to finance training and the greater risks that the investment carries, due both to less certain prospects of future employment on account of domestic responsibilities and also to lower returns to training because of the gap between male and female pay.[4]

If investing in training women is risky, why then should government finance be used? The answer is twofold. First, women's perception of the risk is often exaggerated by their own lack of confidence in themselves. Growth in self-confidence was stressed over and over again by the women who had been through TOPS/OJTS. As one said, 'I believe in myself now, and the course was the basis'. Women who do not believe in themselves will not risk their family's financial security by borrowing to invest in themselves; outside funding is essential. Second, though for each individual woman investment in training carries a risk of failure whose costs may be great, at the collective level the probability of a return on the investment is very secure. The benefit to the economy of enabling substantial numbers of women to exchange low-skill work for skilled jobs where labour is in demand is immense. It is ultimately on this that the case for public investment in adult training rests.

Notes

1. Calculated from Employment Department 1993, Table 1.
2. Own calculations from 1991 Labour Force Survey micro-data. 'Top level jobs' are defined as OPCS socio-economic groups 1.2 and 4 (the self-employed being excluded from the analysis).
3. This work was financed by the Nuffield Foundation, whose support is gratefully acknowledged.
4. Connolly (1991), using data from the 1958 British Birth Cohort, has demonstrated that the returns to training undertaken after leaving full-time education are substantially lower for females than for males.

References

Clarke, K. (1991), *Women and Training: A Review of Recent Research and Policy*. Manchester: Equal Opportunities Commission.

Connolly, S. (1991), *An Investigation of the Labour Market Experiences of Young People who Left School at 16*, D.Phil. thesis (Economics), Oxford University.

Department of Education and Science (1990), *International Statistical Comparisons of the Education and Training of 16 to 18 year olds. Statistical Bulletin 1/90.*

Employment Department (1988), *Employment for the 1990s*. London: HMSO.

Employment Department (1990a), *1990s: The Skills Decade. Strategic Guidance on Enterprise and Training*. Sheffield.

Employment Department (1990b), 'ET follow-up survey of scheme leavers', *Labour Market Quarterly Report*, pp. 16-18.

Employment Department (1992a), *Career Development Loans Newsletter*. London.

Employment Department (1992b), *Career Development Loans Annual Report 1991-1992*. London.

Employment Department (1993), *Labour Force Survey Historical Supplement April 1993: Spring 1979 to Autumn 1992*. London.

Finegold, D. and Soskice, D. (1988), 'The failure of training in Britain: Analysis and prescription', *Oxford Review of Economic Policy*, pp. 21-53.

Green, F. (1991), 'The determinants of training of male and female employees in Britain', University of Leicester, Department of Economics, Discussion Paper No. 153.

Greenhalgh, C. and Mavrotas, G. (1991), 'Workforce training in the Thatcher era - Market forces and market failures', University of Oxford, Institute of Economics and Statistics Applied Economics, Discussion Paper No. 120.

LaLonde, R. (1986), 'Evaluating the econometric evaluations of training programs with experimental data', *American Economic Review*, 76, pp.

Martin, J. and Roberts, C. (1984), *Women and Employment: A Lifetime Perspective*. Department of Employment and OPCS, London: HMSO.

McLeish, H. (1990), 'Who Pays for Skills?', *Labour Market Briefing* No. 3, London: House of Commons.

Metcalf, H. and Leighton, P. (1989), *The Under-Utilisation of Women in the Labour Market*. London: Institute of Manpower Studies Report No. 172.

National Institute of Economic and Social Research (1989), *Productivity, Education and Training: Britain and other countries compared*. London.

Payne, J. (1990), *Adult Off-the-Job Skills Training: An Evaluation Study*. Sheffield: Training Agency Research and Development Series No. 57.

Payne, J. (1991), *Women, Training and the Skills Shortage: The Case for Public Investment*. London: Policy Studies Institute.

Sheldrake, J. and Vickerstaff, S. (1987), *The History of Industrial Training in Britain*. Aldershot: Avebury (Gower Publishing Co. Ltd.)

Wilson, J. (1990), 'High Technology National Training', *Employment Gazette*, 98, pp. 347-52.

Table 12.1
Transition matrix for women trainees' last job
before training and their first job afterwards

	First job after training					
	manag/ prof & rel	cler- ical & rel	less skilled service	manuf- actur- ing	other	Total
	N	N	N	N	N	N
last job before training						
managerial; professional & related	9	16	1	1	0	27
clerical & related	5	102	5	0	0	112
less skilled service	1	67	8	8	0	84
manufacturing	1	7	0	2	0	10
other	1	0	0	0	1	2
Total N	17	192	14	11	1	235

Source: *Evaluation Study*

Note

Based on women trainees who had at least one job before their course and at least one job afterwards.

Table 12.2
Mean earnings (uprated to October 1987 values)
before and after training, by sex

		gross hourly earnings						
		before training		after training		difference	
	N	mean	s.d.	mean	s.d.	mean	s.d.
Men	200	£4.05	2.05	£3.78	1.35	-£0.27	2.10
Women	171	£2.99	1.42	£3.10	.88	+£0.11	1.39
Total	371	£3.56	1.86	£3.46	1.20	-£0.10	1.81

Source: *Evaluation Study. Excludes those who had not worked either before or after their course or were self-employed, those who were under 18 when they left their job before the course, those whose last job before their course was abroad, and those who gave incomplete information on earnings.*

Table 12.3
Logit model for employment in the period April 1987 - September 1987: combined trainee and comparison sample, women

	mean	exponentiated coefficient	t statistic
Constant	..	6.21	..
TTWA unemployment rate	13.26	0.99	0.40
months unemployed in 1985	1.77	0.97	1.28
months in work 1980-1985	40.63	1.01^{**}	2.80
Job (or latest job) in 1986:			
clerical & related	0.34	1.00	..
managerial/professional	0.18	0.98	0.06
personal service	0.34	1.14	0.48
manufacturing blue collar	0.13	0.71	1.02
other	0.01	1.78	0.60
age	35.50	0.96^{**}	3.08
ethnic minority	0.17	0.97	0.09
disability/health problem	0.12	0.54^{*}	2.10
married	0.72	1.18	0.42
number of dependent children:			
0	0.35	1.00	..
1-2	0.56	1.60_{*}	1.50
3 or more	0.09	2.83^{*}_{***}	2.08
child aged under 5	0.21	0.15^{***}	6.06
lone parent	0.12	1.15	0.28
educational qualifications:			
none	0.34	1.00	..
below A Level standard	0.47	1.11	0.41
A Level standard or better	0.19	0.79	0.64
age left full-time education:			
16 or younger	0.70	1.00	..
17-19	0.23	1.48	1.30
20 or older	0.07	2.26	1.55
months in full-time training or education 1980-1985	2.74	1.01_{**}	0.58
went on TOPS/OJTS	0.52	2.21^{**}	3.12

N: 594   deviance: 593 (df 572)
deviance with constant only: 692 (df 593)

Significance levels: *=.05, **=.01, ***=.001

Table 12.4
Logit model for job satisfaction in current job:
combined trainee and comparison sample, women

	mean	exponentiated coefficient	t statistic
Constant	..	0.41	..
TTWA unemployment rate	13.04	0.98	0.94
months unemployed in 1985	1.44	1.00	0.13
months in work 1980-1985	42.39	1.01	1.51
job (or latest job) in 1986:			
clerical & related	0.36	1.00	..
managerial/professional & rel.	0.16	1.69	1.42
personal service	0.37	1.37	1.13
manufacturing blue collar	0.09	1.48	0.86
other	0.02	1.46	0.51
age	35.71	0.97	1.80
ethnic minority	0.17	0.55	1.84
disability/health problem	0.09	0.68	0.92
married	0.72	6.07***	3.92
number of dependent children:			
0	0.36	1.00	..
1-2	0.55	0.40**	2.72
3 or more	0.09	0.27*	2.56
child aged under 5	0.14	1.27	0.62
lone parent	0.11	4.52**	2.58
educational qualifications:			
none	0.31	1.00	..
below A Level standard	0.51	1.58	1.59
A Level standard or better	0.18	1.31	0.62
age left full-time education:			
16 or younger	0.67	1.00	..
17-19	0.27	1.00	0.01
20 or older	0.06	0.26*	2.09
months in full-time training or education 1980-1985	2.56	1.01	0.82
training:			
none (comparison sample)	0.43	1.00	..
TOPS/OJTS, out of trade	0.12	1.79	1.43
TOPS/OJTS, in trade	0.45	2.32**	2.84

N: 382   deviance: 474 (df 359)
deviance with constant only: 519 (df 381)
Significance levels: *=.05, **=.01, ***=.001

Table 12.5
OLS regression model for earnings:
combined trainee and control sample, women

	mean	exponentiated coefficient	t statistic
Constant	..	300.20	..
TTWA unemployment rate	13.02	-2.54	1.88
months unemployed in 1985	1.61	-3.37*	2.08
months in work 1980-85	41.29	0.81*	2.07
Job (or latest job) in 1986:			
clerical & related	0.36	..	..
managerial/professional & rel.	0.16	42.09*	2.24
personal service	0.35	-18.46	1.33
manufacturing blue collar	0.12	-6.65	0.33
construction/mining/transport	0.01	-61.77	0.99
other	0.01	-37.19	0.49
age group:			
18-25	0.14	..	..
25-34	0.31	-29.81	1.29
35-44	0.42	-35.24	1.45
45+	0.13	-38.17	1.41
ethnic minority	0.17	25.13	1.63
disability/health problem	0.08	-11.84	0.58
married	0.71	8.60	0.42
number of dependent children:			
none	0.35	..	..
1-2	0.55	-0.89	0.05
3 or more	0.10	-10.51	0.40
child aged under 5	0.15	-8.71	0.46
lone parent	0.12	-0.08	0.00
educational qualifications:			
none	0.31	..	..
below A Level standard	0.50	23.76	1.19
A level standard or better	0.19	155.00***	5.51
age left full-time education:			
16 or younger	0.67	..	..
17-19	0.26	19.38	1.28
20 or older	0.07	47.69	1.81
months in full-time training or education 1980-1985	2.67	-0.61	0.81

training:
none (comparison sample)	0.42	..	..
TOPS/OJTS, working out of trade	0.13	17.87**	0.38
TOPS/OJTS, working in trade	0.45	82.52**	2.61

Interaction terms

months in work 1980-85 with trainee out of trade	-0.02	0.03
months in work 1980-85 with trainee in trade	-0.76	1.55
below A Lev, trainee out of trade	-4.49	0.11
below A Lev, trainee in trade	-20.86***	0.70
A Lev+, trainee out of trade	-200.10***	3.76
A Lev+, trainee in trade	-141.50***	3.82

R Square	29.99%
N	377
df	345

Significance levels: *=.05, **=.01, ***=.001

Table 12.6
Earnings and career breaks: women who went on TOPS/OJTS compared with members of the comparison sample

	trainee sample	comparison sample
Mean gross hourly earnings in current job[1]:		
(a) in work for the whole of 1985	£3.43	£3.34
(N)	(96)	(86)
(b) away from work for the whole of 1985	£3.35	£2.67
(N)	(82)	(51)
difference between (a) and (b)	£0.08	£0.67

[1] Or, for those not currently in work, the most recent job, provided this was after the TOPS/OJTS course (trainees) or continued to April 1987 or later (comparison sample).

Source: Evaluation Study.

Table 12.7
Comparison between the qualifications gained by TOPS/OJTS trainees and trainees on Employment Training.

	TOPS/OJTS (completers only) (1986)		ET (all leavers) (Jul 89-Mar 90)	
	men %	women %	men %	women %
all gaining a qualification	57	67	19	23
of which:				
recognised	42	51	-	-
not recognised	16	16	-	-
(Base N)	(372)	(318)	(299,845)	((161,455)

Note

ET figures include credits towards a qualification; these are not counted in the figures for TOPS/OJTS.

Sources: Columns 1 & 2: Evaluation Study.
Column 3: Employment Department (1990b) (own calculations).

Table 12.8
Placement rates on TOPS/OJTS compared with
Employment Training

	In work 3 months after training		
	TOPS/OJTS all trainees 1st quarter 1988 %	ET long-term unemployed 1986 %	all trainees Jul 89- Mar 90 %
all in work	67	47	38
in work in trade	51	35	23 (estimate)

Sources: *Column 1: TOPS/OJTS Follow-Up Survey 1987/88.*
        Column 2: Evaluation Study.
        Column 3: Employment Department 1990b (including own calculations).

13   Training and enterprise in France

Eric Verdier

Introduction

Since the beginning of the 1970s, French research on continuing training has been strongly marked by the creation of a unique institutional mechanism whereby firms are required by law to devote a fraction of their wage bill to continuing training. In this way, they have an incentive both to pursue their own immediate goals (improving competitiveness) but also goals that are broader in scope (reducing inequalities among workers).

Among the many studies that have attempted to evaluate the efficiency of this mechanism, a number have brought out the diversity in the firms' applications of continuing training. The question raised here is quite simple: why is such training a resource that can be mobilised only by certain types of firms? The answers we consider have tried to take into account the economic and organisational characteristics of the enterprises concerned. Recognition of the heterogeneity of the productive apparatus has also impelled a number of studies to draw on the theory of labour-market segmentation.

The results of this research cannot however be interpreted without considering the specific characteristics of French firms and the particularities of the initial training system, their organisation of work, and the nature of the French labour market. These have led to the development of international comparisons, notably with Germany and Japan.

It is especially in addressing the forms of flexibility of work that exist in these two countries that certain studies have tried to bring out the most significant shifts in the firms' relations with continuing training.

An innovative institutional mechanism

France has been developing a very particular system of continuing training for the past twenty years. (Indeed, it was only at the beginning of the 1990s that Australia instituted a legal mechanism based in part on the French legislation.) The ambitiousness of the goals of the system reflects the extent of the initial consensus reached by the social partners and the norms underlying the institutional mechanism were the subject of extensive preliminary dialogue aimed at ensuring the optimal efficiency of the measures implemented.

An original system of incentives

In its original conception, this mechanism was intended to break away from an interventionist approach by developing incentives oriented toward two categories of objectives. The first of these could be termed 'civic'. In the most general way, it was deemed important to give men and women, as citizens, greater control over their lives by improving their level of education and training. To this end, inequalities of access to continuing training were to be reduced, and more important, those excluded from initial training and from the culture at large were to be given a 'second chance'. Indeed, at the time this mechanism was being created, the consequences of academic failure were great in that nearly one third of a given age group of young people were leaving the educational system without recognized vocational or general training (the proportion has now been reduced by more than one half). The Act of 16 July 1971 fell within the more general framework of 'lifelong education', which sought to combine initial and continuing training in the hope of transforming the educational apparatus, particularly with regard to its selective character, through a greater diversity of pedagogical techniques (Delors, 1974).

The second category of objectives was economic. The recourse to continuing training was to improve the efficiency of industry and trade by providing businesses or sectors of economic activity with a tool for managing change which would reconcile economic imperatives with the development of employees' skills.

These objectives were not solely the concern of business however: the Act specified that lifelong training was a 'national obligation' jointly incumbent upon 'the State, local authorities, educational institutions, training associations, and vocational, union, and family organisations, as well as firms'.

During the 1970s, the emphasis, in principle at least, was placed on equal access to training; for the 1980s, the main incentive was rather to make continuing training a 'productive investment' for greater competitiveness.

A mechanism resulting from dialogue

The law is, however, not the only basis of the training programme, or even the main one. From the outset, it was preceded by negotiations among the social partners leading to inter-sectoral agreements. Thus, the Act of 16 July 1971, which is the keystone of the continuing vocational training system, followed the preliminary conclusion of collective agreements between unions and employers. The same was true for the February 1984 Act which followed the inter-sectoral agreement of 1983 and which was notably responsible for introducing sandwich courses for young people, as well as new public incentives.

This link between legislation and sectoral agreements responded to a desire to generate incentives rather than prescriptions, and in this way to ensure closer correspondence between general norms and the behaviour of the partners. Thus, every firm with more than ten salaried employees is required to allot a fraction of its wage bill to training expenditures. From an initial 0.8 percent, this legal requirement has been progressively increased to the current level of 1.2 percent, in effect since 1967. What is required, however, is the expenditure, not the training. In other words, a firm can meet its legal obligation by paying its funds directly to the Public Revenue Office or, as is often the case among the SMEs, to mutual funds established on a sectoral and/or regional basis. In the extreme, a firm can make the necessary expenditure without training a single employee.

Unprecedented institutional innovations

The legal obligation generated a vast and ever-expanding market for continuing training. As a result, new institutions had to be created to regulate this market and, in particular, to ensure better coordination between the firms' supply and demand.

This situation gave rise to two kinds of bodies specifically oriented toward the SMEs:

*Training insurance funds (Fonds d'Assurance Formation) which are jointly administered by employers and unions. In certain sectors (e.g., construction and hotel management), firms covered by the collective agreement are bound to belong and to contribute a fraction of the legal requirement to the fund.

*Training associations (Associations de Formation) which were created by sectoral employers, who wanted to retain direct control over the orientation of continuing training policies. Since 1984 their board (which plays a technical rather than a decision-making role) is jointly run.

Like mutual funds, these bodies are able to provide the firm with financing for training in much greater amounts than the firm itself would have been able to set aside in the short run. These institutions are also intended to make SME management more aware of the usefulness of continuing training and to bring about a better adaptation of training content to the specific organisational needs of the SMEs.

The development of this network of institutions mediating between government requirements and the needs of firms is stressed here for two reasons. First of all, the sums of money they collect has increased significantly, with the training insurance funds alone representing 32 percent of training expenditures for firms with ten to nineteen employees. In addition, continuing training represents one of the rare instances in France where institutional structures emanating from the social partners have played a significant role between the traditionally strong and fairly prescriptive intervention of the State and the specific practices of the firms.

The statutes accompanying the 1971 Act established a model for off-the-job training, which was to involve a predetermined sequence of theoretical or practical studies, in principle conducted outside the workplace with specially prepared teaching materials. On-the-job training was excluded; indeed, the law went even further by excluding from the framework of the legal obligation training for adaptation to the work station. By the mid 1980s, this requirement, which strongly reflected the dominant academic model at the time, was relaxed to permit practical training in the workplace provided that employee representatives were informed.

The evaluation of the firms' legal obligation for training

Numerous studies have analysed the effects and impact of the Act of 16 July 1971. (For overviews, see Dubar, 1990 and Berton and Podevin, 1991). The legal mechanism itself provides a statistical source which serves as the basis for such evaluations: in order to demonstrate that they have met the legal obligation, firms with ten or more salaried employees are required to fill out a financial form detailing the amount spent on training, the way in which this training was provided (through the firm's own training resources or through recourse to outside providers), and the participation among the different categories of employees.

Although training in the firm has developed considerably since 1971, its benefits for the individuals involved have diminished somewhat over time. In addition, the disparities between categories remain so large that the founding notion of training as a 'second chance' for social mobility is at best debatable.

The ambiguities of the development of continuing vocational training in firms

From a strictly quantitative point of view, the increase in training expenditures is undeniable. It has more than doubled, to represent 2.89 percent of gross wages (32.6 billion francs) as compared to 1.35 percent in 1972. As such, it greatly exceeds the rise in the legal minimum, which has gone from 0.8 percent of the wage bill in 1972 to 1 percent in 1974, 1.1 percent in 1978, and 1.2 percent since 1987. The question remains, however (see below), whether the legal obligation has actually functioned as a stimulus or whether it has simply revealed or perhaps even reflected the spontaneous development of firms' expenditures.

Over time, the quality of these expenditures has also improved (Ghin 1989). In the first phase (1972-1978), firms' increased training effort mainly consisted of meeting the new legal standards. Thus there was a sharp drop in the payments that firms failing to spend the legal minimum (especially small enterprises) were required to make to the Public

Treasury, since these amounts were increasingly collected by specific institutions (the training insurance funds and the associations mentioned above).

Between 1978 and 1982, the previous increase levelled off, particularly with the growing impact of the economic downturn. Under these circumstances, the firms priority was quantitative: reducing wage costs and including training expenditures. In addition, the widespread recourse to contingent work that began during this period ran counter to investment in training, which requires a minimum stabilisation of the work force in order to be profitable. In 1976, the government had already held back on raising the legal minimum to 2 percent of the wage bill, as mandated by law (and fifteen years later, it still has not been reached).

Table 13.1
Rate of financial participation (RFP) and training possibilities (TP) according to firm size

Employees

	10-19	20-49	50-499	500-1999	2000+	Total
1974						
RFP	0.66	0.66	1.14	1.45	2.59	1.63
TP	2	3	6	10	21	11
1982						
RFP	1	1.10	1.33	1.81	3.06	1.96
TP	2	2	6	10	20	10
1984						
RFP	1.13	1.20	1.46	2.02	3.47	2.17
TP	3	4	7	12	22	11
1989						
RFP	1.31	1.43	2.02	2.92	4.67	2.89
TP	3	4	9	16	27	14

Source: CEREQ (based on employers' declaration 2483

RFP   = total training expenditures
            gross wage bill

TP   = total training hours
            salaried employees

Since 1982 there has been a new phase of growth. Particularly marked in firms with five hundred or more employees, it attests to a more secure place for training in firms' management policies and strategies. Economic goals have come to predominate (favouring the adaptation of skills for greater competitiveness, accelerating the recycling of the work force), and these are supported by the government, which has instituted complementary sources of assistance to the firms, notably to encourage forms of organisation that promote the upgrading of skills and the elimination of hierarchies and compartmentalisation (Kirsch, 1990b; Vesprini, 1990).

The difficulty of raising the legal minimum as planned is symptomatic of the failure, in part at least, of a macrosocial strategy that was the implicit basis for the legislation. Here, the idea was to apply to continuing training existing processes of generalising the behaviours of the most innovative firms to the others, as had already been done with, for example, paid leaves, work hours, and benefits in general. Public firms such as Renault had often been at the source of these 'progressive' transformations (see Fournier and Questiaux, 1976), which represented an extension of what French regulation theory (see Boyer 1987) has conceptualised as the 'monopolistic wage nexus', characterised by highly stable employment, the indexation of wage increases to productivity gains, significant indirect wages, and a high degree of labour specialisation.

The development of continuing training has been caught in a web of contradictions, however. While they predated the crisis, they have been greatly heightened by the change in the macroeconomic context, as demonstrated by the slow-down in the growth of expenditures for training.

Continuing vocational training has been profoundly limited by the social and organisational context in which it developed and, in particular, by its status as a legal requirement. To begin with, the expanded recourse to continuing training obviously runs counter to the well-entrenched principles of Taylorism, and in fact, low-skilled categories of labour have been largely excluded from the new programmes even though the law was intended to reduce such disparities.

In addition, the degradation of work and the organisational 'work crisis' that marked the end of the 1960s and the first half of the 1970s favoured training outside the workshop or the office on principle, since these sites

307

were considered hopelessly tied to the logic of Taylorism. Finally, the domination of the academic model, even for technical instruction, has also led in this direction.

Thus, in one and the same somewhat paradoxical gesture, the Act of 1971 consecrated the firm as a legitimate and efficient site for training but made training external to work. This notion amounted, implicitly at least, to considering that the organisation of work could not upgrade skills and thus could not contribute to training.

The characteristic drawbacks of the French labour market have largely contributed to holding training activities to a logic of short-term adaptation of skills. Their limited duration (fifty hours or less annually per trainee for the entire period) has reinforced the specific character of French employees' skills, which were already strongly marked by management based on seniority. In addition, bound by a very localised concept (i.e., a strictly defined work station), the skills of French employees, even when reinforced by continuing training, have not constituted an adequate resource for mastering reconversions and technical or organisational transformations. In contrast to Japan and Germany, the mobility of French employees, both internal and external, declined during the economic downturn (Silvestre, 1986). In Japan, internal mobility was bolstered by polyvalence and company-wide skills (rather than those limited to the work station); in Germany, the development of the apprenticeship system and transferable skills were responsible for increased inter-firm mobility.

As a result, a number of firms found themselves in a paradoxical situation which is well reflected in the choices of the banks and the insurances companies, two sectors that have traditionally been among the most oriented toward continuing training. On the one hand, these enterprises have tended to neglect the internal potential of skills even though their personnel was less and less mobile with the continuation of employment cutbacks; on the other hand, they favoured the recruitment of young graduates despite the low turnover of personnel which limited this. Certain government measures, such as solidarity contracts and early retirement systems, helped to relax these constraints.

The solidarity contracts, dating from the first half of the 1980s, allowed firms to pay for the departure of the oldest employees from one to five years before retirement age. In exchange, the participating firms were to hire young people with degree levels considerably higher than those of older workers. Applied to early retirees, this policy allowed for a much higher level of initial training of the work force without calling into question the operating rules of the internal market. This produced considerable tensions, however, notably because a number of graduates found their status downgraded at the time of hiring without any significant career prospects opening up. In addition, firms had difficulty recouping the know-how that was lost with the departure of the most experienced employees.

Greatly limited prospects for individual promotion

In principle, acquiring continuing training constitutes an important advantage for the employees involved (Laulhe, 1990). Between 1980 and 1985, 13 percent of those who were trained on the employer's initiative obtained promotions from one socio-occupational group to another, as opposed to 6.5 percent of untrained employees. This is more often the case when the training leads to a diploma (44 percent of the promotions). Furthermore, for those who were employed by private firms in 1980, the risk of being unemployed five years later was two and a half times less when they had undergone training on the employer's initiative during that time period.

Several factors counterbalance this positive effect, however. First of all, the proportion of employees whose training leads to a diploma (from the educational system or simply a 'house' certificate) is well below 20 percent. Secondly, the link between training and promotional mobility has become increasingly remote.

The possibilities open to individuals for capitalising on their training is limited by two determining factors: on the one hand, the nonexistence of occupational markets apart from those for high-skilled occupations (computer scientists, for example), and on the other, the growing competition among those with initial training diplomas, the number of whom rose considerably in the 1970s and even more in the 1980s (Beduwe, 1990).

Table 13.2
(a) Effects of 'employer-initiated' training
completed during the five years prior to the survey
and reported by active employees at the time of the survey

(in %)

Survey	Vertical Mobility	Horizontal Mobility	No Mobility Declared	Other	Total
FQP 1970	55.4	3.4	39.2	2.0	100
FQP 1977	33.6	5.9	59.9	0.6	100
FQP 1985	28.0	7.7	64.1	0.2	100

(b) Effects of 'self-initiated' training
completed during the five years prior to the survey
and reported by active employees at the time of the survey

Survey	Vertical Mobility	Horizontal Mobility	No Mobility Declared	To Find First Job	Other	Total
FQP 1970	35.2	4.1	60.7		3.0	100
QP 1977	29.6	4.4	54.8	8.8	2.4	100
FQP 1985	21.2	6.7	57.2	13.5	1.4	100

Source: INSEE, FQP surveys, CEREQ evaluations.

* Excluding: training that took place upon entry into the firm and before assuming a job, as well as those related to a job-training contract.

In addition, the place of individual choices in the operation of the continuing training mechanism has always been very limited. Thus, legislation had anticipated the possibility for every employee to benefit from a training leave generally for a medium- or long-term course of study. In spite of numerous modifications of the law aimed at facilitating access to this right, the development of training leave has remained very limited (around forty to fifty thousand beneficiaries out of two million trainees falling under the legal obligation). Here too, the weakness of occupational markets and the employers' desire to control internal markets reinforce each other to limit the scope of this component, which, in the beginning of the 1970s, was considered the most innovative insofar as it was likely to help reconcile the interests of the individual and the goals of firms.

The Act of 1971 has also imposed far-reaching conditions which are hardly favourable to investment in the training of individuals (Nallet, 1991). In fact, the regulations provide for training to take place during work hours. In principle, then, night courses (mainly municipal) for so-called 'social advancement' are ignored to such an extent that there are no statistics for establishing their numbers and no particular incentives to take them. Even so, along with correspondence courses, they involve a population in training of the order of 800,000 persons a year. Their impact on the career paths of those taking them is however, not well known.

The predominance of firms' choices over those of individuals is shown by the fact that rates of promotion on completion of continuing training programmes are closely correlated to the profiles of employers. Thus, they increase with proximity to the 'public' pole, and conversely, the proportions are low for SMEs in the consumer-goods industry. For employees who have taken training courses on the initiative of their employer, the promotion rate is 32 percent in nationalised enterprises, as compared to 21 percent for the private sector. Within the latter, employees of small firms will be promoted two times less than those receiving training in firms with more than five hundred salaried employees.

The impact of industrial sector and firm size on training also comes into play in the disparities among occupational groups.

Unequal access to continuing training[1]

The Act of 1971, like the inter-sectoral agreement that preceded it, had the explicit objective of reducing the inequalities generated by the selectivity of the school system and of limiting the access of lower-skilled workers to training during their working lives (Berton and Podevin, 1990).

Greatest benefits for most highly skilled employees
In spite of the extensive penetration of continuing vocational training in the firms, access to it remains sharply differentiated according to the employees' age, sex, or occupational category. Thus, contrary to the

objectives of the legislation, low-skilled categories have remained largely outside training developments, while technicians and supervisors have even greater access than managers and engineers. If, in the past few years, an average of 45 percent of the latter have taken training courses on the initiative of their employer, the proportion is only 20 percent for skilled workers and 12 percent for unskilled workers. In terms of training possibilities (the average number of training hours per salaried employee), the gap between the technicians and the most disadvantaged category (unskilled workers) even shows increases between 1984 and 1989. (See table 13.3.)

However, inequalities linked to individual characteristics appear largely overdetermined by inequalities arising from structural characteristics such as the size and activity sector of the firm.

Large disparities according to sector and firm size
The growth of continuing vocation training since 1971 above all reflects industrial sector. Firms can be divided by sector into three main groups according to the scale of their operations.

Strong tradition of continuing training
Sectors with a high degree of concentration, such as energy or services (transport, banks), have made long and liberal use of training in human relations management: their rate of financial participation in 1989, as in 1976, was greater than 3 percent. These large firms, mainly in the public sector, administer a labour force that is highly skilled and well paid. Negotiation among the social partners is significant and emphasizes the kind of internal mobility that requires continuing training.

Intermediate situations: accommodating change or resolving the crisis
This group includes sectors where the recourse to training is higher than average - i.e., most manufacturing industries, plus chemicals and pharmaceuticals, insurance, and noncommercial services. Thus, the recourse to training often follows from an acceleration of technological change or profound transformations in productive structures brought about by the economic crisis.

Table 13.3
Training possibilities
by occupational category and firm size

(in hours)

	Employees					
	10-19	20-49	50-499	500-1999	2000+	Total
Unskilled workers						
1984	2	2	4	6	11	6
1989	2	2	4	7	14	6
Skilled workers						
1984	2	2	5	9	20	10
1989	2	2	6	11	26	11
Clerical						
1984	3	4	7	12	18	10
1989	3	5	9	14	21	12
Technicians and Superviser						
1984	5	6	11	19	30	20
1989	6	8	15	25	37	25
Engineers Managers						
1984	5	7	12	19	28	16
1989	5	8	16	26	36	22
Overall						
1984	3	4	7	12	22	11
1989	3	4	9	16	27	14

Source: CEREQ (based on employers' Declaration 2483)

TP   = <u>total training hours</u>
              salaried employees

Sectors near the legal minimum
This is a fairly diverse group which includes the whole of the consumer-goods industries, construction, and certain manufacturing sectors (paper and board, metalworking, mechanical construction); commercial activities (wholesale and retail, both foodstuffs and non-foodstuffs, auto sales and repairs, hotels, cafes, restaurants), and two

other tertiary sectors (commercial services to individuals and real estate rental and leasing). In these instances, continuing training remains foreign to management styles that rely on the external market, extensive mobility, a young and little-trained work force and, for certain activities, the massive use of apprenticeships or public programmes designed to facilitate the entry of young people into the labour market.

In terms of firm size, 80 percent of the smallest firms (10-19 employees) subject to the Act of 1971 still remain at the minimum of the required expenditures, and their participation has developed mainly in relation to changes in the legal framework. In 1987, two out of three small firms had no trainees at all, as compared to only one firm out of every hundred with more than two thousand employees. This situation demonstrates the ongoing difficulties of developing or simply undertaking continuing vocational training given the management and strategies of small enterprises.

For SMEs, the legal obligation quickly became a tax levy, which only accentuated the disparity between the legally defined norm and their spontaneous behaviour. Such firms prefer to develop skills through on-the-job apprenticeships and cannot easily part with their employees in order to send them to training courses. Thus, far from favouring SMEs, the intermediate institutions have in fact put them at a disadvantage by limiting their financing to predefined training activities that are hardly compatible with their organisational makeup.

Such problems are further compounded by the very heterogeneity of SMEs and the mediocre quality of the institutional networks they can turn to for access to training and development. It still remains to create new forms of cooperation between firms (e.g., principals and subcontractors), with the employers' organisations as intermediaries, so that all forms of training assistance can be fully effective. In order to have real meaning, the preliminary evaluations must be re-examined in the light of the firms' work-force management strategies.

Continuing training and the heterogeneity of the firms

Following the pioneering studies of Doeringer and Piore (see in particular Doeringer and Piore 1971 and Piore 1975), one line of research into continuing training in France took its inspiration, initially at least, from segmentation theory. More recently, this has given way to two kinds of refinements: the analysis of employee entries and exits relative to the stable work force (for the moment limited to an industrial framework), and the interpretation of data from individual firms.

From structural modes of work-force management to the role of training in adjustments

Drawing on the initial research of Eymard-Duvernay (1981), Grando (1983) attempted to characterise the typical forms of work-force management. The decision to proceed by activity sector[2] was not simply pragmatic: an industry is not only a collection of firms or even an institutional reality with collective agreements generally made in the areas of employment and training, but also an economic reality. As such, its goal is production, and each firm is in fact bound to the others in a dual relationship of industrial complementarity and market competition. On the basis of an analysis of correspondences and a straightforward classification of data, Grando distinguishes two groups of industries. One of these, which he characterises by management 'outside the labour market', includes those sectors with a better trained, stable work force that often benefits from training measures and with a higher than average proportion of managers and technicians. Basic chemistry, metallurgy, electricity and gas production, and the petroleum industry would be the most representative. Firms in these sectors often set up channels of promotion which, through recourse to internal training, permit progress from one skill level to another. These tools have been used to accompany large-scale technological changes. (For the case of nuclear energy at Electricité de France, see Dubar and Engrand, 1986.)

These concentrated sectors, which are among the most highly involved in training, are contrasted with those characterised by 'work-force management through the labour market'. Generally scattered, with prime locations in small rural towns, they expend very little effort on training, the legal minimum at best, for a workforce with few skills and qualifications. Most representative of this pole are the meat and dairy, wood, leather and shoe, construction and mechanical engineering industries.

While integrating many management variables, this segmentation (which is, however, nuanced by the existence of 'borderline industries') remains a static presentation which does not situate training within work-force adjustments.

Continuing training and economic adjustments

A factor analysis of thirty-six industrial sectors brings out several behaviour types, each one corresponding to a specific mode of intervention through continuing training in the economic adjustments proper to different sectors or groups of sectors (Dayan, Ghin and Verdier 1986).

Technological constraint and dynamic adaptation
This first case is characterised by a significant training effort and rapid updating of equipment. The work force assigned to research and development is especially large and the occupational structure is marked by a high proportion of engineers and technicians.

The nature of the goods produced requires the use of the latest technologies, which are quickly updated, and thus the maintenance of permanent processes for adapting production and skills.

Work-force management takes the form of an intensive 'investment' in job quality through the high degree of initial training required, the high level of wages, the predominance of skilled categories among production as well as training personnel, and the considerable resources devoted to continuing training. Respect for contractual agreements with employees (job stability, internal promotion) must be reconciled with continual adjustment to the necessities of rapidly evolving markets. It is this category that comes closest to the practices commonly called 'training investment', but such behaviour is found in only a very small number of sectors. In 1980, they were responsible for nearly 60 percent of all research and development expenditures. The economic impact varies, however: while computer technology and pharmaceuticals are among the most profitable activities, others, such as professional electronics materials, are more precarious.

Reconstitution of the production process to emerge from the crisis
This second kind of behaviour arises from a different context, which involves correcting a situation that has been severely compromised by

inappropriate production structures. The sectors involved need to make up for long-standing deficiencies that were dramatically revealed by the crisis and thus can no longer be ignored.

The rate of financial participation is fairly high, especially in relation to a sometimes modest level of capital intensiveness (automobile manufacture, naval construction) or the low level of initial training among employees. But the recourse to training is distinguished above all by the activity of internal centres. This entails an attempt at reconversion, in the dual sense of the word:

   * the reconstitution of productive structures, thus of work organisation and skills;

   * the social assistance accompanying the sometimes massive job cutbacks, which most affects the least skilled.

This difficult reorganisation is accompanied by a change in the forms of continuing training, with a focus on low-skilled workers.

Distinguishing between the social and economic dimensions of this adjustment thus makes little sense: the two components are equally indispensable and, in practice, most often inseparable. (See Villeval, 1990, for the case of the metalworking industries.) The success of such a strategy is not guaranteed for all the sectors in question, but it appears to be a necessary condition for successfully surmounting the economic and employment crisis.

Vocational traditions and training at the work station
In this third case, continuing training is little developed, most often quite close to the legal minimum; capital intensiveness is below average, and wages absorb a significant part of added value. Profitability and the overall financial situation are moderate.

However, the particular concentration of skilled workers (on the average, nearly one half of the work force) combined with a concentration of the continuing training effort on engineers and managers creates another configuration: while work-force management tends to be of the external type, with youth-oriented recruitment and large turnover, it seems that the process of acquiring and adapting skills is maintained for operatives through the traditional practice of on-the-job training and the informal transmission of vocational knowledge and experience, while the limited resources allotted to formal continuing training are most beneficial to a managerial staff with few degrees and thus serves to bring them 'up to standard'. Nonetheless, it cannot be argued that this kind of practice is adequate for the economic and technological constraints currently weighing on these activities, especially in engineering but also in electrical and handling equipment.

Short-term adjustment and under-training in industries with traditional work forces
These profitable activities which make few gestures toward training their employees represent a final type of behaviour characterised by the preoccupation with short-term adjustment. Given that their positive financial performances depend above all on the low level of wages and capital expenses, while the modest rate of investment results mainly from the absence of capital, profitability must be attained by a strategy that is more or less the opposite of that found in the high-tech industries. Here, short-term adjustment through cutbacks in the work force, the elimination of the weakest units, and the total absence of investment in the quality of manpower (low wages, unfavourable job structure, large turnover) replaces the maintenance and development of medium-term adjustment capacities. This is the price of sustaining a profitability that offers no guarantee of improved productivity or competitiveness in hotly contested markets. (The textile and clothing industry, as well as leather and shoes, is particularly representative of this kind of adjustment.)

Overall, this study demonstrates that recourse to training is closely linked to productive resources (level of skills and capital intensiveness) and to the existence of regulations for personnel management organising internal labour markets. Conversely, there is no correlation between the scale of the training effort and the firms' profitability. This last point has been confirmed by more systematic research on the link between recourse to training and external competitiveness (measured by the import-export ratio in relation to the OECD countries) (CEREQ, 1990). By extension, it may be deduced that in sectors that rely heavily on training (e.g. pharmaceuticals, electronics), such recourse is a necessary (structural) condition of the economic activity, but it is not sufficient to secure an advantageous position on strongly competitive markets.

A recent study (Podevin, 1990) considerably refines this approach by retracing the precise articulations between firms' external recruitments and internal labour markets in relation to the development of continuing training.

Relative to earlier research, this study mainly shows that certain sectors such as engineering have greatly increased their average skills level through passive adjustments (attrition of low-skilled personnel, hiring of younger employees with greater educational qualifications).

The growing role of training in the adjustment of certain categories of sectors, generally those that are quite concentrated, confirms the broad interpretation that had been offered for the resumed growth of training expenditures from 1982 on: it is not linked to the rise in the legal minimum but to the increasing integration of training into firms' strategies.

Beyond the sector: models of the firm

Delattre and Eymard-Duvernay (1983) have shown the necessity of developing sub-sectorial approaches. In this way they have brought out standard categories of enterprises which, within one sector or branch, are representative of a system of industrial positions occupied by firms that are simultaneously competing and complementary. This study has led the way for a more ambitious approach that distinguishes a spectrum of modes of coordination, the impact of which varies from one kind of firm to another. The market model is based on an adjustment of different behaviours through the intermediary of prices. The work force must be mobile in order to follow the market. The industrial model is based on a combination of measures that ensures overall equilibrium while maintaining the compatibility of the different actors present in the firm. The work force is managed through a job classification system that keeps the personnel relatively stable. The domestic model relies mainly on integration into the firm, which is based on strong interpersonal ties. (For more details, see Eymard-Duvernay and Favereau, 1990.)

On the basis of these investigations, an earlier study on the industrial electronics sector (Grando and Verdier 1988) was updated to examine the different reasons behind the low level of training in the SMEs of this high-tech sector which should, in principle, be a high-training sector as well.

An analysis of data from more than six hundred firms of all sizes yields a configuration around two main axes. (See Figure 13.1). The horizontal axis situates the firms relative to the skills level of the work force and capital intensiveness; the vertical axis marks the degree of dependency in relation to the markets.

Figure 13.1:
Training in SMEs: a possible classification

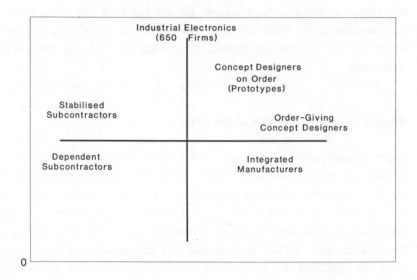

The SMEs are well represented in most categories of firms except for that of integrated manufacturers. Four cases will serve as illustrations:

(a) Dependent subcontractors rely on the markets they receive from the order-givers. Faced with short-term orders, these very unstable firms cannot make lasting investments in training: this would run counter to the instability of the work force and the need to accommodate variations in demand very quickly. This market constraint is often used to explain the low level of training among the SMEs. In evaluating their personnel, moreover, certain firms that manufacture down-market electronic components stress the qualities of 'strength', 'courage', and 'dexterity'. In other words, the use of training to establish a specific qualification within the framework of internal markets is remote from their management principles.

(b) Stable subcontractors benefit from the medium-term commitment of their order-givers. They subscribe to a logic of industrial efficiency that is expressed by the multiplicity of production norms imposed on that is expressed by the multiplicity of production norms imposed on them by the order-givers. More oriented towards the quality of the service rendered, these firms are less dependent on prices; thus, they are in a better position to train their personnel. In reality, their training budgets often remain modest to the extent that continuing training is in large part assured directly by the order-givers, who channel a package of resources (equipment, skills, means of research) toward their subcontractor partners.

(c) Concept designers working to order have control over a product or specific technology. Relations with the client are based on the confidence and loyalty that bind their managers to the purchasing directors in the large firms. On-the-job apprenticeships predominate in this kind of enterprise, which has generally been built around a 'founding father'. Formal training is difficult to use unless on an infrequent basis to adapt to the development of products and techniques.

(d) Concept designers who are order-givers control their markets relatively well. They depend on high skills that must be renewed continually in order to keep up with the evolution of products and processes. Technical and managerial personnel often belong to a professional labour market (high external mobility), which may hinder recourse to training. In effect, the firm runs the risk of seeing its personnel leave after initial training. Although they would like to invest in their personnel, these firms, which are more stable than the other SMEs, are also badly situated to conduct continuing training. Training budgets remain limited for lack of contractual clauses that would oblige employees to remain at the firm sufficiently long to make the sums invested in training them profitable.

Ultimately, it appears that the weakness of continuing training is attributable to a variety of causes each of which reflects a particular mode of coordination:

(a) The market constraint with its uncertainty and short-term adjustments explains why recourse to continuing training is very difficult for dependent subcontractors.

(b) The industrial logic maintained by the network surrounding an order-giver removes any significance from the conception and evaluation of continuing training at the level of a given component of the network.

(c) The predominance of 'domestic' type organisation/personalities in both internal and external relations contributes to making formal training through outside courses inconsistent with skills based on progressive apprenticeships which, through seniority, become criteria for advancement and recognition of the skills.

(d) The weight of professional markets makes it more difficult for order-givers responsible for concept design to create an internal market, with the result that they are faced with an instability among their high-skilled personnel which is hardly conducive to a policy of specific training.

The instruments of government intervention, whether on the level of training requirements or financial incentives, cannot ignore this heterogeneity of the industrial fabric without producing many unexpected results. A general norm on which government intervention is classically based cannot hope to make the interests pursued by public intervention (to produce profitable external effects for the society) systematically compatible with the objectives proper to one category of firm or another.

Investment and training

In another perspective, Margirier (1991) identifies diversified training practices developed by the firms, largely through investments. Only 13 percent of the firms surveyed, mainly SMEs, have not formalised training measures. The other small-scale enterprises behave in a manner which is entirely comparable to those of the largest firms. For at least one firm out of two, training expenditures represent at least 4 percent of their investment. Nonetheless, the large firms are quicker to institute training.

Institutional and organisational innovations

Two main kinds of innovations emerge from the specialised studies of the past few years. One group involves those practices of firms that can be termed innovative in the sense that they use continuing training as a means of introducing new forms of job management and organisation of work that are both flexible and increasingly attentive to work quality. The other group concerns government relations with firms and SMEs in particular.

Training as an organisational principle

The forms that continuing training takes today are sometimes quite removed from the model proposed by the Act of 1971, but this diversification permits its intervention at all stages of the process of change.

Training at the core of the new organisational model
Examples drawn from automobile manufacture will serve to bring out as clearly as possible the break with earlier forms of organisation and management styles in an industry that was for many years the privileged domain for the application of Taylorism and Fordism. The case in point concerns the automation of a Renault sheet-metal shop where the stamped sheets are assembled and welded together in stages to make the chassis. It exemplifies the implementation of new managerial principles that can be summarised in the following terms: 'the inseparability of technical and human factors to guarantee the performance of an industrial system, the necessity of involving the future production department in the research and development process, the necessity of preparing for all aspects of change'. This approach leads to a project logic that establishes the coherence of the new organisation by going beyond the habitual functional divisions that lead to the partial logic of, for example, planning and programming or maintenance operations.

Organisational experimentation: a participatory process and (therefore) one that trains
First of all, it should be noted that the introduction of the new equipment entailed an experimental phase that in itself constituted a training process. Anticipating the arrival of the automated equipment nearly two years in advance, the shop management opted to try out the new organisation with the equipment for the current model of the vehicle. This phase was essential, because, on the one hand, it constituted a full-scale test of the new principles with major production constraints, and on the other, it allowed each operator to try out his new role and the demands it would entail. This shows the extent of the risk that was taken, as well as the confidence placed in the individuals and the work collective. Totally at odds with prescriptive forms of organisation aimed at reducing the uncertainty associated with initiatives left to workers, this new logic

relied on a totally explicit training process to build a learning system that was both individual and organisational.

The first component of the process concerned the totally new relations between production proper on the one hand and the peripheral functions and equipment suppliers on the other. From the outset it was necessary to create a <u>common language</u> for all the protagonists. To this end, the peripheral functions sought to integrate manufacture into the phase of installing the technical means, thus overturning the traditional logic of the 'turn-key' factory. This integration entailed a reciprocal process of information and training, whereby the production personnel were on hand to fill out formal evaluations of the equipment, to participate systematically in the approval process, to take responsibility for the precise definition of work stations the organisation of their environment, and to involve themselves in the formulation of safety procedures.

It was on this basis that the process of training shops and operators was able to develop and generate new managerial principles. Formerly limited to prescriptive roles, the functional departments connected to production became partners providing support, advice, and training. In addition, the maintenance personnel were now explicitly given the task of practical training of line operators, at the work station, when the line was in full operation.

This logic also went beyond the strict limits of the plant, insofar as the methods served to interface between subcontractors and producers in order to establish another double learning process: 'the receiving of new equipment with tests in a realistic industrial situation, with contractual stipulations planning permitting the transmission of subcontractor know-how to the production crew'. The strict client-supplier relationship was thus transformed into a partnership based mainly on on-site training and thus quite removed from classical institutional training.

A second component concerned more formal training modules for machine operators and maintenance professionals. But it must be stressed that these training courses only assumed their full meaning and efficiency in the context of a sequence linking them closely to concrete experiences with organisation and operating modes.

Another adjustment operation, which was the subject of press coverage as well as research (Cabridain and Midler, 1986), demonstrated the same logic: heavy general training, technical training courses, integration into maintenance services, visits to other automated factories, and trials of new equipment constituted a veritable sandwich course. Throughout the process, general knowledge from the training courses was constantly called up by the practical know-how derived from experimentation. This is in effect alternating training, where knowledge, however formalised it is, only becomes meaningful when it is oriented to practice and applied by the individuals and groups concerned.

Recourse to training as part of the new job definitions

Training has become a permanent component of work in two respects:
- Through the establishment of a continuum among different levels of complexity within the same family of jobs (e.g. machine operators), where, as it has been suggested, 'everyone does the same thing but to different degrees'.
- Through the inclusion of a training function within the work stations of the most skilled operators. Thus, in one of the examples studied, the second-level of operators had responsibility for on-the-job training 'through demonstration and explanation of the sequence of operations', while the highest level was to combine 'practice and theory, with the use of elementary educational tools'.

The training-organisation-employment link in response to new social conditions

The creation of an organisation based even partly on a project logic (rather than strict functional divisions) and a principle of cooperation (rather than a prescriptive model) responds to clearly defined social conditions:
- Stabilisation of the work force as a whole through guarantees that there will be no dismissal procedures apart from early retirement (a principle that has been particularly defended in the most recent case);
- Selection of personnel who will take charge of the installation according to the new criteria of initiative and commitment to the training process;
- Negotiated creation of new classifications and jobs corresponding to the new functions;
- Insistence on the training role assigned to the supervisory personnel, who are to accompany the operators as they advance from one

level to another (which goes along with a decentralisation of the evaluation of qualifications);

- Elaboration of career paths (which is a particularly difficult principle to enact, given that hierarchical progressions are to be curtailed).

The implementation of new organisational principles is the product of a broad-based collective effort among the various partners (representing different occupational groups, levels in the hierarchy, functional departments). The diversity of the modalities of change is inseparable from the fact that the current period of sharp transformations has not, for the moment at least, led to a stable model of organisation or at least one that can serve as a point of reference. These tentatives, in the words of C. Midler, are a matter of 'organisational apprenticeships' that have to accumulate. In this respect, planning and human relations departments have a determining role to play in collecting these experiences, drawing the proper lessons from them, and transmitting them to individual enterprises or networks that will subsequently be faced with significant changes. A new form of cross-functional training clearly remains to be created in order to encourage those who are most affected by transformations to take responsibility for them.

Continuing training and job management: toward the management of skills?

New practices, aimed at creating new kinds of occupational environments and strengthening workers' abilities to adapt, are attempting to make training the key instrument for managing current and future job mobility.

Mehaut (1989) distinguishes three categories of measures that often take the form of 'veritable curricula' consisting of a sequence of modules that can be taken at different rhythms according to the progress of the individual:

- Job management and creation of new occupational categories for a particular population (in the electronics sector, e.g., quality-control workers targeted to become shop technicians). The curriculum combines general and vocational training, along with measures directed at the organisation of work, in a long-term programme (more than 500 hours). While it focuses on a particular categories of employees, this kind of training can have repercussions on other groups of personnel. The manpower needs generated by the development of new jobs will activate chains of job mobility that should create additional movement and demand for training in other units of the enterprise.

- 'Vocational' measures preparing for defined positions. More focused on work itself, this kind of measure is hardly different from the classic form of 'training that prepares for the skill required for such and such a position', and does not explicitly continue within a career perspective.

- 'General' measures preceding a reorganisation of work. More removed from the work itself, these measures attempt to provide a base level, such as the baccalaurat, as the minimum level for future operators. Subsequently, related careers can be grafted onto this base. Existing examples suggest that this kind of measure spreads progressively throughout the work force. Greater human and financial resources are mobilised than in the preceding case, and this kind of measure generally benefits from public funding, through the National Employment Fund (Fonds national de l'emploi) and the European Social Fund (Fonds social europen). (On the use of this public aid, see Kirsom, 1990a.)

Several common characteristics of these measures are worth noting.

- They are long-term and more often presuppose individual investments of time outside of working hours. They are totally financed by the firm, which frequently receives assistance from public programmes.

- They attempt to combine an individualisation of the training process with often widespread application. Thus the firm must be capable of monitoring individuals in order to adapt the training process to each of their needs and of closely linking work activities and learning experiences within a course of study that may be very spread out over time. The problem is thus to break with prevailing organisational logic and adapt as much as possible to the particular experience of departments and individuals. Brochier et al. (1989) have shown, for example, that a goal-oriented pedagogy is more compatible with the experience of maintenance personnel than with that of 'production'. The preparation of CAPs (vocational aptitude certificates) in separate units accumulated over several years has become increasingly common. More generally, the large public training organisations play an important if not determining role in the realisation and even the conception of new measures.

- They often serve as a tool for personnel evaluation. Furthermore, when the firm introduces an explicit or even formal link between access to training and the capacity to assume a position, participation in these programmes becomes very selective. Conversely, if it is linked to an anticipated increase in the level of the personnel in the medium run, participation remains voluntary.

- Because of the scope of both collective and individual investments, they pose a problem of certification and recognition of curricula. The solutions are varied: an official degree (CAP), an equivalent degree recognised by the collective convention, or recognition through a change of classification. The choice depends largely on how the firm views these measures: if, for example, they are intended to facilitate not only internal mobility but also outside reconversions, then an official degree is particularly desirable. In addition, it may be argued that such a degree makes the training operation more legitimate in the eyes of the employees and their representatives. But as Berry (1988) points out, this choice runs the risk of falling back on forms that are too close to an academic model and which would hardly be compatible with the kind of alternating training that fully mobilises individual experiences and transforms the workplace into an educational environment. From the cases examined, certification procedures appear to vary from firm to firm, and few guiding principles can be distinguished.

Will these innovations assume sufficient proportions to justify the notion of a new kind of wage nexus that would make employee skills one of the main dynamics for the new organisation of work? (Boyer 1989) How can the establishment of a Japanese-style 'contractual' qualification, which is essentially collective, be reconciled with the desire for greater individual autonomy in relation to internal labour markets? A 'French-style' solution will not emerge from a simple adaptation of the Japanese or German example: the prospects of a 'training firm' where the organisation of work produces skills are still very uncertain (see Kirsch, 1990b).

Principles for a new model
1. Optimisation of the entire productive process.
2. Attempt at total integration of research, development and production.
3. Close and long-lasting ties between producers and users in order to maximise benefits of training.

4. High quality at reasonable costs via a zero-defect objective at each stage of the production process.
5. Insertion of market demand into the production process in order to speed up responses.
6. Maximum decentralisation of production decisions within smaller and less hierarchical units.
7. Networking (and cooperative ventures) as a means of benefiting from both specialisation and coordination.
8. Maximum use of long-term and cooperative subcontracting in order to encourage joint technical innovations.
9. Reorganisation of production, maintenance, quality control and some management tasks for greater technical and economic efficiency.
10 New alliance of general education and effective on-the-job training in order to maximize individual and collective skills.
11. Human resources policies capable of stimulating workers' skills and commitment and providing support for firms' strategies.
12. An explicit and long-term compromise between employees and management in order to obtain broad support for this model: employee commitment in exchange for good working conditions and/or job security and/or a fair share of modernisation dividends (Boyer, 1989).

Improving the coherence of public and private choices

The desire for a stronger link between the SMEs and training lies at the nerve centre of this search for coherence. It takes place on several levels:

- The progressive (and partly unstated) relaxation of the legal requirement defining continuing training;

- The closer link between recourse to training and firm strategy;

- The decompartmentalisation of public aid (for research, investment, employment);

- The revival of an institutional mechanism, with the private sector taking over from public policy.

The last point deserves further attention. (See also Verdier, 1990.) In a large part, the competitiveness of the SMEs depends on the quality of the network of institutions they can rely on for access to innovations, marketing, or even training itself. In the case of the agreements for development of vocational training (EDDF) signed between the national government and groups of employers, notably on the local level, the priority placed on reaching the the SMEs is based on the preeminent role given to the vocational organisations in the distribution of public funding. The idea is to encourage a new dynamic within existing institutions, whether the trade unions or mutual training bodies. In principle these vocational organisations are familiar with the occupational fabric and thus more capable than a government administration of channelling state aid into the specific practices of small enterprises.

Nonetheless, the approach is not free of unexpected effects, as studies suggest (Vespirini, 1990). Obviously firms with the closest ties to the vocational organisations are favoured, although they are not always the most dynamic or the most in tune with the goals of the public programmes. Nor do they necessarily have adequate expertise to direct the implementation of innovative practices.

Conclusion

For greater understanding of the role of continuing training, three complementary lines of research remain to be developed:

(a) Acquiring better knowledge of the mobility of the labour force that benefits from continuing training and especially training that leads to degrees. There are few elements at hand for determining whether that population attempts to make use of degrees and vocational experience on the external labour market.

(b) Refining the analysis of the role of continuing training in the firms' adjustments. Here it is essential to work on sample groups of firms; one such experiment is underway in collaboration with INSEE. (See, Kramarz.)

(c) Monitoring the most innovative experiments in continuing training, in the areas of organisation of work and job management. Are these isolated cases, or has the reputation acquired by such experiments led to the spread of these 'models'? To what extent do partnerships with the public educational system permit these experiments to be stabilised and multiplied?

330

In terms of the legal framework, the current period is crucial insofar as the social partners are in the process of renegotiating the founding agreements of 1970. The Act of 1971 ought to effect compromises between goals that were civic in nature and the interests of market and industry, between firm strategies and individual expectations. Ultimately, its effectiveness has been limited by the rigidity of centralised, albeit negotiated, requirements. The most striking innovations demonstrate that a new 'negotiated law' would hardly need to modify its general objectives. On the other hand, profiting from the disfavour of the Taylorist model which is fundamentally antithetical to it, a replenished and less inegalitarian continuing training (or even one given to "positive discrimination" in favour of those with the lowest skills) should opt for the conclusion of decentralised compromises. Otherwise, to borrow the terms of the special issue on 'life-long training' that the journal Esprit published in 1974, such training will remain the 'dream of the Utopians, (the) line of retreat of the educators, (the) panacea of the technocrats, (the) last resort of devalued managers'.

A recent inter-occupational agreement, signed on 3 July 1991, seems to have recognized what is at stake. In particular, it anticipates the establishment of a closer tie between training and promotion, as well as the organisation of measures for training, language instruction and skilling partly outside of work hours. The decision to make the individual worker assume partial responsibility for continuing training is expected to improve the collective effectiveness of the resulting shared investment.

Notes

1. What follows is largely based on data taken from the annual financial declarations that employers are required to make in order to prove that they have met their obligation. (See CEREQ's annual *Statistiques de la formation professionnelle continue, traitement des déclarations d'employeurs.*
2. At present, the research is basically limited to industry. For the service sector, see the pioneering study of O. Bertrand (1988).

References

Barraquandy, Y. and Maruani, P. (1987), 'Mourir à petit feu de la modernisation', *Gérer et Comprendre*. Annales des Mines. September.

Beduwe, C. (1991), 'Le niveau de diplôme des ouvriers et des employés: la place des jeunes de niveau V', *Formation Emploi*, no. 33. La Documentation Française.

Berry, M. (1988), 'Essai sur les stratégies de changement', *Gérer et Comprendre*, Annales des Mines, no spécial.

Berton, F. and Podevin, G. (1991), 'Vingt ans de formation professionnelle continue: de la promotion sociale à la gestion de l'emploi', *Formation Emploi*, no. 34. La Documentation Française.

Bertrand, O. (1988), 'Qualité et hétérogénéité des emplois des services', *Formation Emploi,* no. 23. La Documentation Française.

Boyer, R. (1986), *La théorie de la régulation: une analyse critique..* Coll. Agalma. La Découverte.

Boyer, R. (1989), *New directions in management practices and work organisation. General principles and national trajectories.* CEPREMAP-CNRS.

Brochier, D. et alii (1989), 'La formation en alternance intégrée à la production', *Formation Emploi*, no. 30. La Documentation Française.

Cabridain, M.O. and Midler, Ch. (1986), 'Apprivoiser les robots, l'expérience ISOAR trois ans après', *Gérer et Comprendre*. Annales des Mines. Janvier.

Cereq, (1990), *Formation contine et compétitivité économique.* Collection des études, no. 51. Cereq (Diffusion Documentation Française).

Cereq, (volume annuel depuis) (1975), *Statistiques de la formation professionnelle continue, traitement des déclarations d'employeurs.* La Documentation Française.

Dayan, J.L., Gehin, J.P. and Verdier, E. (1986), 'La formation continue dans l'industrie', *Formation Emploi,* no 16. La Documentation Française.

Detlattre, M and Eymard-Duvernay, F. (1983), 'Sept catégories d'entreprises pour analyser le tissu industriel', *Economie et Statistique,* no. 159. INSEE.

Delors, J. (1974), 'Au-delà des illusions', *Esprit*. 439.

Doeringer, P.B. and Piore, M.J. (1971), *Internal Labor Markets and Manpower Analysis*. Lexington. Massassuchets.

Dubar, C. (1990), *La formation professionnelle continue*. Coll. Repères. 2e éd. La Découverte.

Dubar, C. and Engrand, S. (1986), 'La formation en entreprise comme processus de socialisation professionnelle: l'exemple de la production nucléaire à EDF', *Formation Emploi*, no. 16. La Documentation Française.

Eymard-Duvernay, F. (1981), 'Les secteurs de l'industrie et leurs ouvriers', *Economie et Statistique*, no. 138. INSEE.

Eymard-Duvernay, F. and Favereau, O. (1990), 'Marchés internes, modèles d'entreprises et conventions de qualitè: matériaux pour une formatlisation non standard du marché des biens', *Communication aux 7 emes journées de microéconomie appliquée*. Université du Québec. Montréal.

Fournier, J. and Questiaux, N. (1976), *Traité du social*. Sirey.

Gehin, J.P. (1989), 'L'évolution de la formation dans les secteurs d'activité (1973-1985)', *Formation Emploi*, no. 25. La Documentation Française.

Grando, J.M. (1983), 'Industrie et gestion de la main d'oeuvre', *Formation Emploi,* no. 1. La Documentation Francçaise.

Grando, J.M. and Verdier, E. (1988), 'L'électronique professionnelle et la formation: ambivalence d'un secteur de pointe', *Formation Emploi*, no. 21. La Documentation Francçaise.

Kirsch, E. (1990a), *Prévoir et former*. Collection des documents de travail, no. 49. Cereq.

Kirsch, E. (1990b), 'Lèntreprise formatrice', Cereq, *Bref*, no. 60. Decémbre.

Laulhe, P. (1990), 'La formation continue: un avantage pour les promotions et un accès privilégié pour les jeunes et les techniciens', *Economie et Statistique*, no. 228. INSEE.

Margirier, G. (1991), 'La place de la formation dans le changement technique. *Formation Emploi*, no. 34. La Documentation Francçaise.

Mehaut, Ph. (1989), 'De l'innovation de formation à la construction d'un nouveau rapport à la formation, in Bel, M. et alii', *Production et usage de la formation par et dans l'entreprise*. Tome I. Rapport de recherche pour le CNRS, le Commissariat Général du Plan et la Délégation à la formation professionnelle.

Midler, Ch. (1988), 'De l'automatisation à la modernisation, les transformations de l'industrie automobile. 1er épisode: une expérience novatrice chez Renault', *Gérer et omprendre*. Annales des Mines Décembre.

Midler, Ch. (1989), 'De l'automatisation à la modernisation, les transformations de l'industrie automobile. 2e épisode: vers de nouvelles pratiques de gestion des projets industriels', *Gérer et Comprendre*. Annales des Mines. Mars.

Nallet, J.F. (1991), 'Le droit de la formation: une construction juridique fondatrice', *Formation Emploi*, no. 34. La Documentation Francçaise.

Piore, M.J. (1975), 'Notes for the theory of labor market stratification, in Edwards R., Gordon, D. and Reich, M., *Segmented work, devided workers. The historical transformation of labor in the U.S.* Cambridge University Press.

Podevin, G. (1990), 'Mobilité interne, promotions et renouvellement de la main d'oeuvre', *Travail et Emploi*, no. 46. Masson.

Silvestre, J.J. (1986), 'Marchés du travail et crise économique: de la mobilité à la flexibilité', *Formation Emploi*. La Documentation Française.

Verdier, E. (1987), 'Incitation publique, mutualisations et comportements privés: le cas de la formation continue', *Formation Emploi*, no. 20. La Documentation Française.

Verdier, E. (1990), 'L'efficacité de la formation continue dans les PME', *Sociologie du travail*, no. 3. Dunod.

Vesperini, F. (1990), *Les engagements de développement de la formation professionnelle, nouvelle modalité d'aide à la formation continue.* Collection des documents de travail. Cereq.

Villeval, M.C. (1990), 'Reconversions et mobilités', *Bref*, no 55. Cereq.

14 Vocational training and productivity performance: An Anglo-Dutch comparison

Geoff Mason and Bart van Ark

Introduction

This paper reports on a detailed comparison of productivity performance and the quality and utilisation of human and physical capital inputs in matched samples of engineering plants in Britain and the Netherlands. It follows an earlier series of Anglo-German comparisons by National Institute researchers which investigated three different manufacturing sectors engineering, furniture-making and clothing and found that in all of them higher average levels of labour productivity in German plants were closely related to the greater skills and knowledge of their workforces (Daly, Hitchens, Wagner, 1985; Steedman and Wagner, 1987, 1989).

Like Germany, the Netherlands enjoys a substantial advantage over Britain in respect of workforce qualification levels. However, in contrast to the German apprenticeship-based training system, the great majority of Dutch vocational qualifications are gained in the course of full-time schooling. In turning to the Netherlands for a new comparison with Britain, therefore, we wished in particular to examine the impact of this very different system of vocational education and training on relative productivity performance.

Within engineering we focussed on plants in three metal-working sectors, namely, centrifugal liquid pumps, industrial hydraulic valves and cold-coiled compression springs. In all we visited 12 plants in Britain and nine in the Netherlands; further details of the two samples are provided in a Statistical Appendix. The median employment size of engineering plants in Britain is substantially larger than in the Netherlands and, in the interests of representativeness, this disparity was reflected in the distribution of plant-sizes in each national sample (see Appendix Tables

A2-A3). Nevertheless, there was still a considerable overlap in the size of plants visited in each country.

The plants were initially identified through trade directories. In both countries roughly three quarters of the plants who were formally asked for a visit agreed to participate. All the visits lasted for roughly half a day and interviews were conducted with production and/or personnel managers. In each case the visit included a period of time on the shopfloor and it was therefore sometimes possible to speak to production supervisors and workers as well. In addition to the manufacturing plants, we also visited machinery suppliers and vocational schools and colleges and compared vocational examinations with the help of college teachers in each country.

Approximately two thirds of the visits were made by two researchers (one from each country) and the remainder were carried out by a single researcher. In order to economise on travelling costs, the plants selected for visits in Britain were geographically clustered in the South East and Midlands. In the Netherlands, the plants visited were widely dispersed in location. All the main visits took place between October 1989 and June 1991; some supplementary visits were carried out in 1992.

Vocational education and training in the Netherlands

By international standards the Dutch education and training system is notable for its relatively early provision of vocational education for a significant proportion of secondary school pupils and the high rate of attendance in full-time vocational schools after the age of 16 (see Mason, Prais, van Ark, 1992).

The majority of those acquiring industrial craft-level skills in the Netherlands do so by first attending full-time junior vocational (LBO) schools between the ages of 13 and 16 and subsequently receiving on-the-job training in the course of their first employment. Other less common but growing means of obtaining craft-level qualifications are through formal apprenticeship programmes where trainees continue to attend college courses part-time after taking up employment, and through two-year full-time college-based courses (known as KMBO courses) which arrange work placements for trainees with local employers.[1]

At technician level the great majority of trainees acquiring qualifications do so at full-time intermediate vocational (MBO) schools, with courses usually lasting four years one of which is spent out of school on industrial training placements. A small proportion (about 6-7%) of people leaving MBO schools go on to study at higher level (HBO) vocational colleges but the great majority immediately enter the labour market where their qualifications, particularly in technical subjects, are highly regarded by Dutch employers.

Table 14.1
Vocational qualifications of the workforce in Britain, France, the Netherlands and Germany, 1987-89

	Britain 1988	Netherlands 1989	Germany 1987
	(Percentages)		
University degrees	10	8	11
Intermediate vocational qualifications			
higher technician diplomas	7	19	7
craft/lower technician diplomas	20	38	56
No vocational qualifications	63	35	26
TOTAL	100	100	100

Source: Labour Force Surveys, NIESR estimates.

Note

For details of classification of qualifications in each country see Mason, Prais, van Ark (1992, Table 2)

The impact of this highly organised system of full-time vocational education in the Netherlands is clearly observable in international comparisons of workforce qualification levels. As Table 14.1 shows, only 35% of the Dutch workforce lack vocational qualifications compared to some 63% in Britain. As in Germany, the main areas of Dutch advantage relative to Britain are in the 'intermediate' qualifications category embracing technical support staff and shopfloor workers and supervisors. Although formal qualifications are an imperfect proxy for workforce skill levels in each case, they remain indicative of inter-country differences in human capital formation.

Productivity comparisons

Estimates based on Production Census data suggest that output per hour worked in the combined metal products and machinery industries was about 30 per cent higher in the Netherlands than in Britain in 1990, slightly below the estimated 35-40 per cent productivity advantage for Dutch manufacturing as a whole.[2]

In our chosen sectors of pumps, valves and springs, most plants produce goods to a wide range of physical dimensions and other specifications. It was therefore not possible to obtain meaningful physical measures of total output for each plant which could be related to total labour input (direct and indirect) in order to compare physical productivity performance in our two national samples. Accordingly we followed the method previously used in Daly, Hitchens, Wagner (1985) of comparing the direct labour inputs involved in the manufacture of similar products in each country.

Six pairs of plants making products to similar specifications were identified, two in each of the three sectors under consideration. In each case the selected products were deemed by production managers to be 'representative' of the plants in question. Detailed information was sought from each plant on actual, not planned or 'standard', output rates and direct labour inputs. Comparisons were then based on the average outputs per direct person-hour associated with specified sequences of operations, for example, the coiling and grinding phases of spring manufacture and, in the case of pumps and valves, the machining of key components and subsequent assembly of the final product.

In all the six pairs of plants yielded some 23 closely-matching operations for which comparisons of productivity levels were feasible (with each pair of plants providing between two and five observations). Across the full set of matched operations, the (unweighted) average difference in output per direct person-hour was 43 per cent in favour of the Dutch plants; the sampling standard error on this estimate is plus or minus nine percentage points. The average productivity gap ranged from 27 per cent in assembly operations and 29 per cent in machining operations to a 60 per cent advantage in machine set-up times for the Dutch plants. If these results are weighted in relation to the distribution of total direct employment in each national sample, the estimated Dutch advantage reduces to an average 36 per cent.

Although our comparisons were based on direct labour inputs only, it should be noted that the ratio of direct to indirect labour was, on average, very similar in both our national samples. The overall result is consistent with Production Census-based estimates of the Dutch advantage in engineering productivity (as noted above) which relate to both direct and indirect labour inputs.[3]

A further comment concerns the variation in average productivity differentials between the six pairs of plants from which data on closely-matching operations were obtained. Analysis of this variation showed that it was not related in any way to the complexity of the products in question or to differences in plant employment-size, rather it simply appeared to reflect the substantial differences in efficiency which exist between plants in each country (a proposition supported by our observations during plant visits).

In summary, our results point to a sizeable gap in average productivity levels in favour of the Dutch industry. In the following sections of this paper, we consider how this gap is related to the age, utilisation and maintenance of machinery and to the skills and training of the workforce in each national sample.

Physical capital equipment

Age of machinery in national samples

In both Britain and the Netherlands precision engineering firms have undertaken substantial new investments in machinery in recent years. As Table 14.2 shows, some 45 per cent of machines in the British plants we visited had been purchased in the last ten years. However, the comparable proportion in our Dutch sample was even higher at 70 per cent. The Dutch plants were also ahead in the use of advanced computer numerically-controlled (CNC) equipment which accounted for some 35 per cent of all machines in use in the Dutch sample compared to about a fifth in Britain.

The faster rate of new investment in the Dutch plants can be partly attributed to the longer payback periods on which they operate: in the Netherlands new machinery was expected to pay for itself within an average of five years compared to an average of three years in the British

Table 14.2
Age distribution of machinery and shares of CNC machines in engineering plant samples

	Britain	Netherlands
	(employment-weighted	percentage
shares)		
Age of machinery (years):[a]		
Under 5	25%	40%
5-10	20	30
Over 10	55	30
Total:	100	100
Average age (years):[b]	12	8
CNC machines as percentage of all machines	20	35

Notes

a: Age-distributions of machinery in individual plants weighted by their respective shares of total employment in each sample; results rounded to the nearest five per cent.

b: Calculated from above distributions: mid-points were taken for the two closed intervals; the top (open) interval was taken as having a mid-point of 20 years in Britain and 15 years in the Netherlands.

plants. In addition, generous tax allowances have motivated many Dutch companies to bring planned capital investments forward in recent years.[4] However, apart from these factors impinging on formal systems of investment appraisal, there were also important inter-country differences in management and workforce skills which affected the speed of introduction of new technology in each sample of plants. In particular, as will be discussed further below, British managers were much less well-supported by the highly-qualified technical staff needed to help assess technological options and get new equipment installed and up and running smoothly.

Machine set-up times and running speeds

It is important to note that the higher productivity levels identified in the Dutch sample relative to Britain could not simply be attributed to the more rapid replacement of conventional by CNC machines in Dutch plants, with associated improvements in changeover times and metal-cutting speeds. In our detailed comparisons of matched operations, all the paired plants were using the same basic type of equipment, either conventional or CNC, and yet an overall Dutch advantage in average machine set-up and processing times was still found to apply.

As noted, the differences in required labour inputs were frequently substantial: where, to take one typical example, approximately 1.5 hours were needed in a Dutch plant to set up a conventional machine tool for a specified series of operations on a particular component, the average labour-time required in a matching British plant was about one hour longer. In this example the sequence of tasks largely consisted of reading and interpreting technical drawings; planning the procedures to be followed; selecting and attaching the tools, jigs and fixtures to be used; and then undertaking a 'trial run' machining the first component in the batch, making adjustments to the equipment as necessary to achieve the required specification.

In part the differences in the average times required by setter-operators in each country to carry out their allotted tasks could be attributed to differences in the age and quality of machinery. In several British plants, for example, managers directly referred to the difficulty of 'holding the tolerances' on older, hard-worked machines or of certain antiquated machines 'always having problems'. In such circumstances the average time needed for setting-up was extended because of the difficulty of getting trial products to conform to specification and, in addition, running speeds had to be restricted to help monitor and maintain accuracy levels.

However, other factors affecting machine set-ups and running speeds in the two national samples relate primarily to differences in human capital. Nearly all the plants visited in each country were operating with a mix of machines of different ages, both conventional and CNC in nature. The efficient use of such diverse stocks of capital equipment requires high levels of management and technical support skills in process and method planning, production scheduling and materials purchasing as well as appropriate levels of workforce skill in setting-up, operation and maintenance of equipment.

In as many as half the British plants visited, managers pointed out problems of factory lay-out and organisation which hampered productivity, for instance, by forcing machine-setters to lose time 'wandering around' looking for the particular tooling and work-holding equipment they needed. In some cases it was suggested that 'compromises' might be necessary if the right equipment could simply not be found. Other concerns related to the flow of raw materials and workpieces around some British factories where machines were still grouped together according to their function (turning, drilling, etc) rather than with regard to common sequences of operations. In the Netherlands most such problems appeared to have been addressed some time ago and only one of the nine Dutch plants visited still had significant difficulties with shopfloor layout.

Breakdowns, maintenance and repair

British plants were also found to be experiencing relatively high rates of machine breakdown. Many interruptions to production were simply caused by machine parts being left unreplaced until they 'burnt out' but we also heard of more fundamental problems applying to new as well as old equipment: in one case we were told of a new machine's 'teething problems' lasting as long as nine months; in another a fairly new machining centre had remained 'down' for a full three weeks and seven conventional machines had to be brought back into production to replace it.

A much smaller incidence of breakdowns was reported or observed during our Dutch visits. As confirmed in our discussions with machinery suppliers, this reflects to a very great extent the more meticulous adherence to prescribed maintenance procedures found in Dutch plants and their greater attention to preventative maintenance in general. Full preventative maintenance programmes were established in two thirds of the Dutch plants visited compared to only one in six of the British sample. The 'emergency maintenance' approach in most British plants was usually justified on the grounds of spare capacity which allows production to be immediately transferred to another machine in the event of a breakdown. However, such transfers still cause delays, particularly if re-setting of the replacement machine is required.

Although the Dutch sample had an edge in the skills and training of their maintenance personnel (all qualified to craft level or above compared to 85 per cent so qualified in the British plants), it should be noted that half the plants in each national sample employed very few (at most one or two) or even no full-time maintenance staff and were content to rely on external service contractors for all or most of their major repairs. In this context the smooth running of production greatly depends on the ability of shopfloor operators to undertake 'first-line' maintenance of equipment (inspection, routine cleaning and greasing, etc) and to anticipate serious problems at an early stage of their development, and at shopfloor level there was a pronounced gap in Anglo-Dutch skill levels (as discussed in the following section).

Workforce skills and training

Shopfloor qualifications and training

In both national samples roughly half the workforce was in direct production (machine tool operators, assembly workers, painters, welders, etc in pumps and valves; machine and press operators and tool-makers in springs). As Table 14.3 shows, over three quarters of shopfloor workers in the Dutch plants were qualified to craft level or above compared to only 41 per cent in the British plants. In the Dutch sample the proportions so qualified were broadly the same in all three sectors; in Britain the proportion of craft-trained workers was much higher in pumps than in valves or springs but still well below that in counterpart Dutch plants.[5]

The marked disparity in craft skills between the two industries is partly the consequence of the relative distribution of initial training costs between employers, individuals and the public authorities in the two countries. The usual way for British employers to develop craft-skilled workers is to incur the full costs of a three to four year apprentice training (including wages for trainees during a first year of off-the-job training and subsequent paid day release for college attendance). By contrast, the employers in our Dutch sample had satisfied most of their skilled labour needs by recruiting holders of LTS (or in some cases MTS) qualifications and putting them through an on-the-job training programme (lasting, on average, roughly a year).

In effect, the bulk of vocational education and training costs in the Netherlands are borne by the public authorities in their provision of full-time schooling and by those individuals who forgo the possibility of paid employment to stay in full-time education past the age of 16. Apart from the costs associated with on-the-job training, the only additional costs to most employers in our Dutch sample arose from trainees' occasional attendance on short courses of off-the-job education and training. Less than 1 per cent of employees in the Dutch plants visited were registered apprentices receiving part-time day release for college attendance.

In our British sample apprentices represented some 3 per cent of total employment with six of the 12 plants making notable efforts to maintain initial training levels in the face of economic recession at the time of our visits. This commitment to traditional craft training reflected the need to preserve a core skills base in an industry where managers are aware of their dependence on the 'black arts' of experienced machine-setters able to carry out high-precision work on a range of different machines.

However, the bulk of shopfloor training in the British industry is confined to developing 'semi-skilled' workers in a narrow range of tasks, capable (as described to us) of carrying out 'repeat work' and 'scaling familiar products up or down' but poorly equipped to undertake new and complex operations on a regular basis. As Table 14.3 shows, when British employers recruit individuals without prior experience as machine operators, the average time invested in their initial training even slightly exceeds the average periods of on-the-job training given to LTS-qualified recruits in the Netherlands; but lacking theoretical education and breadth of experience semi-skilled workers generally remain less versatile and self-reliant than fully trained craft workers.[6]

In the Dutch plants an LTS or equivalent certificate has for some time been a minimum criterion for shopfloor recruitment and the question of initial training to semi-skilled level therefore hardly ever arises. LTS pupils' prior exposure to the use of machinery, and to workshop practice in general, gives them a 'head start' over pupils from general schools in absorbing the content of initial on-the-job training programmes; this is especially true where trainees have followed courses largely based around the needs of locally-important employers. Initial training programmes may also be accelerated by recruiting students from local KMBO courses (as described above) who have previously undertaken work placements at the companies in question; roughly half the plants in our Dutch sample engaged in recruitment practices of this kind.

In consequence, the Dutch industry has been able to raise a much larger proportion of its shopfloor workforce to craft standard and this has produced clear benefits for labour productivity. In Dutch machine shops, for instance, the relative abundance of craft-skilled setter-operators contributed to the lower average set-up times observed in our physical productivity comparisons and, in addition, enhanced flexibility in switching workers from one type of machine (and product) to another in accordance with diverse and rapidly-changing production needs. The higher proportion of skilled mechanical fitters in the Dutch pump and valve plants was also associated with lower average product assembly times.

By contrast, the preponderance of semi-skilled workers in the British industry has negative consequences for both flexibility and the pace of production. In some British plants semi-skilled operators have to be supported by full-time setters and production time is lost if one of these setters is not immediately available every time they are needed. In other cases semi-skilled workers in Britain are trained to set as well as operate some machines but, as we were told during several of our visits, they are likely to be confined to simpler and/or a smaller number of machines than are craft-trained workers and are also more likely to stay within a single area (eg drilling) rather than learn a range of different operations.

In the words of one British manager, 'you have to be patient' with semi-skilled workers: whenever they are transferred to a new machine, the initial drop in productivity is that much greater and more protracted than in the case of skilled craft workers and a greater amount of supervision or 'doubling-up' (one operator teaching or assisting another) is required.   The same applies in assembly departments where semi-skilled workers are likely to need extra time and assistance in order to put together more complicated, customer-specific products.

Table 14.3
Qualifications and training in engineering plant samples

	Britain	Netherlands
Shopfloor qualifications	41% craft 59% semi-skilled 22% semi-skilled	12% technician 66% craft
Average initial training times for machine operators:		
Skilled	3-4 year craft apprentice training	LTS plus 11 months on-the-job training
Semi-skilled	13 months on-the-job training	n/a (New recruits need LTS minimum)
Apprentices	3% of total employment	<1% of total employment
Shopfloor supervisors qualifications	85% craft 15% without vocational qualifications	50% technician 50% craft
Maintenance workers qualifications	85% craft 15% without vocational qualifications	35% technician 65% craft

n/a = not applicable

Note

Classification of formal qualifications in each country:

Craft: British City & Guilds Part II passes or equivalent; Dutch LTS certificates and primary apprentice awards

Technician: British Higher National Certificate/Diploma and (Ordinary) National Certificate/Diploma awards; Dutch MTS certificates and advanced apprenticeship awards.

The Dutch advantage in production workers' skills was reinforced by generally higher levels of supervisory competence. In the British plants visited some 85 per cent of supervisors were craft-trained and 15 per cent remained semi-skilled; in the Dutch plants nearly all supervisors were vocationally qualified, half of them to technician (MTS) standard and half to craft (LTS) level. In addition to these MTS-qualified supervisors, a further 12 per cent of shopfloor employees in the Dutch sample held technician-level qualifications. They had typically been recruited for work which in the British plants was the province of craft workers, for example, CNC machine operation (and, in smaller firms, on-machine programming as well) in situations involving small batch sizes and complex product specifications.

In both countries there was a wide variety of updating and continuing training programmes for existing employees, some of them short courses provided by machinery suppliers and others provided in-house which ranged from one-day courses in Statistical Process Control techniques for nearly all direct employees to two-week courses in electronic control systems for small groups of technicians and skilled machinists. In addition, roughly half the plants in each national sample reported sponsoring small numbers of adult employees to attend one- or two-year college courses leading to recognised qualifications. Although it did not prove possible to gather comparable data on employer-financed continuing training in our two national samples, we formed the view that the annual volume of such training per employee in Britain exceeded that in the Netherlands. However, the difference was in no way great enough to bridge the overall gaps in workforce skills between the two samples.

Managers and technical staff

Senior managers in each national sample held much the same levels of technical qualifications with some 55-60 per cent in each case being engineering graduates or technicians. This category included ten of the twelve managing or general directors in the British sample and six out of nine top managers in the Dutch plants. However, Dutch managers enjoyed far greater support from highly-qualified technical staff than their British counterparts: technical support staff defined as those responsible for research, design and development, production engineering, production planning, office-based programming and test, inspection and quality control accounted for roughly a third of indirect workers in both national samples. As Table 14.4 shows, just under 80 per cent of technical support staff in the Netherlands held technician- or degree-level qualifications against 45 per cent so qualified in Britain. The percentage without vocational qualifications in the Netherlands was only half that in Britain.

As with craft skill supplies, these disparities in technical support skill levels are associated with differences in the extent to which initial training costs are borne by employers in each country. The bulk of engineering technicians in Britain are apprentice-trained at employer expense; by contrast the relatively large annual outflow from full-time intermediate technical (MTS) schools in the Netherlands facilitates the recruitment of prospective technicians on the open market; the main subsequent costs to Dutch employers are those associated with initial on-the-job training.[7] The resulting differences between the two industries in the proportions of technicians with appropriate qualifications for the work they perform had visible consequences for new product and process development in each case.

For instance, several of the Dutch plants visited had expanded their involvement in installing as well as supplying their products and were therefore able to make quick product improvements in response to customer feedback. Some of them had also made good progress in 'modularising' designs so as to allow key components to be produced in relatively large batch sizes without compromising their ability to assemble small batches of final products to customer-specific requirements. British plants in the same lines of business appeared to have a much less systematic approach to product development.

In some British plants we were further told that the introduction of new equipment was being hindered by shortages of qualified production engineers. Although most British plants did not explain their relative lack of new investment in these terms, it was obvious in several cases that the only staff capable of selecting and installing new equipment were already 'over-extended' by involvement with day-to-day production and sales problems. There were few, if any, parallels to this situation in the Dutch plants visited.

Within the British sample, it should be noted, a small minority of plants had clearly been successful in terms of new product and process development and these were precisely the plants which possessed an 'above average' supply of technically-qualified support staff (usually as a result of their own substantial investment in technician apprentice training). However, their performance remains exceptional.

Table 14.4
Vocational qualifications held by technical support staff[a] in national samples

	Britain	Netherlands
	(Percentages)	
Graduate	11	21
Technician	34	58
Craft	24	5
No vocational qualifications	31	16
Total	100	100

a: See text for definition of 'technical support' category.
b: See notes to Table 3 for classification of technician- and craft-level qualifications in each country. Graduate qualifications are classified as follows: British university and polytechnic first degrees; Dutch university degrees and HTS certificates.

Summary and conclusions

In spite of rapid growth in British engineering productivity in the past decade, our comparisons of plants making similar products suggest that output per hour worked in the British industry is still about 25-30 per cent lower than in the Netherlands. This result is consistent with estimates based on Production Censuses in both countries.

Competitive success in the European metal-working industries increasingly requires firms to be able to meet highly specific customer requirements. In response to competition from newly-industrialising countries in the mass production of standardised goods, the majority of British plants visited for this study have indeed moved further into small- and medium-batch production of higher value added products during the 1980's. However, the performance of most British plants relative to their Dutch rivals is still restricted by slower investment in new capital equipment and lower average levels of workforce skills and knowledge.

349

The greater use of new machinery in the Dutch industry partly reflects the longer financial payback periods on which Dutch firms operate and the recent bringing forward of planned new investments in response to generous tax allowances. However, the rapid and effective introduction of new technology also requires managers to be well-supported by highly-qualified technical staff and the Dutch plants were found to enjoy a decisive advantage over their British counterparts in this respect.

The higher skill levels found throughout the Dutch engineering industry primarily reflect that country's widespread provision of full-time vocational education and training. As elsewhere, trainees completing full-time courses of vocational schooling still need to undergo programmes of structured on-the-job training when they first enter employment. However, the relatively high attainments of students at junior and intermediate technical schools in the Netherlands give Dutch employers a considerable 'head-start' over their British counterparts in terms of the 'trainability' of their workforce, both as new entrants to the labour market and subsequently as adult workers who may need retraining and updating.

In this context Dutch employers are able to carry out training to given standards more quickly and cost-effectively than is possible in Britain, and in many cases they are able to set their training standards much higher than is feasible for their British counterparts. Indeed, as was often pointed out to us in the Netherlands, the relatively high levels of wages and accompanying social charges in that country provide sharp incentives to employers to seek the high levels of workforce skill and productivity required to succeed in high value added manufacturing.

Although our comparisons suggest that engineering employers in Britain finance a (proportionately) larger volume of initial and continuing training than is found in the Dutch industry, much of it does no more than compensate for relative deficiencies in the vocational education and training of British workers prior to their taking up employment. In consequence, a majority of British plants are still unable to aspire to average Dutch skill levels on the shopfloor or in technical support departments.

A broad conclusion must be that, in this industry at least, the competitive advantage derived by Dutch employers from a system of vocational education and training largely based on full-time schooling compares favourably with the German skills advantage deriving from the long-established 'Dual System' of apprenticeship training. By contrast, in Britain neither type of system is well-developed. In comparison with the Netherlands, the courses of state-funded full-time vocational education available in Britain cater for only a small proportion of each age cohort. The bulk of British training to craft and technician standards is financed by employers through a traditional apprenticeship system which, however, lacks the institutional and legal foundations of the more successful German system.

A key implication of this and other comparative studies for British policy-makers is that both types of vocational training provision full-time schooling and employment-based apprenticeships need to be strengthened and harmonised. In the case of engineering, for instance, the volume of craft and technician apprenticeship training could be increased if first year off-the-job training took place in full-time vocational colleges, thus delaying trainees' entry to employment and reducing the share of training costs which is borne by employers. Systematic co-ordination of college-based and employment-based training provision for many industries in this way would contribute greatly to the achievement of a 'high skill, high productivity' economy.

Notes

Financial support for this work was kindly provided by the Economic and Social Research Council. We are grateful to the many engineering companies and machinery suppliers who agreed to assist us with this research. We would also like to thank Sig Prais for generous encouragement and advice throughout the study. Responsibility for any errors is ours alone.

1. For details of recent Dutch reforms to apprentice training and to the vocational education and training system in general, see van Dijk et al (1988) and van den Dool (1989); for a description of KMBO ('short intermediate') courses of vocational education, see Mason and van Ark (1993).
2. Estimates of Anglo-Dutch productivity differentials in 1990 for engineering and for manufacturing as a whole are based on

extrapolations (using indices of production and employment in each country) of 1984 'benchmark' estimates in van Ark (1990).

3. For a more detailed discussion of the calculations underlying these productivity comparisons, see Mason and van Ark (1993, Section 4).

4. For further details of recent Dutch tax credits on fixed-asset investments under the 'WIR' scheme now greatly reduced in scope see Financial Times, European Investment Locations Survey, 4 April 1991, p.IV. Dutch managers made clear to us that these incentives mainly affected the timing rather than the volume of new investment.

5. It will be understood that the definition of 'craft-qualified' in each industry involves some simplification of a more complex reality: in the British case, for instance, older 'time-served' employees are included alongside younger craft workers who have completed a standards-based training and further education programme; on the Dutch side, the great majority of employees designated as craft-skilled have acquired LTS qualifications and subsequently followed employer-specific programmes of on-the-job training which inevitably differ in respect of length and breadth of content; only a small proportion have completed a formal apprenticeship. Nonetheless, our comparisons of exam papers in each country leave us in no doubt as to the broad equivalence between the two sets of workers identified as craft-qualified in each national sample.

6. These estimates of average initial on-the-job training times refer to the periods during which new recruits are regarded as being 'in training', ie in receipt of regular instruction and detailed supervision. No attempt has been made to compare the allocation of training times in each country between 'instruction periods' (when there is little or no output) and periods of 'learning by experience' when some productive contribution is made.

7. For a discussion of the relative distribution of technician training costs in Britain compared to France and Germany, see Steedman, Mason, Wagner (1991, pp. 69-70).

Statistical Appendix

Table A1
Number of engineering plants visited by product area

	Britain	Netherlands
Pumps	5	3
Valves	3	3
Springs	4	3
TOTAL	12	9

Table A2
Distribution of plant sizes in national samples of engineering plants

	Britain	Netherlands
Employment size group	(Number of plants)	
1-99	2	3
100-199	6	6
200-299	2	0
300-plus	2	0
TOTAL	12	9
	(Number of employees)	
Median plant size in samples:[a]	260	140

a: The median size is here defined such that half of all employees are in plants above that size and half below it.

Table A3
Medians and quartiles of population plant-size distributions in the engineering industries[a], Britain and the Netherlands

	Britain	Netherlands
	(Number of employees)	
Lower quartile	40	30
Median	140	90
Upper quartile	460	260

a: Refers to local units in Britain and legal units ('enterprises') in the Netherlands in the combined metal products and mechanical engineering industries (Britain SIC 1980, Classes 31 and 32; Netherlands SBI 34 and 35).

Sources:BSO, Report on the Census of Production, 1988; CBS, Statistiek van het Ondernemingen- en Vestigingenbestand, 1987.

References

Daly, A., Hitchens, D. and Wagner, K. (1985), 'Productivity, machinery and skills in a sample of British and German manufacturing plants', *National Institute Economic Review*.

Mason, G. and van Ark, B. (1993), 'Productivity, machinery and skills in engineering: an Anglo-Dutch comparison', NIESR Discussion Paper, New Series, No. 36.

Mason, G., Prais, S. and van Ark, B. (1992), 'Vocational education and productivity in the Netherlands and Britain', *National Institute Economic Review*.

Steedman, H., Mason, G. and Wagner, K. (1991), 'Intermediate skills in the workplace: deployment, standards and supply in Britain, France and Germany', *National Institute Economic Review*.

Steedman, H. and Wagner, K. (1987), 'A second look at productivity, machinery and skills in Britain and Germany', *National Institute Economic Review*.

Steedman, H. and Wagner, K. (1989), 'Productivity, machinery and skills: clothing manufacturing in Britain and Germany', *National Institute Economic Review*.

Van Ark, B. (1990), 'Comparative levels of labour productivity in Dutch and British manufacturing' *National Institute Economic Review*.

Van Dijk, C., Akkermans, T. and Hövels, B. (1988), *Social Partners and Vocational Education in the Netherlands*, CEDEFOP, Berlin.

Van den Dool, P. (1989), 'The Netherlands: selection for vocational education starts early', *European Journal of Education*, 24, pp.

15 Training down under: An overview of the Australian experience

Meredith Baker

Introduction

In the context of the major structural reform and reductions in protection levels currently occurring in the Australian economy, the focus of much debate has been on the extent of training and skills formation both in the public and the private sector. The catch-cry of much of the debate is that training is an imperative in the current and future climate of increased international competitiveness. A well-educated and trained workforce, it is argued, will provide the key to enhanced productivity and flexibility seen as so necessary in an environment of changing international economic circumstances (ACTU/TDC 1987, Minister for Employment Education and Training 1989, Clare and Johnston 1993). Moreover, the extent of investment in worker training has consequences for the rapid and successful adaptation of new technology (Chapman and Tan 1990).

Alongside the need for a strong skills base, flexibility in the deployment of labour is felt to be necessary for industry to adapt and respond in a competitive world market (ACTU/TDC 1987, NBEET 1989, Minister for Employment, Education and Training 1989). Accordingly, changes are occurring on a number of fronts in order to enhance the returns from training to both individuals and employers. In the employee relations environment, for example, changes are occurring which enable more flexible work practices, so long argued to have inhibited Australian industry from becoming competitive. On another front, development of agreed national priorities and goals in training with the establishment of the Australian National Training Authority and the setting of national skills standards, competence and accreditation guidelines via the establishment of the National Training Board it is argued, will underpin the success of the structural adjustment process. Such Federal government initiatives covering the whole of the vocational education and training sector go under the broad heading of the Training Reform Agenda (Clare and Johnston 1993).

However, in the context of the on-going debate on education and training in Australia, it has become conventional wisdom that the main 'villain' responsible for inadequate skills formation in Australia is private industry (Stromback and Moy 1989). This view has since become the rationale underlying the introduction of the so-called Training Guarantee or industry training levy, which commenced in July 1990.

The main aims of this chapter are twofold. First, to establish the extent and coverage of private sector training in Australia and second, to provide an overview of the major policies currently in place which impact, either directly or indirectly, on private sector training.

By way of background, this paper commences with a brief overview of the system of training in Australia, also covering the important institutional features. Following this, evidence on the extent and coverage of private sector training is presented. This is based to a large extent on the *How Workers Get Their Training* survey, undertaken by the Australian Bureau of Statistics (ABS) during 1989 (ABS 1990a). An outline of the various factors affecting private sector training together with the associated policy responses follows. The final section offers some concluding comments.

Structure and institutional background

While this chapter devotes its attention primarily to the extent and coverage of training undertaken in the private sector in Australia, it is conceptually difficult to isolate discussion of job-related training in Australia to the role played by industry. Elaborating the roles played by the government and educational institutions are also important in the context of understanding the relative importance of industry-based training in the overall context of training. Perhaps of most importance to this current analysis, however, is an understanding of the changes currently occurring in the institutional framework governing relations between employers and employees.

Our understanding of the extent and coverage of training in Australia is, unfortunately, muddied by the different concepts and views of what constitutes training - ranging, on the one hand, from a formalised apprenticeship program to the informal 'learning-by-doing' arrangements undertaken at the workplace. Moreover, an analysis of the system of job-related training in Australia is complicated by the apparent lack of formal structure.

While informal training on-the-job represents Australia's largest training resource (OECD 1986), the traditional lynch-pin of formal job-related training has been the apprenticeship system. Indeed, the scale of apprenticeship training in Australia is surpassed only by the German-speaking countries and Denmark, where such schemes offer a broader occupational coverage (*Report of the Commonwealth/State Working Group* 1986). Indeed, based on May 1990 figures, the Australian apprenticeship system currently provides training for approximately 23 per cent of all employed 15-19 year olds — though mostly concentrated among males (ABS 1990b).

The traditional system of apprenticeship training has been criticised on a number of fronts, however. Two of the major criticisms are that the system relies on a time-serving rather than a competency-based approach in the entry to tradesperson status, and the sensitivity of apprenticeship numbers to the state of the economy.[1] The low rates of participation of women have also been a cause for concern. Accordingly a number of federal government subsidies and programs (eg Commonwealth Rebate for Apprenticeship Full-time Training (CRAFT), Special Entry-Level Training (SELT) and 'Tradeswomen on the Move') have been put in place.

Furthermore, the Australian Traineeship System (ATS) has been designed to complement the apprenticeship program and offer an alternative structured training route for post-compulsory training. Focussing on young people who do not continue onto higher education or other formal technical or trade courses, the one year ATS scheme combines work experience with a formal off-the-job training course, usually in the Technical and Further Education (TAFE) sector. In particular, the availability of traineeships is largely governed by employers, who are provided with a subsidy to take on a trainee under this scheme. Commencements represent less than one per cent of the population aged 15-19 (DEET, unpublished preliminary estimates).

Following the Carmichael Report (Carmichael 1991), which outlined a strategy for meeting Australia's training needs by 2001, the Australian

Vocational Certificate Scheme (AVCS) is currently being piloted. The scheme is based on competency-based training — training which is designed to focus on *outcomes* such as the attainment and demonstration of knowledge, skills and application as opposed to training *inputs*, such as time served. Furthermore, competency standards will be set nationally, and established in close consultation with industry bodies. The registration of alternative training providers are also underway, thereby increasing the formal training opportunities in a broader range of industries than hitherto. Thus, the focus of competency-based training is away from an individual's credentials and towards the actual skills they possess. Nevertheless, it would appear the AVCS formalises previously informal training and increases the number of training credentials available.

Alongside the apprenticeship, ATS and AVCS routes lies the system of post-school vocational education and training offered by the TAFE colleges. In 1988 enrolments in TAFE stood at over 900,000 (Minister for Employment, Education and Training, 1988b). Given the typically short duration of courses offered by TAFE, however, at any one point in time the numbers attending TAFE are likely to be around half this number. Moreover, the diversity of courses offered will mean that not all courses may be regarded as job-related in their training content.

The majority of those attending TAFE/technical colleges do so on a part-time basis and are employed part-time at the same time (71 per cent of all TAFE attendees in May 1990 were in this category). Moreover, participation in TAFE by 15-19 and 20-24 year olds represents almost 11 and 8 per cent, respectively.[2] TAFE/technical college participation rates by the population aged 25-64 are much lower, however, standing at just under 3 per cent (ABS 1990b).

The TAFE system is also complicated by the fact that the State and Territory governments have statutory responsibility for the regulation and administration of education and training, and as such are the major providers of such off-the-job training. Generally speaking, each State has established State Training Authorities which are generally empowered to set training standards, approve curricula, accredit training programs and providers, determine the appropriate length and context of training both on- and off-the-job and issue certificates of completion (NBEET 1989). The role of the federal government in the training arena largely reflects this absence of constitutional power, and is traditionally limited to the provision of part-funding for TAFE and other training programs. Nevertheless, the federal government has recently instituted a series of reforms, primarily aimed at achieving a national focus to the accreditation and setting of skills standards thereby overcoming the large state disparities observed in arrangements and statutes and the consequent loss of geographic and occupational mobility. In response to the desire to achieve a nationally coordinated and consistent approach to training, the National Training Board was established in February 1990 and in 1992 the Federal and State governments agreed to establish the Australian National Training Authority (ANTA).

One of the main goals of ANTA is the development of agreed national priorities and goals in training, in association with the involvement of peak employer and industry bodies. ANTA is also the main funding body covering the disbursement of funding to accredited vocational training courses and course providers. The NTB assists in this process via the establishment of a system of recognised training providers, linked in with the endorsement of competency standards across occupations and classifications in industry or enterprise awards or agreements determined by an industrial tribunal. Complementing these developments, the Federal government has increased expenditure in the TAFE sector, thereby increasing its share of total government outlays in the sector. Finally, the TAFE sector has increased liaison with employers and industry in order to better meet market requirements for courses.

The Australian government also provides funding assistance to the unemployed to undertake training with the hope of improving their employment prospects, though it should be noted that by international standards the scale of expenditure on labour market programs for the unemployed has always been relatively small (Sloan and Wooden 1987, Stretton and Chapman 1990, Sloan 1993). The four major training components of the 1992-93 Federal budget are: JOBSTART, a wage subsidy scheme to private sector employers; JOBTRAIN, providing short term vocational training to 'disadvantaged job seekers'; SkillShare, which provides grants to non-profit community groups for structured skills training for the long-term unemployed and disadvantaged; and JOBSKILLS which combines work experience in the community sector and training for those unemployed for 12 months or more. Other minor programs include the Special Intervention program - aimed primarily at improving English literacy and language skills and Job Search Training which includes formal course work with a TAFE or community group.

Finally, discussion of the structure of job-related training in Australia also cannot be divorced from the institutional framework covering the employer-employee relationship. Indeed from a theoretical perspective, institutional arrangements have clear implications for our assessment of the various incentives to train or be trained. Since the turn of the century, Australia has operated under a highly centralised and regulated system of industrial relations. The wage setting arrangements have been typically centralised and set by the (federal) Industrial Relations Commission (IRC) or State wage tribunals and around 80-85 per cent of employees are covered by job-specific minimum wage awards (Borland, Chapman and Rimmer 1990). Moreover, it is important to note that these so-called awards involve a host of other work conditions alongside the minimum wage arrangements and tend to be organised along occupational lines.

An understanding of awards is important in the context of explaining the criticisms of the institutional arrangements with respect to their effects on the amount and type of training observed in Australia. In particular, the existing job classification structures, minimum wage provisions and craft unions have all been blamed for inhibiting the process of skill acquisition. These criticisms are summarised as follows: (i) traditional job classification structures emphasise narrow or rigidly defined occupational classifications, thereby restricting workers to a limited range of tasks and consequently reducing their training requirements; (ii) binding minimum wage provisions for apprentices and trainees are too high, discouraging employers from investing in training and constraining workers wage profiles so that they are unable to accept wages below their marginal product during the training phase; and (iii) the system of craft unionism inhibits the existence of well-defined promotion processes or career structures within firms which in turn leads to under-investment by workers in firm-specific human capital (see Borland 1990 and Chapman and Tan 1990).

In the recent past, however, with the focus on the need to increase productivity and international competitiveness, a substantial transition in the industrial relations framework is currently underway. In the late 1980s, 'award restructuring'[3] was an integral component of this structural adjustment process and one of the major mechanisms by which the link between training and the arrangements governing industrial relations was forged. The process of award restructuring included the following features: establishment of skill-related career paths; removing impediments to multi-skilling; broadening the range of tasks which a worker may be required to perform; creation of 'appropriate' relativities between different categories of workers within an award and at the enterprise level; enhancement of flexibility and efficiency in the workplace through changes in working patterns and arrangements; including 'properly fixed' minimum rates for classifications in awards; and rationalising the list of respondents to awards (Sloan and Wooden 1990). As such, the process of award restructuring encouraged the creation of incentives for firms and workers to invest in job-related training.

Furthermore, the recent introduction of enterprise bargaining arrangements - a move away from the traditional highly centralised bargaining framework - also has implications for job-related training. A holistic approach to the implementation of enterprise bargaining, it is argued, will provide the background structures required for internal labour markets to flourish (see Blandy 1987, Sloan 1992). In doing so, the incentives for internal promotion paths and career paths within a firm are enhanced and consequent reductions in labour turnover levels will be observed. This reduction in labour turnover is one of the keys to increasing the incentives for employers to provide training; under conditions of no labour turnover, firms will have the incentive to finance some or all of this general training (see also ASTEC 1987). Sloan (1992), however, contends that the federal government's vision of enterprise bargaining, being restricted to an add-on to a 'locker' of minimum rates awards, will not in fact bring about much in the way of productivity improvements nor facilitate an enterprise focus to agreements.

Private sector training - who gets it and how much?

Many skills are acquired during employment either informally via on-the-job training or more formally through courses conducted either in-house or outside the firm. Formal study for an educational qualification whilst employed is yet another means of obtaining job-related training.

However, as highlighted in the *Report of the Commonwealth/State Working Group on Skills Shortages and Skills Formation* (1986) and the *Committee of Inquiry into Labour Market Programs (The Kirby Report)* (1985) the Australian research on the extent, nature and coverage of industry training is particularly limited. At that time, the available evidence was limited to a paper by Curtain, Krbavac and Stretton (1986) which presents figures on the estimated proportion of GDP accounted for by private sector investment on training in four countries - Australia, the USA, Japan and West Germany. According to these data, private sector investment in education represented approximately 0.8 per cent of GDP in Australia in 1980 compared with 1.5 per cent in the USA, 1.9 per cent in Japan and 2.1 per cent in West Germany.[4]

This much cited piece has since become the basis for subsequent government policy prescriptions based upon the notion that the private sector under-invests in skills formation. However, the data upon which the Curtain *et al* findings are based, come from a survey of labour costs conducted by the Business Council of Australia which, as Stromback and Moy (1989) point out, involved a highly selective and extremely small sample. Moreover, Stromback and Moy (1989) note that the variations in the cross-country definitions of private sector expenditure on training were substantial, forcing them to conclude that such comparisons were worthless.

Thus, despite the concern of under-training, very little evidence has been gathered on the extent of training in Australia. Recent data collected by the Australian Bureau of Statistics on *How Workers Get Their Training* fills some of this gap and are utilised, together with a number of other sources, to provide an overview of job-related training activities in Australia. First, the extent of private sector training in Australia is examined. This is followed by an analysis of the factors associated with the receipt of different types of training

The extent of private sector training

Data from the *How Workers Get Their Training* (ABS 1990a) survey indicates that 79 per cent of the workforce undertook some form of training during the year prior to being surveyed. However, as Figure 15.1 reveals, the vast majority of such training was in the form of informal on-the-job training - defined to include watching others, being shown, teaching one's self or asking questions of co-workers. Following in importance are the more formal or 'classroom' style training courses associated with in-house training. Defined in this survey as 'training organised by the respondents' employers primarily for their own employees, using the employers' staff or training consultants' (ABS 1990a, p.36), we see that 35 per cent of wage and salary earners participated in such training courses for at least some time during the year. Far less widespread was participation on external training courses; that is 'training which is organised and conducted by training or educational establishments, agencies or consultants other than any of the respondents' employers [but excluding study for an educational qualification]' (ABS 1990a, p.36). Only 10 per cent of wage and salary earners undertook any such training. Finally, 17 per cent of wage and salary earners studied for an educational qualification during the year prior to the survey (ie 1988) - though we cannot be certain of the extent to which such training is undertaken for employment reasons.

Figure 15.1
Participation in training by category of training undertaken and gender, 1989

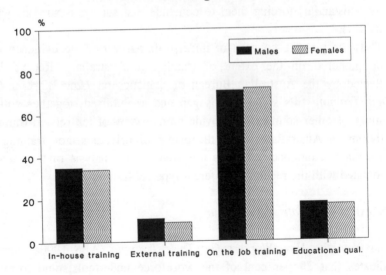

Note

a.   Sample restricted to persons who had a wage or salary job in the last 12 months

Source: ABS (1990a)

364

Further evidence on the amount of employer training is provided in the 1990 ABS survey of *Employer Training Expenditure* which reveals that just under a quarter (24 per cent) of all employers reported any formal training expenditure during the three month survey period (ABS 1991). In dollar terms, this expenditure represented about 2.6 per cent of gross wages and salaries. Disaggregating this data by private and public sector employers reveals that formal training expenditure by private sector firms, as a proportion of gross wages and salaries, represented 2.2 per cent compared with 3.2 per cent for the public sector. Nevertheless, private sector training expenditure appears to have increased between 1989 and 1990 as revealed by Figure 15.2.

Figure 15.2
Average Training Expenditure, All Employers by Sector
July to September 1989 and 1990

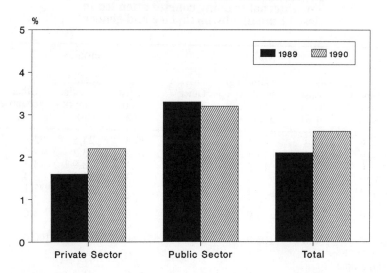

Source: ABS(1991)

Miller and Volker's (1987) examination of the Australian Longitudinal Survey (ALS) data on the extent of training in the youth labour market reveal findings consistent with those from the other two ABS (1990a and 1991) surveys.[5] In particular, their findings indicate that around 70 per cent of young males and 67 per cent of young females reported having received some form of training. The majority of such training was informal (ie from supervisors or other workers) but significant proportions reported the receipt of formal on-the-job training (29 per cent of males and 32 per cent of females) as well as formal off-the-job training (28 per cent and 15 per cent, respectively).

So far, we have concentrated on the evidence on the participation in various kinds of training activities. Information in the *How Workers Get Their Training* data also enables us to examine the amount of time spent on training. These data are summarised in Table 15.1 which provides the distribution of total time spent on in-house or external training courses attended in the last 12 months disaggregated by birthplace and gender. Of those who participated in such courses, we see that females spend less time on in-house and external training courses compared

Table 15.1
Distribution of total time spent on in-house
or external training courses attended in
last 12 months by birthplace and gender[a]

Time spent (hours)	Males			Females		
	Aust born (%)	Main Engl speaking countries (%)	Other countries (%)	Aust born (%)	Main Engl speaking countries (%)	Other countries (%)
1-9	19.3	17.4	19.2	29.8	24.5	23.8
10-19	15.9	15.4	13.6	18.8	23.2	19.3
20-29	12.4	11.5	12.0	13.1	8.9	18.4
30-39	8.8	8.9	8.3	9.3	12.3	8.4
40-119	31.4	31.3	32.3	21.3	25.2	23.1
120-199	6.4	8.7	8.4	3.7	2.4	3.1
200-399	5.8	6.9	6.5	3.9	3.4	3.6
Total	100.0	100.0	100.0	100.0	100.0	100.0
Average time spent (hrs)[b]	62.7	69.2	68.1	45.9	45.8	46.2

Note

[a]   As a percentage of all persons who had a wage or salary job in the last 12 months
[b]   Based on mid-points of the above distribution of time spent on in-house or external training courses.

Source: Baker and Wooden (1991)

with their male counterparts; females experiencing about 46 hours during the 12 month period while males experience between 63 and 69 hours per annum. Since the participation rates in such courses are relatively low, we would expect the time spent in such activities to be much lower when we average such time across all employees. Indeed, data from the ABS survey of *Employer Training Expenditure* reveal that average paid training hours per employee for the three months July - September 1990 is only about 6 hours. This comprises an average of 5 hours for private sector employees and 8 hours for public sector employees.

Information contained in the *How Workers Get Their Training* data and the *Employer Training Expenditure* survey also enable us to explore the level of skills being imparted through an examination of the type of training being undertaken. First, we see in the *How Workers Get Their Training* survey, similar to the findings on training durations, clear gender differences appear in the main types of activities undertaken (Table 15.2). Females are more likely, as compared with males, to undertake training courses concerned with clerical, sales and personal service and general computing skills and are not so involved in courses which concentrate on management and professional skills (though such courses still account for the largest proportion of formal training amongst females), trade/craft skills, skills relevant to the operation of transport and machinery and labouring skills. Such distinctions clearly reflect traditionally sex differences in employment by occupation. Furthermore, details available from the *Employer Training Expenditure* survey reveal the predominance of trade and apprenticeship training, especially amongst private sector firms. By contrast, technical and para-professional as well as management and professional fields dominate the training activities of the public sector (Table 15.3).

Table 15.2
Distribution of the main types of in-house or external training activities by birthplace and gender[a]

Main type of in-house or external training	Males			Females		
	Aust born	Main English speaking countries	Other countries	Aust born	Main English speaking countries	Other countries
Management & professional	27.0	31.9	29.5	25.0	26.1	17.4
Technical & para-professional	9.6	12.0	10.2	9.2	13.2	9.4
Trade/craft	8.4	7.0	5.5	2.3	0.8	2.3
Clerical	4.1	2.6	2.6	12.6	7.7	17.6
Sales & personal service	8.5	10.5	8.6	12.4	10.8	11.2
Transport & machinery operation	5.8	4.1	4.3	0.1	0.2	0.3
Labouring & related	1.7	2.5	1.5	0.8	0.2	1.7
Induction	3.7	1.5	4.0	4.5	2.6	4.7
General supervisory	4.6	3.7	4.3	3.5	5.6	3.9
General computing skills	8.9	5.8	11.6	13.2	12.6	15.7
General health & safety	11.0	12.4	11.1	8.0	12.2	7.4
Other	6.7	6.1	6.7	7.9	8.0	8.5
Total	100.0	100.0	100.0	100.0	100.0	100.0

Note

[a] As a percentage of all persons who had a wage or salary job in the last 12 months

Source: *Baker and Wooden*

Table 15.3
**Average paid training time per employee*,
all employers, field of training by sector
July to September 1990 (hours per employee)**

Field of Training	Sector		
	Private	Public	Total
Induction	0.35	0.36	0.30
General supervision	0.29	0.37	0.31
General computing	0.37	0.60	0.44
Health and safety	0.22	0.42	0.29
Management and professional	0.60	1.79	0.98
Technical and para-professional	0.30	2.24	0.91
Trade and apprenticeship	1.86	0.95	1.58
Clerical, sales	0.52	0.60	0.54
Plant and machinery	0.27	0.31	0.28
Other	0.16	0.40	0.24
All fields	4.95	8.05	5.92

Note

*   The total time receiving formal training averaged over the total number of
    employees

Source: ABS (1991)

It is, of course, difficult to interpret what such data mean. Are these data
indicative of under-training in the workplace environment? There are
two important problems to be borne in mind when interpreting such data.
The first is that we cannot answer the question of whether or not there is
under-investment in training without some notion of what is the optimum
amount of firm provided training. Indeed, as Stromback and Moy (1989)
argue, differences in industrial structure, including protection levels and
production techniques, will mean that optimal training levels will differ
between countries. Consequently, simple cross-country comparisons of
the extent of and expenditure on employer provided training may not be
the relevant yardstick. Second, these broad-brush figures provide little
feel for the *quality* of training undertaken and, in any case, informal on-
the-job skill acquisition is largely unmeasurable.

As discussed in Baker and Wooden (1991), there are, however, a
number of other pieces of related evidence available which enable us to
assess the extent of private sector training in Australia. In particular,

Borland *et al* (1990) point to two other pieces of evidence which they regard as more revealing - at least in a comparative sense. First are empirical estimates of the relationship between wages and work experience. According to the human capital framework, a relatively steep wage profile implies larger returns to investment in training and, therefore, greater investments in training. Borland *et al* draw on the results of a number of previous studies, all of which lead to the conclusion that the wage-experience relationship in Australia is much flatter than in other countries (including both decentralist economies such as the US and Japan, and more corporatist economies such as West Germany and Austria).

The second piece of evidence Borland *et al* draw on are cross-country estimates of the elasticity of labour productivity to changes in the rate of unemployment produced by Dowrick (1990). These figures indicate that this elasticity is relatively low in Australia. This suggests relatively low levels of labour hoarding during the downswing of the business cycle, and since investments in firm-specific training will increase the reluctance of management to lay workers off during a period of cyclical decline, lower levels of firm-specific training are implied.

Finally, survey evidence collected from executives around the world for the *1990 World Competitiveness Report* (IMD/World Economic Forum 1990) indicates that Australian managers generally are not of the view that on-going job training is meeting the requirements of a competitive economy. Scored on a 0 to 100 scale, the responses of the Australian executives gave a mean score of just 45.3 which placed Australia 14th on a list of 23 developed economies.

Overall, therefore, there are reasons to suspect that the level of job training may be comparatively low in Australia.

Who gets training?

One of the major tenets underlying much of the current government's policy focus in the labour market is equity in access (Minister for Employment, Education and Training 1988). In the training arena, examination of the *How Workers Get Their Training* survey, enables us to examine the factors associated with the incidence of different types of training activities. Here, we draw on the first multivariate analysis of

Table 15.4
Probability of receiving training by type of training
(maximum likelihood probit estimates: n = 14448)

Independent variables	Type of training					
	In-house training		External training		On-the-job training	
Constant	-1.37**	(8.32)	-2.82**	(12.25)	1.85**	(10.80)
Lives in metro area	-0.10**	(3.69)	-0.04	(0.95)	0.04	(1.21)
Female	0.11**	(2.77)	-0.03	(0.58)	-0.14**	(3.08)
Married	0.14**	(3.33)	-0.04	(0.67)	-0.03	(0.73)
Children present	-0.05	(1.15)	-0.09	(1.69)	-0.03	(0.78)
Birthplace:						
NESB	-0.26**	(5.99)	-0.10	(1.69)	0.16**	(3.77)
ESB	0.02	(0.52)	0.19**	(3.64)	0.39	(0.91)
Duration of residence	-0.58**	(2.96)	-0.65*	(2.41)	-0.04	(0.18)
Age	0.05**	(6.65)	0.06**	(5.83)	-0.04**	(5.18)
Age squared	-0.0008**	(7.95)	-0.0009**	(6.08)	0.0002*	(2.32)
Tenure	-0.01	(1.46)	0.12	(1.29)	-0.02**	(3.09)
Tenure squared	-0.0003	(0.91)	-0.00	(0.97)	0.0006	(1.91)
Industry:						
Agriculture	-0.64**	(4.43)	-0.13	(0.72)	-0.06	(0.47)
Manufacturing	-0.37**	(4.07)	-0.16	(1.32)	-0.04	(0.40)
Electricity	-0.16	(1.35)	-0.01	(0.09)	0.07	(0.54)
Construction	-0.39**	(3.80)	-0.08	(0.63)	-0.07	(0.62)
Wholesale and retail	-0.23	(2.49)	-0.15	(1.21)	-0.06	(0.60)
Transport	-0.26*	(2.55)	-0.10	(0.77)	-0.14	(1.34)
Communication	-0.23	(1.94)	-0.07	(0.46)	-0.11	(0.82)
Finance	0.03	(0.36)	-0.11	(0.87)	0.03	(0.28)
Public Admin	-0.06	-(0.59)	0.01	(0.11)	-0.07	(0.63)
Community services	-0.04	(0.42)	-0.14	(1.15)	0.01	(0.09)
Recreation	0.40**	(3.96)	-0.13	(0.96)	-0.11	(1.08)
Occupation:						
Managerial	0.71**	(11.94)	0.81**	(9.94)	0.34**	(5.69)
Professional	0.79**	(13.94)	0.79**	(9.88)	0.62**	(10.12)
Para-professional	0.68**	(12.06)	0.65**	(7.97)	0.61**	(10.27)
Trades	0.26**	(5.07)	0.45**	(5.76)	0.26**	(5.54)
Clerks	0.48**	(10.39)	0.52**	(7.15)	0.42**	(9.40)
Sales	0.79*	(16.28)	0.51**	(6.66)	0.37**	(7.79)
Operatives	0.12*	(2.24)	0.08	(0.91)	0.35	(0.70)
Employed cont during previous 12 months	0.04	(1.28)	0.26	(0.06)	-0.20**	(5.58)
Hours of work:						
1 to 15 hours	-0.26**	(4.15)	-0.15	(1.70)	-0.19**	(3.24)
16 to 34 hours	-0.12*	(2.57)	-0.13*	(2.09)	-0.05	(1.05)
More than 40 hours	0.17**	(5.83)	0.17**	(4.76)	0.16**	(5.13)
Public sector	0.21**	(5.83)	-0.09	(1.84)	0.12**	(3.10)
Casual	-0.39**	(8.55)	-0.15*	(2.46)	-0.20**	(4.68)
Firm size:						
less than 10 persons	-0.60**	(16.61)	-0.17	(3.61)	-0.04	(1.09)
10 to 19 persons	-0.47**	(11.56)	-0.24**	(4.34)	0.00	(0.06)
20 to 99 persons	-0.18**	(6.13)	-0.15**	(3.83)	0.02	(0.79)

this data set undertaken in the context of a number of questions relating to immigration and training (see Baker and Wooden 1991, 1992)

Nevertheless, a number of these results are useful in the context of examining who gets training. In particular, the estimations relating the probability of an individual receiving training in their current job to individual and job type characteristics illuminate the relative importance of various characteristics thought to be associated with the receipt of training. Table 15.4 reproduces the three probit equation estimates examining the incidence of in-house, external and on-the-job training undertaken by individuals during the 12 months prior to the survey.[6]

The list of independent variables incorporates all observable variables affecting the benefits from training to the individual and to the firm providing that training. The types of variables considered in previous studies of the determinants of training (eg Lillard and Tan 1986, Greenhalgh and Stewart 1987, Miller 1987, Lynch 1989, Booth 1991, 1992, Tan *et al* 1990, Baker 1991) fall into six main groups, as follows:

(i)   factors associated with the expected length of the employment relationship (eg gender, age, part-time work, casual employment, tenure);
(ii)   education;
(iii)   work experience;
(iv)   the technical requirements of the job (eg as proxied by occupation);
(v)   firm characteristics (eg firm size, private vs public sector, industry); and
(vi)   other demographic characteristics (eg birthplace and duration of residence).

In summary, these results suggest the importance of the following characteristics which are, in general consistent with the findings of international and other Australian evidence.

•   *Age:* an inverted U-shape relationship appears to exist for the more formal training activities, with the probability of receiving in-house being highest at the age of 32 and the age of 36.5 in the

372

case of external training. By contrast, we see that the probability that on-the-job training occurs declines continuously with age, though at a declining rate. A likely explanation for these differences is thought to be based on the fact that the on-the-job training reported in this survey costs employers very little and occurs more at the discretion of the worker. Hence employers stand to lose very little should the worker leave.

- *Hours of work:* the probability of undertaking training rises sharply with hours worked and is significantly lower amongst casual workers.

- *Experience and tenure:* the measure of experience incorporated in these estimates is based on years of *occupational* experience and aims to capture the specificity of skills associated within an occupation. As expected, we see the probability of training falls with occupational experience. Tenure, on the other hand, is not significantly associated with training probabilities.

- *Educational attainment:* consistent with previous studies, education emerges as an important determinant of training with training probabilities rising with level of educational attainment.

- *Employer characteristics:* the probability of receiving of formal types of training improves with firm size (see also Miller 1987 and Tan *et al* 1990), however the same cannot be said for on-the-job training. Training probabilities are also greater in the public sector (with the exception of external training where no significant sector differences emerge). Finally, significant inter-industry differences only emerge for the in-house training equation, with relatively low rates of in-house training in agriculture, recreation, personal and other services, construction, manufacturing and transport.

- *Occupation:* in general, the probability of undertaking training general rises with the skill level inherent in the occupation. Most obviously, the lowest probabilities of being trained are for labourers (the control group) and plant and machine operatives while workers in managerial, professional and para-professional occupations display much higher probabilities. Sales and clerical workers also appear to fare relatively well in the training process, suggesting that differences in access to, and participation in, training reflect not just skills but also blue-collar / white-collar distinctions.

- *Gender, marital status and dependents:* the presence of dependents does not appear to exert any significant impact on the likelihood of receiving or undertaking training. The interaction of gender and marital status reveal some interesting findings, however. Single females undergo more in-house training than males - the same cannot be said of married females, however. By contrast, with respect to on-the-job training, however, the results suggest that while females as a group undertake less on-the-job training than males, married females undertake more on-the-job training than single women. Finally, there appear to be no gender or marital status differences in the probabilities of external training.

- *Birthplace:* immigrants from a non-English speaking background (NESB), in general, are less likely to receive training. Even in the case of external training, while they are not *significantly* less likely to receive training as compared with the Australian born, they are when compared with their English speaking background (ESB) counterparts. While there are a number of explanations which may account for these differences, it turns out that the variable which emerges as being of greatest significance in accounting for birthplace differences in training (at least for the more formal types) is duration of residence: as duration of residence[7] increases, the 'training gap' falls over time. The importance of English language skills, which typically improve with duration of residence, is argued to be the major factor underlying this result.[8]

Under-investment in training and the training levy

It has become virtually a stylised fact that much of the blame for the under-provision of job-related training in Australia lies with the private sector. While there are grounds to suspect that the level of job training may be comparatively low in Australia, the reasons underlying this are likely to be quite complex and arise from a number of different sources. Nevertheless, this view has since become the rationale underlying the introduction of the so-called Training Guarantee or training levy, which commenced in July 1990.

In *Industry Training in Australia: The Need for Change* (Minister for Employment, Education and Training 1988a) a number of options were canvassed which it was felt would increase industry's contribution to training. While it was the government's view 'that it did not want to intervene unnecessarily in enterprise training decisions but that employers must take great responsibility for their own training requirements' (NTB 1991, p.10), government intervention in the training arena has taken place in the form of a minimum expenditure obligation scheme. The Training Guarantee scheme requires every enterprise in Australia (except those with a payroll less than $200,000[9]), from 1 July 1990, to spend an equivalent of one per cent of payroll on training its employees. This subsequently increased to 1.5 per cent in July 1992. If this amount is not spent, then legislation requires that this amount be forfeited and redirected into the financing of training activities.

In assessing the appropriateness, or otherwise, of this scheme, it is useful to consider the possible sources of private sector under-investment of training in Australia. These issues are complicated and inter-related to a certain extent, nevertheless the arguments presented within the literature have been along the following broad lines.

First, it has been argued on numerous occasions that the nature of the industrial relations framework, with its various restrictive awards, binding minimum wages and craft-based unionism, as well as the centralised nature of wage determination has inhibited the potential for training at the workplace. The consequences of these market imperfections has affected the incentives to both employers and employees in various ways. For example, industrial award restrictions and past trade union practices have encouraged the development of occupational labour markets which in turn encourage high labour turnover (Stromback and Moy 1988), consequently lowering a firm's expected benefits of training and hence lowering the level of investment in training. Indeed Krbavac and Stretton (1987) suggest that Australia's relatively high labour turnover rate is an important factor explaining why Australian firms may invest less in training. By contrast, employee demand for training has been limited by access restrictions (eg adults in relation to trade training) and earning constraints (eg flat wage profiles) (Stromback and Moy 1988).

Second, a common view held by the government, is that 'poaching' of trained workers by (non-training) firms discourages training because of the associated capital losses to the training firm. This 'poaching' phenomenon, it is argued, requires corrective action by the government (Minister for Employment, Education and Training 1988b). However, as Sloan and Wooden (1989) point out, in theory at least, this turnover will be confined to generally trained workers - since other employers, by definition, will have little interest in recruiting workers with firm-specific skills - and, moreover, since the trainee finances this general training this 'poaching' does not impose losses on the training firms. More importantly, however, they go on to argue that Australia's wage structure does *not* provide for an appropriate sharing of training costs:

In particular, since the wages paid to workers while being trained, compared with those of trained workers will affect firms' and workers' decisions to invest in training, an age-experience earnings profile which is relatively flat will depress firms' investment in training, while at the same time conduce to high turnover among skilled workers. Indeed, in *Industry Training in Australia: The Need for Change*, it is argued that: 'lack of career paths is one of a number of factors explaining high wastage rates in the trades.' Of course, if the excessively flat age-experience earnings profile is the principal explanation of the under-investment in training, the first-best solution is to adjust the profile in such a way that workers in training receive less in real terms while trained workers receive more. (Sloan and Wooden 1989, p.283-4)

A third area of blame is poor management attitudes toward training. Stromback and Moy (1988) point out that this attitude has been encouraged by excessive levels of protection and poor management

376

training. Conversely, as protection levels fall we would therefore expect management attitudes to improve. Sloan and Wooden (1989) also note that imperfect information on the part of both firms and workers, particularly regarding the benefits of training may produce under-investment in training. Accordingly, they feel that a government-funded information campaign would not go astray. Moreover, Borland *et al* (1990, p.41) note that one of the benefits of being forced to consider formal training commitments 'results in information acquisition and/or attitudinal changes that are in the long-run interests of employers'. Indeed Sweet (1989) in an analysis of the French experience with a similar arrangement, indicates this proposition, suggesting that the initial opposition to the French internal levy changed over time, with the observation those companies that initially financed less formal training than was required eventually financed more than was necessary by law. Hall and Orchard (1991) also argue that a change in industrial culture towards valuing skills is necessary for Australia to prosper and while the training levy alone is likely to achieve this, 'consciousness-raising' at the boardroom level may be a beneficial side-effect.

Another argument which is often given to explain the low level of training is that Australian employers have been able to avoid the expense of training (and retraining) their existing workforce because of the availability of (relatively cheap) imported labour, in the form of immigrants (Minister for Employment, Education and Training 1988, Birrell 1977, Pope 1984, Mitchell 1988 and Joske 1989). The question that then arises is whether this matters; profit maximising employers will presumably opt for the cheapest, most efficient strategy. However, while the importation of labour from overseas may be a cost effective response in the short term, in the long run Australia may be locked 'into a dependency on skilled immigrant labour, leaving us with high levels of structural unemployment (as a consequence of not retraining our current workforce) and an antiquated system of trade and industry training which is increasingly less capable of meeting the challenge posed by industrial restructuring' (Baker and Wooden 1991, 1992). Baker and Wooden (1991, 1992), however, find little in the way of substitution effects as a result of the immigration of skilled workers.

The final argument relating to the low incidence of job training in Australia is based on the existence of externalities which prevent firms from internalising the benefits of training. In particular, Chapman and

Stemp (1992) argue that even regulation-free market economies may provide less than desirable amounts of on-the-job training. This is based on the dual proposition that training increases the ability of a firm to develop, adapt and implement new technology and that the innovations associated with this process are diffused with relative ease to the firm's competitors. Accordingly under-provision of training throughout the economy occurs because individual firms are unable to internalise the benefits arising from innovations. As such, the presence of this externality presents a case for government intervention.[10] Moreover, Chapman and Stemp argue that the assessment of whether or not intervention is appropriate should be undertaken on an industry by industry basis, given the sensitivity of the case to the production technologies and their interaction with externalities. More important, especially in terms of the current policy debate, however, is their finding that there is no general case for the imposition of a uniform levy imposed on all industries. On the other hand, the offering of lifetime employment contracts (viz the Japanese approach) presents a perfect alternative to government intervention as a means of overcoming the problem of internalising the benefits of training and technological change within a firm. Even in the absence of labour mobility, however, information on technological change may be diffused through reverse engineering (where a good is taken apart in order to determine how it was produced), through information transmitted in trade journals, or from the licensing of technology to other firms (Chapman and Stemp 1992).

Thus, for the great majority of cases it would appear that the main 'villain' behind Australia's poor job training performance is the nature of Australia's labour market institutions. No doubt the current industrial relations reform process will go a long way in addressing this issue. Indeed the Business Council of Australia (1988, p.11) argues 'there is no convincing evidence that, once some of the present artificial constraints on skill formation are removed there will be a need for Government intervention'. However, there do seem to be two other pieces of existing evidence which may imply the need for government intervention. The first relates to poor management attitudes regarding the benefits of training, in which case a simple information-raising campaign would probably suffice. The second case relates to the externalities argument outline above. However, it is important to note that there appears to be no general case warranting the imposition of a uniform levy across all industries (Chapman and Stemp 1992). Finally, international experience with regard to the successful implementation (or otherwise) of various schemes designed to improve industry training are not without relevance (see Krbavac and Stretton 1987 and Hall and Orchard 1991). Indeed the *Report of the Commonwealth/State Working Group on Skill Shortages and Skills Formation* (1986) acknowledge that international experience suggests a number of important practical problems likely to be encountered in relation to a minimum expenditure obligation scheme. Drawing on the UK experience, Sloan and Wooden (1989) also note that the scheme may induce some substitution away from informal, ineligible training expenditures towards formal, eligible training expenditures, suggesting that this may not always be desirable or sensible. Unfortunately, with the exception of the report by the Australian Taxation Office (ATO 1992) which details compliance levels by industry, there seems to be little in the way of major research based assessment of the consequences of the current training levy system on the level and distribution of employer-provided training.

Summary and conclusions

We have seen that the training debate in Australia has at least two facets. The first of these relate to the institutional arrangements impacting upon the process of skill formation in Australia. While the second relates to the under-provision of training in the private sector.

The first dimension of the current debate concerns the features of Australia's rather unique system of industrial relations which, it is argued, diminishes the potential for training at the workplace. Such features include narrowly-defined and occupationally-based awards, binding minimum wage provisions and the system of craft-based unionism. In the recent past, however, with the focus on the need to increase productivity and international competitiveness, a substantial transition in the industrial relations framework is currently underway. This structural adjustment process has seen several changes to the system as Australia knows it. Such changes have include the restructuring of wages and conditions of work as set out in awards and more recently a move towards the decentralisation of bargaining arrangements, through enterprise bargaining.

Alongside this background of the need to improve the skills and flexibility of the workforce, concerns have also been expressed about the large disparities observed in the State-based arrangements in the accreditation and setting of skills standards and the consequent loss of geographic and occupational mobility. As a consequence, the National Training Board was established in early 1990 and the Australian National Training Authority in 1992, both as a joint initiatives of the Commonwealth, State and Territory governments of Australia.

In the context of the factors affecting training at the workplace, the current changes occurring in the institutional arrangements, including award restructuring and enterprise bargaining, and the establishment of the NTB and the ANTA, may go a long way toward correcting these problems. However, as Borland *et al* (1990 p.36) point out, 'there is both consensus and discord in this area'. The main Australian union body, the Australian Council of Trade Unions (ACTU), whilst facilitating some of the changes described above, in various places, however, rejects the proposition that lowering wages at career starting points will lead to favourable outcomes (see Borland *et al* 1990). Indeed, the view of the ACTU (which is at odds with conventional theory) appears to be that employers should wholly finance training investments; if not, then the government should compel them via the introduction of a training levy. This leads us to the second dimension of the current debate.

In response to the concerns that there is under-provision of job training in the private sector, alongside the changes occurring in Australia's institutional framework, the major policy tool has been the introduction of the uniform training levy scheme - the so-called Training Guarantee. The major rationale behind the introduction of this levy arrangement has resulted from the view that it is the private sector itself which is somehow at fault for the under-provision of training at the workplace. However, as the discussion in the penultimate section suggests, it would appear that the structure of the existing institutional arrangements is largely to blame for the current state of affairs. The only rationales for direct government intervention in the job-training area would appear to be in the case of imperfect information regarding the benefits of training and/or the existence of externalities, whereby firms are unable to internalise the benefits of training. The provision of an information campaign would address the first problem. With regard to the externality issue, Chapman and Stemp (1992) outline such a case in the context of technological change and training; even in the case of no labour mobility the possibility of the diffusion of new technologies results in firms being unable to internalise completely the costs associated with training and innovation. More important in the context of the current policy initiative, however, is their finding that any assessment of whether or not intervention is appropriate should by undertaken on an industry-by-industry basis and, moreover, they find that no general case can be made in the externalities context for government intervention in the form of a uniform levy imposed on all industries (Chapman and Stemp 1992). It should also be noted that the levy is also likely to impose some other distortions which may well outweigh the supposed benefits of intervention. Such distortions may include: the likelihood that firms may bias training towards training that is firm-specific so that returns accrue to the firm as well as the worker (Borland *et al* 1989); the substitution of informal ineligible training expenditure (or any other related expenditure for that matter) towards formal, eligible training expenditures (Sloan and Wooden 1989); and finally, in terms of the resource allocation problem within the firm, the forcing of employers to spend a minimum amount on training assumes, perhaps naively, that the pay-offs from training exceed the pay-off's from other alternative expenditures (Stromback and Moy 1989). Furthermore, international evidence suggests a number of important practical problems are also likely to be encountered with such an arrangement (see *Report of the Commonwealth/State Working Group on Skills Shortages and Skills Formation* 1986).

On balance, it would seem that the imposition of the minimum training expenditure obligation - the training levy - may not be an appropriate policy response in the current climate. Anecdotal evidence suggests this is the case. Unfortunately there has been no major research conducted that attempts to evaluate the benefits and costs of the Training Guarantee scheme. It is envisaged, however, that 'holistic' enterprise bargaining arrangements (as opposed to add-on arrangements to minimum rates awards) within the Australian industrial relations system will go along way in enhancing the incentives to train on both the firm and the worker side (see Sloan 1992). The major sticking point in this transition process is likely to be a reluctance by the unions to reduce wages at career entry points.

Notes

The author would like to thank Judith Sloan and Mark Wooden for their helpful advice and assistance. The encouragement of Richard Blandy and support of the National Institute of Labour Studies is gratefully acknowledged. Special thanks is extended to Lee Brimble, Lindy Dodd, Annette Gray and Bernice McGrath who assisted in one way or another in the production of this paper. All errors naturally remain the author's.

1. For example, apprenticeship commencements have dropped by about 30 per cent between 1990 and 1991, due in large part to the current recessionary state of the economy.

2. Note that these figures will include those currently in apprenticeships as well as those on the ATS.

3. The term which refers to changes occurring in awards undertaken as a result of the principal of structural efficiency introduced by the IRC in August 1988.

4. The Australian figure does, however, vary across different versions of the Curtain *et al* paper.

5. The ALS is a panel survey began in 1985, with annual observations currently available to 1989, and is based on the National Longitudinal Survey of the US. In particular, the data set focuses on youth, with all of the 1985 sample lying between the ages of 15 and 26.

6. The definitions underlying the three dependent variables are outlined in the previous section and are defined to equal one if the individual undertook the particular training, zero otherwise. It should also be noted that the estimation of the probability of receiving training is based on the observed outcome (or reduced form) of demand and supply decisions of workers and firms and it is assumed that training is observed where there are net positive benefits.

7. Duration of residence is measured as $1/(1+\text{length of residence})$ for the overseas born.

8. The data, however, do not permit us to discount other competing explanations reflecting upward occupational mobility and differences in NESB immigrant cohorts over time.

9. The threshold of $200,000 is also indexed to average weekly earnings.

10. Though it is noted that since governments will have imperfect information then distortions and associated welfare losses will be introduced by some methods of intervention.

References

Australian Bureau of Statistics [ABS]. (1990a), *How Workers Get Their Training, Australia, 1989*, catalogue no. 6278.0.

ABS. (1990b), *Transition from Education to Work, Australia*, catalogue no. 6227.0.

ABS. (1991), *Employer Training Expenditure, Australia, July to September 1990*, catalogue no. 6353.0.

ACTU/TDC Mission to Western Europe. (1987), *Australia Reconstructed*, AGPS, Canberra.

Australian Science and Technology Council (ASTEC). (1987), *Education and National Needs,* AGPS, Canberra.

Australian Taxation Office (ATO). (1992), *Training Guarantee Compliance Results for 1990-91*, Training Guarantee Group, ATO, Albury-Wodonga, December.

Baker, M. (1991), 'The effect of training on earnings: an analysis of the national child development study,' Paper presented to the Australian Labour Market Research Workshop, Centre for Economic Policy Research, ANU.

Baker, M. and Wooden, M. (1991), *Immigration and Training,* AGPS, Canberra.

Baker, M. and Wooden, M. (1992), 'Immigration and its impact on the incidence of training in Australia', *Australian Economic Review,* 98, pp. 31-38.

Birrell, R. (1977), 'Immigration and unemployment: the implications of the Green Paper on Immigration Policies and Australia's Population', *Australian Quarterly*, 49, pp. 36-49.

Blandy, R.J. (1987), 'Labour market policies towards 2000', In Ulyatt. C. (ed.) (1989), *The Good Fight,* Allen and Unwin, Sydney.

Booth, A.L. (1991), 'Job-related formal training: who receives it and what is it worth?', *Oxford Bulletin of Economics and Statistics*, 53, pp. 281-294.

Booth, A.L. (1992), 'Private sector training and graduate earnings', *Review of Economics and Statistics*, 74, pp.

Borland, J. (1990), 'Worker training', *The Australian Economic Review,* 4, pp. 74-80.

Borland, J., Chapman, B.J. and Rimmer, M. (1990), 'Microeconomic reform in the Australian labour market', Paper presented at the

Conference on Micro Economic Reform in Australia, Centre for Economic Policy Research, ANU, Canberra.

Business Council of Australia. (1988), 'Policies for skill formation', *Business Council Bulletin,* 49, pp. 4-11.

Carmichael, L. (Chairman). (1991), *The Australian Vocational Certificate Training System*, Report of the Employment and Skills Formation Council, National Board of Employment, Education and Training.

Chapman, B.J. and Stemp, P.J. (1992), 'Government intervention in the provision of on-the-job training', *Australian Economic Papers,* 59, pp. 354-368.

Chapman, B.J. and Tan, H.W. (1990), 'An analysis of youth training in Australia, 1985-86: technological change and wages', mimeo, Australian National University, mimeo.

Clare, R. and Johnston, K. (1993), *Education and Training in the 1990s*, Economic Planning and Advisory Council Background Paper No. 31, July, AGPS, Canberra.

Committee of Inquiry into Labour Market Programs (The Kirby Report), (1985), AGPS, Canberra.

Curtain, R., Krbavac, L. and Stretton, A. (1986), 'Skill formation in Australia: in search of a research agenda', Paper presented to the BLMR Workshop on Skills Formation, Canberra.

Dowrick, S. (1990), 'An analysis of labour productivity growth', *mimeo*, Economics Department, Research School of Social Sciences, ANU, Canberra.

Greenhalgh, C. and Stewart, M. (1987), 'The effects and determinants of training', *Oxford Bulletin of Economics and Statistics*, 49, pp. 171-90.

Hall, K. and Orchard, S. (1991), 'Human resource development, industrial culture and the training levy', Western Australian Labour Market Research Centre Working Paper 91/7.

IMD/World Economic Forum. (1990), *The World Competitiveness Report 1990*, IMD/World Economic Forum, Lausanne/Geneva.

Joske, S. (1989), 'The economics of immigration: who benefits?', Background paper from the Legislative Research Service, Commonwealth Parliamentary Library, September.

Krbavac, L. and Stretton, A. (1987), 'Skill formation and structural adjustment: the responsiveness of industry training, Department of Employment, Education and Training, mimeo.

Lillard, L. and Tan, H. (1986), *Private Sector Training: Who Gets it and What are its Effects?* Rand Corporation, Santa Monica.

Lynch, L.M. (1989), 'Private sector training and its impact on the earnings of young workers', National Bureau of Economic Research Working Paper No. 2872.

Miller, P. (1987), 'Training in the youth labour market in Australia', Centre for Economic Policy Research, Discussion Paper no. 172, ANU, Canberra.

Miller, P. and Volker, P. (1989), 'Socio-economic influences on educational attainment: evidence and implications for the tertiary education finance debate', *Australian Journal of Statistics* 31A, pp. 47-70.

Minister for Employment, Education and Training. (1988a), *Industry Training in Australia: The Need for Change*, AGPS, Canberra.

Minister for Employment, Education and Training. (1988b), *A Changing Workforce,* AGPS, Canberra.

Minister for Employment, Education and Training. (1989), *Improving Australia's Training System,* AGPS, Canberra.

Mitchell, W.F. (1988), 'The economic implications of high population growth', In L.H. Day and D.T. Rowland (eds), *How Many More Australians? The Resource and Environmental Conflicts*, Longman Cheshire, Melbourne.

National Board of Employment Education and Training (NBEET). (1989), *Training in Australia: The Need for Change,* AGPS Canberra.

National Training Board. (1991), *Network,* 1, pp.10.

Organisation for Economic Cooperation and Development (OECD). (1986), *Youth and Work in Australia: Comprehensive Policy Agenda,* OECD, Paris.

Pope, D. (1984), 'The labour market and employment prospects' In R Birrell, D. Hill and J. Nevill (eds), *Populate and Perish: The Stresses of Population Growth in Australia*, Fontana/Australian Conservation Foundation, Sydney.

Report of the Commonwealth/State Working Group on Skills Shortages and Skills Formation. (1986), presented to the Conference of Commonwealth and State Labour Ministers.

Sloan, J. (1992), 'Until the end of time: labour market reform in Australia', *Australian Economic Review*, 98, pp. 65-78.

Sloan J. (1993), 'Some policy responses to long term unemployment', *Australian Economic Review*, 99, pp. 35-40.

Sloan, J. and Wooden, M. (1987), 'Labour market programs', In Freebairn, J., Porter, M. and Walsh, C. (eds) *Spending and Taxing: Australian Reform Options*, Allen and Unwin, Sydney.

Sloan J. and Wooden, M. (1989), 'The Australian labour market September 1989', *Australian Bulletin of Labour* 15, pp. 259-86.

Sloan, J. and Wooden, M. (1990), 'The structural efficiency principle in action - management views', *Australian Bulletin of Labour,* 16, pp. 199-223.

Stretton, A. and Chapman, B.J. (1990), 'An analysis of Australian labour market programs', Centre for Economic Policy Research Discussion Paper No. 247, Australian National University.

Stromback, C.T. and Moy, P.J. (1988), 'Economic analysis of industrial training policy', Paper presented to Conference on Industry Training, Centre for Economic Policy Research, Australian National University.

Stromback, T. and Moy, P. (1989), 'Industry training: the emerging myth', *Labour Economics and Productivity*, 1, pp. 111-22.

Sweet, R. (1989), 'The institutional context of industry training, with particular reference to the french experience', *Australian Bulletin of Labour,* 15 4, pp. 326-42.

Tan, H., Chapman, B., Peterson, C. and Booth, A. (1990), 'Youth training in the U.S., Great Britain and Australia', Working Draft, Rand Corporation, Santa Monica.

Index